Short *Circuit*

For Mary, whose contribution
to this book is as great
as my own

Short *Circuit*

Strengthening local economies
for security in an
unstable world

RICHARD DOUTHWAITE

A RESURGENCE BOOK
MCMXCVI

A Resurgence Book
first published in 1996 by
GREEN BOOKS
Foxhole, Dartington, Totnes,
Devon TQ9 6EB, England
in association with
THE LILLIPUT PRESS LTD
4 Rosemount Terrace, Arbour Hill,
Dublin 7, Ireland.

A CIP record for this
title is available from
The British Library.

ISBN 1 870098 64 1

Grants towards the research for this book were provided by
The International Society for Ecology and Culture and
The New Economics Foundation.

Cover design by Mary Guinan
Set in 10.5 on 13 Berling
and 9 on 11 News Gothic Monotype by

mermaid turbulence

Printed in Dublin by
Colour Books of Baldoyle

Contents

The world economy has become much more unstable since the early 1970s and increasing numbers of people and places are excluded from full participation in it. Unfortunately, national politicians are powerless to change the factors that created this situation. Communities are going to have to act for themselves.

To protect themselves from the instabilities of the world system, communities can create parallel financial micro-climates within which local resources are used to meet local needs to a much greater extent than would be possible if only world-market prices and interest rates ruled.

If people cannot trade among themselves without using money issued by outsiders, their local economies will always be at the mercy of events elsewhere. Many ways exist for them to create their own money, however. Options run from group currencies such as LETS, through Swiss-style mutual credit systems for businesses and commodity-backed currencies, as in Exeter, New Hampshire, to money issued by local government, like that in Guernsey.

Locally owned financial systems enable people's savings to be lent out in the areas in which they live on terms that allow them to realize their social objectives as well as their financial ones. Here again, communities have a wide range of options open to them, including credit unions, building societies and investment trusts. Interest-free lending along the lines of the Danish and Swedish community JAK banks is another possibility.

The provision of an adequate supply of energy from local resources is fundamental to greater community self-reliance. Fortunately, most places can easily develop a combination of wind, hydro and biomass sources to meet their needs, as examples from Denmark, Austria and Ireland show. Saving energy is as important as generating it, and here Holland and California provide good models.

CONTENTS

Foreword

THIS BOOK IS ONE OF THOSE RARE VOLUMES that will change
the spirit of our age. It is both practical and inspiring. Its inspiration
comes from real-life success stories – accounts of communities that
have taken their future into their own hands and brought back not
only jobs, but real political power and community spirit. Its practical
value lies in a clear analysis of the structures that support a community's economic base, and a description of the hands-on tools needed
to strengthen it. In *Short Circuit*, Richard Douthwaite has undertaken
the most extensive survey yet of community economics in the industrialized world.

To fully appreciate the significance of this book, we need to ask
ourselves why everything we hold dear seems to be threatened. As
individuals, we face increasing insecurity in our working lives, on our
streets and even within our homes. As societies, we face a ruthlessly
competitive global economy, the threat of armed conflict, and a biosphere stressed to the point of collapse. In the face of all this, governments and businesses offer us, at best, a tattered, decaying safety net.
Short Circuit's encouraging message is that the security we need can
be found in our own communities by developing our local economies.

But why are communities and families fragmenting? Why are thousands of species disappearing and the world's climate becoming ever
more unstable? Why is democracy slipping away, and ethnic conflict,
poverty, crime and unemployment growing day by day?

The root cause of all these problems often evades even the most
intelligent and well-intentioned examination. The world economic
system has become so complex, and the attitudes that it has given rise
to so all-pervasive, that we now find it is extremely difficult to gain a
clear perspective. However, there is a common thread running
through these seemingly disparate crises: namely, a system of produc-

tion and distribution that depends for its survival on endless expansion. This continuous growth has led to economic globalization, which essentially means the amalgamation of every local, regional and national economy into a single world system.

Economic globalization is not the result of superior economic efficiency. It is coming about because governments have been subsidizing international and long-distance trade for nearly two hundred years without stopping to assess the impact on society and nature. It is only through tax breaks, cheap fuel, and massive investments in the underlying transport and information infrastructure that apples from New Zealand displace French apples in the markets of Paris, European dairy products destroy local production in milk-rich Mongolia, and Dutch butter costs less than Kenyan butter in the shops of Nairobi. Even a child might ask, 'Why must food be transported thousands of miles, when it can be produced right here?' This is not efficiency but economics gone mad.

Globalization has also led to the growth of huge multinational corporations that have replaced the hundreds of thousands of small businesses, shopkeepers and farmers that traditionally generated most economic activity and employment. And since big firms, unlike small ones, can threaten to move their operations to countries where the fiscal environment is easier, almost every government's ability to raise an adequate amount in tax has been reduced. Consequently, by blindly subsidizing the process of globalization, the nation-state has promoted its own demise.

Moreover, by inducing people everywhere to rely on the same narrow range of industrial resources, the global economic system has greatly increased competition at every level. As a result, unemployment in the industrialized world has soared while, in the cities of the South, populations are exploding because millions of rural families are being drawn away from local self-reliance by the promises of the consumer society – only to be plunged into urban squalor and hunger. Meanwhile, wilderness areas and biodiversity are under increasing pressure as the demand for industrial resources grows.

The system that has emerged suits nobody: in the long run, there are no winners. Even at the highest levels of society, the quality of life is declining. The threat of mergers leaves even senior managers in permanent fear of losing their jobs. As for the burgeoning list of billionaires, try though they might to fence themselves off from the collapsing social order, they cannot hide from the collapsing biosphere.

It is therefore in everyone's interest that the process of globalization be reversed. The most effective way of doing this would be for governments to get together to curb the powers of the multinationals by negotiating new trade and investment treaties that would remove the subsidies powering globalization and give local production a chance. For example, if the hidden subsidies for fossil fuel use were removed, local and national economies would become much stronger. But such international measures would not in themselves restore health to economies and communities: long-term solutions require a range of small local initiatives that are as diverse as the cultures and the environments in which they take place.

Unfortunately, many people are opposed to the creation of stronger local economies for all manner of reasons. Some, for example, imagine that the aim of economic localization is complete self-sufficiency at the village level. In fact, localization does not mean everything being produced locally, nor does it mean an end to trade. It simply means creating a better balance between local, regional, national and international markets. It also means that large corporations should have less control, and communities more, over what is produced, where, when and how; and that trading should be fair and to the benefit of both parties.

It is also sometimes feared that localization will lead to repression and intolerance. On closer examination, however, it is clear that the opposite is true: the global economy is itself nothing less than a system of structural exploitation that creates hidden slaves on the other side of the world and forces people to give up their rights to their own resources. Localization is not about isolating communities from other cultures, but about creating a new, sustainable and equitable basis on which they can interact. In the North, being responsible for our own needs means allowing the South to produce for itself, rather than for us.

All over the world, campaigns against globalization are growing in strength as people see how it affects their lives, their high streets, and their neighbourhoods – and as they become more aware that there *are* alternatives. The significance of Richard Douthwaite's book is that he shows that globalization can be contained by using these alternatives in a coherent way. He also shows we can start to build alternative systems today without waiting for politicians to give us their blessing or for the world to burn.

When community initiatives work (and *Short Circuit* describes both successes and failures) they release the imagination of those involved and enable them to take further steps towards economic

FOREWORD

revitalization, stronger communities, and a healthier environment. But so far, as Richard Douthwaite points out, no community anywhere has implemented more than a few of the many techniques described in this book, so the potential for revitalization is dramatic.

This book, then, is an indispensable tool-kit for communities seeking to initiate their own renewal from within. Those that take any of the steps outlined here will find themselves at the cutting edge of the most powerful movement of the new millennium.

HELENA NORBERG-HODGE
International Society for Ecology and Culture

ED MAYO
New Economics Foundation

Preface

ONE OF THE THINGS I LEARNED from writing *The Growth Illusion* was that policies designed to accelerate economic growth had concentrated so much wealth and power in the hands of multinational companies and financial institutions that national governments had left themselves inadequate powers to safeguard citizens' interests. What could be done to dilute this concentration? I asked myself. Power once gained is rarely given up voluntarily, and governments had become too weak to take it back for themselves even if they were inclined to do so, which, generally, they were not. Intrigued, I thought I might write a book on the topic and circulated an outline to people who I thought might help find the necessary finance.

An enthusiastic response came from Ed Mayo, director of the New Economics Foundation in London, who suggested that I develop a practical handbook on the techniques communities could use to become more self-reliant economically. He raised a small amount of money from the Goldsmith Foundation and I embarked on what we both thought would be a six-month task. I had not got very far, however, when two problems emerged. One was that it became obvious that the sort of brief discussion of techniques I had envisaged would not serve its readers very well without some account of why unconventional, community-based solutions were necessary. The second was that the techniques were likely to give disappointing results if communities simply tried to use them within the existing economic system and their members' thinking went unchanged. A much longer book was required. Discussions with Helena Norberg-Hodge, director of the International Society for Ecology and Culture, led to ISEC agreeing to make it possible, using funds provided by Peter and Máire Buckley for its globalization/localization studies.

Despite the added analytical content, this book is still intended to

PREFACE

be a practical guide and, as such, it has to cover its topics in reasonable depth. Thus no one should feel obliged to read it from beginning to end. I suggest that people read the introduction and chapters 1 and 2 before turning to whichever of the four long core chapters interests them most, and then move on to the final chapter. If I've done my job properly, readers won't skip the other core chapters altogether. Someone keen on wind energy will naturally read the community energy section – chapter 5 – but if he or she wants to finance a wind farm, chapters 3 and 4, on local currencies and local banking systems, have a lot of relevant ideas. Similarly, someone interested in organic farming will turn to chapter 6 and then move back to the money chapters for information on how to make a project commercially viable.

The core chapters include panels in sans-serif type, in which I present practical information and case studies that illustrate or expand upon points raised in the main narrative. Readers, if so inclined, should not hesitate to skip a panel when they first encounter it and return to it before moving to the next chapter.

I resisted the temptation to write this book for a worldwide readership because this would have meant being less specific and, consequently, less useful. It is intended for a British and Irish audience; I have discussed projects from as close to home as possible so that they are from a similar legal and cultural framework and relatively easy for organizers to visit. If there are more Irish examples than, say, Scottish ones, the fact that I live in Ireland obviously has something to do with it. However, it is also because the Irish have recently been doing disproportionately more at a community level than most other countries in Europe. This is because ten years ago they were told by their politicians that if wage and price inflation were moderated and the national debt reduced as a proportion of national income, businesses would increase investment, the rate of economic growth would soar and enough new jobs would be created to make a substantial reduction in unemployment. All this has come to pass except the jobs. Ireland's rate of growth is so high that bankers refer to the country as the Celtic Tiger. It has a large trade surplus and is one of only two or three EU members likely to meet the Maastricht Treaty criteria for participation in a single currency. But despite these 'successes', its level of long-term unemployment shows no sign of falling. As a result, hundreds of people have given up relying on the government or outside firms to bring jobs to their districts and have become involved in community efforts to create work themselves.

Happily, the groups they have joined stand a much better chance of being successful than similar groups in Britain because Ireland's community structures and its social capital are much more intact, even in areas where the population is in decline. This was demonstrated in 1994 when Muintir na Tire, a long-established national community development organization, published a report on the resources that four parishes in North Tipperary could call on 'with a view to creating enterprises as an alternative to traditional job roles that are fast becoming redundant'. Parish C was typical of what the consultants found. It is centred on a village which had a population of 1113 in 1991, down a full 10 per cent from only five years earlier. And yet it had two primary schools and one secondary school, a Roman Catholic church, a new community centre/parish hall, nine pubs, three petrol stations, four supermarkets, a post office, a draper's, a chemist, a hairdresser, a doctor's surgery, a health centre and a credit union. A mobile library visited once a week. It also had five community organizations – a tourism co-op, a festival committee which organizes an annual historical pageant, a Tidy Towns committee to ensure the village looks its best for the annual national contest, a Variety Committee which puts on·plays and revues, and the Gaelic Athletic Association. How many communities in England of a similar size would still have a comparable range of assets? Come to that, how many modern housing estates in Ireland would either?

Admittedly, most of the Irish groups' efforts to develop their local economies are still on the conventional 'what can we supply to outside markets?' lines, but a certain 'which of our needs can we start satisfying from our district's resources?' radicalism is creeping in. I've noted several examples of this. In spring 1995, for instance, some weeks after *The Guardian* carried a brief article about a survey of Hatherleigh, a small town in Devon, to assess the feasibility of supplying all its energy from renewable resources there, I rang the consultants in Bournemouth to request a copy. 'Another Irish address,' the man I spoke to commented. 'That's interesting. We've had more enquiries about the study from Ireland than we've had from this country.' And yet, as far as I know, the existence of the Hatherleigh study was not reported in any Irish newspaper. At any rate, his comment confirmed my view that if a new pattern of community economic development does emerge in Europe in the near future, Ireland will be at its leading edge.

Many, many people helped me to write this book by answering questions, sending information and commenting on parts of the draft; I record their names with gratitude at the end of the book. However, the support of five organizations has to be recorded here. First has to be the Goldsmith Foundation, which provided the seed money for the project, enabling me to visit Germany, Norway, Denmark, the US and Australia to find out what was going on. The New Economics Foundation, besides arranging the Goldsmith grant, provided encouragement, information and advice and read through the typescript at a late stage. As I have already mentioned, funds from the International Society for Ecology and Culture enabled the scope of the book to be greatly expanded. However, its contribution went beyond the financial, as Helena Norberg-Hodge's perspectives on the ways in which happy, stable, self-sufficient communities can be destroyed by external economic forces were very valuable. A remarkable Dutch organization, Aktie Strohalm of Utrecht, also became involved when it employed me as a consultant on its project for the World Council of Churches looking at ways in which local currency systems and credit unions can be developed to meet a wider range of social needs. Here again, its involvement was not just financial; chapters 3 and 4 would not have been so comprehensive without the information and ideas it supplied. Finally, the Schumacher Society in the United States – for which read Robert Swann and Susan Witt – provided accommodation, hospitality and access to its extensive library during my visit to America. Run on a shoe-string, it is the single most important US information source for anyone researching community economics.

This book provides a snapshot of what communities were trying and people were thinking at around the time it went to press and, because ideas and projects are constantly developing, it will date quite quickly in some respects. One way of coping with that would be to publish a revised edition in two or three years' time, but a better way of keeping readers in touch would be to publish a magazine, as this would be more immediate and allow topics not covered in *Short Circuit* to be explored. Moreover, people besides the author would be able to make their views heard. Nothing has been settled yet, but if you would like to receive a free specimen copy, please write to me at the address below.

RICHARD DOUTHWAITE
Cloona, Westport
County Mayo
Ireland
June 1996

Introduction

ON A BRIGHT DAY IN JUNE a small passenger ferry, the *Dún Aengus*, lies among an assortment of small fishing boats beside Cleggan pier in the west of Ireland. Shortly before its two o'clock sailing to Inishbofin, an island with a permanent population of about 180 people five miles off the coast, one of the crew walks down the pier carrying a tray marked *Pat the Baker* containing French sticks and plain white buns. He places it on a hatch cover on the open deck. Five minutes later a forty-foot container lorry with a grocery wholesaler's logo on its side reverses down the pier. Using the tail-lift, the driver places a pallet-load of provisions on the flagstones beside the ferry. 'Haven't you got a derrick so that you can swing it on board?' he asks the crewman. 'We have not,' the latter replies, taking a knife out of his pocket to cut through the heavy plastic cling-film with which the pallet-load is wrapped. The ferry's skipper, Paddy O'Halloran, who has sailed the island's mail-boat for over thirty years, comes from the wheelhouse; I join him, and the goods are transferred from pallet to deck along a three-man chain.

A fair selection of what the island will need for the next week is there; sugar, biscuits, jars of jam, flour, margarine, toiletries and disposable nappies are all passed down the line until a large part of the open deck is three-deep in cartons. I am amazed at the number of packs of non-returnable bottles of Coca-Cola handed to me and wonder if the containers cost more to make than their contents. Later, on the island, I see a half-hearted attempt to dispose of their predecessors by burning them with other packaging material on the beach near the jetty. When the tide comes in, the unburnt rubbish floats off into the harbour. Some of it will be washed up on the mainland because of the direction of the prevailing wind, but most will be strewn along the

1

tideline of the harbour itself. On the jetty I find a stack of baker's trays that somehow never made it back to Pat the Baker's factory in Granard, County Longford, over a hundred miles away.

After a smooth forty-minute crossing over a sparkling sea, the supplies are loaded into a trailer to be hauled by tractor to Day's shop, less than fifty yards from where the boat docked. There, the full extent of Inishbofin's dependence on the outside world is revealed. The milk was packed into waxed cartons sixty miles away in Oranmore on the far side of Galway. The eggs come from County Monaghan, the frozen fish from County Donegal, the cheese, butter and bacon rashers from the Golden Vale in County Cork. Yet this was an island that used to supply large quantities of eggs and butter to the mainland within the lifetime of many of its inhabitants and whose fishing industry once employed over two hundred of its men. What has gone wrong? Why does an island that spun, wove and knitted almost all its own clothing a century ago and even grew flax for its fishermen's lines now produce so little for itself? The question needs to be answered, because only five or six of Inishbofin's seventy-five remaining households are not almost totally dependent for their income on state pensions or the dole.

It's not hard to find factors that contributed to the island's loss of its self-reliance. For example, Margaret Day, who ran Day's Hotel beside the shop until recently and was also the island's nurse for many years, says that the provision of a public electricity supply on the island in the early 1980s enabled people to stop keeping milking-cows. 'Until then, because the ferry could be tied up for days during bad weather, people had to keep a house cow if they wanted to be sure of having fresh milk. After the power came, they could keep bought milk in their freezers.'

There are very few cattle on the island now, because the EU's headage payments for sheep have made that animal more popular, and even those that remain are not generally milked. 'It's very difficult to get them used to hand-milking once they've been allowed to suckle a calf,' says Margaret Murray, who runs the island's other hotel, the Doonmore. 'I'd like to use Inishbofin milk in the hotel, but the health board insists it has to be pasteurized before it can be served to guests. The cost of the equipment means that that's out of the question.'

When a cheese-maker came from the mainland in 1993 to run a course there was scarcely enough island milk for her demonstration, and none of the seven trainees, Murray included, has been able to practise what they learned. No butter is being made now either, although a churn is on display in the Doonmore's dining-room. 'This has meant that there is no buttermilk available for baking soda-bread. We bring it in from the mainland, but having to buy it has discouraged people from making their own bread,' Day says.

Another reason few cattle are kept is the difficulty of getting them to market. Slings have to be placed under their bellies so that they can be winched into the hold of the island's cargo boat, the *Leenane Head*, a fine wooden zulu built in Scotland in 1906. 'The winching and the sea journey set them back,' Murray says. 'They have to be rested for a day before they can travel any further. This makes it difficult and expensive for local people to take them to market themselves. What generally happens is that dealers come over from the mainland and buy the cattle cheaply, asking the farmers to keep the animals until shipment is arranged – which can be as long as two or three months. A farmer can't manage his affairs on this basis: he can't sell when he wants to sell. Sheep are easier to get to the mainland.'

Almost all the island's meat is brought in. Several years ago Murray, who was on the Inishbofin Development Association's committee at the time, investigated the possibility of setting up a slaughterhouse so that the community wouldn't have to go to a mainland butcher just like everyone else. What she had in mind was something small and simple to handle sheep, but the county council had a standard specification and insisted that it be followed. 'Their building was big enough to handle cattle as well and had walls tiled to the ceiling. It was just too expensive, and so nothing was done.' In fact, some sheep are still slaughtered on the island and their meat is sold, but it is done secretly to avoid prosecution. Thus, official inflexibility led to the worst outcome of all: unregulated butchering in totally unsuitable conditions.

Although the island once had curing-sheds to enable its fish catches to be sent all over Europe and to Africa, very little fishing is carried on now; two disused trawlers are tied up at the jetty, unlikely to sail again. The only seaworthy fishing boat of any size left is the *Northern Ranger*, but this is used mainly for taking parties of visitors to the neighbouring islands of Inishturk and Inishark. The main income of its owner, Gustin Coyne, comes from maintaining the island's electricity generating station and from doing electrical work in people's homes. 'A few years ago you could make a good income for the summer by setting three dozen lobster pots,' he says. 'Now you can't make a living if you set three hundred.' The days before the Second

World War, when a Frenchman called Samzun brought in French boats each year to supplement the local effort and shipped the live lobsters to England, are a fading memory.

Most of the fish in the surrounding waters – the mackerel that were caught between March and July, the herring shoals that came at harvest time, the cod and the ling – have gone, destroyed by overfishing or taken by bigger boats further offshore. The decline began in the 1920s. Previously, fish buyers had come to the island from as far away as Germany and Shetland, and the waters around Inishbofin were regarded as among the world's foremost fishing grounds. In the 1840s as many as ten thousand fishermen congregated on the island when the shoals moved that way.

Gustin says the concessions the government made during the negotiations for Ireland's membership of the EEC in the early 1970s delivered the *coup de grâce* to the fishing industry, because they involved exchanging increased access to Irish waters by other countries' boats for higher farm product prices under the Common Agricultural Policy. 'At the time, the government didn't even know how many fishing boats were in this country, or how big they were,' he says. 'That shows how unimportant fishing was to them. I'll give you an example of what that treaty did. Until a few years ago, crayfish were an important and valuable catch around here, but the Spanish found the trench along which they migrate north and began fishing it. So the crayfish began to use another trench, until the Spanish found that too. Very few reach here any more, and there's nothing we can do about it.'

It would be nice to stop being negative and to list the activities the islanders have developed to replace fishing and farming. Unfortunately, apart from a little tourism – mostly day-trippers during the three summer months – there's nothing to report. Instead, the litany of loss goes on. For example, although the island is ideal for raising free-range poultry because it has no foxes – a serious problem for smallholders on the mainland – only a few people keep hens and geese, and Murray says it is difficult to get island eggs to serve in her hotel, although she tries. In any case, keeping hens would not reduce the island's dependence on the outside world to any great extent if, instead of importing the eggs, Inishbofin imported the feed. In the old days the islanders fed their flocks on oats and potatoes they had grown themselves and that were an important part of their families' diets, but only small patches of both are grown today.

The crafts the island had at the turn of the century disappeared as boatbuilders, blacksmiths, shoemakers, tailors, weavers and seamstresses were gathered to their ancestors. No equivalent skills came in to replace them, and the island's children, whose links with their birthplace are weakened when they are sent as boarders to secondary schools on the mainland, look for their opportunities elsewhere. As a result, the number of households dropped from 186 in 1893 to seventy-four a century later, and the population declined even faster – by over 80 per cent – so that a majority of today's households consist of one person or an elderly couple. There are only twenty-one children at the island's primary school. Indeed, because the age structure of the population is so skewed, unless new people move to the island or emigrants return, the number of permanent residents can be expected to fall below a hundred by the time of the next census in 2001. This might bring numbers close to the level at which the authorities decide that the island is too expensive to service and that its people should be encouraged to leave. On the neighbouring island of Inishark the last six families, comprising twenty-three people, were removed to the mainland in October 1960.

During a stay in 1993, some islanders told me they thought that Galway County Council had decided to let Inishbofin run down, because it was several years since it had authorized the construction of any council houses; applicants were being offered houses on the mainland instead. Others disagreed and said that, as the council had spent £2.5 million on building an ugly steel-and-concrete pier the previous year, there was no evidence that it planned a gradual abandonment. (The poet Richard Murphy, who brought the first day-trippers to the island in his sailing hooker *Ave Maria* in the early 1960s, says the 'structure disfigures the most beautiful natural harbour in Ireland as if a forceps were stuck in a womb'.) Both groups were dissatisfied with the level of services the county council provided. Early in 1995, after winter storms had undermined stretches of coastal road so seriously that, in the words of the priest, Father Paddy Sheridan, 'you'd be afraid to walk up the road after your dinner for fear the weight would take you into the sea,'[1] the island's annual general meeting voted to rejoin County Mayo, to which Inishbofin belonged until 1872. The vote had no legal force, but the road repairs were approved the following week and the construction of a council house shortly afterwards.

My suspicion is that the council has no policy for Inishbofin at all and that it built the pier because it was not spending its own money: 30 per cent of the funding came from the government in Dublin and the rest from the EU under its infrastructural development programme. What is certain is that the pier was imposed on Inishbofin from outside. True, the islanders had wanted something done, because the ferry could not dock at the old stone jetty at all states of the tide. However, their idea was to blast away some rocks and extend the jetty to an islet in the harbour called Glasoileán, a solution that would have cost far less than the county council's project and would also have stopped the sheltered moorings at the far end of the harbour silting up. But since no one ever said, 'We've £2.5 million here to spend in any way we like on capital works in Inishbofin: how can we make best use of it?' there was little incentive for the council to keep expenditure down. Had the islanders had control over the money, you can be sure they could have built the jetty extension, a slaughterhouse to official standards, a dairy, and several other projects as well.

Although the pier funds – an amazing £14,000 per islander – should certainly have been spent to greater effect, no one should blame the county council that they were not. The point of the EU's infrastructural spending is not to act as a catalyst for the development of those 'peripheral areas' of Europe in which its ports and roads are built – quite the reverse: the money is spent to improve access to markets on the periphery for goods manufactured by companies in the core. Obviously a road runs both ways, and a pier can be used to ship goods both in and out. But the more cheaply and easily goods can reach Inishbofin or any isolated community from the outside world, the less necessity there is for the people living there to do things for themselves, and the more competition that any goods they do make for the local market will experience from goods made in more convenient locations. The ugly pier represents the EU's bridgehead, an extension of its distribution network, not a glorious entrance to the Single Market for the people of Inishbofin.

Despite the bridgehead, a few islanders are trying to compete against outside producers. A widow who prefers not to be named supplements her pension by baking soda-bread and cakes in her tiny kitchen and selling them to neighbours who call to her door. Her greatest fear is that some day the health inspector who visits the island to check the summer-only restaurants and the two hotels will close her down because she does not meet the recent regulations that require anyone producing food for sale to use a special kitchen quite separate from their domestic one. 'I'll ask him what he thinks I should do and if he could live on £50 a week, which is what I get,' she says with exasperation.

Regina King and her friend Mary Lavelle used to grow vegetables to sell from a stall on Saturday mornings in July and August. 'We've carrots, lettuce, spinach, and mange-tout peas,' she told me in 1993. 'We never have that amount of stuff, and Murray's will take whatever we have left over for the hotel. Everything is completely organic.' Her main problems were rabbit damage – the island is overrun with them and everything has to be carefully fenced – and the salt and sand carried in by the frequent strong winds, which batter and blacken delicate leaves. The two women applied for a grant to help them purchase a polytunnel, in the hope that it would solve both problems and give a longer growing season. The grant was approved, but Regina had a baby and they didn't take it up. Two years later they had changed their minds about a tunnel. 'We can't believe the plastic sheets won't be blown away,' Regina says. 'What we really need is a proper glass greenhouse, but these are expensive, and we can't get a grant for one.'

Some years ago a co-op was set up to bring food into the island at better prices than the shops and also to export the troublesome rabbits, which were caught and sent to England during the Second World War. Unfortunately, the organizers became overly ambitious and proposed buying a refrigerated van to handle sales on the mainland. The capital and recurrent expenses this would have involved killed the whole project, and the co-op itself eventually withered away, its fate sealed when the island's shopkeepers told their suppliers that they would cease to deal with them if they supplied the co-op too.

Dr Steven Royle of Queen's University, Belfast, a geographer who has studied the Irish offshore islands, thinks that life on them was always hard, which is why early systems of state support such as the Congested Districts Board became so heavily involved. 'Although in the past the islands' resources were supporting their populations, this support was at very low levels indeed – levels that would be completely unacceptable in western Europe today. Life was hard and, for many, short. Islanders had few possessions and lived very simple lives, basically as subsistence peasants. The local resources were often stretched to the extent that failure in any one of them could bring real hardship. It was certainly not a comfortable life materially, though the Blasket biographies and other works do present an attractive picture of the social and cultural life.'[2]

Just how difficult life could be on Inishbofin when local resources failed was described by Thomas Brady, an inspector of fisheries, in 1873, when about 1250 people lived there and on its neighbouring island:

INTRODUCTION

In the course of my official business during the early part of the present year, it came to my knowledge that distress, amounting to almost destitution, existed on the islands of Boffin and Shark ... Sheep have died from starvation, the people have little food remaining, no potatoes and very many no seed to put in the ground ... The time for fishing is commencing but the islanders have no fishing gear to follow their advocations. I visited a great many houses in Boffin and Shark ... In one house I found them eating their dinner which consisted of boiled seaweed with limpets in it ... Only three men on Shark have any potatoes.[3]

In 1886 the British government had to send a gunboat, HMS *Banterer*, with meal and potatoes to relieve distress. Housing conditions were bad too. According to a paper written by Charles Browne in 1893 for the Royal Irish Academy, a typical house at the time consisted of a kitchen and one or two bedrooms and was built of dry stones, plastered inside with mud or mortar. The roof was thatched, and the floor was of clay. The windows were small and at the front of the house only, because the landlord would have raised the rent if more had been made. Most of the wood used in construction had been found as driftwood on the beach. Furniture consisted of 'a few stools, a rough table or two, with a dresser containing a scant assortment of earthenware, a spinning-wheel and a quilting frame,' while the bedroom would have two tent-beds, some chairs, and perhaps a small table. Pigs, hens and cattle were brought into the living-room when they needed shelter, because again the landlord would have charged extra had the tenant built outhouses for them.

No one would wish to see Inishbofin return to conditions such as these,s but surely there must be a middle way lying between the extremes of almost complete self-sufficiency on the one hand and near-total reliance on supplies and welfare payments from the outside world on the other. The challenge facing the island is to achieve such a balance, a task that this book is all about.

The fact is that Inishbofin's circumstances are nothing special. Tens of thousands of landlocked communities throughout Europe share essentially the same situation. It is just that, as it is an island, we can see more clearly what its problems are. If it was joined to the mainland it would never occur to us to think it a pity that almost everything it needed was brought in: we would ignore it, just as we do the communities elsewhere that are just as grotesquely dependent on social welfare payments and that are slowly dying too because the economic activities that were once the basis of their existence have withered away. We don't expect people housed on urban estates with much the same level of unemployment as on Inishbofin to bake their own bread and repair their own shoes; but isn't this exactly where our thinking has gone wrong?

The decline in Inishbofin and a multitude of other communities is due to the collapse of ways of life that enabled their people to support themselves successfully for centuries, albeit at what we today would consider an unsatisfactory level. The main cultural collapse has been that of peasant agriculture. In Ireland as a whole, 670,000 people gained their main source of livelihood from the land in 1926, the majority working for themselves or for members of their families. By 1991 the total had dropped to 154,000, only 14 per cent of the national work force, and was falling at the rate of twelve families a day. As a result, 224 villages in County Galway were abandoned completely during the sixty-five-year period; ten thousand people emigrated from Counties Galway, Mayo and Roscommon in 1986 alone.

Similarly rapid changes have taken place throughout Europe, particularly after the Second World War. In the conclusion to the second volume of his book *The Identity of France*, the great historian Fernand Braudel writes that the ancient, peasant France – 'a France of bourgs, villages, hamlets and scattered houses' – survived more or less unchanged until 1945, when 'it fell victim to the "Thirty Glorious Years", that period of unprecedented expansion that lasted until the 1970s'. The final blow that killed it, he suggests, was the introduction of the tractor,

a machine which could pull anything: the most advanced plough, the huge combine-harvester (a mobile factory) or carts piled high with bales or (these days) compressed blocks of hay and straw. If it has been possible to amalgamate properties, and if the size of farm that a family can now handle has increased, it is very largely thanks to the tractor. How else could the huge fields we now see in so many farming areas even be ploughed?[4]

He asks himself why peasant agriculture was able to survive until so recently, and suggests this answer:

Is it perhaps for the simple reason that peasant life offered, to what was certainly an over-abundant population, a balanced way of life? Near Céret, where I live, the Aspre valley has now reverted to nature: today, only brambles, shrubs and broom flourish on the poor and untended soil. Here, 'the equilibrium based on almost complete self-sufficiency, combined with a little trading, which had more in common with barter than with imports and exports, was lost for good in 1950,' Adrienne Cazeilles writes to me (20 January, 1985). The population gave up, leaving everything just as it stood, as if evacuating an untenable position in wartime. But before that, the position had been perfectly defensible. Life in Aspre was not wretched: people were poor, certainly, and it was a hard life, but that is not the same thing. As one of my friends, born in 1899 in a peasant family used to put it humorously but accurately: 'The only thing we were short of was money.'

The people of Aspre did not leave because their way of life was inferior to that in the outside world: they left because it had been undermined by the outside world, and in particular by industrialization. They were displaced, made redundant, by systems of agriculture that used industrial inputs like the tractor to enable food to be produced at progressively lower prices so that eventually they were left with too little income from the proportion of their output they did sell to buy even the limited range of goods and services they needed from outside. Industry also extinguished the settlement on Inishark: one of the reasons the people left was that larger, mechanized vessels began catching the fish stocks previously taken by their sail-powered and oar-powered boats. In both cases – and in thousands of others too – the world lost systems of production that had enabled families to live sustainably for generations from the resources of their areas with very little input from elsewhere. Those affected had no option but to give up their largely independent ways of life and become almost totally reliant on others and on the industrial system for everything they needed. They were never offered a choice. External circumstances compelled them to give up making, catching and growing almost everything they needed and to switch to purchasing their requirements, using wages earned from an employer or money given to them as a dole.

So, just as nomadic herders were displaced by settled farmers, peasant farmers and fishermen were displaced by the industrial system. The main difference about the more recent substitution was the lightning pace at which it came about. The German economist Alexander Rüstow, born in 1885 when his newly unified country was industrializing rapidly, regarded the destruction of the largely self-sufficient peasant way of life and its replacement by the factory system as the advance of an extreme form of tyranny. This was because the factory workers, unlike their peasant forebears, had neither land nor skills to employ on their own account to secure their families' needs and therefore had no alternative to working for whatever wages and under whatever conditions the factory owners chose to offer. The livelihood of the new type of worker was completely outside his or her control. Today we are all dependent. How many of us would survive should the industrial system fail?

Rüstow regarded peasant culture as superior to any other form, a

INTRODUCTION

view that seems ridiculous to those of us who accept the dictionary
definition of peasant as 'uncouth or uncultured' and who would consider being called one a term of abuse. But Rüstow is not alone. In his
book *The Villagers*, Richard Critchfield, an American journalist who
was lucky enough to get commissions from his editors that have
enabled him to report on life in villages around the world for the past
quarter-century, also sees peasant culture as humankind's greatest
achievement and is concerned that industrial culture may not evolve
to provide a satisfactory replacement. This is because the codes of
conduct and attitudes that have enabled peasant cultures to survive
throughout the centuries are the direct opposite of those fostered by
the industrial system.

What are these peasant values? Critchfield quotes the University of
Chicago anthropologist Robert Redfield: 'An intense attachment to
native soil; a reverent disposition toward habitat and ancestral ways;
a restraint on individual self-seeking in favor of family and community;
a certain suspicion, mixed with appreciation, of town life; a sober and
earthy ethic.' The industrial system, on the other hand, has no respect
for the environment or tradition and regards land as a mere factor of
production. Its heroes are individual entrepreneurs, and its predomi-
nant belief is that except in extreme cases the market should limit the
search for profit, not the community. Industrialism's supporters also
accept that family should not stand in the way of an individual's
career.

According to Critchfield, peasant culture is the source of the
world's major religions and concepts of morality, and as urban industrial society is failing to ensure that moral codes are successfully trans-
mitted from generation to generation, it is eroding the ethical basis on
which it is built. He quotes Walter Lippmann:

The deep and abiding traditions of religion belong to the countryside. For it is there
that man earns his daily bread by submitting to superhuman forces whose behavior he
can only partially control. There is not much he can do when he has plowed the
ground and planted his seed except to wait hopefully for sun and rain from the sky. He
is obviously part of a scheme that is greater than himself, subject to elements that tran-
scend his powers and surpass his understanding. The city is an acid which dissolves this
piety. Yet without piety, without a patriotism of family and place, without an almost
plant-like implication in unchangeable surroundings, there can be no disposition to
believe in an external order of things. The omnipotence of God means something to
men who submit daily to the cycles of weather and the mysterious power of nature.[5]

Critchfield fears that civil disorder will break out if the cities' acid
eats away too much of the moral basis of life, and that urban indus-

11

trial culture will be unable to repair the damage caused by the death of morality's rural roots. 'All our culture – our institutions of family and property, religion, the work ethic, the agricultural moral code and mutual help – originated in the villages,' Critchfield writes. 'Farming is hard ... but agriculture creates societies that work ... No substitute for the rural basis of our urban culture has yet been invented ... As President Clinton has reminded us, "Our problems go way beyond the reach of government. They're rooted in the loss of values, in the disappearance of work and the breakdown of our families and communities."' Critchfield therefore urges us to seek 'a substitute for the old rural basis of our soon-to-be global urban culture.'

This book, however, is not about what such a search might find. Instead it discusses a possibility Critchfield probably thought too remote to mention: that communities might find ways of resisting being destroyed by the industrial system and that, out of their struggle for survival, a modern version of a peasant culture might be born.

To those readers who think Critchfield and Rüstow wore rose-tinted spectacles and immediately associate a traditional peasant community with ignorance, extreme conservatism, bigotry, and a chokingly tight level of social control, I would say that the new version does not have to be like its predecessor. In fact it would be almost impossible for it to acquire those characteristics, because attitudes have shifted too far and because of the constant, unstoppable flow of information and ideas into every community, particularly through the Internet. What community in the industrialized world nowadays gives sole moral authority to its priest? Nevertheless a great debate will have to break out in every emerging new-peasant community on the balance it should strike between the interests and rights of individuals and those of the group as a whole. Different communities will find different solutions, but of one thing we can be sure: while no place will opt for the over-restrictive systems of yesterday, very few will find it possible to survive if they adopt the most extreme libertarian positions of today.

Notes
1   Quoted by Lorna Siggins in *The Irish Times*, 7 April 1995.
2   Personal communication, 22 August 1995.
3   Quoted in *Inishbofin through Time and Tide*, Kieran Concannon (ed.) (Inishbofin Development Association 1993), p. 59.
4   *The Identity of France*, vol. 2 (HarperCollins: New York 1990), p. 675.
5   *The Villagers* (Anchor Books, Doubleday: New York 1994), p. 431.

1

Out of Control

The world economy has changed its nature. Since the early 1970s it has become highly unstable and has favoured the rich over the poor. Unfortunately, even if politicians accepted this there would be very little they could do.

FOR A QUARTER OF A CENTURY after the Second World War, most young men in Britain, almost regardless of their level of ability or education, could confidently assume that they would find themselves some sort of job within a few hours whenever they needed one. Admittedly the job might be utterly boring and without prospects, but it would provide an income on which they could live remarkably well. It was a marvellous time to start out in life.

But a sea change took place at the beginning of the 1970s, and twenty years later roughly a third of men aged between eighteen and twenty-four were either unemployed or 'economically inactive'[1] – a term applied to those people without work who have given up what governments see as their economic function of keeping wages down by continual job-hunting and who have thus made themselves ineligible for the dole. At any one time an estimated 100,000 young men were homeless as a result of inadequate incomes, some sleeping on city streets,[2] while theft – the crime for which this age group is most frequently responsible – almost tripled between 1971 and 1992.[3] 'For many youngsters, crime has become a matter of survival in this new society which appears to cater only for the winners,' Stewart Lansley of the Henley Centre for Forecasting wrote. 'Today, denial of the new trappings of consumerism means a denial of full citizenship ... The result has been a growing lack of community cohesion and a declining sense of social commitment.'[4]

Despair engendered by poverty and involuntary idleness drove increasing numbers of young men to suicide: in 1992, 500 males aged between eighteen and twenty-four killed themselves in Britain, 80 per cent more than ten years earlier. Indeed suicide became the second most common cause of death for all young people.[5] Other age groups were affected by the rise in unemployment of course, but it struck most harshly at the young, who, throughout the EU, were twice as likely to be unemployed as anyone else of an age to work. In France, for example, 45 per cent of those leaving school in 1995 with their baccalaureate and 80 per cent of those without any exam successes were unemployed nine months later. Robert Castel, a sociologist, was not alone when he warned of the danger of society breaking down.[6]

What had gone wrong? How did an economic system that had enabled Britain to keep overall unemployment between 1.2 and 2.1 per cent of the working population from 1945 to 1970 alter to such an extent that later governments were entirely unable to hold the problem in check? As the graph shows, unemployment rose rapidly after 1974, only falling back in periods in which the economy enjoyed brief booms but even then never returning to the level of its previous troughs. The difference between the trend in this latter part of the

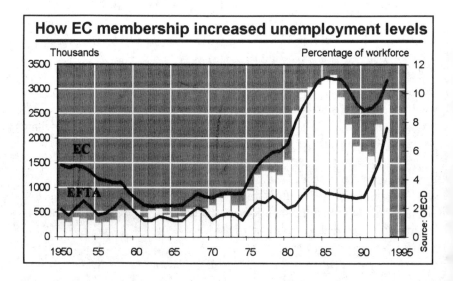

Graph 1.1 *The number of people unemployed in Britain, the white barred area, rarely exceeded 600,000 between the end of World War II and 1974. It then began to climb rapidly as a result of the country joining the EU and reached over 3 million. The grey line shows that European Free Trade Area countries continued to enjoy low unemployment until they either joined the EU themselves or prepared to join it. Their joblessness rates have since tripled.*

graph and that in the earlier one is so marked that by the early 1990s even optimists were forced to admit that full employment would not return when world economic conditions improved and that the problem was 'structural' – that is, created by changes in the way the economy worked.

The first structural change took place on Sunday 15 August 1971. Facing a range of problems that appear like molehills today but seemed like mountains at the time – a trade deficit of $4 billion and unemployment and inflation rates both moving up towards 5 per cent – President Nixon took the United States off the gold standard, thus removing the last fixed link between paper money and real goods. His action destroyed the gold-exchange standard currency system set up by the Bretton Woods agreement of 1944, under which the dollar was convertible into gold and all other major currencies were convertible into dollars. Under this system, countries had been able to expand the amount of money they had in circulation as long as they could keep their exchange rates in step with the gold-based dollar. Without it, the value of their currencies was based on nothing but confidence and fluctuated in response to the whims of the market to an unprecedented extent. The monetary world had no foundation, no fixed point – 'a floating non-system' the German Chancellor, Helmut Schmidt, called it – and central banks were forced continually to adjust interest rates and the amount of money in circulation on the basis of how their national economy was perceived internationally rather than the volume of trade going on. As Joel Kurtzman, a business columnist on *The New York Times*, wrote in his 1993 book *The Death of Money*:

It was a change of monumental proportions that not only redefined money but created the opportunity to dramatically speed up the rate at which transactions between companies and countries took place .... It created enormous arbitrage possibilities and set the stage for the invention of a myriad of new financial products. It also initiated the process of decoupling the 'money' economy from the 'real' economy. As a result, two-plus decades later, the money economy, where transactions take place purely for financial or speculative gain, and the real economy, where the world's raw materials, goods and services are produced and traded, are badly out of balance. That was Nixon's economic legacy.[7]

Another important economic change took place immediately before unemployment began its climb. On 1 January 1973, Britain, Denmark and Ireland joined the EEC, a move that required their governments to gradually harmonize their economies with those of the six existing members. This limited their economic freedom; and these three countries' unemployment levels – and those of the EEC as a whole – became significantly worse than those of other countries that were also coping with the death of the gold-exchange standard but decided to stay in the European Free Trade Association (EFTA) rather than join the Common Market.

The Kennedy (1967) and Tokyo (1979) GATT treaties also restricted the ways in which the British and Irish economies could be managed. The treaties' signatories undertook to reduce the rates of duty they imposed on imports from other participants. This curtailed their ability to create more jobs by protecting home producers from overseas competition and to use import duties to cure trade deficits. As a result, Britain was subjected to a flood of shoes, clothing and textiles from cheap-labour countries, and employment in British firms manufacturing these products fell from 973,000 to 412,000 between 1973 and 1993.[8] Other industrial sectors were similarly affected, and by 1982 a country that had had a trade surplus in manufactured goods in every peacetime year for more than a century and that in 1972 had exported goods worth 55 per cent more than those it imported went into what became a chronic trade deficit. By 1993 this deficit had grown to £13.4 billion. If the goods it represented had been made domestically, the additional activity could have created at least a million extra jobs.[9]

A fourth structural change was the complete abolition of exchange controls in 1979, four months after the Conservative Party came into office under Margaret Thatcher. This concession enabled the banks and financial institutions that had contributed so generously to the Tories' election fund to move their money to wherever in the world they could obtain the highest return: if, after allowing for any differences in risk, a project in New Guinea promised to be more profitable for the promoters than one in Newcastle, that was where the institutions felt their money should be. The fact that the total benefits from a project established in Britain were likely to be considerably higher to the British people than one overseas was ignored. Sectional interests triumphed over the public good.

These four changes left Britain without most of the powerful economic management tools it had previously used to create the space within which governmental policies could be carried out. In particular, the Keynesian methods of economic management that had produced full employment and relative stability in Britain between 1945 and 1970 became unusable, because if a government now ran a budget deficit to stimulate domestic demand and thus increase employment it could no longer use tariffs and quotas to control imports and prevent overseas competitors taking a lot of the extra work away. Indeed, if it was so much as hinted that the Chancellor of the Exchequer was planning to increase the public sector deficit, investors – fearing that the increased demand for imports would depress the international value of sterling – would move their funds to other currencies, precipitating the decline in the value of the currency they sought to escape.

In short, the four changes heightened the degree of instability in the British economy while simultaneously leaving those responsible for managing it with far fewer methods for its control. Other governments got themselves into the same position, of course, with the result that the world economic system became much more liable to catastrophic collapse. As the graphs show, interest rates and exchange rates have been more unstable recently than at any other time in the past fifty years, making it extraordinarily risky and difficult for anyone to try to build up any sort of small business along conventional lines.

Once the British government had signed away its right to use duties and quotas to control imports, it had only one way left to end unemployment. This was to lower domestic costs sufficiently to make home-produced goods and services so competitive internationally that they displaced imports and attracted sufficient export orders to enable all available workers to be offered jobs. This approach sounds fine until one looks at what it entails. There are two main ways in which a country can cut its costs compared with those of its competitors. The easiest and most effective is by devaluing its currency. Unfortunately, however, this method is unavoidably inflationary, because the increased costs of imports in terms of the national currency have to be passed on to consumers, and even if a way of avoiding these price rises could be found it would be undesirable to use it. This is because if import prices fail to rise there is no price incentive for people to switch to home-produced products, thereby creating jobs in the firms making them. One of devaluation's most powerful modes of action is lost.

Since inflation is highly unpopular with the electorate, the banks, and, most crucially, international investor-speculators, both Labour and Conservative governments have avoided devaluing except when compelled to do so, as in the exchange-rate crisis of September 1992, when devaluation proved its worth by generating an export boom. This leaves only one other way of reducing domestic price levels relative to those overseas: by improving efficiency and productivity. All sorts of 'supply-side' measures were taken to boost efficiency, including the elimination of restrictive practices such as union demarcation

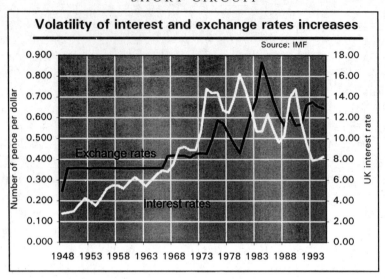

Volatility of interest and exchange rates increases

Source: IMF

Graph 1.2 *Since 1973 exchange rates and UK interest rates have fluctuated much more widely and violently than in the preceding quarter-century. This is shown here by the movement in the value of the US dollar in terms of sterling (scale on left), and UK long-term interest rates (right).*

agreements in the work-place, the 'Big Bang' reforms in the City, and the rules against building societies lending for things other than buying houses. These changes were generally welcomed by people who escaped the human cost of bringing them about, as no one likes the idea of paying a high price for goods or services because one group or another – whether it be printers on newspapers, solicitors in conveyancing, or a state monopoly in telecommunications – has a stranglehold on a particular activity and refuses to allow others to do it more cheaply. Calling a business 'competitive' became the highest form of praise.

The problem with promoting this type of efficiency, however, is that one person's cost is another person's wage packet. If unions, firms or institutions are forced to compete more aggressively against each other because the protective barriers they have erected around their activities over the years are broken down, jobs are lost and the wages and salaries paid to those remaining fall, cutting sales and hence employment in the shops and services that supply them. In other words, in their efforts to create employment, successive governments promoted policies that destroyed it. Only if an industry's turnover increased in real terms after its restructuring was there any possibility that additional jobs would be generated to replace those that the efficiency drive had eliminated. In most sectors this increase in turnover either did not happen or was insufficient to offset the losses from continuing productivity drives. The country found itself struggling up an escalator that was moving down: in any year in which Britain's total turnover as measured by its gross national product did not grow by over 3 per cent – and in the seven years up to 1995, growth averaged only 1.25 per cent – the number of jobs lost because of 'rationalization' and labour-saving technologies exceeded the number of new ones created, and the total amount of employment fell.

Few criticized the thinking behind the methods taken to achieve greater international competitiveness, because the British public and its political leaders had collectively lost their way. I suspect that, if asked, most politicians, regardless of their party affiliation, would have said that they were working to defend and, if possible, advance the welfare of their fellow-citizens. After some prompting, almost all might also have said that the higher the real wages those citizens received, the higher their economic welfare and hence their total welfare, other things being equal.* But no matter how leading the questioning, not one of them would have pointed out that there was a fundamental incompatibility between raising public welfare and the tactics they were pursuing. Nor would they have admitted that, by removing the protective barriers around the British economy, they had inadvertently created a system in which being competitive in both home and overseas markets boiled down to reducing their citizens' wage levels faster than their rivals. Almost no one in politics saw that the commonly accepted goal for the economic system, the welfare of the citizen, was being sacrificed to make the economy perform and that, quite quickly, many people's wages were likely to fall to Third World levels.

But the politicians should not be criticized too harshly: they were blinded by outdated economic theories. The real blame for what went wrong must be taken by the economics profession, which failed to point out that free trade could prove seriously damaging in the circumstances in which it was being introduced.

The conventional proof of the superiority of free trade assumes the economies of both trading partners to be in equilibrium before trading begins – in other words, to be producing at the highest level possible given their technology. This means that all their factors of production

* In *The Growth Illusion* (1992) I show that other things never remain equal whenever an economy grows because the growth process changes everything, including factors outside the economic sphere. However, most politicians and mainstream economists do not realize that growth can have harmful side effects: for them it is unquestionably A Good Thing.

– land, labour, and capital – must be fully occupied. The proof also assumes that the partners reach a similar equilibrium once trading is in progress. If they can assume these two equilibria, most economics undergraduates can show that in a two-country, two-commodity world with perfect competition, the trading equilibrium is better than the non-trading one, because it allows both countries to have more of the two traded commodities than they would if they did not trade.

But it is very doubtful whether a proof based on these limited circumstances has any relevance to our present world. This is because most countries are not generally working at maximum production, since they will not be using the latest technology and all their factors of production – unemployment will exist and their manufacturing companies will usually have unused capital equipment. As a result, even the most sophisticated economist has to struggle to say anything useful about whether the post-trade situation is likely to be better or worse than the pre-trade one, particularly if he or she attempts to take into account any changes in the distribution of income brought about by the growth of trade. Certainly, since the most significant feature of the post-1973 period has been the steady growth of unemployment, equilibria did not exist in most countries that moved towards freer trade. In these circumstances, economists should have admitted that it was impossible for them to say whether the removal of the remaining trade restrictions would prove beneficial. That almost every economist of note failed to do so is a black mark against a profession whose overwhelming support for free trade has been based on faith and intellectual idleness rather than evidence.

No one would open a corner shop without a much more thorough analysis of whether it might prove beneficial for the majority of participants than was ever obtained for the various phases of the EEC and GATT experiments. In an interview with the editor of the *Sunday Business Post* of Dublin in June 1993, shortly before he took up his post as secretary-general of GATT, Peter Sutherland claimed that the world economy would benefit by $200 billion if the Uruguay round of trade liberalization was completed. It was scarcely surprising that he used this figure, as it was the only estimate of the benefits of the Uruguay round available and had already been quoted to such an extent that the public could not be blamed for thinking it reliable. In fact the figure comes from a short briefing document, *Trade Liberalisation: What's at Stake?* produced by the OECD in Paris; and when, several months before Sutherland's interview, French journalists had asked the OECD secretary-general, Jean-Claude Paye, about it, an embarrassed Paye had dismissed the estimate as 'pretty theoretical' and stressed that if benefits on that scale were ever achieved it would be over a ten-year period and at the expense of some developing countries.[10]

The authors of the paper, Ian Goldin and Dominique van der Mesbrugghe, were not surprised that their figure was quoted so widely – 'After all, we were the only ones to try to quantify the gains,' van der Mesbrugghe told me[11] – but were alarmed at the importance being placed on what was in reality little more than an educated guess, which had now acquired an aura of authority. 'I call that $200 billion a biblical number now,' van der Mesbrugghe said, agreeing that it had entered the mythology of our times. And even though later studies have produced similar estimates using different approaches, he doesn't think that makes his figure any more likely to be correct. 'We all used the same trade data and made similar assumptions about which distortions would be corrected and to what extent,' he said.

The one aspect in which van der Mesbrugghe was sure their paper was correct was the one that Sutherland, an Irishman speaking to an Irish audience, signally failed to mention, much less stress. It was that, in the developed world at least, rural communities would lose as a result of the dismantling of agricultural support structures, while urban dwellers would reap the gains. And so, just as five years earlier the potential gains forecast by the equally unreliable Cecchini Report had provided the excuse for remote and rural areas to be sacrificed to create the EU's single market in 1992, so an estimate in which even its authors had no confidence was used, along with selective quotation, to justify a further far-reaching liberalization of world trade.

The forces pushing for these liberalizations were in fact exactly the same groups that had urged Margaret Thatcher to lift exchange controls: financial institutions, transnational companies, and people living on private means. Taken together, free trade and the free movement of capital had a profoundly damaging effect on the share of national income going to the rest of the economy, the people who work for their living and depend on their pay. The figures show this clearly. In 1952 two eminent economic historians, E.H. Phelps-Brown and P.E. Hart, published a classic paper that showed that between 1870 and 1950, wages stayed at between 36.6 and 42.3 per cent of national income, varying only slightly with the trade cycle and showing no clear time trend.[12] Their definition of wages excluded salaries. However, if one recalculates their results taking salaries and wages together, not only is the share of national income taken by labour much more stable from year to year but it rises from 54.8 per cent in 1870 to 65.3 per cent in 1950. In other words, over the eighty-year period during which the well-being of ordinary people improved substantially, the share of national income going to those working in the economy increased at the expense of those receiving rents, interest, and dividends.

If we bring the Phelps-Brown and Hart time series up to date we can see that the trend continued for the next twenty years, until by 1974, 70.5 per cent of the gross domestic product went to pay wages and salaries. After that year, however, the trend went sharply into reverse. By 1987 only 63.8 per cent of GDP was paid for work done, an unprecedented fall in so short a time. It was brought about largely by the introduction of technologies to increase competitiveness that involved the replacement of human labour with two other factors of production, capital and fossil energy.

Interestingly, 1974 was also the year that the Index of Sustainable Economic Welfare (ISEW) for Britain began to decline. ISEWs were devised because using a country's national income per head to provide an indication of the economic welfare of its citizens has several serious drawbacks. One arises because the goods and services produced during a year – which is what national income consists of – might be shared out very unequally. Another occurs because the country's citizens will not get to consume or otherwise benefit from a high proportion of their output, because some of it will be exported (to be replaced by a greater or lesser value of imports), some ploughed back into the economy as new investment, and some used to keep the system running in a tolerable way on tasks such as cleaning up pollution or fighting crime. At the same time some of their production – such as the goods and services they produce for themselves at home – will not be included in the official statistics, which only cover things that are bought and sold. And then some of the production the people do buy may make them no better off but simply keep things as they are. For example, if traffic noise increases so much that they have to install sound-proofing to sleep at night, the products they purchase to deaden the noise count towards national income, but they scarcely represent an overall gain. And finally, some components of national income may have been produced by depleting the country's physical capital – crops grown using methods that cause soil erosion, perhaps – and a correction is needed to allow for this.[13]

Tim Jackson and Nic Marks analysed the British national income figures for 1950–90 along these lines to produce one of the lines in

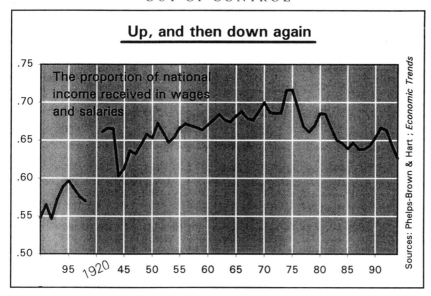

Graph 1.3 *The proportion of national income going to wage and salary earners in Britain was on a generally rising trend between 1870 and 1975. Since then, rents, profits and interest payments have taken a much larger share of GDP, throwing the trend into reverse.*

graph 1.4.[14] For each year they took the figure for total consumer expenditure from the national income statistics and corrected it for changes in the equality of income distribution, arguing that £1000 was likely to be of much more benefit to someone on a low income than to someone who was well off. Then they added their estimate of the value of housework and the other goods and services that people produced for themselves. Next they added the value of the services provided by the washing-machines, televisions and any other consumer durables people owned. Finally they included a proportion of the educational and health expenditure paid for by the state, ending up with an annual total that proved to be closely related to that year's per capita gross national product.

Then they made corrections for such things as the cost of commuting, traffic accidents, water, air and noise pollution, the loss of farmland, the depletion of non-renewable resources, and long-term environmental damage, including that to the ozone layer. Up to 1974 the total deduction they had to make to each year's figures to cover these items grew roughly at the same rate as consumer expenditure, with the result that the residual – their Index of Sustainable Economic Welfare – grew at much the same rate as GNP per head. For example, between 1950 and 1960 the GNP per head grew by 23.3 per cent and the ISEW by 21.0 per cent. In the next decade, 1960–70, the

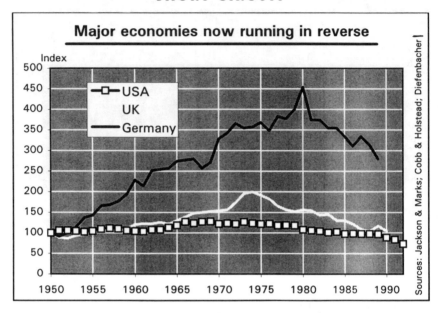

Graph 1.4 *Although national income per head doubled in the USA between 1950 and 1990, the Index of Sustainable Economic Welfare (ISEW) only increased by a small amount and then fell off: it is now at roughly two-thirds of the 1950 level. German and British ISEWs rose more strongly in that period but are now moving rapidly in reverse.*

figures were 26.3 and 27.5 per cent, respectively. After 1974, however, the required corrections grew faster than GNP per head, with the result that the ISEW began to fall, and by 1990 it was only 3 per cent higher than it had been in 1950, having dropped by over a half.*

Attempts to calculate ISEWs for other countries have produced similar results. In the United States, Clifford Cobb and Ted Halstead have produced a 'Genuine Progress Indicator', which shows that economic welfare began to decline there in 1968 and had fallen by over 40 per cent by 1992.[15] The decline in Germany began in 1981 but has been much more rapid: the index calculated by Hans Diefenbacher fell by 40 per cent in just seven years.[16]

---

* If I had been doing the calculation, the 1990 index would have come out much lower. This is because Jackson and Marks valued the goods and services people produced for themselves according to the wages they would have been paid if they had been employed to do them at the going rate rather than on the actual amount of housework, gardening, cooking and child care done. As a cleaner's wages went up by a factor of 2.8 (after correcting for inflation) between 1950 and 1990, this means that unless domestic productivity increased by that amount because of the wider use of vacuum-cleaners etc., Jackson and Marks were inflating the value of these chores and so distorting the ISEW upwards. They were worried about this aspect of their work themselves, remarking that 'it is by no means clear that this impact is fully justifiable'.

I have gone into this degree of detail about ISEWs because they throw an important light on the proposals I make in the next chapter. What the British, American and German indices clearly show is that the world economic system is now running backwards, and although it is producing more goods and services each year, all the increase and some more on top is required to keep the system functioning and to compensate for the damage it does. In other words, as the system gets more centralized and supplies our needs in increasingly indirect ways, using more and more packaging, advertising, capital equipment, and transport, it is becoming much more inefficient: it is not just experiencing diminishing returns to scale as it expands but negative ones.

Part of the reason the British ISEW changed direction in 1974 is that this was the year the distribution of national income began to become less equal; because of the reduced proportion of it going to wage and salary earners, a smaller fraction found its way to those at the bottom of the social scale. In the two decades after 1974, British wages fell sharply in comparison with those elsewhere, in part because of the government's efforts to boost competitiveness, in part because new technologies reduced demand. So, although British pay rates were much the same as those of Italy in 1980, by 1990 they were 25 per cent lower and, according to the European Commission's *Annual Employment Report* for 1993, only 5 per cent above those in Ireland and Spain. As a result, the poorest fifth of the population – the group with the weakest bargaining position in a jobs market that no longer had much use for unskilled or physical labour – saw its share of the fraction of national income going to households fall from 9.6 to 6 per cent during the 1980s.[17] The richest 20 per cent of the population, by contrast, received 43 per cent of total household income in 1991, compared with 35 per cent in 1979.

Similar income shifts took place in the United States and other countries, and when Loic Wacquant, a scholar at the Russell Sage Foundation in New York, compared urban poverty in Europe and America, he found that the economic system had started behaving differently. 'Roughly until the 1970s, the expansion of the economy translated into improvements at the bottom of the class structure,' he told *The Economist*. 'Now, when the economy goes into a downward spiral, neighbourhoods of exclusion get worse. But when it goes into an upward progression, they don't join in.'[18]

Despite the grave social consequences of these massive shifts in the distribution of national income away from payments for work and away from the worst off, the British government felt able to boast of its supply-side achievements in a glossy brochure, *Britain: the Preferred Location*, published in 1992 by the Department of Trade and Industry's 'Invest in Britain' Bureau to attract overseas investment. 'Labour costs in the UK continue to be low – significantly below other European countries,' the pamphlet says. 'The UK has the least onerous labour regulations in Europe, with few restrictions on working hours, overtime and holidays ... There is no legal requirement to recognise a trade union.'

But although by 1996 wages in some parts of Britain had been reduced below those in South Korea, the number of people able to find full-time work had fallen to some 15 per cent below 1978 levels. Unemployment rose throughout the rest of the EU too as each member-state sought to increase its competitiveness in relation to the others by introducing the energy-intensive and capital-intensive technologies that made it possible for less labour to produce a larger volume of goods. In the early 1990s, as Graph 1.1 shows, unemployment began to rise sharply among EFTA countries too as they began to align their economies more closely with those of the EU in preparation for eventual membership. In 1993, shortly before the second Danish referendum on the Maastricht treaty, Professor Sten Johansson, a former director of the Swedish Central Statistics Bureau, told a meeting in Copenhagen that Sweden had started aligning its economy with that of the EU three years previously and that the changes had proved very harmful for groups such as the old, the young, women, public employees, and those living in rural areas.

After the meeting Johansson told me that the Swedish social welfare system had run into trouble because economists had advised the government to remove the remaining controls on currency movements, on the grounds that they were having little effect anyway. However, once this was done, large sums of money had left Sweden, and the monetary system had become extremely unstable. Public sector spending had had to be cut sharply to restore market confidence, undermining the cradle-to-grave social welfare system that had been the envy of most of the world for almost forty years. 'We need to find another system of controlling monetary movements that does not involve locking everything rigidly together and thus causing even more problems,' Johansson said.

Hallvard Bakke, a Labour member of the Norwegian parliament, told the same meeting that politicians in Norway and Sweden were pushing for EU membership although a majority of the people did not want it. 'The Nordic welfare model puts people at the centre. It ensures that they can live a good life without moving their homes. EU policy is the exact opposite: it is that people should move to wherever the work is,' he said. The Nordic countries, Bakke noted, had always been dependent on overseas trade, which made up the same proportion of their national income a hundred years ago as it did today. 'Despite this high level of trade we have been able to build up our own welfare model. The market is good for many things, but not for employment and the good life.'

He was right. When a country with generous social welfare provisions such as Norway or Sweden is forced to compete in an uncontrolled way against dozens of other countries that leave the poor, the sick and the old to fend for themselves, it will inevitably lose markets to them because its traders are carrying overheads their rivals do not. In the past it was argued that the industrialized countries would be able to protect their welfare systems, wage levels and working conditions by keeping several technological jumps ahead of their Third World competitors. Now, however, it is hard to find anyone who believes this because, on the one hand, the technologies used in south-east Asia's export factories are little different from those used in the West, while on the other hand, Western countries are competing ever more fiercely for market shares among themselves, each of them cutting wages and welfare in an attempt to get an edge. The only Western enterprises that can hope to remain relatively unaffected by Third World competition are the manufacturers of sophisticated aircraft and armaments – and then only for as long as the huge public R&D subsidies to these activities continue.

In principle, then, John Major was quite correct when he repeated his opposition to the social chapter of the Maastricht treaty at the EU summit in Copenhagen in June 1993 on the grounds that it would impose higher costs on European manufacturers and make them less competitive in world markets. He was also right to say that social welfare benefits throughout the EU would have to be cut if it was to trade successfully around the globe. 'Long-term unemployment is higher in the European Community than in either Japan or the United States,' he wrote later that year.[19] 'There is now increasing agreement that these problems stem from the inflexibility of European labour markets, from the tangle of regulations, from wasteful systems of welfare, from the burdens of too high systems of taxation, which Europeans have imposed on themselves in the last forty years.'

'European labour costs rose by 4 per cent a year during the 1980s while barely changing amongst our major competitors,' he went on.

'Europe spends proportionately nearly twice as much as the Japanese on public social security and health care and over 60 per cent more than the Americans. The problem will be compounded as the proportion of old people in our population increases. Unless we take action to contain costs, Europe's taxpayers will be paying 30 per cent more for social security and health in real terms by 2020. Unless we act to deregulate our economies, there will be too few earners in Europe to pay those tax bills.'

No one was in a position to dispute his argument that the EU countries needed to cut their taxes and their labour, health care and social security costs, because – largely as a result of the economists' failure to admit that the case for free trade collapsed in conditions of unemployment – alternative strategies less reliant on competing internationally had not been worked out. Even on the political fringes very few people pointed out that free trade was not compulsory and that countries need not trade on externally dictated terms because they could trade on their own, exchanging goods and services with the rest of the world only when and to the extent that they found it beneficial to do so.

In Europe only France, which has had only five years in which the level of unemployment dropped since the middle 1960s, has seriously discussed alternatives to free trade. That it did so was largely because of the work of Maurice Allais, who won the Nobel Prize for economics in 1988. Allais believes that free trade will lead to a surge in imports from low-wage countries and cause many companies to shift their factories there. As a result, he says, Europe will experience mass unemployment, huge wage inequalities, and a social explosion.[20] His thinking gave France the intellectual confidence to oppose the limitations on agricultural subsidies sought by the United States as part of the Uruguay GATT round and for President Mitterrand to tell a television interviewer at the 1993 Copenhagen summit that the EU should adopt rules to enable it to protect its industries against imports from low-wage countries.

However, France is the exception, and unless a trade war breaks out it is impossible to envisage a generation of European leaders that has devoted a large part of its working life and prestige to turning the EEC into the European Union making a 180-degree turn and calling for trade restrictions until unemployment is conquered. And, if there is no trade war, an entirely new generation of politicians will have to emerge before policies that give preference to people rather than to mistaken concepts of economic efficiency are adopted. In other words we are likely to have to wait at least ten years for any national or international restructuring to begin.

In the meantime the outlook for many people is grim. In a state of increasing desperation, our present political leaders and their immediate successors will try ever harder to make their collapsing creation work, hoping rather than believing that the world economy will suddenly start to work perfectly and a more general prosperity will return once the few remaining trade barriers have been brought down, the burden of tax and social spending cut, and the intensity of competition heightened further. This is a forlorn hope. All that will happen is that more and more people will be excluded from full participation in the mainstream economic system. Unemployment will mount rapidly and generate even more crime and misery as social welfare payments are whittled away. Too lazy or complacent to seek alternatives, politicians, academics and commentators will cheer this impoverishment on, arguing that the more rapidly a country adjusts to world market conditions by getting its wages and other costs down, the brighter its future will be.

'The most worrying aspect of the present crisis is that, for the first time in history, the rich no longer need the poor,' Pierre Calame, president of the Foundation for the Progress of Man, told a conference in Paris in June 1993. He went on to explain that in the past the rich had always needed the poor – as servants, to grow food, to build their houses, to fight their wars, and to make the goods they required. Now, however, many of the jobs the poor had done were performed by machines, and, as far as the rich were concerned, it was unnecessary for as many people as previously to be retained within the economic system. The surplus was therefore being expelled and maintained in limbo at the lowest level of public support possible without their becoming a serious threat to the well-being and equanimity of the better-off.

But if the rich can manage without the poor as a result of technology, can the poor manage without the rich? I believe they can, and the ways in which they can do so are what the rest of this book is about.

Notes
1 *Financial Times*, 18 February 1993.
2 Telephone conversation with Centre Point, London, 30 July 1994.
3 The total number of burglaries in England and Wales in 1971 was 451,537, and

the number of thefts and cases of handling stolen goods recorded by the police was 1,003,645. The total number of thefts of all types was therefore 1,455,182. In 1992 there were 1,355,274 burglaries and 2,851,638 cases of theft and handling, giving a total of 4,206,912 crimes, which is 2.89 times higher. Figures supplied by the Home Office Press Office, London, 9 June 1994.

4 *After the Gold Rush* (Century: London 1994), p. 50.

5 *Guardian*, 3 November 1993, 12 October 1994.

6 *Guardian*, 13 April 1995.

7 *The Death of Money* (Simon and Schuster: New York 1993), p. 51.

8 Statistics supplied by the National Union of Knitwear and Allied Trades, 13 June 1994.

9 Author's estimate.

10 See Chakravarthi Raghavan, *Third World Resurgence*, no. 29-30 (January 1993), p. 42.

11 Telephone conversation.

12 'The share of wages in the national income', *Economic Journal*, June 1952.

13 The deficiencies of national income as an indicator of economic welfare are discussed at greater length in my book *The Growth Illusion* (pp. 9-14); there is also a discussion of the pioneering attempts to improve on it.

14 Stockholm Environment Institute (Box 2142, 103 14 Stockholm, Sweden) and New Economics Foundation (London), *Measuring Sustainable Economic Welfare: a Pilot Index, 1950-1990*.

15 Clifford Cobb and Ted Halstead, *The Genuine Progress Indicator: Summary of Data and Methodology* (September 1994), available from Redefining Progress, 116 New Montgomery (room 209), San Francisco, California 94105.

16 Hans Diefenbacher, *Towards a Sustainable Economy: Six Proposals to Take a New Look at Statistical Figures* (n.d.), available from the author at FEST, Schmeilweg 5, 69118 Heidelberg, Germany.

17 *Social Trends* (HMSO: London 1994).

18 Quoted in an article on the growth of an underclass in Europe as a result of long-term unemployment, 30 July 1994.

19 *Economist*, 25 September 1993.

20 *Economist*, 1 October 1994, 'Global Economic Survey', p. 7.

2

Creating Enough Elbow Room

In the world economy only a very limited range of activities is commercially feasible in most communities because of the intensity of competition from outside. We must therefore build independent, parallel economies if we are to fill more of our needs for ourselves.

THE PREVIOUS CHAPTER ATTEMPTED to make two important points. One was that a large part of the world's population has lost the means and the ability to provide for itself and has become dependent on a single, highly unstable economic system that has no use for a growing proportion of it. The second was that for the next few years, unless there is a trade war, politicians are unlikely to be willing or able to protect their citizens from being damaged by this system, even though it is now actually running backwards and making life worse throughout the world.

If both points are valid, is there anything that people like us can do? Can we achieve a better balance between the world economy on the one hand and millions of local economies on the other, many of which have contracted almost to vanishing point? To put this another way, can communities limit the scope of the industrial system and its individualistic culture without governmental help, and by so doing create a protected space within which local, peasant-type economies and collective cultures can be re-created or revived?

Before answering these questions, I need to define two terms. First, by a peasant economy I mean a society in which most families own their own means of making their livelihoods, be this a workshop, a fishing-boat, a retail business, a professional practice, or a farm. In such an economy families would, of course, be free to join with other families to own the source of their livelihoods collectively. Second, by the industrial economy I mean the system under which activities are primarily ways of making profits for shareholders rather than providing ways of life. In the industrial system, groups of investors typically put up the capital and employ workers to carry out their ventures, paying them wages that are regarded as a cost to be minimized rather than a gain. In the peasant system, those wanting a way of life that will also provide them with a livelihood find or borrow the capital to employ themselves, and count their wages as a benefit.

The difference between the industrial and peasant systems is not only that one seeks to minimize the returns to labour and maximize those to capital while the other wants to minimize the return to borrowed capital and maximize a wide range of benefits, including income, for the group involved: there is also a difference of scale. An investor-owned, industrial-system venture can grow extremely large through mergers or by ploughing back its profits, the techniques employed by General Motors – with 251,130 people on its payroll and an income that exceeds the GNP of all but twenty-one countries – to become the biggest company in the world in numbers employed at the beginning of the 1990s. Peasant projects, by contrast, tend to stay fairly small unless they adopt the industrial approach and employ people who are not shareholders or participate in joint ventures with investor-financed firms. Many of the bigger Irish agricultural co-ops owe their size to exactly these non-co-operative strategies.

If it were possible to obtain the political support, a better balance could be achieved between the industrial and peasant systems by enacting laws limiting the size to which investor-financed enterprises were allowed to grow and splitting big businesses into hundreds of employee-owned parts. In addition, shops and factories could be barred from expanding beyond a certain size and restricted in the type of technology and the amount of capital per worker they could use. Similarly, to keep more families working the land, farmers could be prevented from increasing their acreages.

But these top-down tactics are pipe-dreams in the present climate, and we have no alternative but to work from the bottom up. In other words, rather than changing the law we will have to change attitudes and ideas – and consequently behaviour – if we are to build peasant-system economies strong enough to survive the pressures and instabilities of an industrial-system world.

Here are three approaches I think we will have to adopt to achieve a satisfactory co-existence.

CHANGE NUMBER 1
We must begin to use local resources to meet community needs rather than the wants of markets far away

At present all our thinking about the right way to bring prosperity to the places in which we live boils down to identifying goods and services that can be made in or provided from our communities to be sold to people outside. Mainstream economists tell us that with the money we earn from these activities we will be able to buy the goods and services we ourselves need from wherever in the world they are cheapest, and, because each community everywhere will eventually produce and sell only those things they can provide most effectively, everyone everywhere will be able to have more goods and services and be better off than if they tried to do everything for themselves.

This indirect way of meeting needs worked well when most of the goods and services people needed were still provided from their own areas; but now that communities are almost entirely dependent on outside supplies it has become much less satisfactory because of the increased levels of competition and instability in the world economy. For example, if a community organizes golfing holidays for wealthy people from Sweden, as my town has done, it may bring extra money into its area for a year or two, but eventually several dozen other destinations are bound to offer very much the same sort of holiday too, bringing everyone's prices down. This increases the wealth of the golf tourists in relation to the communities competing to serve them and explains why, since world trade has become so important, the gulf between poor countries and rich ones has grown.

After being forced to give price reductions, and paying outsiders for food, drink, heating oil, electricity, replacements, labour taxes, and so on, the communities are left with a much smaller income for themselves than they expected when they first planned the holidays. This might not be too bad if they were able to shrug their shoulders and go back to the way things were, but this is rarely possible: guesthouses and hotels that have borrowed to build extra rooms and take on extra staff now have higher overheads and will find it financially ruinous to revert to previous levels of turnover. Their dependence on an income flow from the outside world has increased, and, consequently, so has their community's. The conventional economic remedy for the reduced margins is usually to suggest that the community find another source of high-paying holidaymakers or take up some other enterprise altogether and make good profits from that – until rivals catch on and, by offering similar products, bring everyone back to square one and force the whole find-a-new-product-or-market cycle to start again.

By offering themselves as holiday destinations in a highly competitive market, the communities have not only become more dependent on outside earnings and seen the wealth of their target customers rise in comparison with their own: they have also increased the risk of economic disruption they run, since, should the exchange rate vary, a postal dispute prevent bookings coming in, air traffic controllers strike, or a recession develop in the overseas economy, those involved in the tourist trade could be very hard hit, with knock-on effects on the rest of their communities.

In current conditions, then, selling things outside our immediate areas to earn the money to buy the goods and services we must have to survive cannot be considered the basis for a sustainable, stable local community. What we must do instead is look at the resources of our areas and see how they can be used to meet our communities' vital needs directly rather than via the conventional, indirect, produce-for-someone-else-and-buy-one's-requirements-in route.

I know we have been taught that this latter indirect route is more efficient because it takes more resources to grow bananas in Ennis, Essex or Essen than in Ecuador. My response to this is threefold. One answer is that the much-touted efficiency of the world trade system is a grotesque myth, as I will demonstrate shortly. For the moment, we only need ask ourselves how a system that condemns so many people to spend their lives in involuntary idleness and uses so many scarce resources to do the simplest things can still be regarded as efficient, particularly as we saw in the previous chapter that as some countries' output increases, their citizens are actually receiving a smaller amount of economic welfare year by year.

Secondly, even if the indirect system was more efficient, we ought to at least discuss how much inefficiency we would tolerate from the direct route in order to reduce the risk of our lives being blighted and our livelihoods disrupted by instabilities in the external world. Most of us pay premiums for house or car insurance every year, accepting the certainty of a small loss in exchange for avoiding the risk of a big one. As communities we should also be prepared to pay for insurance, in this case against economic disruption, particularly as local economies that boast a wide range of activities are not only more sta-

ble but provide much more scope for their members to find nic*l*
within which they can fulfil themselves.

Thirdly, bananas are non-essentials, and if they were imported as a
direct exchange for some non-essential we grew, the fact that we
relied on other people to produce them would not matter: either
party to the trade would be able to terminate it whenever they
wished without seriously harming the other. Our goal should be to
minimize our dependence on external trade, not to phase it out altogether. Trading outside our communities should become something
we can engage in if we choose, and then on our own terms, not something that is vital for our survival.

CHANGE NUMBER 2
World prices must not determine what we produce

Existing levels of prices or profits cannot be allowed to determine
whether or not we should make or grow something in our communities. This is because there is no connection between an item's value to
our community and the price our neighbours pay for it in normal
times. True, most economists and right-wing politicians believe that
market prices should determine what is produced, in what quantity,
by what method, and where, because it is 'uneconomic' and
'inefficient' to take other factors into consideration. But this is
because they believe that the market price of something is equal to its
value and because all their thinking is in terms of the industrial system. Efficiency, however, can only be measured in relation to one's
objectives; and if we have objectives that those running the industrial
system do not share – such as satisfying work, stability, sustainability
and fairness rather than the maximization of returns to investors' capital – our success or failure must be measured with respect to our targets and not theirs.

From the point of view of progress towards community goals, local
production for local use can be much more efficient than production
for outside markets. This is because a community is interested in a
much wider range of benefits than merely the profit a business makes.
It is, for example, interested in the total income – the wages, the
profits, the payments for local materials – that the business brings into
or keeps in the community's area. Investors, on the other hand, are
usually only concerned with the tiny fraction of a business's total
income flow that ends up in their hands, an outlook that, from a com-

munity's point of view, leads to the tail wagging the dog.

Moreover, because a community needs its income for long-term tasks, such as raising children, it wants to be sure that the activity will continue for many years. Investors, on the other hand, tend to have very short time horizons and frequently give up valuable future benefits to get more immediate returns. In a 1994 survey by the Confederation of British Industry, two-thirds of the companies that responded required investment projects to pay for themselves in three years or less.[1] What is efficient for our communities is therefore very different from what is efficient for investors in the wider world.

Unfortunately the future of the planet as well as of communities is clouded by the 'market price equals value' type of thinking. In 1990 a winner of the Nobel Prize for economics, Professor William Nordhaus of Yale University, was keen to calculate how much the United States should be prepared to spend to lower the risks presented by global warming. Because agriculture and forestry, the sectors that would be most affected by any warming, made up only 3 per cent of America's national income (which is, of course, a measure of its output at market prices), he proceeded to assume that this was their value to its citizens. In other words, he overlooked the fact that all the non-agricultural things that go to make up a modern economy and that would be relatively unaffected by the two to three degree rise in average temperature he was assuming – intensive care units of hospitals, underground mining, science laboratories, communications, heavy manufacturing and microelectronics were the examples he gave – would be valueless if people had nothing to eat. This remarkable oversight enabled him to conclude that, as by no means all food and forest production would be lost, the maximum damage likely to be suffered by the United States was in the region of 0.25 per cent of its national income. Consequently, after allowing a generous margin for uncertainties, he argued that for the United States it was not worth spending more than 2 per cent of its national income each year to reduce greenhouse gas emissions. (It is not, of course, spending even that at present.)

Nordhaus's verdict would be amusing if it had not reduced the scale and urgency with which the world's governments have responded to the climate crisis, and if fellow economists were not still citing his paper with approval. By confusing price with value, he failed to recognize that our food, raw materials and energy supplies are worth much more to us than are other products and services on which we might spend the same proportion of our income. Food and transport make up roughly equal shares of the average American's budget, but he or she would give up practically everything to continue eating when faced with death by starvation and considerably less to secure petrol to keep running a car.

We must not make this mistake. In other words, we must not use world prices to determine which activities are profitable and can therefore be carried on in our communities because if we do we might find that the production of items of the greatest value to us, such as food, clothing, light and heat, are ruled out and that increased economic independence is therefore impossible. Indeed we could well find that the only things that are profitable are those we are doing already, along with one or two activities we have only just thought of.

But if many of the types of production necessary to make our communities more self-reliant would be loss-making at current, externally dictated prices, we have a huge problem on our hands because even in a peasant economy no commercial activity will continue long unless those engaged in it get a reasonable return for their efforts and on the capital they have involved. A generation ago, as we saw in the previous chapter, governments enabled national prices to differ from those on the world market by using import duties and quota controls. This widened the range of production that was commercially possible. Now, however, these methods have been outlawed by international agreements, and there is no way of preventing world prices from setting local ones. As a result, unless we can find some way for local producers to make a profit supplying us with a full range of essential goods and services at prices identical with those from outside, our attempts to achieve greater self-reliance are likely to be stillborn.

At first sight a quest for such a way seems doomed to failure, particularly as there are only two basic approaches local producers can use to lower their prices. One is to be so super-efficient that they can match their outside competitors on price, whatever the outside labour costs, whatever the technology, whatever the source of raw material, whatever the economies of scale. The second is for us to reduce the prices at which we supply our labour and capital to local businesses sufficiently to make their prices competitive: in other words, to give them a subsidy. Neither of these strategies seems promising, but let us look at both more closely to see if anything can be done.

OPTION 1
Becoming super-efficient

Whatever Professor Nordhaus might think, agriculture, forestry, fishing, quarrying and mining are primary activities that support everything else. A geography teacher I once had at school explained it roughly like this: 'At one time most people were farmers. As their knowledge and skill increased from generation to generation, they were able to produce more food and raw materials than they needed for themselves, and this surplus was available to support an increasing number of people in other activities, including crafts, religion, the military, and government. Gradually a triangular-shaped social and economic structure developed, with the broad mass of the people involved in agriculture or mining at its base, a manufacturing or crafts sector employing a smaller number of people above them, and a still smaller professional, military, religious and administrative caste higher still, with the apex made up of the monarch and the nobility.'

That was where my teacher left his analysis, but we can take the story on. By 1800, as a result of the increases in productivity brought about by the Industrial and Agricultural Revolutions, the British economy was no longer shaped like a triangle: roughly equal numbers of people were engaged in the primary, manufacturing and service sectors, making it more like a square.[2] Now, two hundred years later, we are back to the triangle again, only this time it is inverted, since only a tiny number of people – just 3.2 per cent of the working population in England, for example – are involved in primary production. The manufacturing sector is shrinking too: in England the percentage of the employed work force in manufacturing dropped from 28.9 to 23.8 between 1981 and 1989. The service sector will probably offer fewer jobs in the future too; meanwhile the number of people who are involuntarily without work has grown.

The whole modern economic structure is therefore supported on a tiny primary-sector employment base. However, everyone not involved in primary production still needs food and raw materials to survive and, somehow or other, must acquire the right to tap into the supply line to siphon their requirements off. There are many ways they can do this. They can sell goods and services to the primary producers themselves, or to others who provide primary producers with such goods and services, or to yet others who, directly or indirectly,

Graph 2.1 The world turned upside down

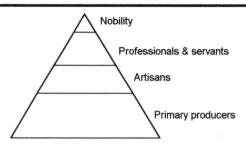

Five hundred years ago, most of the population of working age was engaged in growing food or in some other form of primary production. Output per person was low, so only a limited number of people could be supported in other activities.

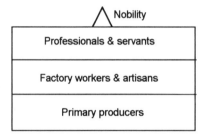

The Agricultural Revolution increased output per farm worker substantially and thus allowed many more people to work in secondary and tertiary occupations. By 1800, British society had a rectangular structure.

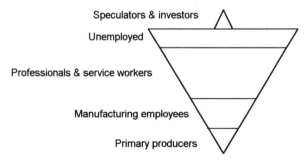

Today, advances in technology have allowed a handful of farm workers, miners, foresters, and fishermen to meet the primary production needs of the rest of the population. Society is now shaped like an inverted pyramid.

perhaps at three or four removes, are involved in the processing or distribution chain. People who are unable to supply such goods and services because they are too young, unemployed, sick or too old must buy their primary supplies with income transferred from people who are.

As the number of people involved in primary production shrinks because of improvements in productivity or imports from overseas, those displaced from the sector must find places for themselves further up. More and more people have to stand on the remaining primary producers' shoulders, balancing themselves and supporting others above them in ways that become increasingly complex. Each person tries to make their activity an inescapable part of some branch of the lengthening and increasingly complex food chain. As a result, the margin between the price the primary producers receive for their products and the price the ordinary consumer pays for them has to grow continually to support the increasing number of intermediaries in the system and the people who depend on them, directly and indirectly.

For example, 2 per cent of the working population produce just over half of Britain's food in expenditure terms, the rest being imported. If the foreign farmers have the same labour productivity as the British, this means that it takes four farmers to support ninety-six non-farmers, a ratio of 1:24. Roughly a fifth of people's after-tax earnings is spent on food. But assuming that farmers earn much the same after-tax income as the rest of the population, an average of only a twenty-fourth of each non-farmer's after-tax income – or about 20 per cent of his or her food budget – will find its way into the farmer's personal bank account. This means that roughly 80 percent of the average food purchase goes to non-farmers: shopkeepers, manufacturers and other intermediaries in the food chain, and firms that supplied the farmer with machinery, fertilizers, and other inputs.

Two comments can be made on this. One is that the 80 per cent estimate gives some idea of the scope for creating incomes in our communities by eliminating inputs and services provided from outside. The other is that if we force the present food production and distribution system – or any other part of the industrial economy – to become more competitive, we will destroy some of the ways in which people support themselves and others in the inverted human pyramid. Those dislodged will either find some other way to stay up there or drop off altogether by emigrating, committing suicide, or dying prematurely, as some unemployed people do, from stress and despair.[4] The unemployed are, of course, still up in the triangle, supported by

[main text continues p.42]

SERVICE SECTOR JOBS MAY BE IN DECLINE

The idea promoted by politicians that the service-sector will absorb all the workers losing their jobs in manufacturing and primary production may be wide of the mark. Professor Jonathan Gershuny of the University of Essex has been pointing out since 1978 that 'with a few exceptions, purchases of services by households in most developed countries have actually been declining as a proportion of total expenditure over the last two or three decades'.[3] This is because families have been doing more for themselves – for example, they have replaced outside laundry workers and inside domestic servants with vacuum-cleaners, dishwashers and washing-machines and do their own painting and decorating.

The reason this trend has not become apparent is that it has been masked in the statistics by an increase in the number of jobs in health services and education as a result of the increase in state expenditure in these areas in the 1950s and 60s and, more recently, by industrial firms contracting out specialist activities, such as cleaning and design work, that were formerly done in-house. Since state health and educational employment is unlikely to increase because of the reluctance of taxpayers to finance even its present level, and since the scope for additional sub-contracting by industry is limited by both the relatively small proportion of the work force still occupied there and the amount of subcontracting that has already been done, overall employment in the service sector is unlikely to grow. 'The services do not seem to offer a very promising basis for the expansion of employment,' Gershuny says. 'We may be seeing now an overall decline.'

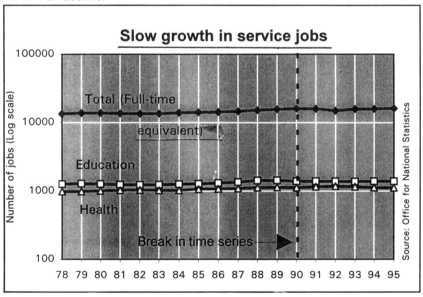

Graph 2.2 If two part-time jobs are equivalent to one full-time, the number of full-time equivalent service-sector jobs in Britain grew by 12.8 per cent between 1978 and 1995, although a break in the way the data is given means that this rise is overstated. The number of full-time equivalent jobs in the health and education parts of the sector barely changed over the period.

41

the rest of the community through its taxes. Analytically, they are a subset of the service sector that provides no paid services in return for the primary products they consume. Achieving increased competitiveness by means that increase unemployment simply shifts people from a place in the triangle where they have an economic role to one in which they have none. Individual firms gain from the shift because the cost of supporting the people involved is moved from their shoulders to those of the nation as a whole. Apart from the companies' shareholders, however, everyone loses out.

It is not only in primary production that the necessity of supporting increasing numbers of people at higher levels of the triangle has widened the gap between what producers get for their products and the price the consumer pays. Exactly the same has happened in manufacturing. Consumer electronics and domestic appliance retailers frequently take a 100 per cent margin, while British clothing chain stores and mail-order houses generally work on retail mark-ups of 150 to 200 per cent. 'Their margins have been high for as long as I've been in business,' says a friend who runs his own clothing company. 'In the last ten years, however, they have been sourcing from further afield, using the lower prices to increase their margins while keeping the price to the customer down.'

The presence of large and increasing margins in highly competitive markets means that the industrial system's long and elaborate distribution network charges as much or more for getting products to the consumer as those products cost to make. These distribution networks are the reason I referred to the reputed efficiency of the modern economic system as a grotesque myth. They are the industrial system's weak spot and a key area for attack in any effort to increase local self-reliance. If a local firm or farm has higher production costs than an external one but can short-circuit the normal methods of distribution by selling more directly to local consumers, the savings it should be able to make by avoiding the network's 150 per cent mark-ups ought to be more than enough to enable it to survive. However, if local producers distribute their products over a wide area through normal channels, they will acquire their external competitors' cost structure and, if they lack any other advantage, will almost certainly fail. Short-circuiting as much as possible of the external triangle by selling direct is therefore the key way to open up a wider range of profitable local production possibilities.

OPTION 2A
Cutting labour costs

The two other ways by which small local producers can come to compete on price with large outside firms are almost as powerful as selling direct. They involve the community stepping in to lower the labour and capital costs of community firms. Let's look at labour costs first.

Workers all over the world are being asked to accept lower wages as an alternative to losing their jobs; can we ask people in our communities to accept lower wages in order to create them? The first thing we need to recognize is that there is an important difference between the two situations. If workers accept less pay from a firm that is selling internationally, there is a very real danger that their sacrifice will compel workers elsewhere to accept lower wages too and thus initiate a worldwide bout of competitive wage-cutting, which impoverishes employees and leaves only those consumers whose incomes have not been cut as beneficiaries.

For example, in 1992 Waterford Crystal made some of its workers redundant, forced the remainder to take a 25 per cent wage cut, and began importing cheaper cut-glass items from eastern Europe. This left its smaller Irish rivals with no option but to cut wages too. 'Prices in the market have reduced, and if you reduce prices you have to reduce your costs. We must maintain our relative position in the market-place,' the managing director of Cavan Crystal, Brian Williams, told *The Irish Times*, explaining why the company was seeking a 15 per cent wage cut after its best trading year for some time. 'Galway Crystal's workers have accepted a wage cut of 20 per cent,' Mr Williams added. A fourth firm, Tipperary Crystal, was also said to be negotiating cuts.[5]

From an economic point of view, all this type of wage-cutting does is shift the world supply curve for the particular product upwards, making more available at any given price, while shifting the demand curve down because of the consumption effects of the lower wages. These consumption effects are often ignored: during the debate in the United States on the North American Free Trade Agreement (NAFTA) and the Uruguay GATT round, pro-free-trade commentators frequently argued that poor Americans would suffer badly if imports of cheap shoes and clothing were restricted in order to protect domestic manufacturers. What the campaigners failed to ask themselves, however, was who made clothes and footwear in *American* factories, and how *their* purchasing power would be affected if their jobs disappeared.

If a firm sells internationally, the purchasing power the workers give up by agreeing to take less pay gets distributed to consumers throughout the world, and there is no way of ensuring that any of it will return to the communities it came from. By contrast, if a group of unemployed people decide to set up a co-op producing goods for sale in their community and pay themselves less than the normal rate, *all* the benefits of their decision stay within the area. No wealth has been lost. Instead, it has been created, to the extent that goods or services are being produced where none were produced before. Moreover, there is no risk of setting off a chain of mutually destructive wage cuts throughout the world. Lower wages should therefore be resisted as a method of creating or preserving jobs unless all the goods or services to be produced by the enterprise will be sold within its own area.

But if we agree to accept less than the going rate from a local company whose market is entirely local, we should seek more satisfying work in return. All of us already quote different wage rates on something approaching a local-versus-international basis. For example, when we paint a bedroom at home we don't charge the family for doing so: we get our reward in other ways. It is the same when we make up costumes for a local dramatic society: we do it, not for money (in fact the chances are we'll end up out of pocket) but because we like being involved. On the other hand, we would never dream of accepting a consultancy contract from an international bank for anything less than the maximum we could negotiate for it.

Both the house-painting and the theatrical costume-making represent one end of a money-to-satisfaction continuum on which most of us operate: they provide absolutely no cash but a great deal of the two forms of satisfaction every normal person craves, one of which stems from successfully tackling an interesting and worthwhile project and the other from being appreciated. The bank job represents the other end of the continuum, delivering a lot of cash and a limited amount of either form of satisfaction because no one outside the bank (and probably within it) will show any gratitude if one fulfils the contract successfully, and there is a fair chance that the high income it brings will arouse envy among one's friends.

This trade-off between wages and satisfaction is highly complex, particularly as money can be the least important thing that people get

CREATING ENOUGH ELBOW ROOM

from a job. Indeed, being paid for doing something can sometimes damage the satisfaction the activity brings. In a goldmine of a book, *The Market Experience,*[6] Professor Emeritus Robert Lane of Yale University describes an experiment in which students were paid to do a boring task and got more pleasure from it than a control group that was unpaid. However, when another batch of students was paid to do interesting work, they found it less rewarding than those who had done the same task for nothing. In fact the paid group doing the interesting job got even less enjoyment than those who had been happy to do the boring task unpaid because they thought it was useful. In another test, unpaid volunteers showed more commitment than paid workers; they were more likely to continue with their tasks when their supervisors left the room.

Lane quotes from a study by F. Thomas Juster that shows that, almost regardless of the nature of their work or their social class, people prefer their jobs to most of their leisure activities:

People do not work for 'nothing' but what they do work for is often not just the pay they receive ... They may work because meeting the challenges of work increases their sense of personal control, or out of a sense of duty, or because of a pressing need to achieve some high standard of excellence. [Whatever] their motives may be, people evade the market's focus on exchange, for these motives are satisfied by internal rewards that do not depend upon exchanging money for work.

In my view, the internal rewards Lane mentions are best provided by firms owned and controlled by those working in them, which see their role as serving their communities and regard work not only as a source of income but as one of the main ways people fulfil themselves. I also think that unless we can construct environments that foster such firms, cut-throat international competition will ensure that in a few years' time, highly paid jobs will be available only to a fortunate few, and the choice for many of the rest of us will be between unemployment and a low-paid job in a large, highly pressured firm scrambling for its place in the world market, a firm to which we can rarely make an individual contribution and matter as people not at all.

If I am right, taking a lower cash wage to work in a peasant-economy firm may turn out in the end not to involve any sacrifice at all. Indeed, in spite of all I have said, these firms may well be able to survive and prosper without paying lower wages than international ones, particularly if the worker-shareholders accept part of their pay in a local currency. This is a possibility we will explore later.

45

OPTION 2B
Cutting capital costs

Local firms can also be helped to match external competitors on price if they have access to capital at low interest rates or, better yet, no interest at all. This is easier to arrange than it might seem: it is largely a matter of enabling firms to avoid borrowing from the commercial banks, using techniques explored in detail in chapters 3 and 4. One method involves the community creating its own currency, which it can lend to companies at very low cost to spend instead of national currency within the local area. This is already being done in Switzerland, where, for the past sixty years, small and medium-sized firms have been able to avoid borrowing large sums of working capital from the banks by creating it among themselves. They pay no interest, just a small service charge to keep their mutually owned system running. (This system is explained on p. 98.)

Even when a firm has to have a national currency loan, it should not have to come from a non-local bank. This is because the difference between the rate of interest that national or international banking groups offer community savers and the rate they charge community borrowers is often excessive and always drains resources from the area. In 1994, for example, Irish savers received between 0.25 and 0.75 per cent interest on deposits of less than £5000, at a time when small businesses were paying up to 10.95 per cent for their overdrafts. Much of this disparity could be eliminated if local savings were channelled to local enterprises through community savings and loan institutions, especially if, as in many credit unions, a large part of the work involved were done on an unpaid, volunteer basis.

In fact, community bank interest rates can be very low indeed, as many people are happy to waive their interest altogether in order to help local projects; as a result, businesspeople in Denmark have been able to obtain interest-free loans from local co-operative banks for an annual 2 per cent service charge. (Details of this are given on page 164.)

CHANGE NUMBER 3
**Our key production processes need to be run
entirely without inputs from the world system**

If we are trying to build a local economy because we can no longer rely on the world system, our new economy needs to be independent of the world system at every step. For example, it makes little sense to replace external food supplies by using agricultural techniques that lead to crop failure if fertilizers or sprays cannot be brought in from outside. That is just exchanging one form of dependence for another, and Murphy's Law predicts that, if we took such a route, the price of agrochemicals would go through the roof. Airliners are built with at least one completely independent back-up to every important system, and our economies should be the same.

In the recent past, local economies had back-up because, as transport systems improved, it became increasingly possible for communities to turn to the outside world whenever their crops failed or some other disaster happened. Localized famines became much less frequent. Now, however, the easy availability of goods from outside has all but eliminated local production for local use, and the back-up has become not just the main system but, in effect, the only one. Worse, this sole system now has very little back-up within itself because the giant corporations that control so much of world trade deliberately eliminated spare capacity and duplications whenever they took over firms that had built up the trade.

Not all the components of the world system are equally unreliable, of course; but since they are interlinked, a failure in one is bound to have knock-on effects on the others, distorting their price or affecting their availability. There is therefore no alternative to eventually duplicating them all. Nevertheless, it obviously makes sense to give priority to building alternatives to those parts of the world system where the risks are highest. This is undoubtedly the financial system, which could break down completely at any time, as the next panel explains.

A community wishing to minimize the hardships it would suffer if the world financial system collapsed should obviously make monetary independence its first priority. A currency and banking system that can continue to serve a particular area regardless of whatever financial convulsions take place outside that area is fundamental to the construction of a self-reliant local economy, particularly as it also creates

[main text continues p.50]

JAPANESE BANKS COULD CAUSE FINANCIAL MELTDOWN

'The scope for a catastrophic debt deflation, with its epicentre in Japan, is much larger than in 1929,' Peter Warburton, the chief economist at a London firm of securities dealers, wrote in the *European* in early 1994.[7] He was concerned that after making huge capital write-offs as a result of the collapse of the Tokyo property market, the big Japanese banks faced the prospect of having to call in many of their loans prematurely if the Nikkei stock market index fell below 16,000 for very long. And that, in turn, could cause the world's financial system to collapse.

The banks' situation has not improved since then. Their problem is that a large part of the capital left after their property losses is in the form of unrealized gains on shares they own. If those gains are wiped away by a stock market fall, the Bank for International Settlements, the central bankers' central bank, will insist that their lending be reduced to restore their capital-to-loan ratios to international standards. But if this meant the banks had to call in loans on any scale, forced asset sales by their borrowers would cause property prices to crash around the world. This would weaken the loan book of almost every large bank, possibly forcing them to call in loans too and leading to a rapid worldwide deflation – a long-term fall in the general price level.

Such a deflation could come about, Warburton said, if share and property prices began to fall so sharply as a result of the forced asset sales that people and institutions that had put all their wealth into fixed assets found themselves with no money and no way of borrowing any. Those hit in this way would cut back their spending sharply, driving wages and prices lower still and causing companies to collapse as they became unable to service their debts, thus pushing prices down another notch. 'This is a description of a classic deflationary spiral,' he wrote, suggesting that governments might be powerless to prevent it. 'Unfortunately, few governments used the opportunity of the late 1980s economic expansion to straighten out their finances. Their ability to fund large-scale deficit spending in the event of a global emergency is therefore called into question.'

At the time Warburton wrote his article the Nikkei index was being artificially maintained at around 20,000 by the Ministry of Finance, which was discouraging firms from issuing new shares. The previous year, before this restriction came into effect, everyone had had a nasty fright when shares sold during the part-privatization of a railway company had caused the Nikkei to drop to the crucial 16,000 level.[8] It returned to the danger zone in early 1995 when a 20 per cent rise in the value of the yen – as a result of the 'flight to quality' during the Mexican peso crisis – damaged Japanese companies' export prospects. The authorities were able to save the day briefly by reducing interest rates but had to cut them again later that year after four insolvent financial institutions had to be wound up. This second cut brought the prime rate down to only 0.5 per cent and, since interest rates cannot be negative, meant that the tactic could not be used again. International credit-rating agencies reacted by marking down the Japanese banks' creditworthiness, with the result that they had to pay higher interest than multinational companies for funds borrowed from non-Japanese banks. The risk of a collapse became so acute in October 1995 that the United States felt it necessary to announce that it had $150 billion ready in case a bank collapsed and caused a run on the whole system.[9]

The threat from Japan is not the only one the world's monetary system faces. Other risks have been created by the lifting of controls on the way the financial markets can operate. 'The weakest link in the chain will give, and financial deregulation is a predictable way of creating more weak links in the world system,' Rudiger Dornbusch of the Massachusetts Institute of Technology told a conference on the risk of an economic crisis in 1989. Laurence Summers, then chief economist at the World Bank, told the same meeting that technological and financial innovation had made speculative bubbles that ultimately burst more likely today than they had been historically. 'The risk of a currency crisis is now greater than it was when exchange rates were fixed,' he said.[10]

Although events such as the collapse of the Bank of Credit and Commerce International (BCCI) in July 1991 and the speculators' success in forcing sterling, the franc and several other European currencies to devalue in 1992 proved both speakers right, nothing has been done to buttress the system. In 1994 even money-market traders began to complain about the activities of 'hedge funds' – huge pools of capital, much of it borrowed from the large banks, that speculate massively in the market. One of the funds' favourite ploys is to sell large quantities of a stock or a currency that they do not own in the hope of forcing its price down sufficiently so that they can buy enough to fulfil their sales contracts at much less than they were paid, thus making a good profit. The four biggest funds control over $25 billion between them and include Quantum, the fund run by George Soros, which claimed to have made £1 billion when sterling was forced out of the European Monetary System in 1992 and then lost $600 million speculating against the yen eighteen months later.

It is not unusual for hedge funds to borrow twenty times their assets. This means that in the unlikely event that Soros wished to bet everything on movements in a single currency he could put $200 billion into play; all 800 funds operating throughout the world could mobilize $2 trillion. 'They have undoubtedly produced volatility beyond all previous bounds,' one trader said after the markets had taken a dramatic fall in early 1994.[11] 'Seldom can so many highly paid economists and analysts have been at such a loss to explain what was happening,' The Economist commented, reporting widespread fears that if the funds' speculation turned badly sour they could endanger the banks that had lent them money. Soros himself agreed that there was such a risk in evidence he gave to the US House of Representatives' banking committee a few weeks later.

Although the future, indeed the survival, of hundreds of millions of people has been affected by the hedge funds' activities, no government has yet acted to keep them in check.

an environment within which other aspects of self-reliance can be achieved more readily. Accordingly, the next two chapters describe how such community currency and banking systems can be built.

Once a local financial system is in place, the community should turn its attention to meeting its irreducible energy, food and clothing needs from its own area. In fact I rate community energy independence second only in importance to monetary independence because food production and many other activities depend on energy use. Moreover, external supplies of energy are highly centralized and insecure; wars have been fought recently to safeguard them. But food production needs to be local too, and not just because outside sources might dry up or price fluctuations throw the local economy out of balance. Another reason is that unless a community can feed itself it will need to generate a substantial external income to buy its nourishment from outside, and the enterprises it will need to operate in order to do so will not only be subject to the fluctuations of the world economy but will also absorb more and more local resources as the outside economy becomes increasingly competitive. The four basic steps towards greater local self-reliance therefore are:

STEP 1: The establishment of an independent currency system, so that a community can continue to function economically, even if at a reduced level, whatever happens to money supplies in the world outside.
STEP 2: The establishment of an independent banking system, so that an area's savings can be made available to projects serving the community at interest rates such ventures can afford without passing through institutions that would be affected by an external financial collapse.
STEP 3: The production of enough energy from local renewable resources to meet an area's needs, however difficult this might seem.
STEP 4: The production of the area's basic food and clothing requirements without the use of inputs from outside.

This immediately raises a set of questions: 'Are there more steps? How far need a community's quest for greater self-reliance go? Inishbofin islanders may have grown flax to make their own fishing-lines, but many of the things we consume today cannot be produced in our communities on any realistic basis. Cotton clothes, for example – do we have to switch over to locally grown, locally spun linen and woollen garments instead?'

The answer is in two parts. The first is that we only need to produce the essentials of life within our communities, and once this has been done we can be entirely pragmatic, taking things further only if it suits us. Some clothing is obviously essential, and every community should therefore use part of its agricultural resource to produce fibres to turn into garments. However, clothes are a fashion item as well as a necessity, and many of us buy more than we need to stay decent and warm. There is no need for a community to go out of its way to produce this surplus.

Once its essential food, fuel and clothing needs are satisfied, a community should only replace external products with those of its own if it still has people who want to do more paid work than is available. In other words, a community should operate as far down the outside-production triangle as necessary to generate the jobs it needs. In the case of materials it cannot produce for itself, such as cotton, this might involve buying the raw cloth so that it can be printed and finished locally before being cut and sewn into clothes. This, according to the managing director of an Irish firm that weaves its own fabric to make into duvets, would save about 20 per cent of the price of the finished cloth.[12] If a community went a stage further and did the weaving locally with bought-in yarn, it would save an additional 32 per cent. And, since the raw cotton comprises only 29 per cent of the price of the cloth, spinning yarn from imported cotton would save another 12 per cent.

The further a community goes down the external inverted triangle, the more scope it has to create a substantial rectangle or triangle of its own. Once everyone is fully occupied, though, any further extension of the local economy is impossible unless the community can increase its labour productivity or persuade those of its members still employed in the mainstream economy to give up their jobs there.

The second part of the answer to the question 'How far need we go?' is 'Not as far as you think.' This is because many products that it would be difficult to make on a community scale are not required in a peasant economy. For example, shipping containers are unnecessary to someone delivering their product next door, and small firms are unlikely to want to use complex, high-output machinery for their limited production runs. As we saw in the previous chapter when we considered indices of sustainable economic welfare, a high and increasing proportion of everything produced by the industrial system is consumed by the system itself to keep running and is never enjoyed or used by people at all. Much of this internally consumed production consists of goods and services that a peasant economy does not require.

Another question frequently crosses people's minds at this stage: 'What should be the boundaries of the area within which we seek to become more self-reliant?' Fortunately the answer has been provided for us by the proprietors of our local newspapers, who, through trial and error over the years, have established the spatial limits within which we, their readers, are interested in each other's doings.[13] If the circulation area of a paper becomes too local it will lack the advertising and commercial base on which to survive; on the other hand, if it spreads itself too widely its readers will become tired of turning page after page on which there is little to interest them and will switch to papers with a more limited coverage. Advertisers, too, resent paying high prices to reach readers living too far away to become customers and will move their budgets to smaller papers covering a more limited area in greater depth. There is therefore a permanent dynamic tension between the benefits a paper enjoys if it expands its circulation area and the advantages it maintains by keeping a tight local focus. Of course newspaper circulation areas overlap, and so will our local economies; each product or service is likely to have a different distribution area.

A local newspaper's circulation area approximates to what sociologists term a social field, which they define as 'the spatial reach of kinship, occupation and friendship within which people react in economic, social and cultural terms'. In an essay on social fields in Ireland prepared as part of an EU-financed four country study into the appropriate scale for sustainable development, Dr Kevin Whelan of the Royal Irish Academy wrote:

Effectively the social field may be partially, but not exclusively, defined by the local town and its hinterland. This applies to small towns with a population of 1500 to 10,000 and their hinterlands extending within a ten to fifteen mile radius ... Through commuting, services and shopping, many cementing institutions now operate at this level – the factory, the supermarket, the secondary school, the bank, bus and rail links, the night club. In many ways these newly strengthened town hinterlands are the most important level in the territorial organization of rural communities, especially since the advent of mass participation in post-primary schools. The new patterns of social interaction can be seen in marriage fields: those relatively cohesive territories from which marriage partners are drawn and which now tend increasingly to mirror the economic hinterlands of these towns. The more localized social field has been extended and the traditional territorial order of the countryside has been reshaped. However ... only the local newspapers offer some expression of the nature of these town/country interactions.[14]

Although Whelan says that 'long-term economic and ecological needs may best be met at a regional level,' which encompasses a

[main text continues p.56]

BIOREGIONS OR SPATIAL FIELDS?

Over two hundred groups in the United States and others in Europe are working to increase economic self-reliance within 'bioregions' rather than within social fields. Does this make much difference? How do the areas derived by the two approaches compare?

'Very closely' is the short answer. Kirkpatrick Sale, the author of one of the few books on bioregional thinking, Dwellers in the Land,[15] defines a bioregion as 'part of the earth's surface whose rough boundaries are determined by natural rather than human dictates, distinguishable from other areas by attributes of flora, fauna, water, climate, soils and landforms, and the human settlements and cultures those attributes have given rise to.' Thus a bioregion might be the watershed of a river, bounded by hills on one side and the sea on another, physical characteristics that quite obviously influenced the way human settlements and transport links developed over the centuries and hence the shape and size of the inhabitants' social fields. Of course if a motorway is cut through the hills it will enable some people to widen their social fields without affecting the size of the bioregions it links, and the correspondence between bioregions and social fields will be weakened.

In such circumstances, most British bioregionalists would regard human ties as more important than natural barriers and, tacitly at least, work on the basis of the social field. Whether Americans would work on the same basis is open to question. Indeed it is significant that the bioregional concept was developed in San Francisco in the late 1970s by Peter Berg, a writer, and Raymond Dasmann, an ecologist, in a country with notoriously weak community ties. Could it have been this that led them to reject social links as a way of delineating the areas within which to aim for greater self-reliance and to choose the features Sale listed? If so their idea merely enabled them to exchange one problem for another because in many cases, particularly in the United States, individual bioregions cover such large areas that they contain much bigger populations than is desirable if a true democracy is to be made to work.

Sale – who took Schumacher's idea that 'small is beautiful' and looked in Human Scale[16] at the damage wrought when countries, companies and organizations grow too large – knows this problem well. Consequently, in Dwellers in the Land he suggests that bioregions can be divided into subregions and sub-subregions, 'like Chinese boxes, one within another,' depending on their dominant natural characteristics. 'Ultimately,' he says, 'the task of determining the appropriate bioregional boundaries – and how seriously to take them – will always be left up to the inhabitants of the area, the dwellers in the land, who will always know them best.'

He goes on to suggest that the size of communities and social institutions should also be left for the locals to decide, provided they have 'undertaken the job of honing their bioregional sensibilities'. However, they are likely to be small:

The human animal throughout its history, regardless of continent, climate, culture or character – seems to have favored clusters of 500 to 1000 people for the basic village or intimate settlement and 5000 to 10,000 for the larger tribal association or extended community. Only rarely did agglomerations ever exceed this size, as with the capital cities of various empires, and even then they typically lasted for less than a century before shrinking to smaller sizes ... Certainly, there is no question that the city of a million people, or even half a million most probably, has gone beyond the ecological balance point at which it is able to sustain itself on its own resources ... By contrast, the small community has historically been the most efficient at using energy, recycling its wastes, reducing drawdown and adjusting to carrying capacity. A kind of unconscious wisdom operates at that level, I would argue, that is not necessarily available at other scales: the sensors of the society are most receptive, the feedback systems and information loops most effective, the decision-making mechanisms most adaptive and competent. This is the level, too, at which people have been shown to solve social problems most harmoniously, to survive randomness and change most easily, to know the maximum number of other people with some intimacy, and to retain a sense of the self-amid-others most salubriously. It is not by accident or divine decree after all that the limited community has lasted all these many millennia.

Bill Mollison, the originator of permaculture – the conscious design of land use and human settlements on a low-input, sustainable basis, which shares many common features with bioregionalism – has suggested that the population of a region aiming at greater self-reliance should be between 7000 and 40,000 people. In other words, human scale is more important than landscape; and his unit, like that of Kirkpatrick Sale, would be almost indistinguishable from most social fields as defined by the circulation areas of local newspapers.

Problems over the boundaries and sizes of bioregional units have not prevented a considerable amount of useful thought and research from being carried out under the bioregional banner. For example, one of bioregionalism's important characteristics is the emphasis it places on the individual's relationship with the place in which he or she lives. Angus Soutar, who has been active in developing local currency systems in Britain, most recently in Manchester, expressed this very well in a lengthy article he contributed to Benign Design, the newsletter of the British Green Party's policy group on permaculture. 'The aim of bioregionalism is simply to know home,' he wrote. 'We aim to re-establish a sense of place, a sense of rootedness, as a counterweight to the damaging tendency of rootlessness and drift which tends to characterize our current society.'[17]

In order to come to 'know home', he suggests that people should study some aspect of their area that interests them. 'Perhaps you study local plants, maybe traditional building materials and methods, or perhaps old watermill sites. Through these observations you begin to understand that a sustainable way of life is possible and that many of our ancestors achieved it or were close to it.' This knowledge in turn leads to an understanding of the interconnectedness of people and the environment. As a result, members of the community begin to feel that their lives are part of the continuing history of their region, the ideal perspective for them to have when they help to plan the region's future:

One of [bioregionalism's] fundamental assumptions is that local control of the environment is the easiest way of regulating the use of resources. By local control, we mean control at the neighbourhood or village level. The most intimate understanding of the natural environment can only be obtained by people who are living in the midst of it, constantly observing as they go about their daily activities. That understanding can then inform their decisions and actions – whether it be to harvest, build, quarry, chop down trees and so on. In short, local people have a vested interest in resource use and the carrying capacity of their region and can ensure that they do not run down their natural resource base. An outsider will find it more difficult to recognize the subtle patterns of interactions between people and the land. And an outsider's decisions may be swayed by ideas of exploiting resources in the short term at the expense of sustainability.

Peter Berg can be contacted at the Planet Drum Foundation, PO Box 31251, San Francisco, California 94131; tel. +1 415 2856556; fax +1 415 2856563. Membership of the foundation costs $25 a year outside the United States and includes two issues of its attractive magazine, Raise the Stakes, which Berg edits. Apart from his own books, Reinhabiting a Separate Country: a Bioregional Anthology of Northern California and A Green City Program for the San Francisco Bay Area and Beyond, Berg refers enquirers to the series of bioregional books published by New Catalyst (PO Box 189, Gabriola Island, British Columbia V0R 1X0, Canada), and particularly to Home: A Bioregional Reader, one of the series.

In Britain the Bioregional Development Group are the people to contact (The Ecology Centre, Honeywood Walk, Carshalton, Surrey SM5 3NX; tel. +44 180 7732322; fax +44 181 6436419). The group aims to revive traditional, sustainable land-based industries through the introduction of new, efficient and appropriate-scale technologies. 'Though traditional land use is of great interest to us, traditional backbreaking work is less appealing,' they note in their brochure. So far they have produced a detailed report (S. Riddlestone, Bioregional Fibres, 1994; £30) on the potential for a sustainable regional paper and textile industry based on flax and hemp, and have looked at the prospects of reviving charcoal and coppice production in the Weald. Their forty-page report on this costs £12. They have also produced a £20,000 mobile kiln, the Viper, which makes four tonnes of charcoal worth up to £2800 a week. (See New Scientist, 14 May 1994, for more details.)

Movements seeking regional autonomy or independence have been established throughout Britain. Genuine political independence is impossible without economic independence, but few seem to have thought much about this, although the Campaign for the North published a paper calling for a regional banking system some years ago. The Movement for Middle England (10 Bartholomew Street, Leicester LE2 1FA), which covers the English Midlands, is an exception. It wants to develop a sustainable, decentralized regional economy and to introduce a democratic structure based on local 'moots' of about fifty households each, which would, when necessary, delegate power upwards to neighbourhoods, districts, counties, and finally the region. An up-to-date list of these movements' addresses can be obtained by sending £2 for a copy of the latest issue of The Regionalist to David Robins, 16 Adolphus Street West, Seaham Harbour, Co. Durham.

dozen or more social fields, this is largely because he was trying to identify subnational units in Ireland big enough to suit the European Commission's planning and grant-administration purposes. Significantly, his quest was unsuccessful and he was forced to admit that in Ireland at any rate 'there is no appropriate regional tier which can attach to or foster local initiatives.'

The idea that a social field consisting perhaps of a small country town and its hinterland should be the area within which greater economic self-reliance is sought upsets many city-dwellers. 'What about communities like mine?' a friend living in London asked when she came to visit one summer. 'Your ideas may be fine for people in rural areas, but you can't write off the millions of us in the cities.'

Of course one can't, but big cities cannot become self-reliant and have never been so. They depend for their survival on an uninterrupted flow of fuel, raw materials and food from outside their boundaries and only grew to their present size when transport powered by fossil fuel enabled them to gain access to increased supplies. This is not to say that they are unsustainable – there is no reason to believe that it will prove impossible to develop transport systems powered by renewable energy that will allow their inhabitants to continue to be clothed, warmed, housed, and fed – but their economic function will be undermined if rural communities become more self-reliant. The cities house many of the people towards the top of the industrial system's pyramid; if country-dwellers find ways of eliminating the burden the cities impose on them by building independent small pyramids of their own, jobs in urban areas are going to disappear altogether or move to the country. The dependence of cities on their supply areas and the lack of economic self-reliance in those supply areas are two sides of the same coin, and we cannot reduce one without affecting the other.

City-dwellers can do a lot to make themselves less reliant on the world economy by manufacturing more of their imported requirements and by entering into arrangements with producers in their immediate hinterland for their essential energy, food and raw material supplies. Even so, city populations are likely to fall if the approaches outlined in this book prove successful. A better balance between city and country will emerge, and rural decline and depopulation will end. Indeed, as we will see in the final chapter, it is not only the retired and the rich who are already moving to the country in search of a better life.

LIVING WITH LIMITS

In the past, before transport systems developed enough to allow almost everything to be brought in, the challenge facing a community was to develop a culture, a way of life, that enabled it to live for generation after generation within the confines of its own place. Some communities, even some entire civilizations, failed to do so and disappeared. Other places managed extremely well and imported surprisingly little until recently. 'So little trade went on with neighbouring towns that one carrier with a donkey cart was able to do it all, and even he, it was understood, went to town weekly only if he had orders enough to make the journey worth while,' writes Walter Rose in his book *Good Neighbours*,[18] an account of life in the village some thirty miles from London in which he was born in 1871. George Bourne, who is best known for *The Wheelwright's Shop*, his classic description of the business his father ran in Farnham, Surrey, until 1884, also stresses how little was brought from outside in *Change in the Village*, a fascinating account of the decline of rural self-reliance first published in 1912:

> It is really surprising how few were the materials, or even the finished goods, imported at that time [the 1850s]. Clothing stuffs and metals were the chief of them. Of course the grocers (not 'provision merchants' then) did their small trade in sugar and coffee, and tea and spices; there was a tinware shop, an ironmonger's, a wine-merchant's; and all these were necessarily supplied from outside. But, on the other hand, no foreign meat or flour, or hay or straw or timber, found their way into the town, and comparatively few manufactured products from other parts of England. Carpenters still used the oak and ash and elm of the neighbourhood, sawn out for them by the local sawyers: the wheelwright, because iron was costly, mounted his cartwheels on huge axles fashioned by himself out of the hardest beech; the smith, shoeing horses or putting tyres on wheels, first made the necessary nails for himself, hammering them out on his own anvil. So, too, with many other things. Boots, brushes, earthenware, butter and lard, candles, bricks – they were all of local make; cheese was brought back from Weyhill Fair in the wagons which had carried down the hops; in short, to an extent now hard to realize, the town was independent of commerce as we know it now, and looked to the farms and the forests and the claypits and the coppices of the neighbourhood for its supplies. A leisurely yet steady traffic in rural produce therefore passed along its streets because it was the life-centre, the heart, of its own countryside.[19]

Now the limits of place have gone, and goods can be transported from anywhere on the globe for those with the money to pay. As a result, one of the strongest bonds holding a community together has been broken. Although the negative feedback mechanisms that warned communities to mend their ways when they had overstepped the mark still operate, they have lost their power: if the fertility of a district's soil declines, if its forests are felled, its mines exhausted, its seas fished out, the better-off know they can always buy their requirements elsewhere or, if necessary, move on. Positive feedback rules most aspects of life in the industrial system because it rewards the countries that consume the Earth's resources most rapidly with incomes that enable them to purchase and destroy even more.

There is therefore a close link between local economic self-reliance and sustainability. The most commonly accepted definition of sustainability – 'meeting the needs of the current generation without compromising the ability of future generations to meet theirs' – is too pat. We need to spell out what sustainability means in concrete terms. The fact is that living within limits and sustainability are one and the same thing, and until humankind learns to live within limits again, its future and that of the planet is threatened. Theoretically it might be possible to develop a worldwide industrial culture that enabled humanity as a whole to live sustainably within the limits of the world, but I doubt it: the scale and the complexity of the task are too great, and there's very little time. Moreover, diversity rather than uniformity is desirable if we are to exploit every available ecological niche. A more practical approach is therefore for each social field to achieve ecological sustainability by and for itself. This entails meeting at least five targets, three of which we have already established as necessary also for economic sustainability:

1. Every system used in its area should be able to be continued, and every production cycle repeated, without environmental deterioration or other problems emerging in the next thousand years.

2. The population should be stable, and the district's economy should be growing or changing very slowly, if at all. The district must certainly not depend on economic growth for the maintenance of employment and prosperity.

3. The district must produce at least enough food and raw materials to enable its members to live simple, comfortable lives while staying within the limits of their environment and not exploiting other parts of the world.

4. All the energy used in the district must come from its own renewable resources.

5. To avoid being exploited or disrupted from outside, the district must have its own currency or currencies and its own banking system. Because investors' interests are rarely compatible with those of a com-

munity, capital should not be allowed to flow in or out, and interest rates, if any, should be determined internally.

A sustainable world will not be one dominated by large companies and run according to the conditions necessary for maintaining international competitiveness and speeding economic growth. It will be one of small communities that run their own affairs and that, rather than trading across the globe, meet or make most of their requirements from their local resources. For it is only if communities develop cultures that enable them to live indefinitely within the limits of their own places that humankind as a whole will be able to live sustainably within the limits of the natural world.

Notes

1 Reported in the *Independent on Sunday*, 7 August 1994.
2 See Graeme Shankland, *Wonted Work: a Guide to the Informal Economy* (Bootstrap Press: New York 1988), p. 10.
3 From Orio Giarini (ed.), *The Future of Service Employment in the Emerging Self-Service Economy* (Pergamon: Oxford 1987).
4 See Richard Wilkinson (ed.), *Class and Wealth* (Tavistock: London 1986).
5 Report by Tom McEnaney, 14 September 1994.
6 (Cambridge University Press 1991).
7 25 February 1994.
8 *Economist*, 17 September 1994.
9 *Independent on Sunday*, 5 November 1995.
10 Quoted in Martin Feldstein (ed.), *The Risk of Economic Crisis* (University of Chicago Press: Chicago 1991).
11 Quoted in the *Sunday Times*, 6 March 1994.
12 Telephone conversation.
13 I owe this idea to Gillies MacBain.
14 *The Territorial Spiral: Historical Evidence of Scale-Appropriateness, Working Paper 4, Landscape and Life: Appropriate Scales for Sustainable Development* (Cross-Disciplinary Forum, Department of Geography, University College, Dublin), November 1993.
15 (New Society Publishers: Philadelphia 1991).
16 (Secker and Warburg: London 1980).
17 Issue 4, autumn 1993. *Benign Design* appears three times a year and is available from Spencer Fitzgibbon, GPPPG, 21 Meade Grove, Longsight, Manchester M13 0SG, tel. +44 161 2254863, for £6 a year.
18 (Cambridge University Press 1942).
19 Quoted from the edition published by Augustus M. Kelley (New York 1969), p. 103.

Local currency cheque form and tokens as used in the Westport LETS system.

3

Cutting the Monetary Tie

If people living in an area cannot trade among themselves
without using money issued by outsiders, their local economy
will always be at the mercy of events elsewhere. The first step
for any community aiming to become more self-reliant is
therefore to establish its own currency system.

THE ESTABLISHMENT OF A LOCAL MONEY SYSTEM is fundamental to greater economic self-reliance. This is because, at present,
the level of trading activity in almost every part of the industrialized
world is determined by the amount of money that flows in from outside. Unless that flow is adequate, even jobs that local people could
do for themselves without any outside resources will be left undone.
For example, I might have the materials for painting my house, and a
neighbour, an experienced painter who is temporarily under-
employed, might be keen to do the job for me. However, if I have no
national currency to pay him with I will not be able to use his services, unless we can work out a barter arrangement – something that
might be difficult, as I may have nothing I am prepared to give up
that he wants from me and that is roughly equivalent to the value of
his labour. As a result, I may be forced to do the painting rather inex-
pertly myself.

The conventional solution to this problem is for me to try to earn
more national currency. Individually I might be able to do so by
working for someone else in my community; but if the community as
a whole is to increase the number of things its members do for each
other on a permanent basis, we will need to get a larger stock of
pounds into circulation permanently among us. This can be done by
increasing the amount of goods and services we sell to – and hence

our reliance on – the outside world. However, quite apart from the risks this exposes us to, the new money tends to flow out again nearly as fast as it came in, so that a big rise in external sales is likely to be needed before we can achieve a significant rise in the local national currency stock.

A better alternative is therefore for us to try to stop what national currency we are already earning outside from leaking so quickly away by making more of the goods we are buying from elsewhere for ourselves. This is a valuable strategy. However, even when we have replaced a proportion of the goods imported into our communities with those of our own, the link between the level of economic activity and the flow of money from outside remains; only the ratio has changed. By cutting the leakage rate we have simply moved to a higher activity level for a given amount of money flowing in.

The best approach is therefore to make our internal transactions independent of the external money flow by using a special currency with which to carry them out. After all, the only role the national currency plays in transactions between neighbours is that of a measuring stick, a scale by which the value of the work done by the man who comes to paint my house can be compared with the value of the work I do for him or for another of my neighbours. It is a way of ensuring that no one takes out more than they put in. Families and small stable communities do not need to use money to measure each person's input in order to ensure that everyone pulls their weight: members just do things for each other without keeping count, in the confidence that it will all balance out in the end. The community on Árainn (Inishmore), one of the Aran Islands, still functions this way. In larger groupings, however, most of us seem to feel the need for some way of keeping score.

In the past, all successful societies had systems under which people worked for each other and for the common good without the intervention of cash. Hugh Brody writes in his well-known book on Irish rural life, *Inishkillane*,[1] that some form of mutual aid 'compounded of claims and counter-claims between farm households has prevailed in virtually every society where small farming has been the basic activity,' and he quotes a phrase from Isabel Emmett's study of a Welsh village: 'To farm this district, a man must either have the constant daily co-operation of his fellows, or he must have a very large sum of money behind him.'

In Ireland, Brody says, there is little evidence that the households involved in a mutual-aid relationship ever bothered to keep an account of each other's obligations. 'It seems that the details were vague and the fact of the relationship more important than the memory for particular exchanges that occurred in it. What a household knew was the neighbours they could look to for help, and to whom they would not refuse to give help if asked themselves.'

He likens the relationship to that of savers to a bank. 'The giver, by giving, guaranteed that he would be the receiver in the future. In that way, the giving of surplus to friends and neighbours is not very far from the giving of surplus to the cashier in a bank. The quality of integrated society, like the legal rules of banking, guaranteed that the gift would not be forgotten and a future claim ignored.'

However, as subsistence farming gave way to more specialized production for sale to exporters, it became possible to save cash for a rainy day rather than storing up favours with one's neighbours. Remittances from family members overseas also helped reduce the household's near-total dependence on its own resources and so reduced its need to have neighbours available for back-up should those resources fail. Nevertheless, examples of mutual-aid systems still exist, or have ceased to operate only very recently. A friend of mine can remember neighbours coming to her father's farm in the west of Ireland each autumn up to the middle of the 1960s to help bring in the crops and then, after this work was done, her father, his five men and his threshing machine going off to help harvest the neighbours' crops in return. 'No money changed hands, even though the contributions to the overall effort varied,' she says. 'It was the *meitheal*.* The imbalance just did not matter.'[2]

In general, however, economic relationships are now too complex and too transitory throughout most of the industrialized world to allow systems of exchanging labour without a measuring stick to survive, apart from those involving relatives, close friends, and immediate neighbours. Our intra-community transactions have consequently become highly dependent on the flow of cash from the outside world, a change that makes us very vulnerable should the external money supply fail to leave us with enough measuring units to do all the trading we would like with each other.

It is for this reason that developing an independent local supply of measuring units to facilitate local exchanges is an essential step towards greater community self-reliance. Several hundred communities have already established such systems of measure. Most of these

* Lit. 'working party': the Irish word for this system of mutual support and help.

are based on one developed in the early 1980s by a Scottish-born Canadian, Michael Linton, in the Comox Valley in British Columbia and use either the national currency or time as their units of measure, although other units have been proposed – such as litres of milk or cords of firewood (in certain areas of Canada and the United States more or less anyone can go out and cut wood, thus turning their time into a readily measured amount of winter heat).*

Most of the Linton-inspired LETS (local exchange trading systems)[3] issue their members with chequebooks and operate their own computer-based cheque-clearing system to record payments in and out of each person's account. In the system I belong to in Westport in Ireland, on the last Thursday of each month we each collect all the cheques we have received and post them to the member who operates the computer system. Our statements of account are available to us by the following Thursday. It's simple, and it works well.

The unit in which we write our cheques is not the Irish pound but the 'Reek' (after a local name for the nearby mountain, Croagh Patrick), and every six months or so we bring out a new issue of a directory listing the goods and services that members are prepared to supply. Of course members need to know what is going on more often than that, and so each month, along with their statements, everyone

[main text continues p.68]

---

*In ancient Egypt, grain was the monetary unit. The farmers would deposit their crops in government-run warehouses against receipts showing the amount, quality, and date. These stores suited the farmers because they protected the grain against theft, fire and flood and also saved them the cost of providing their own, or selling their crop immediately after harvest, when prices were low. The stores also enabled them to pay their rent and to buy goods simply by writing what was in effect a cheque transferring grain from their account in the store to that of someone else; people using another grain store in another part of the country could be paid with these cheques. The various stores would balance their claims against each other, just as banks do today, and the grain itself would only be moved if there was a net flow of cheques from one town to another and the grain was actually needed there for consumption. In other words, the weight of corn was merely a basis for accounting and the corn itself was not a standard barter good. The tobacco stores in the New England states operated in much the same manner and enabled the crop to serve as legal tender in Virginia for almost two hundred years and in Maryland for a century and a half. As J.K. Galbraith points out in *Money: Whence It Came, Where it Went* (Penguin 1976), this was longer than the gold standard managed to survive. An important feature of both grain and tobacco as currencies was that whoever held a deposit was not only charged for keeping it in the warehouse-bank but knew that it would deteriorate there and consequently ate, smoked or spent it as soon as reasonably possible. As a result, money was not hoarded but circulated well.

DIFFERENCES BETWEEN LOCAL AND
NATIONAL CURRENCIES

Money, according to Michael Linton, the developer and popularizer of LETS (an acronym for 'local exchange trading system', although some people substitute 'employment' or 'enterprise' for 'exchange'), the most widely used local currency system, is 'the unreal stuff that we swap for real stuff,' and in his well-practised public address he goes on to highlight three fundamental differences between national currencies and their local cousins.[4] The first is that a national currency is acceptable anywhere – in some cases all over the world – while a local currency can only be used in a very limited geographical area. This restricted acceptability is a plus rather than a minus, he explains, because the smaller the system the sooner any spending power introduced to it by a member is likely to find its way back to him or her in the form of increased demand for their goods and services.

'If you spend money in the national system, it has gone. The individual's spending power has no effect on the overall level of demand and on the ability of other people to trade with him. On the other hand, in a local currency system, if you buy from a fellow-member his spending power is increased, and, directly or indirectly, the extra purchases he makes are likely to increase demand for whatever you are offering. The smaller the system the sooner your money comes back.'

The second key difference is that national currency is always scarce because its supply is deliberately restricted for fear of inflation, whereas the supply of a local currency, since it is created by people doing things for one another, is always adequate for their needs. All LETS schemes create money by allowing – indeed encouraging – their members to go into interest-free debt because it is only if one member runs up a deficit by buying another member's goods or services that the other members can move into credit. At any time and in every LETS system, the total of all the accounts in credit will equal the amount by which the rest are in debit; and if everyone trades so as to bring their account back to nil, all the purchasing power will disappear. Some systems – such as the first attempt to set up a LETS system in Totnes, Devon – failed because members were so reluctant to run overdrafts that they were never able to trade at all. 'If you are prepared to do something other people want in the national system, the money will not necessarily be there for them to hire you, but with LETS it will,' Linton says.

The third difference is that as the national currency comes from outside the community and is in short supply, it can be used by those with a lot of it to gain power over those without. A local currency, on the other hand, can never be an instrument of power and domination because no one is ever desperate to get it: they can simply make their own. Consequently, although a person may have a lot of local units in their account, they cannot avoid having to persuade a heavily indebted member to work for them because, as no interest is payable on overdrafts, the only pressure the indebted member will feel to do so will stem from their sense of obligation to the rest of the group to return the equivalent of the goods and services they have had from the system within a reasonable time. If they dislike the other member, this might well override their wish to fulfil their commitment to the group as a whole. In LETS it is the member rich in local units who is in the exposed situation rather than the indebted one.

Linton encourages LETS systems not to place formal limits on the extent to which members can overdraw, suggesting that they rely on group pressures and gentle advice from an active co-ordinator to prevent members from becoming so heavily indebted that they despair of ever meeting their obligations and cease to participate. Although many schemes have not taken this advice and have imposed limits, it is certainly possible for a system to operate satisfactorily without them because if a member withdraws leaving a badly overdrawn account behind them, no one in the system suffers unless a crisis of confidence causes the system to break down. All that has been lost is the goods and services the missing member would have supplied to the group if they had discharged their obligations before their departure; and since those goods and services can be supplied just as well by a new member as by the old one, so long as the system keeps recruiting and trading, nothing is lost. Every member who supplied the defaulter has been paid.

Provided they are kept small enough, LETS systems can be nicely self-regulating. In many places members get a bank-style statement of their account each month, showing the cheques they have written and lodged. They also get a sheet showing the state of every other member's account, so that anyone who feels that another member is drawing rather too much from the system can decline to do business with them. In other words, each member has the power of sanction over every other member's descent into the red. However, once the group gets too large, this type of control becomes less effective. Because of this, and because of the benefit of having one's own LETS spending come back quickly in demand for one's own goods and services, many people think that five hundred members might be about the maximum desirable for such a system.

Linton's views on size can be confusing. On the one hand his seminars stress the advantages of small scale and present the vision of a future in which towns will have several systems, some operating in particular districts, others based on churches, sports clubs or other organizations and drawing their members from a wider area. Most people, he thinks, would be members of more than one system. On the other hand, the last time I met him he was hoping to arrange for his consultancy company, Landsman, to undertake the setting up of a three-million-member system in Sydney, Australia, on a profit-sharing basis. When this project failed to get beyond the proposal stage he tried to start a massive system in Manchester and made himself unpopular with LETS enthusiasts in the area, some of whom disliked the fact that a considerable amount of national currency was being invested in the project, on which it was hoped there would be a commercial return. However, Linton insists there is no inconsistency because all sizes of systems have their role, 'like gears on a bike'.

The biggest system in the world at present, and the one that Linton says is the best he knows, is the one operating in Katoomba and other towns along the road and railway line to Bathurst as it passes through the Blue Mountains about forty miles from Sydney. It was started in February 1991, and by the end of 1993 it had 1000 accounts representing perhaps 1200 people (as not all the accounts were individual ones). About 70 per cent of the accounts were classified as active, having traded more than 100 Ecos (regarded as equivalent to an Australian dollar) since they were opened. 'In a typical month we process more than eight hundred transactions, worth more than forty thousand Ecos,' Peter Furnell, one of the early members, told me.

So large has the number of accounts become, in fact, that in 1993 the decision was made to post each member's statement out quarterly rather than monthly. 'That seems often enough for most people,' Furnell says, 'and it enables a new issue of Green Pages, the directory of all the services our members offer, to be posted in the envelope as well.' To supplement the directory, the group also publishes a weekly bulletin – a single sheet printed on both sides – which lists goods that members have for sale and news about the system. This is distributed to pick-up points in shops and pubs throughout the towns. 'For a lot of things you just can't wait until a new edition of the directory comes out,' Furnell says.

The system's rapid growth (after its first nine months it had 120 accounts, so roughly 400 people must have joined in both 1992 and 1993) has meant that it has become much less personal. 'People no longer feel that they know everybody or that they could do so. That's a loss. They now say, "LETS should do this" or "LETS should do that" rather than "We should do it",' Furnell comments. There are no signs that the system has suffered in other ways, though. In particular, no one has abused the system by running up large debits and putting nothing back. In September 1993, 2 per cent of the accounts were overdrawn by more than 1000 Ecos, but all the holders had traded more than 2000 Ecos during the system's life. 'We do have a 2000 Eco limit on overdrafts, but it's not enforced very strictly,' Furnell says.

To overcome the increasing anonymity of the system, Kaiya Seaton, the coordinator of the Development Group, says they intend to turn it into a 'multi-LETS' by encouraging the formation of subgroups in each of the towns they cover, each group issuing its own newsletters and trading as far as possible among themselves. She adds that when new systems have set up in neighbouring areas and suggested ways in which their members can trade with those in the Katoomba system, she has discouraged them from doing so. 'I told them, Don't trade with our system, as it will cause you to lose your own.'

Michael Linton can be contacted at Landsman Community Services Ltd, 1600 Embleton Crescent, Courtenay, British Columbia V9N 6N8, Canada; tel. & fax +1 604 3380213; e-mail lcs@mars.ark.com; http://www.unet.com/gmlets.html.

receives a set of supplementary pages for the directory listing new entrants' skills and a news-sheet reporting what's going on. It's a lot of work preparing this material, but those who do it find it enjoyable – and get paid in Reeks for their efforts.

When we were planning the Westport system we were worried that settling all our transactions by cheque could prove cumbersome because each cheque would take a member's time (for which he or she would have to be paid in Reeks) to process through the computer system, an elaborate procedure just to buy a pound of carrots. And, just as people without bank accounts are reluctant to accept payment in ordinary cheques, we felt that people outside our system would be reluctant to be paid in our cheques, even though they would be able to spend them with members by endorsing them on the back. This, we thought, would make the system undesirably exclusive because there would be no way for waverers to use it casually before committing themselves to becoming members and paying the entrance fee. We therefore decided to issue Reek tokens for use in small transactions and for paying non-members, who could spend them at the stall we operate once a week on market day or in the cafés and shops that have joined our system.

Because other things got greater priority, it was almost eighteen months after trading began that the tokens appeared. They were designed by a member and run off on a laser printer, ten to an A4 sheet. They were laminated in clear plastic and the individual tokens validated with an embossing stamp bearing the words *Meitheal na Mart* (the name of the co-operative society we had registered to run our system). Each of the five denominations – 1, 5, 10, 20 and 50 Reeks – was printed on a different-coloured paper, and the tokens were the right size to be kept in a credit-card wallet.

How did they work? Well, physically they were excellent. Tests showed that they could be washed in a jeans pocket twenty times without losing legibility. But in practice, for all the good they were doing six months after they came out, we might as well not have bothered. 'They've never really been promoted, but the number of people using them is slowly increasing,' commented Ben Ryan, who ran the market stall and issued tokens in exchange for a cheque to members who wanted them. 'The thing is, they are not really necessary, as members can buy from the stall without using cheques just by signing for their purchases in the book. But I did pay two non-members with them and they joined afterwards.'

Besides experimenting with tokens, Westport is slightly unusual in that the Reek is a time-based unit, representing a minute of average working time. We use this non-national-currency-based measuring stick because we do not want prices within the system to be automatically identical with those outside, and also because we do not want the tax and social welfare authorities to be able to treat local currency earnings as if they were cash.

A LETS scheme that claims that its unit is of equal value to the pound or the dollar is deluding itself; everyone would always prefer to take payment in the national currency instead of the local one if they were given the option, since the latter can be spent in only a limited number of ways among a limited group of people. In view of this it seemed best to make our local unit as different from the Irish pound as possible.

Both time-based and currency-based units work well as measuring sticks. However, on balance I feel that non-monetary units are preferable, if only because they make it more difficult for people to quote prices in a mixture of national and local currencies – something that LETS members quite reasonably wish to do, since they cannot live by earning local units alone. However, since the need to use national currency alongside LETS units undermines the object of establishing the scheme in the first place, it is also quite reasonable to make rules that restrict it. The system in Katoomba, for example, specifies that members cannot use its directory for advertising if more than half the good's price has to be paid in Australian dollars.

Groups should be constantly striving to eliminate national-currency supplements. If a mechanic working within a LETS system has to buy parts to mend a car, he or she will naturally pass on whatever they cost in national currency. Ideally, however, the charge for their time should be billed in the local unit alone. True, because of their overheads, repairers will need to cover, say, 30 per cent of their labour costs in national currency, but they do not have to collect that 30 per cent on every job; and they can charge LETS members 100 per cent local currency because non-members will be paying 100 per cent cash. All they have to do is balance the amounts of each currency they get over a month, not on each transaction. The fact is that every LETS member incurs some national currency cost on every transaction, even if it is only that of making a phone call. However, as long as everyone's national-currency costs are more or less the same, none of us will be any worse off if we don't charge each other for them, and we won't need to have national currency moving around between us to keep our local currency system running.

[main text continues p.72]

HOW LETS EARNINGS ARE TREATED FOR TAX

One of the first questions many people ask about local currency systems is how they are treated for tax. For members, however, the question rarely arises because either their national-currency incomes are insufficient to place them in the tax net in the first place or they do so little of any one thing within the system that the tax authorities are happy to ignore the tiny amounts of imputed income involved. 'There's nothing like a detailed account of dog-walking or granny-sitting to convince an inspector that further investigation is likely to be less than cost-effective,' says Angus Soutar, who has advised British LETS systems on tax and worked with Michael Linton to set up Greater Manchester LETS.

As a result, only those members who do part of their normal business or profession through a LETS system are liable for income tax on their local-currency earnings. For example, if a solicitor agrees to accept payment of her fees in the local unit, she would have to declare these earnings for tax at the national-currency value they placed on them. Even in a system that nominally tied its unit to the national currency, this would not necessarily be one-for-one; but systems using some other basis of valuation obviously have an advantage when it comes to convincing the tax inspector that this should not be the case.

'Two of our members, both alternative health care practitioners, have submitted tax returns listing their LETS earnings,' Val Oldaker wrote in the LETSlink newsletter.[5] She belongs to the Newbury system, whose 'NewBerry' (NB) is a time-based unit with no fixed parity with sterling. 'In one case the inspector took the view that since the standard, listed rate for the treatment was £20, this meant that the value of the 25 NB currency received was £20. In fact one of the reasons that the alternative health people are so keen on LETS is that they are primarily interested in health, not money, and if a patient who needs help doesn't have any money, they will often be treated for nothing, or very little. If such a patient joins LETS, at least the practitioner gets something. So we managed to convince the inspector that the choice in treating a LETS patient was not between 25 NB and £20 but 25 NB and nothing. He said that "as long as you can prove that the practitioner has treated the patient for little or nothing, then we can use this figure as an exchange rate".'

The other practitioner produced a 25 NB cheque, which the inspector was claiming was worth £20, endorsed it on the back, and handed it over to his receptionist in payment for an hour's telephone answering. 'How can you explain the fact that this cheque, by your calculation, has devalued from £20 to £3.50?' the practitioner asked. 'The officer tied himself in knots trying to be fair, by realizing that the value of the NewBerry is dependent on what it is spent on, rather than what is earned. So we'd be taxing spending, not earnings, but the Inland Revenue has no way of doing that,' Oldaker commented.

The best way out of this valuation problem would be for the revenue authorities to agree to accept any income tax due on a local-currency income in the unit in which it was earned, but there seems little chance of this; throughout the world they insist on payment in the national currency.

70

Many members of LETS systems are equally insistent that if a transaction is completely in the local unit, that unit should also be used to settle any tax liability incurred, because a system designed to enable people to manage with less official money is obviously weakened if users are obliged to earn national currency to make their alternative arrangements work.

A lot is at stake here because if governments accepted locally produced money in payment of taxes it would give that money enormous credibility. Moreover, since this revenue could only be spent in the area it came from, among members of the group that generated it, the area would benefit twice: first, in the jobs created when the tax was spent and, second, as a result of whatever the spending achieved. The payment of taxes in local units could suit local councils too, since it would give them an additional source of income independent of central government, something they badly need. But national governments are going to be very unhappy to see even a trivial part of their financial power slip away.

Sooner or later someone who has sent their tax inspector a cheque drawn on their LETS account and refused to replace it with one in national currency will court imprisonment on this issue. In Australia several systems have opened accounts for the tax authorities, and substantial sums have accumulated in them, which the government has refused to touch. In one case, after waiting two years for the their local-currency taxes to be used, LETS members spent them themselves on the projects they felt were of most benefit to their area, a wonderful first for true local democracy.

The other big issue dividing local-currency earners and the tax inspector involves determining just how much of a particular activity they can do before they are judged to be carrying on a business and therefore liable for tax. So far there is no definitive answer. John Bolger, a former tax inspector who now has his own practice as an accountant and tax consultant in Kilkenny (where he played a leading role in setting up a LETS system), puts it this way: 'The Revenue is not interested in someone who is doing very small bits and pieces. Whether someone is carrying on a business is a matter of degree, and a pragmatic approach must be taken. However, if the person is not carrying on a business, whatever he or she receives is not taxable, irrespective of whether local units or national currency is taken in payment.'[6] Frank Brennan, perhaps the leading Irish tax consultant, agrees. 'Nothing in the LETS system would bring a person within the tax net who might not otherwise be there. If, for instance, I give someone a lift in my car, even though they might give me a gratuity that will not constitute taxable income in my hands, since I am not in the business of providing taxi services. The position is obviously different for somebody who is in that line of business.'[7]

An identical position has been taken by the Inland Revenue in Britain: anything earned from one's normal line of business is taxable, whatever the currency used in payment. Other activities constitute 'social favours' and are exempt from tax. In both countries, therefore, there is a strong incentive for anyone paying income tax to forget their day job and do other things entirely when they join a LETS system.

Indeed it is sometimes possible to charge 100 per cent local-currency prices even when one has had to cover considerable national-currency costs. During Westport LETS's first summer, a woman who baked wholemeal bread every Thursday for sale on our market stall found that she could charge all-Reek prices to members because sales to non-members, many of them tourists, provided the national currency to meet the costs of her gas and flour. During the autumn, however, two other members began baking bread after the first had started a drama course in Dublin, and they found that, as the tourists had gone, so few cash sales were being made each week that their national-currency costs were no longer being met. Unfortunately but understandably, they began charging mixed prices, asking members to pay half the cost of a loaf in Irish pounds, the rest in Reeks. Sales fell off alarmingly, dropping from sixteen loaves a week to two and cutting their net earnings from baking to the point at which it was not worth carrying on. 'They used to spend all their Reek earnings at the stall anyway buying eggs and cheese,' a committee member said when we discussed this. 'Now they've got to buy those things for cash, so they are not saving themselves any national currency by charging the mixed prices, and they've got fewer Reeks to spend in the group.' Today, three people are baking for the stall, charging all-Reek prices on sales to members.

Apart from tax, the other big advantage of not fixing the value of a system's unit in national currency is that it makes it easier for LETS prices to differ from those quoted in pounds or dollars. Prices in the Westport system began to move away from straight conversions after three months – and not in the way one might expect, since for the most part they went down. This was because some members found that their services were not being used often enough to pay off the overdrafts they were running up on their accounts, so they cut their rates to get more business. Others found when the first directory appeared that their rates were seriously undercut by other members and brought them down when it was reprinted. A third group cut Reek prices to give the system a boost.

Some rates moved both down and up. A builder adopted the entirely reasonable view that if someone wanted to hire him, his time had to be worth at least as much to the other member as that member was listing as an hourly rate in the directory. He therefore began adjusting his charges to match the other member's. 'If they could do the job themselves they wouldn't bother to hire me, so I must be worth at least as much as they are.'

The Westport core group's policy is not to recognize or support any exchange rate between the local unit and the national currency and to discourage members from selling one to buy the other. Members are required to quote a Reek price for goods sold on the market stall but are free to quote a cash price for the same items to enable them to be sold to non-members. However, it is up to them to set both prices, and the exchange rate therefore varies from member to member. Some suppliers of goods in short supply – free-range eggs, for example – refuse to set a cash price at all because they want them to be sold solely to other members in order to develop the system.

Michael Linton's view on the exchangeability of currencies is quite different: he sees nothing wrong in people with a good cash income but insufficient time to offer services through the system spending local units they don't have in, say, a restaurant and then balancing their accounts by buying units from someone with plenty of time and an inadequate national-currency income. 'That way everyone benefits. The people with a high income and no time support the LETS system, and the member with plenty of time and no cash gets the cash income he needs,' he argues.

In Westport, however, we think that this approach weakens a LETS system by underlining the inferiority of the local unit and that it is much better for people with cash but insufficient time to balance their LETS accounts by finding something they no longer want that they can sell through the system – particularly as so few actual goods are available through some LETS systems that they amount to little more than diversified babysitting circles. In Westport we make a real effort to ensure that an attractive range of goods is always on offer: this was one of the reasons we opened the stall. If someone offers, say, a bicycle for Reeks to balance their account, that's really good because it widens the members' range of options and thus strengthens our currency.

Another of Linton's ideas we have decided not to adopt is his strongly held belief that systems should not set limits on the amount by which members can overdraw their accounts. Linton thinks that if the debit or credit balance of every member's account is circulated regularly, no one's overdraft will get out of hand because if other members see that he or she is taking too much out of the system, they will refuse to deal with them until they have brought their indebtedness down. He adds that members with big overdrafts are in a poor position to refuse offers of local-currency employment because of the group pressure to cut their debts.

All this is true, and the Westport system publishes members' account balances by pinning them up on the stall. After all, all Reek overdrafts are debts, not to the system itself, as with an overdraft at a bank, but to every other member, so it is right that members should know what they are. However, we felt we would all be happier if we issued some guidance on what was a reasonable deficit to run and suggest to new members that they limit themselves to an overdraft of 4000 Reeks (approximately £200) for their first month and then keep below whatever figure represents three months' average Reek earnings for them. What everyone fears is that some members might get themselves so deeply in debt that they will feel unable to pay off their obligations within a reasonable time and then withdraw from the system, damaging both it and themselves.

Other systems have similar guidelines, even those that claim not to. For example, Stroud LETS in Gloucestershire, one of the most successful in England, says that if it imposed credit limits it would destroy the atmosphere of mutual trust and empowerment it is trying to build up. However, though it may not set explicit limits, it does have implicit ones, and whenever an account seems to the co-ordinator to be getting its holder into trouble, she contacts the person involved, frequently with an offer of work, and helps them come back into line.

Perhaps the only system genuinely not to have had limits was Michael Linton's own in Comox Valley. When this slowed almost to a standstill for several years, for reasons we will discuss shortly, Linton's own account was the most seriously extended (his commitment* was the equivalent of $17,000, out of a total of $60,000 outstanding in a system that had turned over $300,000); and outsiders have criticized him for using the system to get goods and services for his own benefit without putting enough back. Linton rejects their charge. 'During those three years there was no appropriate way within the system to pay me for my more than full-time work. My function was design, development, promotion, publication, and training, and it was related to longer-term issues and required wider resources than the local network could possibly provide. Since I couldn't be paid I ran up my own commitment.'[8]

Linton acknowledges that this probably damaged the Comox Val-

---

* Linton dislikes using words like 'debt' and 'overdraft' in relation to LETS systems, preferring to refer to a member's obligation to provide goods and services of equivalent value to those they have received as their 'commitment'.

ley system. 'Any non-providing negative can tend to detract from system performance, and certainly in this instance mine did. However, it can also stimulate. And equally, mine did. We worked that out beforehand and took the risk with, in my view, considerable success. The system operated with these biases for almost half its first successful period.'

An overdraft on a LETS system's own account is often a substantial 'non-providing negative' and thus a source of danger in itself. It can arise because once a LETS is running there is no need for the committee or anyone else who works for it to do so unpaid, since they can always be given local units to recompense them. Moreover, committees often feel that membership subscriptions do not have to be adjusted to cover all the setting-up costs while the system is going through its development phase. Why should early members have to bear the entire cost of something that, everyone hopes, will benefit a far greater number of people for many years to come? And so the deficit on their system's account is allowed to mount up steadily. The question is, how far can it go without damaging or endangering the system? The answer is, nobody knows.

Up to a point, a deficit in the system's account is good because it means that the average balance in individual members' accounts is positive, and this encourages them to spend. No one likes incurring debts they can avoid or defer, even in a LETS system. In Westport we even considered giving new members several hundred Reeks the moment they signed up, in order to get them trading immediately. Instead we decided it would be more effective to subsidize the stall's running costs until its turnover had grown enough to pay the members staffing it an adequate amount for their time. Everyone in the system benefits from having the stall because of the goods it offers and the meeting place it provides. On top of this it is a good advertisement for the system, and most new members are recruited through it.

But we were running a risk covering the stall's deficit. The beauty of a LETS is that the number of units circulating within it is always adequate, but never excessive, for the volume of trade going on. If trade contracts, units will be extinguished as long as members fulfil their obligations to each other by restoring their accounts to their opening nil balance. But if trade contracts within a scheme like that in Westport, in which the system itself is significantly overdrawn, the lack of activity may mean that it is impossible to bring the system's account back to nil, and the sort of inflationary problem that I fear in

Ithaca (see next panel) might develop. If it did, members would be left with units in their accounts they could not persuade anyone to take at anything approaching their original value.

Even if it avoids the problems associated with a serious decline in trade, any LETS whose account is in deep deficit is bound to be afflicted by a subtle, insidious malaise because of a lack of balance between supply and demand. This arises because many members – a majority perhaps – will have credit balances in their accounts and feel that they ought to be able to spend them, whereas only a small number will be in deficit and will feel that they ought to work their indebtedness off. Everyone's statement will give false signals because the system itself is not trying to provide goods and services to members to reduce its debts to the same extent that individual members owing the same total sum would undoubtedly be. As a result, people find credit balances difficult to spend and tend to lose confidence in the system. Management committees should therefore err on the side of safety and keep their system's own overdraft very small.

Six months after trading began, the deficit on the Westport system account was equivalent to 80 per cent of the monthly turnover, which seemed a lot.[9] On the other hand, it was only 300 Reeks (approximately £15) per head for each of the sixty-five members, which seemed nothing in comparison with the value of the system we had built up. Eventually we reduced the deficit by holding a party that people paid to attend. (LETS systems should always organize plenty of parties, as experience shows that members generally trade only with members they know, so an enjoyable event strengthened our system in two ways.)

But what was the Westport system's value? In economic terms it is fair to say that, so far, most LETS systems have been disappointing. The Stroud system has a monthly turnover per member equivalent to only £15, which probably amounts to less than 5 per cent of participants' average monthly incomes. In Katoomba the comparable figure would be about £20 a month, and Westport's is much the same. Similar figures were produced by a survey of five English systems by Jyll Seyfang, which showed that even when the least active 30 per cent of members were excluded, turnover per head ranged from a miserable £75 to a respectable £220 a year.[10]

These figures hide more than they reveal. In general, turnover is low in Britain because the Department of Social Security does not permit anyone who is unemployed to participate in a LETS scheme without risking losing all or part of their benefits. This is on the grounds that for at least some of the period for which the benefit is paid, the claimant was 'unavailable for work' – despite the fact that in most cases no jobs with wages payable in national currency were available. As a result, not one unemployed person became involved in Stroud LETS in its first two years' trading, although the unemployed are one of the social groups that stand to gain most from such schemes. My impression is that British LETS members are generally people with low national-currency incomes and some free time who join up for pleasant optional extras that they would otherwise be unable to afford. 'Your members are only getting involved to the extent that they can afford to lose,' an eastern European visitor told the Stroud co-ordinator, Sandra Bruce, on one occasion. However, in Diss, Norfolk, Jyll Seyfang found members to be 'predominantly middle-class people with "alternative" or "green" ideals and an adequate cash income who were attracted to the system by its relevance to these beliefs rather than for the economic benefits of the system'.

Turnover per member is generally higher in the best Irish systems than in Britain because the unemployed can participate wholeheartedly without risking their benefits. This happy situation came about because the Department of Social Welfare accepted arguments by Meitheal na Mart on behalf of all the Irish LETS systems that it was in the public interest that the unemployed be free to take part because this would keep their skills alive, maintain their work habits, and, since informal networks are so valuable to job-hunters, raise their chances of hearing about national-currency-paid jobs. Participation was also likely to maintain their health, we said – because many studies had shown the damaging effect unemployment has on the health of those experiencing it and their families – and therefore to save the state resources it might otherwise have to spend on medical, psychiatric and social care.

In August 1993, only two months after the first Irish system started trading, the department wrote a letter saying that it would not withhold benefits so long as LETS systems did not 'begin to encroach on regular taxed and insured employment'. Such an encroachment would not, of course, be in anyone's interest, and immediately after this ruling the Westport group introduced a rule that restricts members from doing more than thirty-two hours' work a month on a regular basis for any one person for which they are paid in Reeks. We have also tried to convince our members that, now that a LETS system is running, they should never pay cash to anyone working in the black economy. If they do, we point out, they will undermine both the national social welfare system and their own local currency network.

Both the New Zealand and Australian governments have adopted the same policy as Ireland and do not withhold welfare benefits from LETS members. Including lone parents and pensioners, over half the Westport participants are on some type of social welfare benefit, and LETS has greatly improved the quality of their lives. One young couple, the wife unemployed, the husband temporarily disabled after an accident, used the system to transform the garden of a semi-derelict cottage they had just rented: rank grass and scrub was cut, a 200-tree shelter belt was planted, and a rockery and herb garden were built and stocked. 'If we had been paid in real money rather than Reeks we'd never have felt able to spend it this way. Other things would have seemed more important,' the husband told me. 'But it's had a wonderful effect on the house and how we feel about living here.'

In fact, as with most things in life, those who put most effort into a LETS get most out of it, and every survey seriously underestimates the systems' economic importance to particular members. Just ignoring those members who did not trade in a particular month increases the average turnover in Westport to £30, for example; the average level of trading each month by the most active twenty-five members over an eight-month period was £40, with the top four participants doing over £100 a month each. Other Irish systems do much more. In the Beara peninsula in County Cork, where a great deal of effort has been put into building a strong system, the weekly stall did £600 worth of business in a single four-hour period in November 1995, and the most active twenty-five members are estimated to do an average of £120 business each every month. In east Clare the record sales figure for the system's stall, which operates only one day a month, is £800, and its twenty-five most active members are estimated to do an average of £80 worth of business each a month.

The main thing any community contemplating starting a LETS should realize is that getting the system running is not enough. A local currency cannot show its full potential until those behind it have made a real effort to develop businesses doing a substantial part of their trade through it. These businesses obviously get an enormous marketing advantage over firms that have to insist on full payment in pounds or dollars and in effect acquire a degree of protection against outside competition that, as we have seen, national governments are no longer allowed to provide. In addition, to the extent that they can spend local units instead of national ones to cover their start-up costs, they can benefit from what is in fact an interest-free loan.

Naturally a business selling a proportion of its output for the local unit will have to pay for some of its inputs in that unit too, and the willingness of its workers to accept part of their pay in the local unit could be crucial to its survival. At first these firms can be expected to have to limit the proportion of business they do for local money, but as the number of them grows and linkages between them develop, the limits will relax and the amount of national currency that individual members need for living their daily lives will fall.

The members-only nature of a LETS system can be used to create commercial advantages. For example, it provides a way around EU food preparation, labelling and hygiene regulations that might otherwise make it financially impossible for anyone to begin making food products on a small scale. When the environmental health officer called at the Westport LETS stall recently he told the member minding it that as the food available there was only sold to members, the conditions under which it was made were of no legal concern to him. Other EU restrictions also might not apply. For example, it might be possible for a farmer to supply milk to other members through a LETS system without it counting towards the sales he or she is allowed to make under their milk quota.

In its early days, all one can expect economically from a LETS system is that it will provide a useful supplementary income for the weaker members of the community and a safety net the stronger may have to rely on if the world economy crashes. That's a lot in itself; but the real benefits at this stage are not so much economic as personal and social, and many members feel that it would be worthwhile launching a system for these alone. On the personal level, being forced to think of services to offer other members enables people to escape from the confines of their job and to develop skills that would otherwise have lain dormant. For example, many people play a musical instrument reasonably well but would never dream of advertising for engagements. But when a fellow-member of their LETS system asks them to play at a party, they are delighted to do so, not because of the local currency they will earn – that just shows that their ability is valued – but because of the fun they will have giving pleasure to others. Trading through LETS, particularly if they do not confine their activities to their normal profession, introduces members to a wider circle of people than they would probably have come to know so well in any other way. A member of the Newbury system wrote in the LETSlink Newsletter that a 'virtual village' had been created in her town since trading began.[12]

[main text continues p.86]

PAPER CURRENCY REPLACES LETS IN AMERICA

The most successful local currency system in the United States was started as a reaction to the Gulf War in 1991. 'Our country was just being dragged along by the huge armaments manufacturers and the need for oil to fuel the automobile,' says Paul Glover, the person responsible. 'I felt that something had to be done to build a local economy which would enable people to supplant these forces.'

Glover – a journalist, graphic designer, ecological urban planner and draft resister who once walked from coast to coast across America along back roads – had been back home in Ithaca, a city of 30,000 people in New York state, for several years before he started the system. In fact he had already helped establish a LETS there, but this, having traded for ten months and attracted about sixty members, ceased operations when the Community Self-Reliance Center, which had set it up and operated its computer system, closed down in 1988. The experience convinced Glover that a much simpler system was needed – specifically one in which the currency unit actually passed from hand to hand without the necessity for computer records.

It was not just the high level of administration connected with a LETS that drove him to this conclusion. 'Paper currency is more readily used for smaller transactions. Our local farmers' market could not be bothered to report dozens of small LETS transactions on market days. Now that we're using paper money we find it moves faster than LETS credits, involves more people spontaneously, and is more fun.'

A friend of Glover's, Patrice Jennings, had analysed the LETS experiment for her master's thesis at Goddard College, and together they devised the Ithaca 'Hours' scheme to avoid the worst snags her research had revealed. 'There's no law against issuing a hand-to-hand currency if it doesn't look like US dollars, and it gets around all the record-keeping problems that we had encountered with LETS,' Glover says. 'I got about ninety people to back me by paying a minimum of a dollar to advertise whatever goods and services they were prepared to sell for Hours in a newspaper I told them I was going to bring out. I don't think many of them really thought that very much was going to happen. In return for their money I paid everyone four Ithaca Hours, so that they had some currency to use when trading began.' Each Hour represented a typical hour's work and had no exact monetary value at this stage in the system's development.

Glover then spent $300 to print five thousand copies of an eight-page tabloid newspaper, Ithaca Money, that contained 260 advertisements and gave details of how the system would operate. He distributed the paper throughout the city in November 1991. 'One of the problems with LETS is that the lists of members and the goods and services they want or are offering are distributed only to members: this means that only a limited circle of people get the chance to participate. You've really got to get information about the system into the hands of the whole community, not just part of it. A newspaper seemed to me to be the best way to keep everyone informed. Moreover, like other newspaper editors, I'm not

responsible for supplying the tax authorities with information about the business affairs of my advertisers. If I was co-ordinator of a LETS system I would have to do so, as in the United States barter transactions are tax-able.[11] We are not a tax-avoidance scheme, and I announce in every issue of the paper that it is each participant's responsibility to report to the IRS [Internal Revenue Service] the dollar value of any professional trades made.'

Trading began slowly once the paper appeared but grew month by month. By late 1993, when I visited Ithaca, thirteen editions had been published and 4300 Hours, worth $43,000, were in circulation – the national-currency value of an Hour having been fixed at $10, the average level of wages and salaries in the area. 'Initially we just said to people, "Value them at whatever you think an hour's work is worth," and different businesses used different rates, which varied from $6 to $12.50. Eventually, though, we decided to standardize on $10. It makes life easier. This does not mean, though, that offering an Hour will buy you sixty minutes of every member's labour. We haven't felt it necessary to require profes-sional people to accept the same rate of pay as other types of worker. It seemed more important to try to get the lower rates up, but we've seen professionals cutting their rates in the spirit of equal pay. Most partici-pants are getting far more spending power per hour when they are paid in Hours than they do when paid in cash, so we can more readily afford pro-fessional services.

'Hours are real money. They are backed by real people, whereas federal money is backed by nothing at all, unless you count four trillion dollars of national debt. If critics tell me Hours are just Monopoly money, I point out that, on the contrary, they are anti-monopoly money because they would never be accepted by the huge corporations,' he said. Glover is proud of the fact that a thief who robbed a restaurant that accepted Hours went out of his way to take the Hours as well as the normal cash. 'They were kept separately. He didn't just pick them up with the rest of the money. That really demonstrates the extent to which they've been accepted. Hours have also been used as the pot in a game of poker; and because my landlord will take my rent in Hours, I can pay for about 95 per cent of what I need with them.' Glover earned 447 Hours in 1993 from selling display advertisements in Ithaca Money.

Almost every conceivable trade and profession offers its services through the newspaper, and the list of 250 businesses that accept Hours is impressive. At the end of 1995 it included two locally owned supermarkets, six delicatessens, thirty of the stalls in the weekly farmers' market, and several restaurants on at least one night a week. The city cinema was not only taking them but giving change for them in federal notes and coins, while the credit union, although not maintaining Hours accounts, would take them for loan repayments and other fees.

'When our printer started keeping the Hours printing-plates in his safe, I knew they were being taken seriously,' Glover comments. What about the possibility of forgery? 'Everybody asks that!' Glover laughs. 'In the US it's

been found that forgers don't bother with notes of less than $20 in value, so we've taken great care to make our two-Hour [$20] especially difficult to counterfeit. It's printed on watermarked paper hand-made from cat-tails [reedmace] here in Ithaca, using rare antique numerators for the matching serial numbers and a type of printing ink which is no longer manufactured.' The other denominations have embossed serial numbers and are printed with several colours. Notes are also date-stamped when first issued, in a colour sequence only Glover knows.

Glover spends a lot of time checking that retailers who earn plenty of Hours are able to spend them satisfactorily so that they will be happy to continue taking them. 'I encourage businesses to start accepting Hours in a limited way and then gradually extend. That's much better than having them go in too big and then cutting back drastically,' he comments. 'It's best for a high-volume business likely to have [a queue of] customers at the till to take a fixed maximum amount in Hours rather than a percent-age.' If he finds a business with a build-up of Hours, he goes through the complete list of goods and services available with the owner or manager and helps them draw up a shopping list.

These visits to businesses and contacts with individual participants (the Ithaca system has no formal membership) allow Glover to assess whether it is safe to put more Hours into circulation, although the actual decision whether or not to do so is taken by a twice-monthly meeting over a pot-luck meal to which anyone can turn up. So far the rule has been to provide each new participant with four Hours when they place their first advertise-ment and to allow them to claim a further two Hours as a loyalty bonus if they are actively using the system eight months later. Interest-free loans are also available, subject to the offer of suitable collateral. 'We've also put Hours into circulation by making grants to local community organiza-tions who spend them on participants' services,' Glover says. 'In fact we've been tithing: 9.5 per cent of our total currency issue is given to groups according to decisions taken at our fortnightly meetings.'

Since the Ithaca system has been growing, these methods of adjusting the number of Hours in circulation have worked well. However, serious problems are likely to arise should the level of trading ever contract, as it might well do if the US economy picked up and participants found that, since they could earn federal dollars more easily, they did not really want to be bothered with dealing in Hours as well. In these circumstances peo-ple might find it increasingly difficult to find anyone to accept their Hours, and the system could go into a tailspin, with holders dumping their Hours for whatever goods and services they could still get from the diminishing number of people prepared to accept them. Such dumping would cause an inflation that would further undermine confidence in the system and could well lead to its collapse.

The chief structural weakness of the Ithaca Hours system is that it lacks any means of withdrawing Hours from circulation if the level of trad-ing declines. Indeed, although his antennae are highly sensitive to changes in activity level, Glover has no precise idea of the total amount of trading taking place nor of how many people are actively participating: he employs two part-time workers (paid in Hours) to check that people are still prepared to accept the Ithaca unit before repeating their listing in a new issue of the newspaper. The beauty of a LETS system, on the other hand, is that no one ever needs to decide how many units ought to be in circulation or to make adjustments to it: each transaction creates the purchasing power needed to carry it out, and if participants pay their obligations off and drop out, the number of units in the system automatically declines.

Glover replies to this type of criticism by arguing that even if the US economy improved dramatically it would not remove the need for local currencies. 'In the Great Depression, local currencies were issued primarily as emergency money when banks closed; and when federal programmes gradually returned dollars to communities, the local issues faded away. Today, however, we can expect local currencies to become secure and permanent money supplements because millions of well-paying industrial jobs have been shipped overseas, forcing many communities to reinvent their economies on non-industrial lines. Consequently, these communities will not see dollars return even if what is left of American industry prospers. Moreover, the supply of dollars has become so monopolized by the big corporations that money will have to be created locally for use by small enterprises and traders, whatever the national economy does.

'Minimum-wage service jobs keep 20 per cent of Americans below the official poverty level, forcing millions onto public assistance or into crime,' Glover told me in a letter. 'Ithacans need so much more money than we have for food, rent, clothes, fuel and pastimes that we need to create it ourselves. Government, industry and the big corporations are leaving us behind. That situation is permanent. So, therefore, is our money.'

Although it might have seemed at the outset that much less work was going to be required to operate a hand-to-hand currency than a LETS system, this has probably not been the case, although Glover points out that a lot of his time was taken up by the continuing process of inventing the system and responding to contingencies. When I met him he had just completed almost three years of much-more-than-full-time unpaid work to get the system going, not even issuing himself with Hours to compensate for the effort he was putting in, although he had received five small grants during the period. Fortunately, that period of hardship was ending: he was finding it increasingly possible to delegate work, and the local credit union was paying him a regular stipend.

Glover thinks that discussing whether LETS or Hours are superior is a waste of time. 'We will prosper by experimenting and learning from each other rather than theorizing. I'm impressed by what I hear about LETS in Australia and include a news story I wrote in 1986 about the Ithaca LETS when that started up, in case people want to try a LETS system,' he wrote in a letter.

No local currency of any type will thrive and develop unless there is at least one person prepared to put a great deal of effort into its first two or three years; and if at any stage Glover had limited his commitment, the

Ithaca Hour system would have been just as likely to collapse as the LETS system that preceded it. 'If I was hit by a truck even now, people would look at their money and start to question it, so I'm institutionalizing the system to make it less dependent on me,' he says. At the moment the only formal structure behind him is an advisory board, which meets monthly, but the system is a legal entity, as it is covered by the charter of the former Community Self-Reliance Center. Glover intends to hand over to others some of the work of selling advertising. 'I've exhausted all my contacts by now,' he says. 'New people will be able to gain access to groups that are culturally inaccessible to me.' Another project that will help make the system less dependent on him is the opening of a shop through which people can sell things for 100 per cent Hours. 'We had one on the main street last month but we had to close it after three weeks when the owner changed his plans. The store will provide an outlet for people who do things like baking bread or knitting sweaters and make it even easier for people who have earned Hours to spend them.'

Glover hopes that in a few years' time it will be possible to pay local taxes in Hours and that almost all locally owned shops will accept them. In the longer term he hopes they will help make the Finger Lakes bio-region far less dependent on distant corporations and resources as part of a national change that turns the United States into a country of strong ecological local economies rather than a single national one. For the present, however, there is no doubt that the Ithaca Hour works well for almost everyone who uses it. Hundreds of thousands of dollars' worth of trading has been done, and at least three thousand people have participated. Moreover, by the end of 1995, twenty other places had started Hours systems.

'Hours changed my life,' said Bill, an architect, in the system's newspaper, which carries success stories in every issue. 'I had no jobs, was out of money, and was scared. I got two jobs through Ithaca Money which kept food on the table and turned out to be steady work. One of these employers has become a good friend. Now I've got a third major Hour job, very creative and exciting. There's a lot less stress associated with Hours and they're fun to spend.' Susan, another satisfied user, added: 'I trust a person more who has Hours in their wallet. It means they've invested in Ithaca and that they are willing to be open-minded about the value of labour.' The two hundred similar testimonials that have been published demonstrate that, despite the Hour's undoubted economic impact, its most important achievement so far has been to bring people together, create friendships, and build community spirit. As Lynn, another user, told Ithaca Money, 'Hours bring back the sense of co-operation and interdependence, of a more personal and caring economy.'

Paul Glover can be contacted at Ithaca Money, Box 6578, Ithaca, New York 14851; tel. +1 607 2738025; e-mail ithacahour@aol.com. A Home Town Money Starter Kit, giving details of how to set up a similar system, can be obtained from him for $25, including postage to Europe.

Despite these benefits, a LETS system will only work well if there is underemployment and an inadequate supply of national currency in a region or among a social group: if everyone is fully occupied and finds that their activities are not seriously restricted for lack of cash, why should they bother to join a LETS, and what economic benefits could it bring them if they did? A service credit system such as Time Dollars (see later panel) would be better in such a community.

LETS systems are therefore very vulnerable to changes in the state of the mainstream economy. Since every LETS member prefers to be paid in national currency whenever it is available because that currency can be spent on a wider range of things, LETS schemes will tend to develop during recessions as the national currency gets scarcer, and to weaken or collapse whenever the national economy improves. In my view it was the improvement in the Canadian economy in the middle 1980s that hit Michael Linton's original LETS in the Comox Valley, although he attributes its period of dormancy before it was revived by a women's group to the departure of a dentist who had been prepared to take payment in the local unit while he was reconstructing his surgery so that he could spend the proceeds on the building work.

'Our problem was that although we had six hundred account-holders at one point, we never had more than about five shops that would accept our Green Dollars,' Linton told me. 'And these weren't large shops either. So when the dentist left the district, a lot of the builders and handymen who had joined the scheme in the early days and had sent their families to him for treatment found that they couldn't spend their Green Dollars that way, and they weren't greatly interested in the services of the rest of the members, like the single mothers offering babysitting or aromatherapy.' So the tradesmen stopped working for Green Dollars, which left the rest of the members with nothing substantial that they really wanted to buy either, as they had been treating the LETS primarily as a way to get their houses done up. Trading more or less stopped. Linton disagrees with my belief that the underlying reason the builders stopped participating was not that the dentist had gone but that the economy had improved and they found it easier to get paid in cash. His explanation and my theory are not incompatible, and both probably contain part of the truth. However, there is no doubt that the Comox experience underlines the importance of ensuring that people's real needs, as opposed to their peripheral pleasures, can be met through a LETS.

Comox Valley LETS was by no means the first local currency

experiment, and Linton says he spent almost a year researching earlier systems before launching it. 'All the components of LETSystems were drawn from other sources, but the precise arrangement of them seems to [have been] unprecedented,' he says. The commercial barter networks were one source, and the Useful Services Exchange established in Reston, Virginia, by Harry Ware in the early 1970s was another.* Where Ware got his ideas from I have been unable to discover, but records of people setting up systems to enable exchanges to take place without the use of official currency go back a long way. In 1696, John Bellers, a Quaker, proposed that unemployed workers be paid in labour notes for goods they had produced with materials supplied by the system's central office. The office was to recover its notes by selling the goods either to the workers themselves or to others who had received notes from the workers in payment for food or rent. The idea was tried out in Bristol and failed but was revived almost 140 years later by the philanthropist Robert Owen, who republished Bellers's book. Owen, however, was no more successful than Bellers: his National Equitable Labour Exchange opened in 1832 and closed

[main text continues p.89]

---

* The immediate precursor of LETS in Britain was Link, a scheme to help elderly people develop new social contacts and to keep mentally and physically fit by carrying out small tasks for other members. The first Link was set up in the London borough of Merton in 1976 by a health insurance company, British United Provident Association, and a group of charities, including Age Concern. By 1978, thirty-five systems were operating, all in urban areas, but a survey by Age Concern the following year showed that twenty-two had become inactive. The last surviving system closed in Bath in 1990. A local system was run by an unpaid volunteer manager who would pin up a card for each member on a notice-board in the system's office giving details of the work that that member was prepared to do; members would then try to match their requirements with the offers on the cards. However, although membership was open to all, most of those who joined were elderly, and there was an acute shortage of people offering to do tasks requiring physical strength. (The Bath scheme overcame this by getting schools involved.) Members were given enough tokens to pay for four hours' work on enrolment and could only get more by earning them from other members. The running costs of the system were covered by charities or by bring-and-buy sales and coffee mornings. This meant that they were almost always seriously underfunded: the Bath system managed on £1000 a year, including office rent. There seem to have been two main problems with Link apart from its age structure. One was that its attempt to treat everyone's time as of equal value (one token per hour) was not seen as realistic by many members, who frequently had to enhance their tokens with cash to secure someone with the skills or strength to do a particular job. The other was that members used the office only to make initial contacts with people living in their district and then made further contacts directly. This meant that people joining an established system found it difficult to get involved.

CASH ATTITUDES V. LETS ATTITUDES

It is a serious mistake to think that approaches and attitudes customarily applied in the cash economy will work equally well with LETS. Here are four points to notice:

1. While anyone being paid cash to do some work is at their employer's disposal, anyone being paid LETS units is at their own. LETS members tackle jobs as friends wanting to help out, not as people in financial difficulties prepared to do anything to be paid. This means that they must be allowed to arrange a time to do the job that suits their convenience as much as yours. And if they need to be collected from home because their partner has the car, you have to do it: only if you were offering cash would it be reasonable to suggest that they be inconvenienced. And, naturally, you offer your helper coffee and make them lunch. If someone doesn't like working for you, they'll never offer to help you out for LETS units again.

2. A LETS is just as much a social organization as an economic one. If there is a big job to be done such as clearing scrub, don't try to find one member to do it alone over several days. That's too much like paid work. Provide food and drink and get enough people to come together so that the whole task can be completed in a day. This turns the task into a party, and its successful completion will leave everyone with a sense of achievement. This way you'll strengthen your system and have no trouble recruiting enough volunteers.

3. Banks like customers with large credits in their accounts. LETS co-ordinators do not. In fact members with large local-unit credits in their accounts present a much more serious threat to a system than those who have run up large deficits. This is because those with hefty credit balances are among a system's most valuable members since they must have been providing goods and services that other members like in order to have reached their surplus position. Consequently, if any member amasses more units in their account than they are able to spend and cuts down the amount of LETS work they are prepared to take on, every other member will find their units less useful and harder to spend. In short, the system will begin to unravel. The top priority of every LETS coordinator should be to approach members with big positive accounts to find out if they are experiencing any difficulty spending their units. If they are, the coordinator must find other members to supply goods and services they want so as to help them bring their surpluses down.

4. 'Money is a way of finding out who you can trust. After you have established that, it just doesn't matter any more,' Edgar Cahn, the originator of Time Dollars, an American system of service credits, told me once. This certainly proves true with LETS units much more quickly than it ever does with national currency; and your relationship with some LETS members you are dealing with regularly will soon begin to seem much more important than the balance in your account. After a little while it feels almost petty to put a value on each transaction and to give or receive a cheque. Each party begins to give as they can, confident that they will always be able to take as they need. Mutual trust becomes paramount; the spirit of the Irish meitheal begins to emerge.

less than two years later. The Bank of Exchange set up in 1848 by the French socialist Pierre-Joseph Proudhon – best known for his view that 'property is theft' – was an equally unsuccessful variation on Bellers's idea.*

For our purposes, however, the most relevant experiments with local currencies were carried out in the 1930s in response to severe shortages of national currencies at the time. These arose mainly because a national currency has to perform two functions: that of a means of exchange, so that people can express the value of different goods and services and can transfer that value to each other, and also as a store of value, which holders can save up until they are ready to buy. These roles can conflict with each other. During an inflation, for example, the monetary unit fails as a store of value, encouraging people to exchange their cash for goods as quickly as possible, thus speeding the inflation along. Conversely, when prices fall in a depression, those who can hold on to their money do so because they expect to be able to buy whatever they need more cheaply later on. Naturally their hoarding removes money from circulation, thus reducing other people's ability to buy things and accelerating the rate at which prices fall.

Reichsmark hoarding became a severe problem in Germany during the economically depressed period immediately after the First World War, and the Freiwirtschaft (Free Economy) movement developed to tackle it. In 1919 one of its members, Hans Timms, set up an organization to issue a supplementary currency based on the writings of a friend, Silvio Gesell, who, having made his fortune as an importer and manufacturer in Argentina, had returned to Europe in 1906 able, as Keynes put it, 'to devote the last decades of his life to the two most delightful occupations open to those who do not have to earn their

[main text continues p.94]

---

* Proudhon believed that the ideal rural society was one based on small peasant farmers who supported themselves by working independently on land they owned. This brought him into direct conflict with Marx, who believed that big farms, like big factories, were bound to displace smaller ones because of their superior efficiency, and called for the social ownership of the land. Marx, who ridiculed Proudhon as a petty-bourgeois, also saw the small farm as a barrier to social and economic development and a 'leaden weight' on the working-class movement. One of the great tragedies of modern times is that when these ideas were debated at the Second Congress of the International Workers' Association in 1867, Marx carried the day, and henceforward the socialist movement not only gave its support to the destruction of the peasantry but also to industrialization.

THE DOLLAR THAT DOESN'T WANT TO BE MONEY

In early 1994 only about ten LETS systems were trading in the United States, and their total membership was small. There were, however, more than 150 Time Dollar systems operating, with anything from a few dozen to several thousand members in some thirty states. Were they filling much the same economic need? Since the cover of their inventor's book refers to Time Dollars as a new currency, one might be forgiven for thinking so, particularly as Ralph Nader's foreword says that 'citizen action must rest on a new economic base: one that makes it possible for people to meet their own needs while working to rebuild community and revitalize democracy at a grassroots level'.

But while they have similarities, the two systems differ in many important respects. Dr Edgar Cahn, a campaigning lawyer who began developing the Time Dollar idea in hospital when recovering from a heart attack, would be appalled if his creation ever became as acceptable as national currency, a situation that would be every LETS enthusiast's dream. 'Money is ideal for strangers because you can get things with it regardless of whether you know the person you are dealing with or not. Its use preserves a degree of anonymity and does not build community and trust,' Cahn says. For him the fact that Time Dollars can only be spent in a limited number of ways is an advantage, since he wants them to empower people to meet social needs that can no longer be afforded in most modern economies. 'Real money is all-purpose: you can buy anything with it,' he says. 'Time Dollars can only buy things of special value such as companionship, love and caring. Maybe we don't really want the things we value most to be up for grabs to the highest bidder.' Revitalizing a community economically is no part of his brief.

Time Dollars are earned by providing care for other people and can only be spent in buying similar care for oneself or for one's relatives and friends. The largest system is in Miami, where volunteers' services include light housekeeping for the sick or elderly, deciphering Social Security rules, companionship, respite support for carers, lifts to the doctor's, the church, or the supermarket, letter writing, reading to the blind, pet care, babysitting, language classes, sewing classes, and adult day care. Whichever service volunteers provide, all earn the same rate – one Time Dollar per hour – and, as with LETS, records are kept on a computer in the coordinator's office. Unlike LETS, however, the coordinator matches volunteers with clients, rather than having the latter hunt through a directory for a volunteer who seems right.

Many volunteers are elderly people who, on one level, rationalize their participation with the thought that by providing help now they are earning the right to call on other members should they need care in the future. However, many schemes find it difficult to get volunteers to report their hours, and since only 15 per cent of Time Dollars are ever spent and no one is refused care because of a deficit in their account, Cahn believes the real reason people join is to be of service to others. 'People must request help, but it doesn't matter if they haven't the Time Dollars to pay for it. You lose your volunteers if you don't keep them assigned.'

It is the fact that the volunteers primarily want to give rather than to earn that makes it so important that Time Dollars not be seen as money and that they have no monetary equivalent – that they not be bought and sold. 'Yet the fact that they receive something for their efforts is important too because it validates their contribution,' Cahn says. 'A teenager here in Washington, DC, who was earning Time Dollars doing yard work for elderly neighbours told me that the Time Dollars meant a lot to him because if he wasn't getting something his buddies would think he was a chump. Earning something he could give away gave him status. Time Dollars are a hybrid of the psychological rewards of volunteering and of payment. They are a form of money which is not a commodity.'

As such, they permit people to do things they would never do for cash. 'A retired bank president would never mow a sick person's yard for money, but he'll do it for Time Dollars,' Cahn says. 'Market wages incorporate status hierarchies. Ask yourself if you would ask your mother to accept market wages to go next door to clean up a neighbour's house. Then ask yourself if you would have the same reservations about asking her to go over and help a sick neighbour by cleaning up and accepting Time Dollars so that Granny, living across town, could be picked up and taken into the doctor. Price is not the issue. It is status. To accept money for such a task implies one has accepted the market status defined by the wage.'

Cahn lists other ways in which Time Dollars differ from national currency and yet are superior to it if one is trying to build community. 'Money is frictionless and "efficient", yet what an economist calls inefficiency and friction are sometimes the glue that holds society together. Unlike the national currency, Time Dollars are issued and spent locally. What we are doing by recording them on our computer is acting as the community's memory in a way which wouldn't have been necessary a generation or two ago when people were less mobile. Real money knows no loyalty to community or even country. A dollar put into a poor community can exit in hours to a cigarette manufacturer or a Japanese electronics firm. It is estimated that of every dollar the Federal Government puts into an Indian reservation, 75 cents flows out within forty-eight hours. Moreover, the supply of real money is limited. The supply of Time Dollars is not – it only depends on the willingness of people in an area to help each other.'

Cahn and his wife, Jean, were the co-founders of Antioch Law School in Washington, which trained – and radicalized – its students by having them work under supervision on cases for the poor. 'It was founded on the quaint idea that law and justice should have something to do with each other,' Cahn comments wryly. But recovering after his heart attack in 1980, he found the tables were turned. 'I'd always been the doer, the person who made things happen, and now here I was, lying in bed, and people were doing things for me. I was an object, a taker, and I didn't like it. I'd been reading about other people – single mothers, the elderly, minority teenagers and the unemployed – that society puts on the scrap heap and then regards as takers draining its resources. And I thought, "Those other people don't like being takers any more than I do. There's got to be a way to enable them to meet some of society's needs."'

91

As Cahn sees it, these needs arise because the informal, non-market economy has broken down over the years as households bought for cash more and more of the things they had previously provided for themselves. 'McDonald's now provides the meals, Nintendo and video tapes the entertainment, insurance companies and the police the protection, Medicare and Medicaid the nursing care and so on. Unfortunately, these suppliers can generally provide only 70 per cent of what's needed – the police cannot be effective without community help, for example, nor can the schools educate children properly without parental support. But with both partners working to provide the money for these services, parents seldom have the time to fill these gaps. It's not that nobody has the time, but the available hours have been dumped on the elderly and the unemployed. The fact is that very few families, and certainly not the nation as a whole, can afford all the services they need if they have to be bought from specialists at market rates. To give you an example – supposing I gave up brushing my teeth myself and called in a dental hygienist to do the job for me. Whatever do you think that would cost? In the market economy one cannot even buy an hour of one's own time with one's take-home pay from an hour of work.'

After his recovery the Cahns moved to England for several months so that Jean could complete a course. This gave Edgar, whose doctorate is in English literature, the chance to develop his ideas at the London School of Economics. He remembers some lively discussions on the relationship between economic efficiency and equity. 'My argument was that you can only say something is efficient in relation to your objectives. The superior efficiency of the market economy turns out either to be illusory or to have hidden costs. It only functions as well as it does because it assumes continued uncompensated contributions and support from the very non-market institutions it is undermining.'

In 1986 the Suntory Toyota International Centre for Economics at the LSE published Cahn's ideas under the title Service Credits: a New Currency for the Welfare State. The same year, back in the United States with their ideas formed and three pilot projects under way, the Cahns persuaded the Robert Wood Johnson Foundation to give $1.2 million to finance Time Dollar programmes for three years in Missouri, Washington, Miami, San Francisco, Boston, and New York. Five of these six schemes are still running, the sole closure caused by the commercial takeover of the voluntary hospital where one was based. 'If you pay a full-time manager and two part-time assistants it costs $50-60,000 a year to run a typical system. This works out at about $1.25 per hour of care given, much cheaper than anything which can be provided in any other way. In fact, there are very real economic savings because people can be discharged from hospital sooner if they've got someone to look after them at home.'

Since Time Dollars and LETS have different objectives, one primarily social, one more heavily economic, there is no conflict or incompatibility between them, and many communities ought to seek to establish both, particularly as the people who would become involved in each would tend to differ. At the very least, LETS groups can learn from Cahn's ideas on the conflict between community and national currency and seek to ensure that, in their enthusiasm to make their local unit as useful and as versatile as possible, they do not reintroduce too many of the bad features of the monetary system from which they are trying to break away.

Jean Cahn died in 1991, and since then Edgar Cahn has been working up to eighty hours a week with students and volunteers at his house in Washington to spread the Time Dollar idea as a memorial to her. When I met him he was working on ways in which Time Dollars could be used on public authority housing estates to develop tenant management systems, help families under stress, assist tenant-operated enterprises, and reduce vacancy rates and building deterioration. 'Too often what we call growth in the Gross Domestic Product is simply a transfer of functions from the household economy to the market economy. Every time we put a grandmother in a nursing home, that is a contribution to GDP. Every time we enable her to continue to live at home, it's not,' he told me.

'Although there's a widespread feeling that the disintegration of the family is the source of most social problems, no one asks how we can rebuild the non-market economy. This has led to a simplistic fixation on entry into the job market as the panacea for eradicating poverty. Yet the non-market economy is the only economy we control: the other, the market economy, is irreversibly embedded in the new global economy. We lack a viable strategy for dealing with poverty because we are concentrating on the wrong economy.'

Enough detailed information to start a Time Dollar system is given in a leaflet, The Time Dollar, by Edgar Cahn, available for $2 together with a self-addressed DL (110 by 220 mm) envelope from Time Dollar, PO Box 19405, Washington, DC 20036. Existing Time Dollar systems are described in Time Dollars by Edgar Cahn and Jonathan Rowe (Rodale Press, Emmaus, Pennsylvania, 1992; $19.95).

Womanshare (680 West End Avenue, New York, NY 10025 USA; tel. +1 212 6629746; email Wshare@aol.com) is a highly successful time-exchange system that has operated in New York since 1991. As with Time Dollars, credits cannot be exchanged and members work for each other on an hour-for-hour basis in order to value 'the resources of each individual ... independently of the prevailing economy'. Membership, which costs $50 a year, is limited to eighty women to foster group cohesion; the result is a long waiting list. 'Having just women [is] easier,' Jane Wilson, one of the founders, comments. She says that men tend to want to take over and to keep an exact account of trades. The group has a strong social side and potluck meetings are held every month in someone's home. Members are required to attend at least two a year and also to do at least six hours' work for other members each quarter. The wide variety of skills and services available within the group is publicized in a directory that is revised every three months.

living, authorship and experimental farming.'[13] Keynes devoted five pages of his major work, *The General Theory of Employment, Interest and Money*, first published by Macmillan in 1936, to a discussion of Gesell's contribution to the theory of money and interest. Keynes regarded as 'sound' Gesell's idea of increasing the cost of holding on to money by requiring stamps to be fixed to it to revalidate it regularly, although he pointed out that people would switch their savings to substitutes such as foreign money, jewellery and precious metals to escape the levy. 'I believe that the future will learn more from the spirit of Gesell than from that of Marx,' he wrote.

The currency was called the Wära – a combination of *ware* (commodity) and *währung* (currency). Notes were issued for 0.5, 1, 2 and 5 Wära, each Wära being worth exactly a Reichsmark – indeed it could be exchanged for one in emergencies, since the entire proceeds from the sale of Wära notes were lodged in a redemption fund. The key difference between the Wära and the Reichsmark lay in the fact that the former were costly to hoard, since anyone holding some at the end of a month had to buy special stamps costing 2 per cent of each note's face value to revalidate them for use during the following month. Naturally this meant that anyone who received Wära tried their best to spend them before they needed to be stamped again, and the new currency began to circulate rapidly among Freiwirtschaft enthusiasts throughout Germany. Timms's organization used the 2 per cent monthly levy for promotional purposes.

Gesell got the idea of making it expensive to hang on to money from bracteates, the thin silver-alloy coins issued by the rulers of the

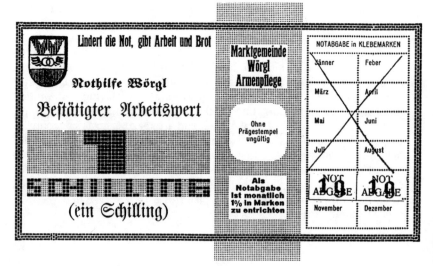

dozens of small independent states in the Holy Roman Empire from the twelfth to the fifteenth century, which were at least as risky to hold as any of the commodities they could be used to purchase. Most of this risk originally stemmed from the fact that they could lose up to a quarter of their value overnight because whenever a ruler who had issued a batch died, all the coins bearing his head became invalid and had to be exchanged, at a 20–25 per cent discount, for new ones bearing his successor's features. Predictably, however, rulers soon began to recall bracteates as a form of tax, sometimes as often as three times a year; in the fourteenth century Johann II of France changed his currency no fewer than eighty-six times.

Having to use money that lost its value so quickly meant that people spent it as soon as they received it, since even holding it overnight involved a risk. So, according to Fritz Schwarz, a Gesellian writing in 1931, instead of saving this fast-depreciating cash, people spent any surplus they might have on improving their houses and property, and he points to the fine houses relatively ordinary people were able to build during the period.[14] The construction work meant that there was a high demand for labour, and wages were consequently good: an ordinary day-labourer could expect to earn six or eight groats a week, enough to buy four pairs of shoes or two sheep. Working hours were short – there was trouble in Saxony when the mine-owners wanted to increase daily hours from six to eight – and there were at least ninety religious holidays a year. This meant that craftsmen, who took Mondays off to recover from over-indulgence on Sunday, worked less than a four-day week. It was a time of great prosperity, Schwarz claimed, with 'no difference between the farmhouse and castle'. Farmers wore coats with golden buttons and had silver buckles on their shoes.

Ironically, it was gold that brought this golden age to a close. A bracteate was generally 'a totally wretched and ugly little disc of metal, very thin, of low fineness, easy to lose, and easy to break,'[15] which had no intrinsic value because of its low silver content, and was therefore useless for international trade, particularly as it could be recalled at any time. Realizing this, the Genoese and then the Florentines issued gold coins in 1252, and Venice followed in 1284. These new coins could act as a store of value as well as a means of exchange and allowed people to build up their assets in ways that did not involve employing others and thus passing their surplus around. Moreover, as they spread, trading itself became more difficult. 'The means of exchange disappeared into socks and mattresses,' Schwarz writes; and as money became scarce, interest rates soared, despite the opposition of the church. Some merchants found it more profitable to sell off their stock and lend out their capital, and a gulf developed between families with an income based on interest and the rest of the population. The demand for labour dropped, wages fell, and unemployment appeared. And to cap it all, rulers had to find other means of taxation.

No one in authority took much notice of the Freiwirtschaft currency until 1931, when the purchaser of a defunct coal mine at Schwanenkirchen, a village in Bavaria with a population of five hundred, was able to reopen it by paying the miners in Wära, which he had arranged they could spend in the village shops. In their turn the shopkeepers forced their wholesalers to accept Wära, and the wholesalers passed them back to their suppliers, who spent most of the notes they received on buying Schwanenkirchen coal – since there were few other ways in which Wära could be used.

According to an account published in August 1932 in the American magazine *The New Republic*, the effects on the village were dramatic. 'One would not have recognized Schwanenkirchen a few months after work had been resumed at the mine. The village was on a prosperity basis, workers and merchants were free from debts and a new spirit of life and freedom pervaded the town ... Reporters came from all over Germany to write about the "Miracle".' The article pointed out that if Reichsmarks had been used in place of Wära they would have been hoarded because of the uncertain times, and the venture would have failed. Moreover, even if they had not been hoarded they would have dispersed all over Germany, and there would have been little likelihood of their returning to Schwanenkirchen and increasing demand at the mine.[16]

Although only 20,000 Wära were ever issued by Timms's central organization, some 2.5 million people handled them in 1930-31 as a result of their high velocity of circulation. Their success in Schwanenkirchen terrified the German government, which feared they would cause inflation, and after an unsuccessful court action on the grounds that Wära infringed the state's sole right to issue money, it passed emergency legislation in November 1931 to bring their use to an end. The mine in Schwanenkirchen closed, and its workers were plunged back into unemployment.

Not far over the border, in the Austrian Tyrol, another enthusiastic supporter of Gesell's ideas had been following events closely. He was Michael Unterguggenberger, the mayor of Wörgl, where local tax payments were seriously in arrears and the official treasury was in crisis because 1500 of the town's 4300 inhabitants were out of work. The type of auxiliary currency used in Schwanenkirchen – technically known as 'stamp scrip' – seemed the answer, and, after negotiating a loan from the local Raiffeisen (credit union) savings bank, the mayor printed notes with a face value of 32,000 schillings, in denominations of 1, 5, and 10. Only a third of these were ever put into circulation. In August 1932 the scrip was used to pay half the wages of the council staff, including the mayor; and because the businesspeople of the town knew it could be used to pay local taxes, they reluctantly accepted it in payment for goods, the fear of losing sales to competitors bringing stragglers into line. As the scrip, like the Wära, had to be stamped each month to maintain its validity, it was passed quickly from hand to hand, generating a rapid increase in trade. It was in fact spent in preference to national currency, and in its first year, according to a later German account of the experiment, each local note changed hands 463 times on average, whereas a typical national note was involved in only 213 transactions. Quite soon only the railway station and the post office were not accepting the local money.[17]

The traders took no risk in accepting Wörgl scrip, as it was completely backed by the national-currency loan the mayor had obtained from the savings bank and left on deposit there. This enabled anyone holding scrip to swap it at any time for 98 per cent of its face value in national currency. Very few people appear to have made the exchange because at 2 per cent it cost more to do so than to pay the 1 per cent monthly revalidation fee, but any local money that was returned to the bank or paid to the council in tax was immediately relaunched into circulation in the town.

Just as in Schwanenkirchen, the effects of the 'auxiliary money' were impressive. In the first month 4542 schillings were paid off in tax arrears, allowing a new public works programme to begin that employed fifty people, their wages paid entirely in scrip. In the second half of 1932 Wörgl spent 100,000 schillings rebuilding and asphalting four miles of streets and extending the sewerage system, the entire cost being covered out of overdue tax receipts. The savings bank benefited too, and deposits exceeded withdrawals for the first time for many months. In January 1933 the town began to build a ski jump and a reservoir; both were completed without incurring any debt.

As one might expect, other towns started planning to copy the scheme. Although the Austrian government had not been hostile to the Wörgl experiment, the Central Bank felt it had to prevent the spread of such systems for fear it would lose control over the amount of currency in circulation nationally and hence over inflation. It began legal proceedings against the Wörgl council, and on 1 September 1933 the scheme was stopped, thirteen months after it had begun.

'Wörgl had a community currency but it was not a personally issued currency like LETS; its issue was institutional,' Michael Linton comments. 'It was just a substitute for the national currency issued by a local government rather than by the Austrian Central Bank. Many local money schemes in the past have merely been small-scale versions of national currencies, and they don't work any better at the local level than they have at the national. Because they are kept scarce like national currency they create a climate of competition, which still leads to local unemployment and local rich and local poor. More seriously, they are also inherently less stable than national currencies and prone to irrecoverable collapse, so the authorities were in some ways quite right to suppress the Wörgl one, although almost certainly they did so for the wrong reasons.'

The story now moves to the United States, where several hundred communities, ranging from villages to the state of Iowa and cities such as St Paul, Minnesota, either issued their own scrip or seriously considered doing so. The pioneer was Hawarden, a town of three thousand people in Iowa, in October 1932, but unfortunately the promoter, Charles Zylstra, departed from the Wörgl-Wära model and did not set up a redemption fund to guarantee the issue. Instead he proposed that every person who received a scrip note with the face value of a dollar should stick a special 3-cent stamp on it before passing it on and that after it had been used for thirty-six transactions and had collected $1.08 worth of stamps it could be redeemed for a US dollar.

Unfortunately there was no way, apart from public honesty, of ensuring that a stamp was applied after every transaction. Moreover, although the scrip itself was dated in an effort to prevent hoarding, the absence of dates on which stamps had to be applied meant that there was no incentive to pass the money along as quickly as possible. In fact as the scrip was used to pay part of the wages of people engaged on unemployment relief projects, the whole scheme amounted to little more than an optional tax to meet the cost of the work that was paid by those using the local money.

Despite its problems, Zylstra's system was adopted in several towns with mixed results. Eventually, however, it was replaced by closer approximations to the Wörgl scheme as that became better known, notably through the efforts of a professor of economics at Yale University, Irving Fisher, who published a manual on how to set up and run a stamp scrip system in 1933.[18] Fisher described at length a type of scrip proposed for the city of Reading, Pennsylvania, in which the note had fifty-two squares on the back, each printed with the date of consecutive Wednesdays in the year after its issue. Before they could be used, special 2-cent stamps had to be stuck in these squares by whoever held the note on the previous Tuesday night. By the end of the year $1.04 would have built up to allow the note to be redeemed at par, leaving 4 cents to cover expenses. According to newspaper reports of the time, scrip of this type was widely adopted.

By 1933 more than three hundred communities had introduced some form of barter system, scrip or local currency to try to overcome the nationwide currency shortage. Tenino, Washington, even used wooden money: it printed 25-cent, 50-cent and $1 tokens on spruce wood after the local bank collapsed, freezing everyone's assets. Wooden coins worth $6500 were put into circulation; but when the day came for them to be redeemed in US currency, only $30 worth was presented: coin collectors and tourists had taken the rest, leaving the town council with enough cash to buy the bank building and open it again.

'Scrip permitted if soundly backed' was the headline in the *New York Times* on 10 January 1933, but it was too good to last. Three months later, on 4 March 1933, President Roosevelt forbade any further issues although existing schemes were allowed time to wind themselves up. It was not that the government had any objections to scrip being issued to create jobs, but it had been advised by Professor Russell Sprague of Harvard University that the American monetary system was being democratized out of its hands.

Within the past few years, as we have seen, unstamped scrip has reappeared in at least twenty-one communities in the United States thanks to Paul Glover. The most recent version of stamped scrip I know of was that issued in the historic French town of Lignières-en-Berry in August 1956 in an effort to generate more business and thus counteract the town's decline (its population had halved to 1700 in the previous fifty years, and of those who remained, three hundred were over seventy).[26]

At first the scrip, which was issued by a group of the town's traders, was exactly like that in Wörgl. It was backed by national currency, into which it could be converted at 98 per cent of its face value, and had to be revalidated each month with a stamp costing 1 per cent. The early results were encouraging, but the project started

[main text continues p.106]

MUTUAL CURRENCY SYSTEM PROVIDES BUSINESSES WITH CHEAP CAPITAL

Perhaps the best example of the benefits that can flow to businesses that join an arrangement to create a private currency is provided by WIR, the Wirtschaftsring (Economic Circle) co-operative in Switzerland. Since its inauguration in October 1934, WIR has grown into a massive organization, turning over 2521 million Swiss francs (£1200 million) in 1993 among its 60,000 account-holders. Indeed the WIR system is so simple and so successful and saves its participants so much money by enabling them to obtain zero-interest working capital that it is surprising that similar systems have not been set up around the world.

Essentially, WIR is an independent currency system for small and medium-sized businesses. A company wishing to join contacts one of the six regional offices and sets up a meeting at which its credit requirements and the collateral it is able to offer are discussed, just as they would be if it sought a loan from a bank. As first mortgages in Switzerland do not usually exceed 60 per cent of the purchase price, the collateral most frequently offered is a second mortgage on a house or business premises: in recent years over 80 per cent of WIR's loans have been secured this way. If the meeting is successful a loan application is sent to the WIR credit approval committee, which checks the security and obtains a report on the applicant from a credit-checking agency. If the report and the security are in order, the new participant is given a WIR chequebook, a charge card, and a fat catalogue listing other participants with whom the loan has to be spent.

Although the sums in WIR accounts are denominated in Swiss francs, they are not Swiss francs at all, since, unless one breaks the rules, they cannot be turned into cash, paid into banks, or given to non-members. We will therefore call the system's units 'Wir'. Even when someone wishes to leave the organization they cannot get national currency out. As a result, the purchasing power created when the credit committee authorizes a loan stays entirely within the 'ring', generating increased business for all participants. Secured loans of this type are cheap. In 1994 WIR mortgages carried a service charge of 1.75 per cent, and relatively long repayment terms could be negotiated; the charge for ordinary current-account loans was 2.5 per cent.

The credit committee has a policy of restricting the total value of the loans it authorizes to one-third of the system's annual turnover in order to maintain the Wir's value. All repayments are made in Wir earned when the member sells his or her goods and services to other participants. Only the service charges on them have to be paid in Swiss francs, since the co-op itself cannot function without some national currency. Its other charges – a quarterly subscription of eleven francs to cover the cost of the WIR magazine, a new edition of the catalogue and a levy of 0.6 per cent of the value of each cheque lodged to a participant's account – are all in Wir.

WIR's summer 1994 catalogue included 1853 architects, 167 lawyers, 18 chimney-sweeps, and 16 undertakers. 'The main areas are gastronomy and the building trade, while the odder categories are astrologers, piano tuners, matrimonial agencies, genealogical researchers and magicians. There's even a circus,' says Claudia Horny from WIR's public relations office.[19] Not all suppliers will take 100 per cent payment in Wir, but with several sources listed for most products and services it is generally possible to find at least one who will, particularly at slack times of year or during sales. Prices and payment terms for transactions in Wir are just the same as they would be for cash, and until recently, if a supplier insisted on getting a proportion of an invoice paid in national currency, two cheques, one in Wir, one in Swiss francs, were handed over at the same time. However, since the beginning of 1995 it has been possible to make combined payments of cash and Wir using a single charge card.

In fact the percentage of the Swiss franc price of the goods and services that participants will supply for Wir is discussed with each member when they join, and the service charges mentioned so far only apply to 'official' members, who have guaranteed to accept at least 30 per cent of the payment in the system's unit. Members unable to give such a guarantee are called 'unofficial' members and pay higher charges: 3.5 per cent for current-account loans and a 1.2 per cent levy on the value of each cheque.

The system was set up as a co-op in 1934 by Dr Werner Zimmermann and Paul Enz with some of their friends to overcome the currency shortages of the time. The group, influenced by Silvio Gesell, had as its motto 'Free exchange of goods and services without exploitation of our fellow-man and without government coercion', and saw high interest rates as an aspect of exploitation. At first the idea was simply that businesspeople who knew and trusted each other would extend credit to each other for purchases within their group, cutting down their need to borrow from banks. According to a 1971 report on the system, 'they thought they could transact business among themselves with a system of chits similar to IOUs that would cover at least part of the price of any transaction, the balance being settled in the conventional way ... [However,] it was soon found that in order to bring about wider acceptance of these chits, and also to comply with existing banking laws and avoid financial losses, collateral was essential.'[20]

This insistence on collateral might partially explain why WIR has survived and similar systems established at the same time in England, Germany, France and Austria have disappeared without trace.[21] However, an official history of WIR produced in 1984 for its fiftieth anniversary suggests that WIR is the sole survivor because the other circles did not realize the significance of what they were doing and wound themselves up when the financial crisis was past.[22] But opposition from vested interests played a part in some cases too. Zimmermann and Enz visited circles in Norway and Denmark before starting WIR, and when they returned to Denmark for a second visit they found that the circle there had been closed by the government after pressure from the banks.

The structure of WIR reflects the original small-group concept. Although by the end of 1935 the co-op had three thousand account-holders, only sixteen shareholders had any say in how the organization was run. After 1939 additional shareholders were permitted, but even today only about 5 per cent of participants hold shares entitling them to select the board of directors.

A Dutchman, Hendrik Bor, tells me that in the late 1970s he attempted to set up a rival to WIR that would be open to anyone, but the venture was closed down by the Swiss police. Bor, a computer expert, had become familiar with the way WIR worked in 1977 when he was asked to devise an electronic data-transfer system to prevent members from breaking the rules and selling Wir for Swiss francs. At one stage the exchange rate dropped as low as 55 per cent, and as this figure was quoted on an electronic news screen at the main entrance to Zürich central station, WIR's prestige suffered.

Bor says that he structured his organization, SYS Network, to enable it to avoid the constraints placed on WIR by the Swiss central bank. Two members of the Economic Crimes Police attended one of his presentations; he repeated the presentation at police headquarters a few days later, and when he had finished, Bor says the senior officer present told him that SYS could wipe out Switzerland's banking institutions and it would not be allowed to do so. Shortly afterwards his Swiss partners were threatened with long and detailed investigations into their tax affairs and so much pressure was put on the Swiss president of SYS that he committed suicide. The network was wound up.

When Bor tried to set up a similar system in the Netherlands in 1983 the reaction was equally hostile, and the Central Bank ordered an investigation. During this, according to Bor, one of his associates told the bank's inspectors: 'You can never stop Bor doing what he's doing. You'd have to beat him to do that.' A newspaper got hold of the story and embroidered the words so that they read 'beat him to death', and next day, when Bor was walking in the street, one of two youths on a moped took off his helmet and swung it at him. Bor saw the pair coming and tried to get out of their way but the helmet hit him in the mouth, damaging his teeth, some of which had to be extracted later. He is convinced that the attack was not a random incident but had been ordered by a commercial bank.

Then the tax authorities began their own investigation, and in April 1984 a Dutch business magazine, FEM, published an eight-page story about the network. 'It gives the impression that he's a crook,' a Dutch friend told me after reading the copy I gave her. 'It doesn't say so explicitly, of course, but if you read between the lines.' Bor's wife was so upset that five days later she applied for divorce. 'She could no longer carry the burden of living in fear with a man who had decided to go against the banking wind,' Bor says. 'I decided to liquidate the network, but before it was wound up the Central Bank's eight investigators had completed their report, saying it was the cleanest fiscal operation they had ever seen. The tax people said the same.' He left for the United States and began using the name Monrobey ('Bor' backwards and inserted into the middle of 'money'). 'I arrived in the US almost penniless because when I got there I found that my English partners had blocked my bank account in Europe to try to force me to go back there,' he told me.

Today, however, he is back on his feet financially and busy developing a network of 'liquid capital circuits' (LCCs) in the United States. An LCC is a community-controlled payments system: members lodge national currency to their LCC account and their account balance is recorded as 'electronic capital' on a microchip in a special credit card, the DCN-Passport, which they carry. DCN stands for 'Dynamic Capital Network', which links local LCCs and enables 'each member of the network to buy and trade with every other network member' wherever in the world their LCCs are located. In an explanatory brochure Bor writes:

The LCC system revolves around consumers using the DCN-Passport for their normal purchases. Businesses which accept the DCN-Passport as payment will see a tremendous influx of new business as members of the LCC choose to patronize firms which support their local economy. As your business grows, the LCC will be there to provide you with the needed capital to fund your growth. The LCC will establish interest-free financing for additional inventory, new employee training, improved facilities etc. As your local LCC grows it will begin to replace any current bank financing you may have. Your overhead will drop substantially as the LCC eliminates any interest expense. So you could lower prices, become more competitive, and still make larger and larger profits. The LCC quickly expands up your chain of suppliers, dropping their overhead and their prices. The net drop in retail prices soon becomes very large. It is a well-researched fact that 30 per cent to 50 per cent of retail prices consist of overhead created by the cost of capital in the supply pipeline. Imagine the competitive edge LCC businesses will have over others who fail to see the advantages of interest-free capital.[23]

Where does this interest-free capital come from? Bor explains that, just as American Express or Thomas Cook always have a large amount of cash that they can invest from the sale of their travellers' cheques because of the days or weeks that elapse between the time a customer buys the cheques and the time they spend them, an LCC has a lump sum too, as there is always a period between the moment a member's national currency becomes electronic capital and the moment the electronic capital is converted back to cash to purchase something a member needs from a supplier outside the system. 'As the system grows, the electronic capital begins to have a life much longer than the life of simple travelers' checks ... this greatly increases the average time each cash dollar is at the disposal of the LCC for interest-free financing,' Bor says. In effect, an LCC aims to keep its electronic credits circulating among its members for as long as possible before they are converted back to cash, and by linking individual LCCs the Dynamic Capital Network stops credits leaking from the system even if they are spent out of town. By early 1996, however, Bor was still some way from establishing a viable system. Not one of the LCCs was really working, he told me, and none had more than fifty members.

Bor is very critical of WIR, which he says is not a good model for the rest of the world and is only able to continue because the Swiss are enormously self-disciplined in the way they think and work. He claims that the rate at which Wir circulate has been kept very low under pressure from the banks. As a result, the prices charged by member-firms have not gone down in the way they would if the system had been working well because of the interest payments it would have enabled members to save. Too many members, he says, build up large surpluses of Wir, which they use to build properties to rent. Construction and the restaurant trade are the activities that underpin the system, he says.

Current proposals for a mutual credit network in Britain seem simple by comparison with Bor's. They were developed in the middle 1980s in complete ignorance of WIR by Christian and Diana Schumacher, the son and daughter-in-law of the author of Small is Beautiful, Fritz Schumacher. However, neither has had time to follow the idea up, and so far no system has been established, although talks took place with local authorities in the Sheffield area in 1994 and a hunt for market research financing is going on.

What the couple suggest is that businesspeople in a particular area should set up a committee that would determine how many 'bonds' each of their companies should be allocated by the rest of the group.[24] These bonds, which would be interest-free for three months and have parity with the national currency, could only be spent with other members of the group, exactly as with WIR. At the end of every three-month period, however, members would be obliged to bring their total holding of bonds back to its original figure; so if they had sold more to the rest of the group than they had bought from it and had a surplus of bonds in their account kept by the central committee, they would receive cash for the surplus amount. On the other hand, if they had sold less to the group than they had bought they would be required to pay cash to cover the shortfall. As the total cash sum due to accounts in surplus would be exactly equal to that received from the accounts in deficit, the committee would not be required to do any balancing itself, unless a business in difficulties failed to remit cash to cover its shortfall.

'The quarterly repayments ... give a regular opportunity for the scheme's administration to detect problem signs in advance of a major crisis and for help and advice to be given,' the Schumachers write in their project proposal. 'If a member business collapses, its outstanding debt to the system would be legally recoverable in the same way as other liabilities. If this were not possible out of the proceeds of liquidation, then guarantees [under a mutual cross-guarantee arrangement] would have to be called.' In other words, all the remaining members of the system would share the loss.

The Schumachers' aim in designing their scheme was to enable a network of linked businesses to grow up in a particular area so that if one of them failed, perhaps because an outside customer had switched an order for components elsewhere, there would be a high probability that other opportunities could be found. 'Where there are already many businesses trading, these businesses themselves generate new business opportunities for other businesses and vice versa,' they write. 'Equally, where there are few businesses, then the possibilities to start new businesses are correspondingly fewer.' They argue that the bonds would encourage businesses to place their orders with suppliers in their own areas and thus foster business development there.

Although the Schumachers mention that bonds would be of considerable help to businesses unable to raise adequate working capital, they deliberately avoid saying that banks would lose business as a result of the scheme, for fear of alerting a powerful opposition. Nor do they stress how much interest participants might save. 'We've checked the legal aspects as far as possible and it seems that there are no problems there,' Diana Schumacher told me. 'As a result, I don't see how the banks could stop a local trading bond scheme being started, but it seemed a good idea not to provoke them too much.' In view of Hendrik Bor's experience, this seems wise. A really effective alternative economic system will inevitably damage the profits of one of the most powerful groups in the world, and their reaction to it is liable to be frightening and extreme.

How would the Schumachers' trading bond organization differ from the business barter networks that have been operating for thirty years in the United States and are now spreading in Britain and Ireland? The answer is very considerably, largely because of the difference in the motives of the people behind them. The commercial networks' aim is to make a profit for their proprietors rather than to boost business in a particular area. They usually charge a joining fee of £200 to £300 and a 10 per cent commission on each purchase. Their rules require all trades between members to be passed through them so that they can take their cut, although in return for this they generally try to find a customer for whatever stock or services a business wishes to sell or a supplier of whatever it wishes to buy. The barter networks also limit the extent to which a company can take goods and services from the network without balancing it by supplying another member. 'If we were doubtful about the saleability of a business's product we would make it an associate member and not allow it to purchase through the network until it had made a sale,' says Pat Naismith, a co-founder of the Irish barter network, Contranet.

No commercial barter organization would have reservations about extending membership to multinational corporations. Indeed it was to facilitate giant companies that the first American networks were set up.[25] Moreover, although they might have a local base, they would see nothing wrong in arranging deals anywhere in the world. In short, commercial barter networks are part of the world economy rather than a means of promoting a local or regional one.

WIR, Auberg 1, 4002 Basel; tel. +41 61 2779111; fax +41 61 2779239.
Hank Monrobey and Associates Ltd, PO Box 15656, Ann Arbor, Michigan 48106-5656; tel. +1 313 4266929; fax +1 313 4266935; e-mail monrobey@ix.netcom.com.
Schumacher Projects, Church House, Church Lane, Godstone, Surrey RH9 8BW; tel. +44 1883 744577; fax +44 1883 744522.
Contranet, 6 Lower Kilmacud Road, Stillorgan, Co. Dublin; tel. +353 1 2782774.
British Barter Association, c/o Alan Cartledge, 48 New Street, Three Bridges, Crawley, Sussex RH10 1LW; tel. +44 140 3791917.

to enjoy real success when, in April of the following year, wage earners were told that if they converted their money into scrip they would be given 5 per cent extra. Naturally it was necessary to stop people who bought scrip this way from converting it back immediately for a quick profit. The new notes were stamped with their date of issue so that they could only be changed into francs at the 98 per cent rate after four months: if converted earlier, a bigger discount applied. This deal proved very attractive to the people of the district because if they converted their cash into scrip and spent it immediately they were in effect getting a 5 per cent discount from the traders. However, if they simply held on to the scrip for four months and then stamped it to bring it up to date, they could convert it back to cash and earn 3 per cent interest for the period. As a result, the new money was widely used in the town and tended to circulate for at least four months before being cashed in.

Many communities moved to copy the system, alarming the Bank of France so much that in July 1957 it sent a team of police specialists to investigate what it saw as 'a virus about to contaminate the whole country'. Laws carrying penalties of up to two years' imprisonment and a fine of twenty million francs were passed to frighten off people planning similar systems, but Lignières scrip continued to circulate at least until the early 1960s, and another small town, Marans, introduced a variant of it in 1959 without anyone being prosecuted.

Scrip – of the unstamped variety – is currently being used in some Argentine provinces as a result of a decision in 1984 by the governor of Salta, Roberto Romero, to give public employees and creditors the choice of being paid in promissory notes immediately or in national currency some days later. As prices were rising rapidly at the time, many employees chose not to wait and accepted the new notes because the banks would exchange them at par for national currency if necessary anyway. However, to encourage people not to exchange them, Romero organized a lottery, offering prizes to the holders of the notes bearing the winning numbers. The provincial government naturally accepted the new money for the payment of taxes, and shops and businesses rapidly began to accept it too. Three other provinces took up the idea and have since issued their own money on similar lines.

Local currency systems can avoid the conflict between money's function as a medium of exchange and as a store of value if they develop different currencies to do different jobs. A LETS unit can be a satisfactory medium of exchange; it can also fulfil money's third function – that of being a unit of account – because it allows people to keep track of how they stand with each other. But by no stretch of the imagination can it be considered a store of value, and anyone who built up a large surplus of units in their account so as to be able to obtain goods and services when they retire in twenty years' time would be foolish because no one can guarantee that the system will still be operating then.

This is both a strength and a weakness. It is a serious weakness with LETS because people earning more local units than they can immediately spend stop accepting them so readily and thus damage the system for everyone else. However, rather than trying to enable LETS units to duplicate all the functions of national currency, it is probably better to create a local store of value in some other way.

Robert Swann, a co-founder of the E.F. Schumacher Society in the United States and one of North America's leading thinkers on economic alternatives, has taken part in two attempts to devise currencies that are also stores of value. One of these was the 'Exeter Experiment' – the successful launch in Exeter, New Hampshire, in 1972 of the Constant, a currency devised by Dr Ralph Borsodi, a leader of the decentralist movement in the United States and the author of a book, *Flight from the City*, that encouraged a back-to-the-land movement during the Great Depression in the 1930s. Despite his background, however, Borsodi – as his book about the experiment, *Inflation and the Coming Keynesian Catastrophe*,[27] reveals – was motivated more by what he saw as the dishonesty, theft and embezzlement that inflation involved than by any thoughts of achieving greater community self-reliance. Indeed, prompted by President Nixon's decision a few months earlier to break the dollar's link with gold, he did not intend to launch a local currency at all but was running a small-scale experiment to demonstrate the viability of a new type of national or international currency.

The first Constants were sold on 21 June 1972 at a conference organized by the School of Living, an organization Borsodi had founded and for which Swann then worked. Borsodi deposited the proceeds and those from subsequent sales with two banks in Exeter so that they had funds to cash any Constants presented to them. Alternatively, if the holder wished, the banks would lodge the Constants in a special account in the holder's name. The value of a Constant was based on that of specific amounts of thirty basic commodities – gold, silver, iron, aluminium, lead, copper, nickel, tin, zinc, oil, wheat, barley, rice, rye, oats, soya, maize, wool, cotton, cocoa, coffee, copra, hides, jute, rubber, cement, sulphur, sugar, peanuts and cotton seeds – and holders could sell them at any time for the total of whatever the constituents were then worth. Borsodi's organization, Independent Arbitrage International, recalculated the Constant's underlying value monthly and let the banks know. 'People who bought Constants from Borsodi's organization at, say, $2.18 a 10-Constant note were surprised later when the bank paid them $2.19 for it,' a local journalist, Mel Most, wrote after the experiment had been running for seven months.

As Borsodi realized, the Constant was potentially far more than a way of protecting one's purchasing power against commodity-price inflation. If firms had begun to quote prices in Constants rather than dollars and the banks had offered Constant loans, the new units might have proved so much more reliable than the steadily depreciating dollar that the national currency would have ceased to be used. Before this could happen, however, the experiment was terminated, a year after it had begun, because Borsodi thought he had proved the point that a commodity-based currency was entirely workable. He did not feel that at the age of eighty-six he could take on the responsibility of setting up and running an international currency-issuing bank.

For our purposes, the significance of Borsodi's experiment is that a small town (Exeter had a population of just under nine thousand at the time) readily adopted an alternative currency despite the fact that it was not backed by the local government, as had been the case in Wörgl. 'Thousands of dollars [worth] of bank money orders and personal checks for Constants have circulated like money and been used for buying and selling, and have been cashed [by banks],' Most wrote. 'Even the staid, wealthy Philips Exeter Academy paid in Constants for thousands of dollars [worth] of printing and supplies.' Swann adds: 'The Town of Exeter accepted them as payment for parking fines. Very few people ever redeemed them for dollars at the bank.'[31] No legal problems over issuing the notes emerged.

With the exception of silver and gold, Borsodi never intended that his proposed Bank for the Issue of a Stable Currency (BISC), for which the Exeter Experiment was a trial run, should buy physical stocks of the thirty commodities backing the Constant. Instead he proposed that BISC should buy commodity futures with part of the money it received for Constants and that it should sell the futures and buy replacements as they approached maturity. The rest of the purchase money was to have been invested in securities or issued as loans and the income used to cover BISC's administrative costs. The bank

[main text continues p.114]

Did President Kennedy's decision that the US government should issue its own notes like this one lead to his assassination? Some conspiracy theorists believe so.

WHY DO GOVERNMENTS LET BANKS CREATE MONEY?

One of the most perplexing problems future economic historians will face will be that of explaining why almost every nineteenth and twentieth-century government allowed private banks to create almost all the money their citizens used – even to the extent of requiring their state treasuries to pay interest for the loan of money the private banks had created merely by making entries in their account books – when the governments could have created an equivalent amount of currency the same way themselves and financed, interest-free, whatever they wished to do. At the very least the practice constituted – and constitutes – a massive subsidy to the banking sector and to the wealthiest groups in society.

According to John Hotson, who retired as professor of economics at the University of Waterloo in Canada in 1992, roughly 95 per cent of a typical industrialized country's currency is created by privately owned banking organizations granting loans to their customers.[28] One of the few occasions on which governments put interest-free money into circulation is when their central banks decide they need new premises and simply issue the currency to pay for their construction. At almost all other times, governments feel constrained to borrow all the funds they need and therefore pay interest on money the private banks have created.

Why governments feel unable to create money for, say, public capital projects, and run up massive national debts in their determination not to do so, has never been adequately explained, although bigots with hypotheses abound. Neo-fascists claim it is due to a Jewish conspiracy and sell books about it through mail-order catalogues alongside works that claim the Holocaust never happened. An equally silly though less dangerous theory comes from the 'Order of St Michael' in Canada, where 'social credit' (the idea that a society should create its own purchasing power) was a powerful political force in the 1930s. The order's members, who call themselves 'slaves of Mary' and 'Catholic patriots' working 'to deliver nations from communism and the banking dictatorship', hold the freemasons responsible but, like the fascists, fail to produce any evidence.

Another group of conspiracy theorists, this time in the United States, have placed documents on the Internet that purport to show that President Kennedy was assassinated because he had allowed the Treasury to issue a limited number of US currency notes directly and avoid using those issued by the Federal Reserve which, like the Bank of England until 1946, is privately owned – its shareholders include all the major American business families. The documents on the Internet include the text of executive order No. 11,100, made by Kennedy on 4 June 1963, authorizing the Secretary of the Treasury to issue $1 and $2 bills backed by the silver held in government reserves. It is said that $5 billion worth of these notes were issued but that, immediately after Kennedy's death, President Johnson revoked the executive order on his first day in office and had as many as possible of the notes recalled. Some, however, still exist. A little-known contender for the Republican Party's nomination as its 1996 Presidential candidate, Charles E. Collins, made allegations about the death of Kennedy and a promise to issue US currency directly the main plank of his campaign.

Three extremely serious consequences flow from allowing banks to create almost all a country's money by issuing loans for which they charge interest. The most pernicious is that the need to pay this interest creates the capitalist system's constant need for economic growth and thus makes it unsustainable in a finite world. (We will be discussing this more fully in the next chapter when we consider how interest should be managed in a local economy.)

The second consequence is that governments have too little control over the amount of money put into circulation. For example, if the banks issue so many loans that the economy overheats and the inflation rate rises, one of the few ways governments can respond is by raising interest rates. They do this by selling government stocks to mop up the excess funds – in other words, by borrowing some of the excess money themselves. This can seriously distort the distribution of national income because if the interest rate rises above the rate at which the gross domestic product is growing in money terms, the wealth of lenders begins to increase faster than that of borrowers, and the total debt owed to financial institutions by everyone in the country, including companies and the state itself, grows in relation to GDP. This is exactly what happened in Britain in the 1980s: because inflation was suppressed by raising interest rates, and real growth rates were low, the proportion of national income going to moneylenders significantly increased.

The third consequence of not issuing money is that governments cannot do what Paul Glover has done with his Ithaca Hours and what the Westport LETS system has done with its Reeks: pay to get things done without incurring a debt on which interest must be paid indefinitely. Only two places in the world have issued their currencies on a non-debt, non-interest basis – Jersey and Guernsey – and the results have been remarkable.

The Guernsey system dates back to the period just after the Napoleonic Wars, which had seriously damaged the island's economy because they prevented smuggling, the people's most important source of income. As a result, according to Olive and Jan Grubiak's pamphlet The Guernsey Experiment,[29] the island was in a distressed state. 'The deep roads ... in wet weather became muddy rivers between steep banks. The town was ill-paved and unattractive, and there was not a vehicle for hire of any kind on the island. There was no trade, nor hope of employment for the poor. Worst of all, the sea was encroaching [on] the land, and washing away large tracts of it, thanks to the sorry state of the dykes.'

110

There seemed little possibility that the island's government would be able to erect the necessary sea defences, which were expected to cost £10,000, since the £2390 interest on Guernsey's public debt of £19,137 (equivalent to approximately thirty times that amount today) absorbed all but £600 of its annual income. In view of the people's poverty, there was no scope for further taxation. However, a committee was set up to see how money could be raised for a smaller project: the erection of a covered market. The group reported in 1816 with the proposal that the cost of the market and various other public works be met by issuing 6000 'States notes' (the States is the Guernsey parliament), each with a face value of £1, to circulate alongside the £50,000 worth of banknotes then in use on the island. The idea was accepted, although notes worth only £4000 were issued at first; and since it was proposed to redeem them with British money in stages, the arrangement amounted to little more than an inge-nious interest-free way of borrowing the funds to finance the island's capi-tal works programme. Other tasks, however, including the sea defences and the construction of schools, were taken on and further note issues made, so that by 1829, States notes worth £48,000 were in circulation.

In 1826 a complaint was made to the Privy Council in London that the States had no right to issue currency without royal consent. The States submitted a lengthy report to the Privy Council on the ways in which the local currency had been spent, and demonstrated that the income from the projects it had financed was more than enough to redeem the notes issued. Satisfied, London took no action. The complaint was probably instigated by the promoters of the Old Bank, which set up in Guernsey the following year. A second private bank, the Commercial, opened in 1830, and the two 'flooded the island with paper money'. The States held dis-cussions with both banks and, as a result, withdrew £15,000 worth of its own notes from circulation and agreed to keep the total issue below £40,000. This agreement remained in force until 1914.

During the First World War the local banks were prohibited from increasing their note issue, while the States was under no such restriction and issued a further £100,000 worth of its currency to meet demand. Since then the two local banks have become part of British banking chains and have ceased to issue currency – instead British notes circulate in Guernsey alongside the island's own.

Today, if someone uses a bank on the island to cash a cheque or draws money from an automatic teller with a bank card they will receive Guernsey currency, which the banks obtained from the States' Treasury in exchange for a sterling cheque for the same amount. The treasury then returns the sterling cheque to the bank that issued it, to be lodged in a deposit account in the States' name. Each Guernsey note in circulation is therefore backed one-to-one by its British equivalent.

'We've got about £14 million worth of notes and coin in circulation at the moment,' Michael Browne, the States' Supervisor, told me in early 1994. 'It fluctuates a little with the seasons. It constitutes a £14 million interest-free loan for us – in fact it's a loan we collect interest on. The pay-ments we get on it from the banks make a small but useful contribution to the island's budget.'[30] Although Browne says it would be possible for the States to spend the sterling it receives from the banks in payment for its currency, it no longer does so. 'Our policy on this island is, if we can't afford a new school building or something like that, we don't borrow but wait until we can pay for it before we put it up. As a result we have almost no public debt, apart from some money owed by the state trading boards, which run the telephone and electricity systems. Even that is covered by sinking funds,' he explains.

According to Browne, Guernsey's absence of debt is a result of its conservative financial policies and is the main reason why the island's income tax rate is only 20 per cent. He regards the States' refusal to spend the funds obtained as a result of its currency issue simply as prudent book-keeping and suggests that the success of the 'Guernsey experiment' is largely a myth. With the presumption of an outsider, I would suggest he is mistaken. There are two ways in which Guernsey could handle the sterling it receives from the sale of its currency. One would be to spend a high proportion of the £14 million it has already collected on capital works immediately, leaving just enough on deposit in the banks to ensure that a Guernsey pound can always be exchanged for a British one. But if this course were followed the amount of capital spending the currency issue made possible in future would fluctuate wildly from year to year, as it could never be more than a prudent proportion of whatever amount of additional island currency had entered circulation during the previous twelve months. In some years there might be no increase; in others the amount of local currency in circulation might even decline because of a fall in economic activity, requiring the island not only to halt its capital spending programme but, in the event that the Guernsey pound's fractional sterling backing proved inadequate to cover the withdrawals, to use some of its tax revenue to pay interest on British pounds borrowed to ensure that the exchange rate was maintained. In other words, basing the island's capital spending on how much more local currency went into circulation in a particular year would prove highly destabilizing: the States would spend more when the island was booming and have to cancel its capital programme and slash its current spending when it went into decline.

The second way open to the island is to do exactly what it does: to limit itself to spending the interest on the capital sum that issuing its own currency creates. This avoids the destabilization entailed by the first course and ensures that a relatively steady amount of capital spending can be undertaken annually. After all, if the States are able to get 7 per cent interest on their £14 million sterling deposit, this will earn them enough to cover a third of their £3 million capital budget year after year.

Jersey issues its currency in the same way. Could counties and towns elsewhere follow suit and enjoy similar benefits? There seems no reason why not because the Guernsey arrangement suits both the island and the banks. Lending is any bank's most important source of income, and whenever a bank hands currency notes over to a customer, both its assets and its liabilities are reduced, cutting its capacity to make revenue-earning loans. When it hands out Guernsey currency, however, the sterling it used to buy them is deposited in another of its accounts, so there is no fall in the bank's assets and hence in its capacity to make loans. Guernsey, as we have seen, benefits too.

Someone appears to be getting something for nothing. How do the benefits arise? The answer is that they come from the creation of £14 million that would otherwise not have existed, by essentially the same process banks use to create money when they grant a loan facility on which the customer writes cheques. So, given that both sides benefit, the only obstacle likely to arise would be if central banks objected to county councils convincing their residents that it was in their interests to insist on getting county currency whenever they withdrew cash from their banks.

Alternatively, county or town councils could create their own money by following the Wörgl model almost exactly; working in close collaboration with local businesses, as local authorities did whenever scrip was issued in America in the 1930s, they could arrange loans from their local credit unions and leave them on deposit so that anyone who wished to exchange their local money for national currency could do so on payment of a small fee. Wörgl's monthly revalidation stamping system could also be adopted to ensure that the local money was always spent in preference to that from outside.

The benefits to any council adopting either approach are clear: no longer would it have to depend almost entirely on central government or on bank borrowings to finance low-income housing, industrial starter-units, a library, or a better swimming-pool. Local builders would get more work – indeed, if the council was wise it would only embark on a big spending programme when there was spare capacity in the local construction trade. Even the national government would be better off, as a result of increased tax revenues and lower social welfare claims. But would these gains be sufficient to enable it to ignore dire warnings about inflation that would undoubtedly come from its central bank or treasury department, upset by the loss of some of its powers?

John Hotson is associated with the Committee on Monetary and Economic Reform (COMER) (c/o Robert Good, RR2, Puslinch, Ontario N0B 2J0; tel. +1 519 6218978), which describes itself as 'composed of economists and non-economists, both academic and non-academic, whose goal is a sustainable financial system in a sustainable world economic/ecologic/social system.' Membership costs $35 per year. COMER is one of the few groups in the English-speaking world doing serious work on monetary reform. It has links with Economic Reform Australia, which is working on similar lines (Frances Milne, 14 Gallimore Avenue, Balmain, Sydney, NSW 2041; tel. +61 2 8107812). An unsurpassed microfiche source of historical material on free money and free banking is the Libertarian Microfiche Publishing Company, 7 Oxley Street, Berrima, NSW 2577. Another good source is the Monetary Freedom Network, c/o Siegfried Schwenke, Wissmannstrasse 15, 12049 Berlin; tel. +49 30 6213861.

was likely to prove highly profitable, Borsodi wrote, because only fractional commodity backing for the Constant would be necessary.

Today, however, Swann thinks that energy is a better backing for a currency than a collection of commodities because the long-term price of every product is related to the amount of human, animal, renewable and fossil energy that went into making it. One of his proposals would in effect turn electricity producers into currency-issuing banks. 'Almost every community has renewable resources for producing energy,' he writes in one of the chapters he contributed to *Building Sustainable Communities,* a book on the methods communities can use to become more self-reliant.[32] 'All such energy resources can be converted into electricity or measured in kilowatt-hours.' He envisages community companies established to develop these resources financing themselves by selling energy notes. 'For example, if local utility rates are presently ten cents a kilowatt-hour, then one dollar would buy ten kilowatt-hours for future delivery. Owners of the notes, sold in lots of 10, 50, and 100 units (comparable to current values of one, five and ten dollars), would hold them for future redemption no matter what their future dollar rate ... The community organization or corporation would issue the notes only in amounts equal to their projected output of electricity, thus avoiding inflation of the currency.'

Since the notes would always be worth the current price of the amount of electricity they represented, they would be accepted instead of national currency by people living in the generating plant's service area in payment for goods and services – particularly if, as with the Constant or the Wörgl schilling, a local bank stood ready to redeem the notes for cash. Although Swann has not tried such a system out, he was associated with the successful launch of the Deli

Dollar and the Berkshire Farm Preserve Note (discussed in the next chapter), which share the sale-of-product-in-advance feature with his energy note idea. As a result, there is no reason to believe that an energy-backed currency would fail.

Wära, stamp scrip, Hours, Time Dollars, Wir, Reeks, Constants – a wide range of currency systems is available for local economies to use. Which would suit a social field with a population of a few tens of thousands of people? The answer is 'Most of them', because each excels in specific functions and only a range of systems can fulfil them all.

The first step is undoubtedly to get several LETS systems established, each limiting its membership to about 250 people so that the necessary social controls operate well. Then, for those who neither want nor need to join a LETS system because they have adequate national currency incomes but would like to use their leisure to help others, a Time Dollar type of system should be considered. Business-people will want their own WIR-type system in which their unit and the national currency are equal in value so they do not have to distinguish between the two in their books. These business systems will have to control the amount of credit they allow much more stringently than would a LETS because their membership is likely to be larger and less amenable to social pressures.

There is no reason why a district should not also have its own equivalent of a national currency, which would be accepted by everyone for all transactions. This could be a store-of-value, commodity-based unit, Borsodi-style, operated by a local group,[33] or an energy note, backed by one or more power producers, or a national-currency-backed banknote issued by the local council on the lines of that in Guernsey. Indeed there is no reason why a single area should not have all three in operation simultaneously. There would be some inconvenience, certainly, but computerized cash-registers would minimize it, and shops in border areas at present readily cope with keeping three or four currencies in their tills. In any case, if a combination of several local currencies and a national or international one works significantly better than a national or international one alone, should the fact that traders would need to do a little extra bookkeeping be allowed to prevent it?

In the past, several different types of money could frequently be found in use in the same place at the same time. Some ancient civilizations used one form of money, generally silver, for long-distance trade and another, perhaps barley, as their unit of exchange closer to home. This meant that, unlike the mainstream system today, a shortage of external currency did not prevent internal trading.[34] In the Middle Ages, coins from several countries would often be used to make a single payment, the value of each type based on the weight of precious metal it contained. Later still, notes issued by innumerable private British banks circulated alongside sovereigns from the Royal Mint, and it was only in 1844 that the Bank of England was given the exclusive right to issue paper money. Previously its monopoly had extended just sixty-five miles from London; this limited monopoly allowed about twenty Scottish banks to issue their own money in 1800, each backing its notes with its own gold reserves. This system was very stable: losses to note-holders and depositors amounted to only £32,000 between 1727 and 1844, the entire period during which they were allowed to operate, and Scottish notes were preferred to English ones as far south as Yorkshire.[35] In Ireland in the eighteenth century the currency consisted of a mixture of foreign coins, bankers' bills and notes, and locally issued silver and copper tokens, the result of a British ban on the export of English gold and silver coins to pay for imports purchased there.

In common with other aspects of life, this diversity has now been lost. The money supply has been standardized and nationalized, and although banks in Northern Ireland and Scotland still issue paper currency carrying their name, they do so as agents of the Bank of England. But it is only in the issue of notes and coin that the state has a monetary monopoly: two other important forms of money – cheques and credit cards – still enable the banks to create spending power privately, and government controls over the extent to which they do so are indirect and ineffective. Uncrossed cheques are essentially a near-currency since they can be passed from hand to hand in settlement of successive transactions; during an eleven-month bank strike in Ireland in 1970 they allowed economic life to proceed more or less normally.

Quite soon, forms of privately created electronic money like the Mondex system tested in Swindon in 1995 may displace the state's cash and notes altogether. 'Users would carry a plastic card that would let them download funds from their bank account using a mobile phone or cashpoint. The card could then be used to make purchases [by passing it through a reader] up to the value of the sum downloaded,' Giles Keating, the head of global economics at the CS First Boston Bank in London, explained in the *Financial Times*.[36] He argued that holders would be able to use their cards at home and abroad because the readers would automatically convert the currency held in the card to the one in which the purchase was priced. This would give people complete freedom to choose the currency they downloaded into their cards. 'The effect would be dramatic. Smaller currencies could almost disappear – especially if there is any hint of systematic depreciation. Even larger currencies would face a substantial decline in usage if they were weak ... Long-term credibility as a strong currency would become even more important than it is at present.'

But even though state control over the supply of money and the issue of currency is at present only partial and, if Keating is right, may well disappear altogether, we can expect considerable resistance from governments to community monetary systems once they threaten the status quo. The only reason that LETS systems have escaped problems so far is that they are having so little effect on what is conventionally regarded as the 'real' economy that they do not warrant the effort of closing them down. But when communities get serious, the opposition will become serious too. The big banks, who are developing the electronic money systems, will not allow their power to create money to be eroded without a struggle and will find ready allies in politicians hoping to retire to a seat on their boards. Power is never given away by the powerful, it has to be taken by the weak. If we are ever to achieve independence in our lives and communities, the right to issue our own currencies is one of the issues over which we must expect to have to fight.

FURTHER INFORMATION

Every group considering starting a LETS system should acquire a copy of *The LETS Info Pack* (£10, post paid, from Letslink UK, 61 Woodcock Road, Warminster, Wiltshire BA12 9DH; tel. & fax +44 1985 217871). This provides a step-by-step guide to setting up a system, supplies a model constitution, advises on tax and social welfare, and includes samples of existing groups' cheques and directories so that new ones do not have to reinvent the wheel. Even though a lot of the same ground is covered in Peter Lang's book *LETS Work: Rebuilding the Local Economy* (Grover Books, Bristol, 1994; £8.99, or £10 post paid, from Letslink UK), it is worthwhile having both. So is the magazine *Lets-link* (£10 for four issues in Britain, £15 elsewhere in Europe).

Groups in Ireland should contact Letslink Ireland (c/o Bill Walsh, Lower Aiden Street, Kiltimagh, Co. Mayo; tel. +353 94 81637). Both the British and Irish organizations will put enquirers in touch with good systems as close to them as possible prepared to offer a speaker or other assistance. Letslink UK also has an archive of research material on LETS.

In continental Europe the Letslink function is performed by the organization Aktie Strohalm (Oudegracht 42, 3511 AR Utrecht, Netherlands; tel. +31 30 314314; fax +31 30 343986), which launched the thriving and innovative Dutch movement and has contacts with systems in Denmark, Germany, Switzerland, Belgium, and France. It is actively exploring ways in which local currency and local banking systems can be developed and linked with each other to make more self-reliant local communities possible.

An increasing amount of information about LETS is becoming available on the Internet. 'econ-lets' is the main site for the discussion of 'the economic, social and telematics issues surrounding the development of LETS'; you can join it by e-mailing the request 'join econ-lets [firstname lastname]' to mailbase@ mailbase.ac.uk. Dana Hofford maintains a list of World Wide Web sites related to money, which he will e-mail to enquirers. Contact him at dhofford@nn.apc.org. See http://www.u-net.com/gmlets/design/dml~3.html for details of Michael Linton's systems. Try http://www.prairienet.org/community/religion/idf/currency .html for details of Australian systems and operating software for LETS accounts computers; software is also available by post from Richard Knights in Totnes, Devon (tel. +44 1803 867098). The E.F. Schumacher Society's Web site is at http://members.aol.com/efssociety.

Notes

1 *Inishkillane: Change and Decline in the West of Ireland* (Penguin 1974).
2 For a painstaking account of this system see Anne O'Dowd, *Meitheal: a Study of Co-operative Labour in Rural Ireland* (Comhairle Bhéaloideas Éireann, University College: Dublin 1981).
3 LETS has become a generic term covering a wide range of local currency systems, and Linton therefore distinguishes between 'LETSystems', which have five essential characteristics, and LET schemes, which he describes as the 'committee-managed, small-is-beautiful, no-business-please [i.e. no commercial motivation], politically correct variety'. The five characteristics of 'LETSystems' are: (1) they operate on a not-for-profit basis, and the costs of administration are paid by each account-holder in the local unit; (2) all accounts start at nil, and the account-holder has sole control over the movement of money in and out of his or her account: there is never any obligation to trade; (3) any account-holder may know the balance and the volume of trading of any other account-holder in the system; (4) the local currency unit is equivalent to the national currency; and (5) no interest is charged or paid on balances. There is a wide range of systems with these characteristics, as Linton encourages them to experiment. When this chapter refers to LETS systems or schemes it is talking about all types, including those that meet the 'LETSystem' specification.
4 The quotations from Michael Linton come from talks he gave in Dublin in 1993. They have since been checked by him.
5 February 1994.
6 Letter to author, 21 February 1994.
7 Letter to John Bolger, 16 February 1994.
8 E-mail to author, 27 November 1995.
9 Confusion often arises when the turnover of different LETS systems is compared because some systems quote turnover figures derived by adding together all the changes in members' accounts, both positive and negative, thus doubling the value of trading apparently done. This is eliminated here.
10 'The Local Exchange Trading System: Political Economy and Social Audit' (MSc thesis, School of Environmental Sciences, University of East Anglia 1994); avail-

able from Ms Seyfang at PO Box 18, Diss, Norfolk IP22 3NS, for £6, post paid. Studies of the Totnes and Calderdale LETS systems by Colin Williams of the Centre for Urban Development and Environmental Management (Leeds Metropolitan University, Brunswick Building, Leeds LS2 8BU) indicate that LETS members have below-average incomes and that the unemployed among them generally make more trades, although each trade is of lower value than that of those in work, and their total earnings are less. The average annual value of trading per member was £40 in Calderdale and £153 in Totnes, Williams found.

11 Particulars of each barter transaction must be submitted by whoever is running the system with both parties and the revenue service, unless the system has fewer than a hundred transactions a year. See *Journal of Taxation*, 1983; also *Standard Federal Tax Report*, 3 September 1983. The law is PL 97-248, paragraph 5093.

12 February 1994.

13 The only book by Gesell (d.1930) readily obtainable in English is *The Natural Economic Order*, probably in the edition published by Peter Owen, London, in 1958, although there was a Berlin edition in 1929 and an American one in 1933.

14 'Sechs-Stunden-Tag im Mittelalter' in *Vorwärts zur Felten Kaufkraft des Geldes und zur Zinsfreien Wirtschaft* (1931).

15 Carlo Cipolla, *The Monetary Policy of Fourteenth-Century Florence* (University of California Press: Berkeley 1982).

16 Quoted by Irving Fisher in *Stamp Scrip* (Adelphi: New York 1933), p. 20. The *New Republic* article was written by Hans Cohrssen, who became Fisher's assistant and contributed a valuable account of the stamp scrip movement in the United States to Dieter Suhr's book on the necessity of developing a type of neutral money that encourages neither hoarding nor spending, *The Capitalistic Cost-Benefit Structure of Money* (Springer: Berlin and New York 1989).

17 Fritz Schwarz, *Das Experiment von Wörgl* (Genossenschaft Verlag: Bern 1952), cited by Margrit Kennedy in *Interest and Inflation-Free Money* (third edition) (Permakultur Publikationen: Steyerberg 1990).

18 *Stamp Scrip*, cited above. Fisher also wrote *Mastering the Crisis* (George Allen and Unwin: London 1934), which covers a lot of the same ground.

19 Letter to author, 11 August 1994.

20 Erick Hansch, *Initial Results of WIR Research in Switzerland* (International Independence Institute: Ashby, Mass. 1971).

21 *50 Ans Cercle Économique WIR*, WIR Basel, 1984.

22 *Ibid.*

23 *DCN-Passport to Interest-Free Living* (n.d.).

24 *Local Trading Bond Scheme: Proposal for a Feasibility Study* (Schumacher Projects: 1993).

25 See *For Polygamy in Currency* (Abraham Rotstein, University of Toronto, and Colin Duncan, York University, Ontario n.d.), which states that the growth of barter networks in the United States was partly due to anti-trust laws, which may forbid direct barter between firms but not if mediated through a third party. 'Several of the largest transnational corporations in the world are members of their own barter networks,' they say. Another motive was tax avoidance, and there were some spectacular tax and other frauds in the past, although the networks are now trying to improve their image.

26 Details of the Lignières and Marans systems are given by Marino-Bertil Issautier

in *Perspectives d'une Révolution Économique et Monétaire*, a special issue of *Cahiers de la Pensée et de l'Action* (Paris 1961).

27 Available from the E.F. Schumacher Society, 140 Jug End Road, Great Barrington, Massachusetts 01230.

28 'Financing Sustainable Development', a paper given by Hotson at the first 'TOES' (The Other Economic Summit) in Australia, 26–28 November 1993. He can be contacted by phone and fax at +1 416 2921036.

29 (Omni Publications: Hawthorne, California 1960).

30 Telephone conversation.

31 In Swann's introduction to *Inflation and the Coming Keynesian Catastrophe* (E.F. Schumacher Society: Great Barrington, Mass. 1989).

32 C. George Benello, Robert Swann, and Shann Turnbull, Ward Morehouse (ed.), *Building Sustainable Communities: Tools and Concepts for Self-Reliant Economic Change* (Bootstrap: New York 1989).

33 Professor Lewis Solomon of the National Law Center, George Washington University, Washington, DC, devotes almost a quarter of his book *Rethinking our Centralized Monetary System: the Case for a System of Local Currencies* (Praeger: New York 1996) to local currencies pegged to commodities and the practical steps that would have to be taken to issue one. He also provides an authoritative survey of the legal aspects of issuing local currencies in the United States.

34 Karl Polyani, 'The economy as an instituted process' in Polyani, Pearson, and Arensburg (eds), *Trade and Markets in the Early Empires* (Gateway: Chicago 1957).

35 Lawrence White, *Free Banking in Britain: Theory, Experience, and Debate, 1800-1845* (Cambridge University Press: London 1984). An excellent bibliographic essay on free banking by Kurt Schuler appeared in *Humane Studies Review*, vol. 6, no. 1 (autumn 1988). See also F. A. Hayek, *Denationalisation of Money* (Institute of Economic Affairs: London 1976).

36 2 November 1995.

4

Banking on Ourselves

High interest rates are not the only way in which people can get a healthy return on their savings. Organizations that re-cycle savings locally provide social dividends as well.

EVERY WORKING DAY, every week of the year, the three banks with branches in Westport, County Mayo, send large converted lorries out into the surrounding countryside to bring money in. 'My branch is one of the most successful in the country in terms of the amount of funds we are able to remit to head office for use elsewhere,' one of the banks' managers, now retired, told me proudly some years ago. 'We take in very much more in deposits than we lend out.'

This pattern is repeated throughout most of rural Ireland and Britain: the mobile banks go out and the cash comes in. 'I know of branches in the west of Ireland where the ratio of local deposits to local loans would be six to one, but that would be extreme,' another retired bank manager told me; 'Four to one would be quite usual, and the ratio for the west of Ireland as a whole would be two to one because places like Galway and Letterkenny are expanding and spending more than they save.'

Despite the ex-managers' evidence, there are few published statis-tics to indicate the extent to which financial institutions are draining resources from rural Ireland. The banks claim that this is largely because they do not keep their records in a way that would permit the data to be assembled easily. Since 1991, however, the Central Bank has collected figures for bank deposits from the farming sector; it had been publishing data on bank advances to that sector for many years. In 1993 these figures showed that Irish farmers owed £1225 million to the banks and were owed £946 million by them. But, as the *Irish Farmers' Journal*[1] pointed out when these statistics were published, the deposit total did not include farmers' money held by building societies, credit unions, pension funds, and other investment institutions, a much greater sum in view of the better return. As a result, the agricultural sector was a significant net lender to other parts of the economy.

Professor Patrick Honohan of the Economic and Social Research Institute in Dublin, who has done considerable research into monetary flows between economic sectors, told me that although he had no data he would expect to find that savings moved out of rural and depressed urban areas. 'After all, financial institutions lend to borrowers who look as if they have plans that will result in a cash flow sufficient to repay the loan. By definition, such borrowers are less plentiful in depressed regions.'[2]

This means that the economic system has 'positive feedback': prosperous parts of the world get more investment because better returns can be had from projects there, which makes them still more prosperous, while poorer areas have what capital they possess taken away. As a result the poorer areas fall further behind and people living in them are forced to leave to seek work wherever investment is going on. They take up residence in the expanding areas and add their spending to its rising income flow, generating further investment possibilities. A significant cause of the emigration of young people from rural Ireland is that their parents have allowed their savings to be invested away from home.

Economically this population shift is an undesirable and inefficient outcome because it leads to vacant housing and underused assets in declining areas as well as to overcrowding and congestion in the prosperous ones. Unfortunately, however, conventional economics is based on the assumption that there will always be negative feedback in the shape of diminishing returns and not a positive feedback, like the investment-causing-a-population-shift-and-hence-more-investment case we are discussing. The discipline is therefore ill-equipped to recommend ways to stop the flow.

W. Brian Arthur, professor of population studies and economics at Stanford University, is one of the few members of his profession to have tried to work out what happens when a positive feedback occurs. He described his results in *New Scientist* in 1993:

Increasing returns have interesting implications for the characteristics of economies. There are many possible patterns of world production and consumption, so it is not possible to predict which one will occur. The particular pattern that falls into place builds up organically – that is, new firms and industries grow on what is already there. This is partly the result of historical accidents – who set up what firms where and when. Once in place, such concentrations become hard to dislodge; they are 'locked in'. The resulting pattern probably does not coincide with the best allocation of resources. Even if all countries start with equal concentrations of each industry, the slightest tremble in the marketplace tilts the outcome to an asymmetric one. So with positive feedback in the form of increasing returns, the economy acquires very different properties: multiple potential production-consumption patterns, unpredictability, history-dependence, lock-in, inefficiency and asymmetry.

When I first came upon these properties I was surprised – and fascinated – by them. They showed that there were theoretical reasons, not just practical ones, why the economy is unpredictable. But mere hints of these ideas alarmed economists of previous generations. In 1939, the English economist John Hicks warned what would happen if they tried to incorporate them into mainstream economics: 'The threatened wreckage is that of the greater part of economic theory.'[3]

Arthur points out that many parts of the economy – the high-technology sector in particular – do not run into diminishing returns. 'To produce a new pharmaceutical drug, computer spreadsheet program or passenger jet, perhaps hundreds of millions of pounds have to be spent on research and development. Once in production, however, incremental copies are comparatively cheap. Once a product gets ahead of its rivals it gains further cost advantages and can get even further ahead. High technology is subject to increasing returns.'

Governments obviously need to counteract the effects of increasing returns, of positive feedback, if they wish to have an even spread of economic activities throughout their countries and prevent the concentration of economic power in very few corporate hands. However, most mainstream economists are strongly opposed to such strategies and react to proposals to, say, subsidize emerging domestic producers facing competition from established giants overseas by warning that such a course would limit the workings of the free market and thus lead to gross inefficiencies. This response ignores the widespread evidence that gross inefficiencies are generated by the market itself and that intervention might be needed to correct them. It also ignores the historical evidence that the governments of virtually every continental European country provided protection for their infant industries to enable them to counteract Britain's head start during the Industrial Revolution.

The idea of intervening in the market by restricting capital flows is particularly unacceptable to many economists because it would prevent investors moving their money to wherever it can gain the highest return. 'A standard view would argue that the greatest national benefit is achieved if savings are put to the most productive use,' Professor

Honohan told me after making his comments about capital flows from depressed areas. In the context in which he used it, 'profitable' might well be substituted for 'productive'.

The existence of positive feedback means it is not just movements of capital across national boundaries that are harmful. Substantial, continuing capital flows from one part of a country to another are destabilizing too, leading to prosperity in one area and decline in another. However, in the absence of any political recognition of both facts, endangered communities are going to have to limit such flows themselves if they are to survive.

One way of doing this might be for a community group to attempt to draw up a league table of the financial institutions in its area, showing the proportion of the savings each takes in that it re-lends locally. If such a table could be prepared it would allow people to move their savings to the institution with the best local-retention ratio, thus putting pressure on its rivals to increase the proportion of local loans they make. However, I say 'attempt to draw up' because, if the Irish Green Party's experience in the 1994 European election is any guide, it will prove impossible to assemble one outside the United States where the relevant data are freely available under the Community Reinvestment Act. Elsewhere, banks are likely to refuse to supply the necessary figures, arguing that because account-holders do not necessarily live in the districts in which each branch is located, any statistics they supplied would be flawed and potentially misleading.

The counter-arguments – that their computers could quickly sort out account-holders' addresses, and that even imperfect data would be better than nothing – are unlikely to change bankers' minds, and unless information can be obtained secretly from sympathetic (or disaffected) bank staff, the league-table project is likely to run out of steam. Nevertheless it is well worthwhile attempting to compile one in order to alert people to the effects of money flows. Moreover, the near-inevitable refusal of the bank chains to tell savers what they are doing with their deposits will strengthen some people's resolve to set up a mechanism of their own through which their capital can be channelled to local projects without the intervention of secretive outsiders.

There are several reasons for wanting to end, or at least drastically reduce, the involvement of outside banks in one's community. One is that using an external bank's services to do a job that can be done within the community causes a significant loss of purchasing power, which can only be restored if the community sells goods and services to the outside world and thus stays dependent on it. The farmers who lent £943 million to the Irish banks in 1993 would have been paid about £10 million in interest, while farmers borrowing the same amount would have paid perhaps £113 million for the privilege, making a net loss of £100 million to the farming community. Not all this difference would have left rural areas because some would have gone to pay the bank staff and thus have been returned to the local flow of national currency. However, since branch operating costs are usually less than half a bank's income, using outside banks to effect a transfer from one group of farmers to another causes a substantial net drain from rural areas.

The most important reason for wanting to short-circuit local money flows, however, is that discussed in chapter 2, namely that once our savings have been passed over the mahogany counter of the bank, they will not return to our communities except at interest rates determined on world markets. These rates have nothing to do with local conditions or the rates of return we are able to earn by producing local goods for local sale at prices set by the lowest-cost producers in the world. And, as we also discussed, these externally determined interest rates are so extremely unstable that the cost of borrowing money can vary by over 100 per cent within a short period, jeopardizing the survival of every enterprise with an outstanding loan. During the ten years in which I ran a factory, the rate of interest the bank charged on its loans varied between 8.5 and 21 per cent. What business, local or otherwise, can easily cope with so wide a variation?

In many places it is not necessary to start from scratch to set up a local banking system. Ireland and Britain already have almost a thousand independent, co-operatively owned community organizations busy recycling their members' savings locally at stable interest rates: the credit unions. The Irish movement began in 1958; its British counterpart started in 1964 and only began expanding rapidly in the late 1980s. Now, however, a new British credit union is established on average every week. But the movement's stronghold is the United States, where 66 million people – almost a third of the population – are members. Irish credit unions, with 1.33 million shareholders in 1993 out of a population of 5.14 million (including Northern Ireland), have achieved almost as good a penetration rate. In Britain, membership in 1993 was about 100,000, up an amazing 40 per cent on the previous year.

The credit union movement traces its origins to a loan bank set up by the burgomaster of Weyerbusch in Germany, Friedrich Wilhelm Raiffeisen, who was appalled by the activities of moneylenders who 'fastened like a vampire on the rural population' during a famine in 1846–7. Raiffeisen Credit Societies were set up all over Germany and were used by the founders of the Irish co-operative movement, Horace Plunkett and George Russell (Æ), as the model for the agricultural credit societies or 'village banks' they helped set up around the turn of the century. By the middle 1950s, however, of the 310 originally established only 176 survived, and their activities were on a very small scale; roughly half of them were so disorganized and weighed down by bad debts that they even failed to meet their legal obligation to make annual returns.

The Raiffeisen model was followed rather more successfully in Canada and the United States, however, and no American credit union defaulted as a result of the 1929 crash. By 1955 there were 16,201 US credit unions with a total of about three million members, most consisting of people employed by the same firm; and it was information, letters and encouragement from these and from credit unions in Canada that enabled a schoolteacher, Nora Herlihy, to set up the first Irish credit union in 1958. Similarly, the first British credit union was set up in Wimbledon as a result of contacts with Nova Scotia.

Before being admitted to a credit union, new members must prove they share a 'common bond' with the existing members, either because they live in the same area or, in the case of an employee credit union, work in the same firm. If their application is approved they will then have to purchase at least a £1 share, although some credit unions impose a minimum of five shares. Any savings they then lodge – up to a maximum of £6000 in Ireland, £5000 in Britain – are also described as shares because they go to augment the union's working capital.*

Shareholders receive dividends rather than interest on their money, the actual amount being determined by the union's financial results. Shares can be cashed at any time, but the manager has the right to require sixty days' notice in order to preserve the union's liquidity. In most credit unions, shares are not cashed if the member holding them

---

* Sums above the £6000 limit can be accepted by Irish credit unions as deposits rather than shares up to the amount of its paid-up share capital. Interest is paid on these deposits at a variable rate determined periodically by the committee, but they are not covered by insurance; nor, under Irish law, can they be lent out to members: they are simply consolidated and invested in government stocks through the investment management arm of one of the banks. They therefore represent a leak of national currency from the community, and the only good thing to be said about them is that they help credit unions to cover their overheads.

receives a loan but are held as partial security. This can make support for that credit union expensive. Recently, well-established Irish credit unions have been paying tax-free dividends on shares of about 6 per cent and charging an annual rate of 12.68 per cent on their loans, the same rate as in Britain. As a result, anyone needing access to their money but too loyal to insist on selling their shares pays their credit union roughly 6.5 per cent to borrow their own funds. The only miti-gating feature of this arrangement is that the borrowers are insured, so that if they die the loan is written off and their estate receives a gratuity of twice the value of their shareholding.

The risk that shares in a credit union will be lost if lenders default or directors defraud is covered by insurance, and no saver in Ireland or Britain has ever lost money. In any case, credit unions experience remarkably few bad debts, in part because of the common bond, in part because of the character and ethos of the movement. In 1992 my credit union in Westport feared that loans totalling £8826 might not be repaid out of a total loan book of almost £3 million – a record many banks would envy. Another safeguard is that, in both Ireland and Britain, each union's accounts books are inspected regularly by the movement's own auditors and by the Registrar of Friendly Societies.

Since it took an angel in Frank Capra's classic film *It's a Wonderful Life* to show the small-town savings and loan manager the difference his life had made to his community, we shall never be able to quantify the benefits credit unions have brought. Their contribution has undoubtedly been substantial, most notably in getting members out of the clutches of moneylenders and in building up the saving habit. A founder-member of the first Irish credit union to be organized for workers at a single company wrote to Nora Herlihy: 'It has done one good thing for our members. It has got them out of the moneylen-ders' offices and none of them will ever go back. Some of us were charged £2.10s. interest for a loan of £10 – the principal and interest to be paid back in 25 weekly instalments of ten shillings each. The credit union charge for a similar loan is about one-eighth of that amount and it remains in the credit union for our benefit.'[4] Even today the president of the newly established credit union for employ-ees of British Airways, Graham Tomlin, talks of the credit unions' role in fighting loan sharks, who are still a serious social problem in most British and Irish cities.[5]

In Britain credit unions play another role: that of providing banking services to deprived communities after the commercial banks have pulled out. For example, St Columba's Credit Union in Bradford, which operated from a church after it was founded in the middle 1970s, responded to the closure of a local branch of the Trustee Savings Bank by acquiring its own premises in 1991. 'For the low-incomed and pensioners on the estates here, the closure meant spending money to go into town to pay bills,' the manager, Joseph Yewdall, told me in 1995. 'We now have 720 members and £250,000 assets and are growing daily. We call ourselves a one-stop community bank.'[6] Southwark Council established South London's first high-street credit union to meet the same needs. In Birmingham, where five of the city's thirty-nine wards no longer have a bank or building society and a further six have only one branch left, the Birmingham Credit Union Development Agency has been set up to help establish credit unions to fill the gap. An estimated 28 per cent of Birmingham's population has no local access to banking services or is on the verge of losing it.

But can credit unions do more than fulfil the valuable role of 'poor man's bank'?* Specifically, can they provide finance at interest rates low and stable enough to help community ventures using local resources to meet local needs to compete in their local markets with goods and services supplied from outside? Or should communities develop other financial intermediaries to perform that function?

At present, credit unions are not geared to lend to small businesses, and most of their directors and members think in social-service terms rather than economic-development terms. Moreover, although their interest rates are not only usually lower than other sources of personal finance but amazingly stable (in Ireland they remained at 1 per cent a month on the outstanding balance – 12.68 per cent APR – from the time the first credit union opened until 1995), in 1994 they were unattractive for anyone seeking to borrow for non-speculative business purposes, since they were about twice what the banks were asking large, established companies to pay.

The few credit unions that believe they should channel savings into local economic development have generally done so by providing premises from which small businesses can operate. One such is Blessington Credit Union in County Wicklow, which spent £90,000 in 1987 buying and restoring a derelict courthouse – the architectural centrepiece of the town – to provide offices for itself and to rent to others and then in 1992 invested a further £84,000 in building a five-

---

*One of the reasons credit unions are much stronger in Ireland than England is that the Irish do not regard them as largely for people who cannot afford a 'proper' bank account: they are seen as community assets, and the better-off not only save with them but play an active part in their management.

unit enterprise centre in the overgrown garden at the back. However, the best Irish example is probably to be found in Tallow, a village with nine hundred inhabitants in County Waterford whose credit union was set up by sixteen people in 1968. The first honorary secretary was Sheila Ryan. 'It took us five years to be taken seriously,' she says today, 'but what gave us real credibility was when we were able to buy our own offices in 1975 for £4000. We only had shareholdings of £12,000 at the time, so we took out a five-year loan from Kanturk Credit Union, which we were able to repay within three months, so great was the impact of the opening.'

All the work involved in running the union was carried out voluntarily by the directors until 1984, when Ryan became its paid manager. 'The voluntary ethos is very important, but members also want a professional service,' she says. Her employment left the directors free to fulfil their true role: setting the organization's policy. 'The board became seriously concerned about the growth of unemployment in the town and encouraged the establishment of the Tallow Enterprise Group. We offered them our office facilities and meeting rooms, but they were never used because the unemployed just didn't have the confidence.'

Another approach was obviously necessary, and so a solicitor, an accountant and three of the directors who had set up their own businesses re-formed the enterprise group and began to run training courses on the top floor of the credit union building. Twenty-six people attended; of these, half set up projects. But where were these new businesses to work from? In 1989, rather than mark the organization's twenty-first anniversary with a lavish dinner-dance, as other societies might have done, the board decided to buy a derelict four-storey grain store for £3500 and spend a further £10,000 on doing it up so that it could be used by the enterprise group. Not that this meant there was no anniversary dinner: a meal was prepared by credit union members and served in the refurbished building, Nora Herlihy House.

A playschool, a crèche and a picture-framing business started up in the new premises, along with a secretarial services company and a plastic display goods firm. 'But it wasn't just used for economic development,' Ryan says. 'We've had classes and exhibitions there and used it for Tallow's international sculpture festival.'

In 1993, with the old grain store fully occupied, the credit union board was keen to buy the premises of a motor dealership that had gone into liquidation. 'Twenty thousand square feet of space was being offered for £35,000,' Ryan says. 'However, we didn't feel we could bid for it until the family that had owned it gave us permission. We don't profit from other people's misfortunes around here.' Permission was given, but a problem arose: the Registrar of Friendly Societies had visited Tallow three years earlier and expressed the view that owning and operating an enterprise centre was no part of a credit union's function. This, naturally, damaged some directors' confidence. 'But he never put anything in writing,' Ryan says. 'If he had found any legislation that we had infringed he would have certainly put it on paper. It was ridiculous: we had an enterprise centre worth £60,000 on our books for £10,000, and the registrar was unhappy.' (Incidentally, Tallow's purchase and conversion of the grain store would have been illegal in Britain, as the Credit Union Act, 1979, prevents credit unions from buying property except for their own use.)

So, instead of buying the garage itself, the credit union lent the necessary funds to the enterprise group, which bought it instead and got £100,000 in Government grants and soft loans to do it up. 'This solution made very little difference because the enterprise group operates more or less as a subcommittee of the credit union anyway,' Ryan continues. 'However, it would have been better if the credit union had bought it directly, as we would have had another very valuable asset on our books. I think the enterprise group will probably assign the credit union the title one day.' When the garage had been refitted, the businesses in Nora Herlihy House moved into it to allow an adult language-tuition centre to be established in their old home.

By 1995 the Tallow Area Credit Union had a full-time staff of four, almost three thousand members, and savings of £3 million. These statistics make it one of the smaller Irish credit unions, a fact that makes its achievements all the more remarkable. But it will not stay small for long. Its rate of growth has become exponential – it took it eleven years before it had £100,000 worth of savings and twenty years to reach £1 million, but the second million took four years and the third million two. Part of its attractiveness is due to its policies. 'Although we have the right to require sixty days' notice, we've never asked anyone to wait longer for their money than it takes the time-lock on the safe to open,' Ryan says. 'Nor have we required them to borrow against their shares. It's not fair to do that, and it's quite possible to avoid it if you have adequate liquidity. Normally we keep between a quarter and a third of total savings in short-term investments or in other liquid assets.'

Tallow Credit Union lends 'quite a lot' to members to use in their businesses. 'It would be more difficult if we were in a bigger town,'

Ryan says. 'We know the seed and we know the breed, and if a family is honest you can be fairly sure that the children will be too, although you do get the odd black sheep. In some cases we would already know quite a lot about the project before it comes to us for a loan because it has been assessed by the enterprise group, although it's not necessary that it comes that way. We recently made loans of £12,500 each to two members so that they could establish a joint project. That total of £25,000 would be about as much as we would ever put into one venture. The risks are higher with this sort of loan, so you need a balanced portfolio.'

Ryan thinks that the main problem with business loans from a credit union is their short term: by law they have to be repaid over five years in both Ireland and Britain. 'I'm hoping that there will be a change in the legislation and we'll be able to lend for ten years, but I suspect it will increase to seven,' she says. If she were managing a credit union in Britain she would almost certainly also complain about the £5000 loan ceiling, but in Ireland there is no limit on how big a loan to a member can be as long as it does not exceed 10 per cent of the assets of the credit union concerned.

In 1994, when the Irish banks were paying their ordinary customers about 0.5 per cent interest on their savings accounts and lending to small businesses at between 8 and 10.25 per cent and to big business at 6.65 per cent, Tallow, which was paying a dividend of 4 per cent – half its surplus – had more savings on its hands than it could lend to members at its 12.68 per cent rate. However, like most credit union managers, Ryan did not favour cutting her interest and dividend rates, for fear that at some time they might have to be put up again. 'That's one thing that people like about our loans: they know exactly what the interest rate will be in four years' time. They are about 1 per cent more expensive than an overdraft now, but during 1992 they were very much cheaper because the banks' rates went up to 20 per cent.' Would she favour reduced-rate loans for local businesses? 'Definitely not. They would be against the rules anyway because all members have to be treated equally. In any case, the risk on business loans is higher than that for personal ones.'

As credit unions are likely to stick to this position, they will be unable to channel local savings into local productive enterprises at interest rates lower than those available to the big firms they must compete with. Special organizations will have to be set up to fulfil this function, although these may be able to adopt the credit union structure, share existing premises, and learn from their experience;

the close relationship between the Tallow Enterprise Group and the credit union is something any new community lending organization would wish to duplicate.

'There is a case for a "credit union of credit unions",' says Philip Flynn, a veteran of the Irish credit union movement. 'In other countries, central credit unions facilitate mortgage lending and handle investments in co-operative and community enterprises: the French Caisse Populaire, for example, must invest 20 per cent of its reserves in enterprises that benefit the community. Having a central structure would let credit unions spread the risks entailed by such investments and let them do something positive with a proportion of the funds they now have invested in government securities. Certainly, credit unions can do more for community economic development. Lack of self-confidence, imagination, vision and understanding may be the reasons they haven't. But then, maybe nobody has ever asked them to do so within a coherent context.'

A tiny lending institution in south Devon might be a prototype for future community economic development loan funds, although it has yet to show that it can beat the interest rate problem. Its name is TILT (Totnes Involvement in Local Trading), and it must be one of the smallest lending institutions in the world: when it launched an appeal for more deposits in early 1992 it had only three loans outstanding and £2315 available for new lending. One of the loans was to a photographer for darkroom equipment, another to a bicycle repair shop, and the third to a woodworker who wished to buy out his partner's share of their business's equipment when the partnership broke up.

'Before we opened up, in 1989, we thought we would be able to raise a total of perhaps £50,000 in large amounts from a few individuals,' Mark Beeson, a founder-director, told me in 1994, when the amount under its control had risen to £6000, the highest ever. 'Unfortunately, however, deposits on that scale never materialized, and as a result we've never been able to make individual loans of more than £750.'

Several years' thought and study went into the establishment of TILT, however, and the fact that it survives and does a useful job despite its small size makes it a more relevant model for communities elsewhere than an organization that started big and experienced few problems. 'Under the present system, money is inevitably drawn away from those areas which need it and loaned out in places which are already thriving,' Beeson says. 'We set up TILT because we realized

132

[main text continues p.136]

GRAMEEN LENDING METHODS SUCCESSFUL IN CHICAGO

A combination of peer support and peer pressure can make lending to members of a group much safer than lending to an individual, even if the group has to be constructed first. This at least is the experience of the Women's Self-Employment Project (WSEP) in Chicago, which was set up in 1986 by a foundation and three professional women to help lone mothers on welfare with no credit records to break out of poverty through self-employment. 'Fifty-two per cent of the Chicago homes where mothers are raising children alone are below the poverty line,' says Connie Evans, executive director of the project, 'and in 1992, when a charity, the United Way of Chicago, studied the city's needs, it reported that loans to emerging businesses or start-ups of under $10,000 were virtually non-existent. That was for all social groups, so the chances of the sort of women who participate in our programme getting a loan were, realistically, nil.'

WSEP uses an approach to lending developed by a former Bangladeshi economics professor, Mohammed Yunus, who became concerned about starvation among people marginalized by the economic system during the 1974 famine in his country and went out onto the streets to try to find out just what the barriers to their reincorporation into the mainstream were. He met a woman who was being paid just over a penny a day by a shopkeeper to make bamboo stools. She would have been able to earn a great deal more had she sold the stools herself but could not afford the cost of the materials – about a pound. Within a few days, Yunus met forty-one other people whose lives could also have been greatly improved if they had been able to borrow trivial sums of money: the total amount they needed was just £20.

His first reaction was to give them the money himself, but then he realized that, while his gift would help those he had met, it would do nothing for millions of people with similar needs: he had to help change the system. When he approached a bank to see if it would lend to his group, the idea was treated with scorn. 'The poor are not creditworthy,' he was told. He persisted, however, and the loans were eventually granted on his personal guarantee. The Grameen Bank was born. Over a million loans later and with a 98 per cent repayment record, Yunus has proved the conventional bankers' view wrong. 'The Wright brothers demonstrated that humans could fly,' he says. 'Grameen has demonstrated that the poor can borrow. Our statistics show that the poor are more creditworthy than the rich.'

Grameen's secret is the use of borrowing circles. In Chicago, self-selected groups of five women from the same area, who must not be related to each other or be in business together, each of whom wants to borrow to set up or continue a small business, attend part-time courses lasting six to ten weeks. During these they develop a sense of commitment to each other and are taught business skills and how the WSEP Full Circle Fund works. They also open accounts at banks where the WSEP has negotiated special low-cost or no-cost terms for them, so that they can manage their money better and have a place to save. When the women are judged to be ready, the group is recognized as a circle, selects a name for itself, and chooses two of its members to receive the first loans, which may not exceed $1500 each and are repayable over a year. The interest rate is 15 per cent, which Connie Evans believes is not excessive in view of the high administrative costs lending this way involves.

The circle then meets for about three hours every second week 'for continuing support and assistance'. In districts where several circles exist, the meetings are arranged so that after each circle has finished receiving loan repayments and discussed any new loan applications it can join three or four other circles in what is termed a centre to discuss issues of interest to them all. 'The neighbourhoods in which we work have not only been drained of economic resources but also of many of the institutions which exist in healthy communities,' Connie Evans says. 'Through these meetings the Full Circle Fund is evolving into a vehicle which enables women to begin replacing them.'

One centre has set up several committees to handle its members' needs, both as borrowers and members of the wider community. 'One of these committees helps people prepare well-thought-out loan applications. Another concentrates on arranging the types of training the women feel they want. A third is concerned with crime and violence and has developed a plan to put decals [signs] in their front windows so that children in the community can recognize a "safe" house if they run into trouble on their way to and from school.' All the districts in which WSEP works are infested with crime: one of them was described in the Wall Street Journal as 'a neighborhood where every block has a boarded-up building, and two inches of bullet-proof plastic separates workers from customers at Kentucky Fried Chicken.' Another journalist said of the same area that 'the most conspicuous entrepreneurs were the ones dealing drugs on the corners.'

Repayments on a circle's first two loans begin two weeks after the money is received, and if the three fortnightly payments are made on time, another two of its members qualify for their loans. The final member gets her loan after a further six weeks, provided all her colleagues' accounts are in order. This is the key to the circles' success: if anyone falls down on her repayments, the four other members of her circle will be unable to get their loans or additional ones; she will have let down her friends. 'Peer support and peer pressure really serve as a good way to lower credit risk,' Connie Evans told me in 1995. 'Each year we make 100 to 125 loans totalling $250,000 to $300,000 through the Full Circle Fund and have seventeen circles in two centres in operation,' she said. 'The repayment rate is 97 per cent, and we estimate that about six hundred businesses have been started since the programme began, 85 per cent of which are still operating.'

When a circle member has successfully repaid her first loan she can apply for another one, this time of up to $3500; and each time she pays off a loan her credit limit increases by $2000, until she reaches the fund's $10,000 ceiling. WSEP does not rely solely on pressure from other members of the circle to see that these larger loans are repaid: most are also 50 per cent backed by some form of collateral, although frequently this takes an unconventional form. One borrower was allowed to offer her dining table and chairs as security for a loan, while others have used paintings and craft items. 'Almost anything the women value can be accepted,' Evans told me. WSEP is not just going through the motions – it will seize whatever is pledged if the loan turns sour. The woman who pledged her table saw it taken away and sold.

'We also give loans tailored to a woman's business needs, such as thirty, sixty or ninety-day short-term loans and revolving lines of credit for the purchase of stock,' Evans says. Besides collateral, access to these further funds is usually conditional on the prospective borrower's completion of one of the courses WSEP runs, such as its entrepreneurial training programme, which involves attendance at a weekly class for twelve weeks at a cost of between $8 and $52 weekly, depending on the woman's means.

WSEP classes are therefore not cheap, but then neither is running the programme, which, with its four full-time workers, costs about two-thirds as much as the annual amount lent out. Most of its costs are in fact covered by grants from government agencies and foundations.

WSEP was not the first such programme in the United States. 'Besides Grameen, we also modelled ourselves on WEDCO in Minnesota, and we helped a similar programme in Los Angeles get started,' Evans says. 'There are probably twelve or more organizations using lending circles now.' One of these is the Lakota Fund on the Pine Ridge Reservation in South Dakota. It made sixty-eight individual loans in 1987 and found that half the repayments were late and 28 per cent of its money had to be written off. It then established borrowing circles, and the default rate dropped to 7 per cent.

Evans believes strongly in the importance of what WSEP is doing. 'The employers in the neighbourhoods in which we work are usually large companies and fast-food and retail chains, which offer women low-wage and service-oriented jobs that don't provide them with the experience and opportunities necessary for their personal and economic advancement. Self-employment can be a way of escaping these limitations. It gives women a chance to provide their children with positive role-models, to increase their own self-esteem, and to raise the quality of life of their families. It also keeps economic resources within the community. Profits gleaned from local money do not end up reinvested in some other neighbourhood, city, or state.'

Mohammed Yunus thinks that work should not be separated from the ownership of the means of production. 'We have to instil in everybody's mind that each person creates his or her own job,' he wrote in the Grameen Bank newsletter, Grameen Dialogue, in 1994. 'The more we can move towards home-based production by the self-employed masses, the more we can come close to avoiding the disasters of capitalism.'

Connie Evans, Executive Director, Women's Self-Employment Project, 166 W. Washington Street (suite 730), Chicago, Illinois 60602; tel. +1 312 6068255; fax +1 312 6069215.

that while people might be ready to set up small businesses and to trade on a local scale, buying from producers they knew who used methods of production which were environment-friendly and community-friendly, their surpluses, their savings, would tend to stay in big institutions, which might invest them in projects completely at variance with their depositors' ideologies and which could indeed undermine whatever those depositors were working for in their careers.'

Although discussion of the need for a local bank began as early as 1981 in the first issue of the *Dart*, a bi-monthly community magazine that Beeson founded and edits, it was 1987 before Norman Duncan, a retired consultant to the oil industry, and Andy Langford, a founder of the Conker Shoe Company – one of the two co-operatively run shoe manufacturing businesses in Totnes – began to plan to set one up.

'Originally, Andy and Norman thought that we could model TILT on investment funds in the US and New Zealand, but it soon became clear that British law meant that the structure of any organization here would have to be rather different,' Beeson says. 'So, in July 1987 they sent an outline of their idea, together with their CVs, to a number of organizations connected with alternative finance asking for advice and help. Most of the replies were discouraging because they pointed out that if we were to set up as a proper bank we would need at least £5 million in capital, an impressive board of directors and a three-year track record in lending before we could even apply for a licence from the Bank of England, which even then we would be most unlikely to get. The one positive idea came from Mercury Provident, an ethical bank based in Sussex (now called Triodos and based in Bristol), which suggested that TILT should act as a broker for investors who wanted to put their money into various forms of community enterprise, which is more or less what Mercury does itself.

'A lot of attention was given to the form TILT should take. Andy and Norman investigated the possibility of setting up a charitable trust, only to find that TILT could not be registered as a charity because its activities were to be mainly concerned with assisting commercial operations – even though its objective in providing that assistance was to benefit the community and the environment. Another idea was to set it up as a friendly society or co-op, particularly as this would have given us the sort of democratic decision-making structures we wanted; and for a time it looked as though we would be taking that road. Indeed at the meeting to launch the TILT Setting-up

Association in February 1989, that was the plan outlined. The meeting raised £750 to cover fitting out the community office on the High Street in Totnes, from which TILT now operates, and to provide TILT's legal registration fees. A large number of people were interested in the project, and there was a hard core of five or six individuals who believed in directing their energies towards changing things at the local as opposed to the national level. I joined the Setting-up Association at its first meeting.'

Two months later, however, a letter arrived from the Registrar of Friendly Societies to say that, under the Industrial and Provident Society Acts, a co-op could not make investing on behalf of its members its main business. Although this ruling was correct, had the Totnes group had access to specialist advice or had the Registrar gone out of his way to be more helpful it would have been possible to have restructured the application and registered TILT under the provident society legislation. Instead the project took another direction.

'By now, regular meetings of the Setting-up Association were taking place, and the letter seemed a great set-back,' Beeson says. 'However, Norman had discovered that an ordinary limited company carrying out investment business on behalf of its shareholders was exempted from having to register under the Financial Services Act, 1986, and could raise capital from those shareholders without having to register the issue or circulate a prospectus. This was a way out of the legal impasse, although it still meant that we became more hedged around with restrictions and limitations than we had hoped to be.'

The most serious of these limitations was that TILT cannot publicly solicit deposits, which, as Beeson says, is 'a considerable handicap for a company with a yet-unknown name.' Nevertheless, registration as a limited company and its licensing under the Consumer Credit Act went ahead, and the organization was launched in November 1989. Andy Langford had left Totnes by this time (he now lives in Oxford, where he teaches permaculture design and helped establish the city's first LETS), and the founding directors were Beeson, Duncan, Prem Ash from Conker Shoes, Alison Hastie from Green Shoes, William Hubbard, a solicitor, and Amiten O'Keeffe, a builder. All except Duncan were still serving at the end of 1995.

Anyone borrowing from TILT or lending to it is required to hold a £10 membership share, which enables them to help make policy and elect directors. Members are allowed to purchase an additional voting share for each year's membership, up to a maximum of five, on the grounds that their knowledge of TILT and their commitment to it are likely to be greater than that of someone who has just joined, but so far no one has. Members wishing to invest can choose between buying ordinary TILT shares and making it a loan. The ordinary shares cost £100 each, carry no vote, and entitle the holder to a dividend should TILT's profits ever become adequate for its board to declare one. 'Members understand that we're not likely to become a vast profit-making concern,' Beeson comments.

Loan stock is issued each year at interest rates determined by the sum involved and the term for which it is lent. The rates also vary with the Bank of England's minimum lending rate (MLR). Thus, for example, someone depositing the minimum amount, £100, for the minimum period, six months, will receive MLR less 6 per cent, while someone depositing over £5000 (which no one has done yet) for five years will get MLR minus 2.75 per cent. 'At present we lend at 6.75 per cent above MLR, which is a lot cheaper than a personal loan from the bank, even if such loans were available to our borrowers, which is generally not the case,' Beeson told me when MLR was 5.25 per cent. 'Loan stock holders get an average interest rate of 2 to 3 per cent because most of their deposits are quite small and lent for short periods and our administrative costs are relatively high. TILT cannot be an easy source of cheap money because we can only survive if we balance our books. Any member can join the Loan Consideration Committee, which selects projects on the basis of their potential contribution to the local area. However, only projects which give firm evidence of financial viability will be assisted, and all lending is conditional on the borrower having guarantors.'

Mark Beeson admits that although TILT takes 'inordinate time and care' in vetting loan applications, one or two of the projects it has assisted have run into difficulties. 'In such cases we waive repayments for a month or two, but we keep in touch with the businesses weekly, coaxing them along, and they have survived. Successful lending can't be done in isolation from the business and those behind it. We quite frequently help prospective borrowers in preparing their forecasts, and sometimes our loans are conditional on borrowers accepting technical or managerial advice. The experience of similar funding systems abroad shows that close links between borrowers and lenders reduces defaults to almost zero.'

TILT has only continued to operate because of a considerable amount of unpaid effort put into it by its directors. 'We've helped four or five projects to continue and in some cases to flourish,' Beeson says, 'so we feel that we've achieved something. We're also the first

 [main text continues p.144]

NOVEL WAYS OF RAISING SMALL LOANS

Perhaps it doesn't matter too much if a small business has to pay a relatively high rate of interest if it can raise a loan when it needs one urgently and if the interest it pays stays within the community. This was certainly the case when Frank Tortoriello's popular delicatessen in Great Barrington, Massachusetts, faced closure in 1989 because no bank would advance him $4500 to move to new premises when his lease expired. Fortunately Tortoriello knew Susan Witt, who runs the Self-Help Association for a Regional Economy (SHARE) from the offices of the E.F. Schumacher Society in the wooded hills five miles outside the town. And fortunately too Witt knew that a Massachusetts newspaper, the Springfield Union News, had survived by paying its staff in its own notes after a 1930s bank failure closed its operating account. The staff spent the notes with local merchants, who used them in turn to buy advertising space. She also knew that a restaurant, Zoo-Zoo, had issued its own notes in Oregon in 1977 when faced with a situation similar to Tortoriello's.

'SHARE suggested that Frank print his own currency – Deli Dollars – and sell them to his customers in order to raise the capital he needed to renovate the new spot,' Susan Witt says. 'What he did was to pre-sell meals to his customers. He sold a $10 Deli Dollar for nine dollars in October, to be redeemable at the new business once it was renovated for ten dollars' worth of sandwiches. However, to ensure that all the Deli Dollars didn't come in during the first month, they were dated over a ten-month period.' This meant that the rate of interest Tortoriello paid ranged between 44 per cent a year on a four-month Dollar – the earliest maturity sold – to 13.3 per cent on one due in ten months. 'To Frank, though, it was a low-interest loan, because he was paying back in sandwiches rather than federal dollars,' Witt says.

'I put five hundred notes on sale and they went in a flash,' Tortoriello told a Washington Post reporter. 'Deli Dollars turned up all over town. It was astonishing.' One was even put in the collection plate at the local Congregational church, because the minister frequently ate at the delicatessen. 'Frank's customers liked helping him move,' Witt comments. 'They felt that they were beating the system by keeping the business open through their own efforts. Even people who never ate there bought Deli Dollars to help out.'

Dan and Martha Tawczynski, who run an organic market garden in Great Barrington and sell most of their produce from their own roadside shop, heard about the scheme from their daughter, Jan, who was working in the delicatessen at the time. They wondered if they could do something similar. 'During the winter months they have high heating bills for their greenhouses growing plants for spring and summer,' Susan Witt explains. 'They thought perhaps their customers would help them by pre-buying plants in the same way that the deli customers were pre-buying sandwiches. At about this time Donald and Ruth Zeigler's roadside farm shop was badly damaged by fire. The two requests for help came to SHARE simultaneously, and we suggested the two farms work it out together. Out of this grew Berkshire Farm Preserve Notes, which were sold and

Two of the notes issued by the Self-Help Association for a Regional Economy in Great Barrington, Mass.

redeemable at either farm, so it was more of a currency than the Deli Dollar. The Notes had different redemption dates between June and October. If one farm accepted fewer Notes than it had sold, it had to pay the other farm for them. The Zeiglers ended up with about $70 more than their share and took payment for them in Dan's organic potatoes, which are particularly good.'

The issue raised over $7000 and has been repeated each year since. 'I think it would have been impossible to survive without the Notes,' Dan Tawczynski says, looking out over land that was once farmed but where the forest has now grown back. The Zeiglers also appreciate what the scheme has done. 'We have a special pick-your-own day for Farm Preserve Note buyers,' Ruth says. 'We send out invitations in May.'

More recently, SHARE has helped a village shop, a Japanese restaurant and a coffee-roasting company to raise capital – and generate extra business – by the print-your-own money route. However, it has another, more conventional way of raising money for small local businesses – finance that is badly needed, because, as Witt points out, 'these days a lot of banks won't touch small commercial loans. Their costs are so high they are often not interested in discussing anything less than $100,000.'

Great Barrington is about a hundred miles from New York, and a lot of New Yorkers have bought weekend retreats there. These temporary residents are generally a lot better off than the local people, and some of the more enlightened ones feel they ought to put something into an area that gives them a lot of enjoyment. One way Witt has encouraged them to do

140

this is by lending money to SHARE for collateralizing loans to local businesses. 'Anyone who wishes can walk into our participating bank – which
is locally owned and has a good track record of investing in the community – and open a ninety-day-notice passbook savings account jointly with
SHARE,' she explains. 'They leave their passbook at the bank, so that
SHARE can use up to 75 per cent of the amount in it as collateral for
loans. The money in the account still belongs to the depositor, who gets
the interest which accrues on it and is the only person able to draw it out,
except in the event of a default. When SHARE has decided to back a loan
to someone, we formally lodge enough passbooks with the bank to cover
the amount. We have a $3000 loan limit, although some places which
have adopted the SHARE model go up to $30,000, and we only support
loans which will lead to greater regional self-sufficiency – food, shelter or
energy projects – or the provision of basic community services.'

Naturally the bank likes the scheme as it doesn't have to spend time
checking loan applications submitted by SHARE, which has already done
so. Another advantage is that SHARE loans increase the total of local
loans the bank can declare to the regulatory authorities, thus winning it
benefits under the Community Reinvestment Act. Moreover, as each loan
is fully secured, the bank carries no risk and still enjoys a healthy margin
between the rate of interest it pays to the passbook depositor and the rate
charged to the borrower. 'We think it's worth allowing the bank to make
that margin because of the bookkeeping work it saves us,' Witt says.

What happens if depositors need to get their money back? 'They have
to give us 120 days' notice, which gives us time to find someone else,'
Witt says. 'There's never been any problem paying depositors back
because of the liquidity we preserve by only collateralizing three-quarters
of the savings in each passbook. However, we do reserve the right to make
depositors wait until loan repayments allow passbooks to be released.'
And what if a borrower defaults? 'We haven't had a loss in the seven years
we've been operating, but if we did it would be shared by all SHARE depositors and not just those whose passbooks were lodged as security for the
problem loan. In fact, however, we know all our borrowers well and can
often help them overcome any trouble.'

SHARE's first loan was to a maker of goat's cheese who needed a milk-
ing-room built to government standards in order to sell her produce to
shops and restaurants but had no record with a bank. 'SHARE investors
are kept informed about the products they are investing in,' Witt says.
'They go down to Sue's farm to look at what she's been doing. The little
goats are so cute that next time they bring down their grandchildren to
see them. The following week they come to get a big supply of cheese for
a party. Gradually the loans they've made begin to work into their social
and cultural life. The goat cheese becomes their goat cheese. It takes on a
different nature just in their house.'

In Australia, where small commercial loans are just as difficult to
obtain from banks as they are in the United States, James Evans, director
of the Eastern Suburbs Business Enterprise Centre (ESBEC) in Sydney,
has developed a loan scheme, First-Business Finance (FBF), a joint ven-

ture between ESBEC and its neighbouring BEC in Botany and with a number of high-powered external directors. It has several features in common with SHARE but operates on a much larger scale. It also makes a neat link between local savers and small local firms needing funds.

FBF made its first loans in early 1995. Like SHARE, it aims to help people wanting to start businesses who cannot borrow from banks because they may have no collateral or are unemployed or have only the briefest credit record, if any. A case history given in FBF's business plan is that of a 'retrenched' (redundant) 52-year-old cabinet-maker with a wife and three children who had never run a business, whose tools had belonged to his former employer, and who had no assets that could be offered as security. As a result, although he was offered several jobs, including a subcontract from his old company, no bank would approve a loan to enable him to purchase tools and to provide a small amount of working capital.

ESBEC helps this type of would-be borrower to develop a business plan and prepare a loan application, and those applications it is happy about it passes on to Sydney Credit Union, which releases the cash – usually between $5000 and $10,000 – without any further investigation. When the scheme began, the credit union charged an interest rate of 12.95 per cent, which was 2 per cent less than its personal loan rate but 4 per cent more than for a fully secured home loan. 'That's its premium for the perceived higher risk in the small-business market,' Evans says. 'FBF is working on the basis that access to capital rather than its cost is the thing that matters for our sort of borrower.' The costs of setting up each loan are low – about $350 – of which $300 can be added to the amount borrowed.

FBF guarantees the loans but, remarkably, only to the extent of 1 per cent of the total amount outstanding. This means that it can authorize loans worth a hundred times more than the total amount in its guarantee fund, which was initially provided by the New South Wales government, whereas SHARE can only approve loans worth 75 per cent of the money its supporters put up. 'If we do it right, that guarantee money will never be touched,' Evans says. The reason he is so confident that the guarantee funds will stay intact is the level of support the Eastern Suburbs and Botany BECs offer FBF borrowers. The organizations – and another forty-eight BECs throughout New South Wales – were set up by the state government in response to pressure from Rotary Clubs that had seen how well partnerships between the public and private sectors had worked in England during the 1970s. 'The government funding for us decreases over time, so the BECs must gain funds from the local community,' Evans says. 'Our core role is to provide a free counselling service to anyone wishing to start a small business, to existing businesses having problems, and to those wishing to expand. However, we also get involved in anything which can strengthen the economic capacity or increase employment in the local area.'

Many of those using the counselling services eventually join the BECs, which are non-profit companies run by their members, who pay a fee based on their turnover, with a minimum of $240 a year. 'Members pay

142

their fees out of enlightened self-interest,' Evans says. 'Most offer their skills to help our advisory and training service clients and attend the social events, training courses and monthly business workshops we organize. It can be very lonely running a small business, but ESBEC gives them the feeling that they are not alone.'

Members also make valuable contacts. 'Networking is about giving, not expecting something back,' Robyn Henderson, the author of a book on networking, told them on the night I attended a meeting of more than a hundred members in a tennis club lounge. 'Business these days is built with people who trust you and with whom you have rapport. Sixty per cent of people who stop dealing with companies did so because they thought they weren't valued. Make ten new contacts a day. Be honest and open with complete strangers.' After her talk it was amazing to see the rate at which business cards were being exchanged. (Although ESBEC developed quite independently, in many respects it is equivalent to the Briarpatch Network in San Francisco, discussed in the final chapter.)

'We will not be advertising FBF loans in the papers,' Evans says. 'All borrowers will come from community networks like ESBEC, many of which provide pre-start training, mentors, business advisory services, ongoing training and income support in the first year of business. They will all have been helped prepare a business plan and be able to call on continuous support during the operation of their business.'

Evans accepts that some people who get loans will cease business before their debts are repaid but does not think this will necessarily cause them to default. 'A 1992 survey showed that 30 per cent of those who ceased business did so because they had accepted a job, and our experience indicates that in any case they do not accumulate large debts. At present in Australia no one is lending to micro-entrepreneurs on a large enough scale for the risks to be properly assessed. We hope to do that, and our target is to prove that this sort of lending is viable so that other places around Australia copy the concept within the next five years,' he says.

Susan Witt, Self-Help Association for a Regional Economy, Box 76, RD 3, Great Barrington, Massachusetts 01230; tel. +1 413 5281737.
James Evans, Eastern Suburbs Business Enterprise Centre, PO Box 604, Bondi Junction, NSW 2022; tel. +61 2 3692844.

organization of its kind in Britain and have provided a model because I don't see why our system should not be repeated elsewhere.' Nevertheless he agrees that it would be better if TILT were bigger. 'Then we could support a front person. At present, operating the company can weigh quite heavily on the directors' time.'

In mid-1995 Beeson told me that be believed TILT would now expand steadily. 'When something like this is established there is an enormous surge of support and enthusiasm. This dies away, to be followed by a tough period in which you have to prove to potential investors that you are going to survive. We've just about got through that period now, and more offers of deposits and applications for loans are coming in. We've just received a deposit of £2500 for four-and-a-half years, our biggest and longest ever, which is a good sign. We need to have about £10,000 available to us, and I hope we'll get up to that figure in the next two years. At that level we would be able to break even and continue indefinitely. At present, after covering all our expenses (although the directors get nothing for their time) we are making a loss of between £50 and £100 a year, which is funded from our share capital. That is obviously not sustainable.'

Beeson is not alone in thinking that the TILT model is applicable elsewhere. Andy Langford adopted it almost entirely when he set up Shared Visions Ltd in 1994 to make small loans available to permaculture and sustainable agricultural projects throughout Britain. 'Shared Visions differs from TILT in one crucial respect,' Beeson says. 'TILT's whole ethos is local, and we see it moving up and down the local class and interest strata building community. Mercury Provident and Shared Visions are national: they move horizontally along national class and interest strata, catering for special-interest groups. Before Andy left TILT he had come to feel that it was not going to be sufficiently national for what he wanted to do in the permaculture movement.'

Would TILT have gained any advantages if it had taken Mercury's advice to follow its example? Its founders might have registered it as a provident society – 'a form of savings-club-cum-investment-fund devised … in the last century for small depositors,' as Mercury once put it in one of its brochures. All deposits in provident societies are legally share investments, which, unlike the share capital of a limited company, can be repaid if the society's liquidity allows. Anyone who invests in a provident society automatically becomes a shareholder, and all their investment is at risk – there is no deposit insurance as with a bank – but societies have two classes of shares, and the brunt of the risk is carried by the membership shares, which carry no interest and of which members must buy a certain minimum. Interest – which is strictly a dividend, as in a credit union – can only be paid on deposit shares, the second type. The fact that the provident societies cannot pay interest on membership shares, their risk capital, probably circumscribes them more than the limited company that TILT became, since TILT can offer the hope of future dividends to entice people to buy its equivalent.

Mercury itself ceased to be a provident society in 1986 because of the difficulty it was having in selling enough of the higher-risk, zero-interest membership shares to its members to meet the highly confidential capital-to-loan ratio for deposit-takers specified by the Bank of England at a time when its lending was growing rapidly. Its solution was to become a public limited company and a fully fledged bank, a route that would be closed to it and to similar bodies today. 'We were able to do so only because we had been licensed as a deposit-taker – which essentially means a bank – just before the secondary banking crisis in the early seventies which led to the regulations being tightened up a lot,' Glen Saunders, a Mercury director, told me.

Mercury converted the provident society's membership shares into membership shares in the PLC, enshrining in its new memorandum and articles of association the original principle of one shareholder one vote, no matter how many shares they own, and no dividends. The change meant it could issue ordinary shares for the first time. These, like the membership shares, count towards the risk capital required by the Bank of England but, unlike the former, carry no vote, and purchasers can specify what rate of interest they wish to be paid, within a certain range. The new shares have increased Mercury's risk capital but by barely enough to keep pace with the rapid growth of its loans, which rose from £1 million in 1985 to £2 million by early 1988 and £4 million by the end of 1992. A deterrent for purchasers is that ordinary shares cannot be readily sold: Mercury undertakes to find a customer for them but warns that 'resale may take some time.'

To be approved for a loan by Mercury, a proposal has to be not only financially viable but also likely to produce a significant amount of what the bank calls 'added value' for society or the environment. In some cases the project's supporters are asked to provide personal guarantees to cover the loan if the venture proves unsuccessful. 'The bank accepts normal forms of collateral but we prefer guarantees, provided they are spread thinly so that guarantors are not seriously affected in case of a bad debt,' Saunders says.

Whereas TILT got its initial deposits and then looked for projects to lend them to, Mercury has always done things the other way around, approving projects before attempting to raise funds. This seems to have worked very well, as the organization has always had more deposits than projects approved for loans – so much so in fact that at the end of 1992, £3.9 million was held in a variety of liquid financial assets, roughly £200,000 more than it had out on loan to its projects. This ratio was in Saunders's view 'higher than desirable, given our fundamental goals,' and the bank was working to reduce it. Two factors had caused this situation: Mercury's rapid growth, since deposits can be taken in more quickly than they can be prudently lent out, and the need to keep large sums on hand in order to allow depositors – some of whom can request their money back with as little as one day's notice – to withdraw whenever they wish. 'We are trying to educate our depositors to understand the consequences of short periods of notice where longer terms will allow us to use the money more effectively in terms of our and their real intentions,' Saunders told me in 1994, predicting that an optimal liquidity ratio would be achieved in a few months' time.

Depositors in Mercury are invited to 'target' their money by specifying the activity they would like it to be used in and the interest rate they would like to be paid. Mercury then adds its fixed service charge – typically 4 per cent – to the interest rate the customer has specified, and this is the amount the borrower will be charged. In mid-1994 depositors were invited to specify rates between nil and 2.5 per cent and could deposit a minimum of £10 for as little as a week, with only a day's notice of withdrawal required. Fixed-term deposits did offer better interest rates, ranging from 2.5 per cent on £500 deposited for one month to 5 per cent on £50,000 for six months, but no targeting of loans was permitted. Deposits with Mercury are covered by the Bank of England's Deposit Protection Scheme. This ensures that 75 per cent of deposits up to £20,000 – that is, a maximum of £15,000 – will be refunded should the bank collapse.

Potential depositors target their savings using a list of projects that have already received their loans from untargeted funds or from funds for which the depositor had merely specified the sector. Thus, if someone says they would like to make a loan to the Henry Doubleday Research Association or to the Glasgow Steiner School (both of which were among the 110 projects on Mercury's summer 1994 list), their money would be placed there and the untargeted funds released for use elsewhere. Of course there is always a chance that well-known bodies will be offered too much money, and Mercury warns that 'we cannot always allocate your money exactly to the projects of your choice.' If the project a depositor chooses runs into trouble, he or she will not suffer: any loss will be made up out of Mercury's reserves. 'We've only had three bad debts in twenty years,' Saunders says. 'The last one was for £75. Of course more projects than that have ceased trading, but we've got our money back. People often perceive the sort of project we lend to as being risky, but in fact they are more stable than commercial ventures as a rule.'

Mercury was set up in 1974 with seven directors, all of whom had been influenced by the work of the Austrian philosopher Rudolf Steiner and were members of the Anthroposophical Society he founded. Only one had any experience in banking; the rest were an economics journalist, a junior business executive, a farmer, an accountant, and two teachers. It got off to a slow start, and it was 1976 before it processed its first loan – for a cow-shed. 'Then things began to come thick and fast,' says Saunders. 'They had to employ a secretary, and the loan committee spent most of each Saturday morning meeting applicants and developing policy. However, there was still no office or telephone on which they could be reached. None of them received regular remuneration, and they seldom charged fees for their time. But money came in fast enough: every loan for which they sought funds was oversubscribed.'

Despite its success, Mercury was smaller than its directors would have liked. This led them in mid-1995 to merge with a similar Dutch bank, Triodos, and to take its name. 'We cannot service the needs of many interesting social and environmental projects,' Saunders told me some months before the merger. 'Our maximum loan before we make what is known as a large exposure is £140,000, whereas a small social housing project will need at least £250,000. A satisfactory balance to the loan book in terms of risk, exposure, work load, etc. has to be achieved by mixing the larger loans with the many smaller ones we take on.'

Before the merger Mercury was approached by several groups wanting to start similar but locally focused lending organizations. 'We support the local circulation of funds, but with caveats,' Saunders says. 'There can be difficulties with too circumscribed a circulation area. Small local funds have difficulty generating the capital needed, except for the very smallest types of enterprise, and the liquidity of such funds is often highly restricted. The danger of local collapses of circulation is considerable. At present we are looking to see whether we can create something with and through Triodos – by, for example, local targeting – which will achieve the benefits of local circulation without these disadvantages.'

Because of the massive hurdles that have to be cleared before the Bank of England will permit registration as a bank, only one organization in Britain is currently attempting to establish itself as a fully fledged, locally oriented bank to foster community initiatives. This is the Aston Reinvestment Trust, whose foundation was promoted by the Birmingham Settlement, a charity working for the regeneration of life and business in disadvantaged areas of Birmingham. 'We've modelled our project on the community development loans funds in the US. There are now fifty of these, and their loss rate is only about 1 per cent,' Pat Conaty, the project's development manager, told me in late 1994. 'We've set up two companies, Aston Reinvestment Assurance, an insurance company, and Aston Reinvestment Company, an investment company, and one underwrites the risks of the other. We are now trying to raise £3.5 million from churches, foundations, and ethical investors. If we are successful and the investment company can establish a good track record, we hope to be licensed as a bank and be able to accept deposits from the public in three or four years.' Six months later, enough seed money had been received for the trust to be launched at the Bank of England premises in Birmingham, with Joan Shapiro of the South Shore Bank, Chicago (see next panel), as the principal speaker.

Against this, at least three British groups involved in ethical investment have recently decided not to try to become banks and have used the Industrial and Provident Society Acts – basically the same as those in Ireland – to become provident societies. The pioneer was Shared Interest in April 1990; this grew out of a wish by Traidcraft PLC, the alternative trading organization based in Newcastle, to set up an institution to lend largely to groups of producers in the Third World, although poor people anywhere would have been eligible. Traidcraft was already making loans to co-operatives and similar bodies overseas to help them produce the goods it sold through its catalogue.

Its original plan was to persuade one of the bank chains to offer ethical deposit accounts that would place 75 per cent of the investments they took in with the new fund and 25 per cent on the money markets in order to maintain liquidity. Four banks considered the proposal but eventually turned it down as they felt they would have to remain entirely responsible for whatever happened to their customers' money. The possibility of raising capital by selling shares in an investment company was also explored but rejected, since no one was confident that an adequate amount would be subscribed within forty days of the publication of the prospectus, the maximum period the law allowed. Then Chris Ruck, a former chief executive of the Co-operative Bank, suggested forming an industrial and provident society, since shares could be sold without issuing a prospectus.

This course was adopted. The legal work was carried out by a Leeds solicitor, Malcolm Lynch, who was later involved in two similar formations, one of which was Radical Routes Ltd, a co-op of co-ops in Birmingham that by mid-1994 had raised over £100,000 from investors to provide its member-co-ops with loans they found impossible to obtain from the banks. The other was ICOF Community Capital, launched in 1994 by an existing industrial and provident society, Industrial Common Ownership Finance Ltd (ICOF), to provide loans to community enterprises.

ICOF had itself been set up twenty-one years earlier to provide funds for workers' co-operatives and, like Mercury, found that too few people were prepared to buy zero-interest membership shares to allow it to expand. To get around this problem, in 1987 it launched a public limited company, ICOF PLC, which was able to raise £560,000 by the sale of non-voting preference shares. But the costs of this issue were high – £50,000 – and because the shares had to be repaid in 1997, ICOF found it needed to begin setting aside funds three years earlier, reducing the amount it could lend. As a result of this experience it decided not to take the PLC road again.

'Social economy businesses have had problems with accessing money from mainstream finance organizations,' ICOF Community Capital said in its prospectus. 'Traditional institutional investors are sceptical about any legal structure which denies personal wealth accumulation and emphasizes common ownership and local democracy ... We recognize that [the] level of profitability [of social economy businesses] may be constrained by the achievement of social or environmental profit and we expect our investors to share this recognition. We accept money as an investment and although no guarantee can be given, it is expected that results will enable interest to be paid. It will be a goal to provide interest in line with inflation. The minimum investment is £250, the maximum is £20,000 and normally withdrawals can be made on six months' notice. We hope the monetary value of your investment will be maintained but it may go down.'

Despite these and other warnings, such as the right of the trustees to suspend withdrawals – which in any case can only be made on six

[main text continues p.154]

149

HOW A BANK CAN TRANSFORM A COMMUNITY

'In deteriorating neighbourhoods, capital flows out of the area; people cease upgrading their homes, and landlords fail to maintain their buildings; property values fall; store owners quit investing in their businesses and close or move; and neighbourhood residents lose hope, stop investing effort in education and developing work skills, and fall into unemployment,' Milton Davis, the chairman of the bank responsible for perhaps the world's best example of what a financial institution can do to rescue a declining community, told the US Senate Committee on Banking, Housing and Urban Affairs in February 1993. 'Revitalizing such neighbourhoods requires recognition that disinvestment is itself a market phenomenon and, consequently, will only be reversed by fundamentally reinvigorating neighbourhood markets. Permanent, self-sustaining neighbourhood renewal results from creating an environment where private investors inside and outside the neighbourhood are confident their investments will be reciprocated and rewarded as healthy neighbourhood dynamics are restored.'

In the 1940s and '50s the South Shore district of Chicago was considered one of the pleasantest, most convenient places in the city to live because of its location beside Lake Michigan, just south of the central business district. As late as 1960 it had a predominantly white middle-class population; ten years later, however, many of the whites had moved to the suburbs, and South Shore had become 70 per cent black – a remarkable demographic switch in so short a time. Most of the area's banks moved out with the whites and by 1973 only three were left to serve a population of 78,000. Two of these were badly run banks on South Shore's periphery which were later closed by the government regulator. The third, the South Shore Bank, had increased its capitalization in order to gain official permission to open a branch in central Chicago, and, had the permit been granted, it would almost certainly have allowed its South Shore branch to run down. It had already switched its lending activities elsewhere: of the $33 million it had taken from South Shore in deposits only $120,000 had been returned on loan to customers living in the area, which it feared would become a slum.

Essentially, Chicago's banks had made a self-fulfilling prophecy: because they expected South Shore to decline, they refused to lend in the area, thus making it certain that the predicted decline would occur. That it did not was because a miracle happened. South Shore Bank was bought by a company set up by a young team of idealistic bankers (a phrase that sounds like a contradiction in terms) who had worked together at another Chicago bank, the Hyde Park Bank and Trust. They were led by 36-year-old Ronald Grzywinski, a former president of two banks, including the Hyde Park. 'Under pressure from Adlai Stevenson, a former Democratic presidential candidate, the Illinois state treasurer had made a $1 million time deposit in the Hyde Park Bank, on condition that it was used to make loans to minorities,' Grzywinski says. 'I was president and part-owner of the bank at the time, and the demand for these loans was very high. So, in February 1968 the Hyde Park board approved the establishment of a permanent division to handle this type of business.' Milton Davis, Mary Houghton and James Fletcher, all of whom later moved to South Shore, were recruited to work in the division. In 1969, Grzywinski left Hyde Park to become a fellow at the Adlai Stevenson Institute for International Affairs, and then in 1971 he began to work full-time on plans that eventually led to the takeover of South Shore in August 1973.

'The first thing that we did was to close the directors' dining-room, so that every employee had lunch in the same place. Then we called all the loan officers together and told them that although we thought that they were very good at their jobs, they must not turn down loan applications from the South Shore area without the express consent of Mary Houghton or myself. The bank was profitable but its previous management just had not understood the changes taking place in the area. For example, the bank closed early each afternoon, preventing working people using it. We went round to all the voluntary organizations in the district such as the PTAs [parent-teacher associations] in order to learn from them.'

The immediate effect of the takeover as far as customers were concerned was that mortgages for the purchase of good-quality single-family houses became available for the first time in several years. Previously every financial institution in the city had 'red-lined' (excluded) South Shore and refused to finance mortgages there – a practice outlawed two years later under the Home Mortgage Disclosure Act.

'It was four years before we were able to lend for the purchase and rehabilitation of units in multi-occupancy housing blocks, a type of business which other banks had found to be very high-risk,' Grzywinski says. 'The delay was because we didn't have the capital to set up the bank subsidiaries which now take this task on.'

According to Malcolm Bush of the Woodstock Institute in Chicago, which studies community financial institutions, once the bank felt able to lend on apartment blocks it concentrated on several close together in a part of South Shore where their renovation would be most obvious, to try to change the inhabitants' perception of the area. By the end of 1993 the bank had financed the renovation of more than nine thousand flats, over a third of the total in the entire district. Indeed, Grzywinski attributes the bank's success with this type of lending to the scale on which it was done, saying that other banks have failed with it elsewhere because they have not lent enough to make a difference to public attitudes in the areas where their renovations have taken place.

The way South Shore typically operates today is that its subsidiary, City Lands Corporation, will initiate a large-scale housing rehabilitation, for which it can generally obtain government subsidies. This enables dozens of local property owners to carry out smaller-scale rehabilitations in the same area, knowing that each investment they make reinforces every other investment's viability. Grzywinski admits that other banks have criticized South Shore for the risk it is taking by concentrating all its lending in the same geographical area. 'We did sell some of our loan portfolio to Equitable and to Metropolitan Life [large life assurance companies], just to prove we could be liquid if we needed to be, so that's a non-issue now. Our proudest achievement is that other banks are now invest-ing in the area, demonstrating that the market has begun to work again.'

South Shore writes off only about a twentieth of its property loans annually as a result of sticking to areas it knows, helping its borrowers with advice, and steering them to properties to rehabilitate that suit their skills and financial resources. Leroy Jones, a plumber, and his wife, Josephine, say that they learned to renovate property successfully as a result of meeting other landlords at fortnightly breakfasts sponsored by the bank. Today they own five buildings, all mortgaged by South Shore, which keeps close tabs on them. Their first building was financed by another bank. 'You know, I don't think that they ever came by,' Mrs Jones says. 'But Mr Bringley [the South Shore vice-president responsible for their loans] is always saying, "I drove past your building. I see you put another tree up."'

Grzywinski says it was eight or nine years after the takeover before even the bank was sure that the techniques it was using would work pre-dictably. It returned to profit in 1983 and has not made a loss since. In 1992 its net profit was $2.2 million on assets of $229.1 million, of which $161 million was out on loan. Losses were 0.4 per cent, a figure many banks would envy. All told, it pumped $41 million into this area of Chicago during the year, most of it deposited by savers outside its service area attracted by the work the bank was doing. 'We've got depositors in every American state and in seventeen foreign countries,' Milton Davis told BBC radio's The Financial World Tonight in 1993.

Not surprisingly, this level of investment has not cured South Shore's social problems, although it has certainly alleviated them. 'South Shore was a middle-class community before the whites left and it is still middle-class,' Grrzywinski says. 'The demographics changed surprisingly little. Seventeen to twenty per cent of the population are below the poverty line, and 50 per cent can be regarded as high-income. The mass of working people would earn between $15,000 and $25,000. We have people on welfare, of course, and a lot of single female heads of households. Crime has gotten worse recently, largely because we've too few entry-level jobs for single young men ... Crack cocaine and the ridiculous attitude we have in this country to guns don't help.' Milton Davis told the BBC: 'The miss-ing building block is jobs. We need help on this one.'

Four years after South Shore was taken over, Congress passed the Community Reinvestment Act, which encourages banks to reinvest deposits received from their service areas by ranking their performance in this direction. Any bank with a below-average record of reinvestment finds it difficult to get permission from the regulators to merge with another bank or to move its premises. As a result, banks are increasingly trying to move in South Shore's direction and are reopening in places they deserted twenty-five years before. 'I heard a banker from Milwaukee com-plaining last week that he'd offered loans in a low-income area but very few borrowers had taken them up,' Grzywinski told me. 'My attitude is that he just wasn't trying hard enough. You can't start doing our sort of business by printing a brochure and taking TV time. It's more complicated than that.' Malcolm Bush comments: 'South Shore have found that they need to be very close to their customers and to know their area street by street.'

At present there are only three other 'community development' banks like South Shore in the United States, although President Clinton called it 'the most important bank in America' during his 1992 election campaign and said he wanted to see a hundred more like it set up. This was not just campaign rhetoric: during Clinton's term as governor of Arkansas, South Shore set up the Southern Development Bancorporation at his request. Grzywinski is chairman of the board. Southern works in the small towns in the south of the state, where it sees its role as 'to channel financial and informational services to local entrepreneurs so that residents can build thriving, diversified economies independent of large, distant corporations'. The two other development banks are the Community Capital Bank in New York and the Self-Help Credit Union in North Carolina.

'The most important characteristic these institutions share is a mission to work towards the economic development of a community and its residents,' says Kate Tholin, Malcolm Bush's colleague at the Woodstock Institute. 'They target a specific geographical area, use credit as a tool for revitalization and empowerment, provide technical assistance and education on financial matters, and work in partnership with other community organizations and professional lenders.'

Could the South Shore model be used outside the United States? Many people are dubious, pointing out that it took twenty years for South Shore to establish its credibility and that about £10 million would be needed in share capital before any new bank could operate on a similar scale. Any smaller level of lending in a target area might be inadequate to change perceptions about it, and thus fail to get others to invest as well.

Grzywinski prefers not to talk about why South Shore was America's only community development bank for over fifteen years and why he and his colleagues were the only bankers to respond so wholeheartedly to a pressing social need. 'Answering questions about why we did it could take a lifetime. For myself, I think you could say that it was a combination of boredom – I'd had two very senior jobs in banking at a very young age and earned a lot of money very quickly – and my feeling that I needed to make myself the opportunity to apply my talents to something I really cared about. I wanted a challenge in a job I knew I could do well.'

Joan Shapiro, Senior Vice-President, South Shore Bank, 71st and Jeffery Boulevard, Chicago, Illinois 60649; tel. +1 312 2881000; fax +1 312 7535699.

Malcolm Bush, President, Woodstock Institute, 407 South Dearborn (suite 550), Chicago, Illinois 60605; tel. +1 312 4278070; e-mail woodstck@wwa.com.

months' notice – Community Capital received deposits of £140,000 in its first four months. Three-quarters of the depositors waived their interest payments to allow them to be used to build up a guarantee fund to cover any loan losses that are incurred, thus increasing the safety, if not the return, of their investments.

In Ireland no similar provident society has been established in recent years, and an official at the office of the Registrar of Friendly Societies described them to me as 'a dying breed', their historical role in mobilizing workers' savings taken over by the highly successful credit unions. However, Malcolm Lynch is confident that the legal work involved in forming one would present no difficulties, since the Irish law is still based on the original British Act. He estimates that fees, including stamp duty, would be between £1500 and £2000.

Workable legal structures therefore exist – three in Ireland, two in Britain – that community groups could use for setting up their own enterprise loan funds. These are the limited company and the provident society models in both countries and the credit union format in Ireland (where Britain's stifling £5000 loan limit does not apply). All the organizations using these structures are, however, very small and lending very little. Even the best-known, Mercury, had more limited resources before its merger than any of Ireland's twenty biggest credit unions. Moreover, apart from TILT and the emerging Aston Reinvestment Trust, all have a national rather than a local focus. And, except for Mercury, their bad-debt record is generally poor. Could these problems arise because they are using the wrong approach?

And what about interest rates? Although some Mercury and Community Capital savers have shown themselves willing to accept little or no interest from organizations whose aims they support, community businesses seem unlikely to be able to get enough low-interest funds through local organizations modelled on the lines of those we have discussed to enable them to compete with multinational corporations. And even if they could, what would be a reasonable interest rate to demand from a local business? Should interest be demanded at all?

Economists justify charging interest by arguing that people need to be rewarded if they are not to spend all their money the moment they receive it and agree to allow others to use it temporarily instead. Their argument is flawed, as most people would still save if they were paid no interest at all because everyone faces financial uncertainty and likes to have something put by for a rainy day. Moreover, everyone grows old and wants to have savings to draw on when they retire. What people need to be paid for is not saving itself but allowing others to use their savings instead of hiding them in their mattresses. After all, there is a real risk if they lend their money that it will not be paid back. In addition, if a borrower benefits financially from investing someone else's funds, it seems right that part of the benefit should be shared with the saver who made it possible.

Then there is the question of inflation. While people still wish to save when inflation is rapid – indeed there is evidence that they save a higher proportion of their incomes in order to maintain the real value of their security cushions – they will want to put as much of their savings as practical into assets, such as land or antiques, that can be expected to retain their value in relation to other goods and services and can be converted back to cash by being sold later on. If people are to agree to keep their wealth in money in order that others might use it, they therefore need to be compensated by the borrowers for any loss of purchasing power.

In summary, then, a fair interest rate does three things: it rewards the lender for the risk he or she runs when making the loan; it compensates for any loss in the purchasing power of money; and it shares between borrower and lender the benefits that flow from the way the money is used. In practice, of course, the first and third reasons can be rolled into one; the promise of a share in the potential benefits should cover the risk inescapably involved in making a loan.

Despite these justifications, the charging of interest was condemned by the Catholic Church until the 1830s, and Islam still bans it today. Indeed many thoughtful people of all faiths and of none continue to have serious reservations.* One root of their unease runs back to the time when gold was used as currency. Since gold did not increase itself, and very little was being mined, where, people asked, was the extra bullion to come from to pay the interest when both principal and interest had to be handed over at the end of the year? Obviously the borrower could only obtain more gold if someone else had less, so lending money at interest meant that either the borrower impoverished himself when he paid over the extra or he impover-

---

* Keynes, for example, in his *General Theory* set out fifteen arguments against charging interest, the chief of them being that 'the average rate of interest which will allow a reasonable average level of unemployment is one so unacceptable to wealth-owners that it cannot be readily established' (pp. 308-9). Such a low interest rate 'would mean the euthanasia of the rentier, and, consequently, the euthanasia of the cumulative oppressive power of the capitalist to exploit the scarcity-value of capital'. He adds: 'Interest today rewards no genuine sacrifice ... There are no intrinsic reasons for the scarcity of capital' (p. 376).

ished someone else. And as neither outcome was socially desirable, usury (as all forms of moneylending were called, no matter how low the interest rate) stood morally condemned.

Even though we now use paper currencies, this source-of-interest problem has not gone away. As we saw in the discussion of the Guernsey Experiment in the previous chapter, almost all money in circulation is issued on loan. This means that money to cover interest payments can only be obtained by borrowers if other borrowers have borrowed sufficiently more. Moreover, the necessity to pay interest on these additional borrowings means that the economy needs to expand if the proportion of world income that is paid over in interest to the lenders is not to increase. This in turn explains why the capitalist system is unsustainable: it depends on borrowing money at interest that can only be paid without impoverishing the borrowers if the economy continues to grow. If growth stops, the borrowers find themselves having to service loans that have not generated any return. Their profits fall and they therefore cut back on their borrowing and investing the following year, throwing out of work many of those who would have built the factories, shopping centres and office blocks they would otherwise have ordered. This cuts demand, and, unless governments take up the slack by borrowing themselves in order to spend more to compensate, the economy sinks into a depression.

In short, the borrowers' need to pay interest means that governments have no choice but to allow growth to continue, despite the damage that the changes involved may well do to the natural environment, to communities, and to the social order. Consequently, whether we are concerned with countries or communities, unless we can develop an economic system that avoids interest we cannot hope to achieve a sustainable way of life.

Muslim economists have been trying to develop such a system. They reject the payment of interest because of what they see as the basic injustice of transactions in which the borrower has to return more than he or she received. 'An equitable transaction is equal for equal. Usury is something for nothing,' wrote Fazlun Khalid and Umar Ibrahim Vadillo, members of the progressive Murabitun movement of European Muslims, in a crystal-clear essay, 'Trade and commerce in Islam'.[7] 'The profit of usury is like a parasite in the market – it sucks wealth without giving anything in return. The parasite forces the market to increase artificially in size, like a diseased body, just so it can feed. But as the market grows, the parasite also grows. Usury produces an imbalance in natural trading, and this has now penetrated everything.' They explain that Islam forbids the taking of a guaranteed fixed return on an investment regardless of the way the investment turns out. 'A profit from money can only be justified if it is invested in a business and that business produces a profit. Money by itself cannot produce a profit. Islamic law requires that the investor shares both in the success and the failure of a venture [according to a] mutually agreed contract.'

The only way that devout Muslims can therefore hope to make a profit by letting someone else use their savings is by taking what is in effect a share stake in the borrower's venture, recovering their money when it is completed, or by selling their shares in it later on. Anyone wanting to avoid the risks inherent in putting all their savings in one project would have to join with other investors and set up a fund to take shares in a number of businesses, a route that would also make it easier for them to get their money out. Umar Chapra, an economic adviser to the Saudi Arabian Monetary Agency, proposes exactly this approach in *Towards a Just Monetary System*,[8] which is essential reading for anyone interested in how a zero-interest financial system might be built. However, as Chapra points out, Islamic law imposes two requirements on such funds. One is that all those who have invested in a venture have to have equal decision-making powers, regardless of the amount they have invested, because one party would otherwise have an advantage and the others would cease to be effective owners. Voting at shareholders' meetings must therefore be on the basis of one shareholder one vote, exactly as with a co-operative society. The other stipulation is that the results of the venture be shared among the co-owners in proportion to their investments, which need not be in cash or property: time, skill and effort can count as investments as well.

Chapra, who holds a PhD from an American university and taught economics in the United States, devotes a chapter of his book to countering conventional arguments that an interest-free system would lead to a misallocation of resources or simply would not work. On the contrary, he argues, it would be more efficient, since a prospective profit-sharing investor would undertake a much more careful investigation of a potential project than conventional, interest-oriented lenders who shift the entire risk to the entrepreneur by demanding property deeds or other types of security for their loan, thus assuring themselves of a predetermined rate of return irrespective of the success of the borrower's business. Moreover, Chapra says, the use of interest rates to allocate capital between competing borrowers is itself inefficient:

The rate of interest tends to be a 'perverted' price and reflects price discrimination in favour of the rich – the more 'credit-worthy' a borrower is supposed to be, the lower the rate of interest he pays and vice versa. The result is that 'big' business is able to get funds at a lower price because of its 'higher' credit rating. Thus those who are most able to bear the burden because of their bigness or claimed 'higher' productivity bear the least burden. In contrast, medium and small businesses, which may sometimes be more productive in terms of contribution to the national product per unit of financing used and at least equally 'credit-worthy' in terms of honesty and integrity, may be able to secure relatively much smaller amounts at substantially higher rates of interest. Hence many potentially high-yielding investments are never made because of lack of access to funds which flow instead into less productive but 'secure' hands.

Therefore, the rate of interest reflects, not the 'objective' criterion of the productivity of the business but the 'biased' criterion of 'credit rating'. This is one reason why in the capitalist system, big business has grown bigger beyond the point dictated by economies of scale, thus contributing to monopoly power, while small and medium businesses have often been throttled by being deprived of credit. This is particularly so when interest rates rise and create a liquidity crunch by reducing the internal cash flows. Small businesses are rarely given a respite by the lending banks. Loans to them are called in at the slightest sign of trouble, thus causing widespread bankruptcies. However, when big businesses are in trouble, there is rescheduling accompanied by additional lines of credit. Does this indicate an optimum allocation of resources or an efficient banking system?

Instead, if credit is made available on the basis of profitability, then not only will the banks be more careful and rational in evaluating projects but also small, medium and big business would stand on an equal footing. The higher the rate of profit, the greater will be the ability to secure funds. Big business, if it is really more profitable, should pay a higher and not smaller rate of return to the lending institutions. The Islamic system could reflect an innate ability to favour entrepreneurs with talent, drive and innovation but who, as Ingo Karsten has put it [in an IMF staff paper, 'Islam and Financial Intermediation', in 1982], 'have not yet established their credit-worthiness'. Thus resources would not only be more *effectively utilized* but also *equitably distributed*.

Chapra maintains that a zero-interest system would also lead to greater economic stability, since, as all companies would be debt-free, they would not have to make interest payments during economic downturns. This would avoid the human and material waste that occurs whenever businesses close and are sold up at the bottom of the trade cycle, only for the lost capacity to be replaced when prosperity returns. Chapra believes that the recent growth of corporate borrowing in the United States is an ominous development because it raises firms' break-even points and makes them more vulnerable to cyclical downturns by increasing their fixed costs; and he quotes Milton Friedman's reply to the question 'What accounts for the unprecedentedly erratic behaviour of the US economy?' – 'The answer that leaps to mind is the correspondingly erratic behaviour of interest rates.'

Even the *Economist* likes Islam's theoretical framework for a zero-interest economy. 'It gives the provider of money a strong incentive to be sure he is doing something sensible with it. What a pity the West's banks did not have that incentive in so many of their lending decisions in the 1970s and 1980s. It also emphasizes the sharing of responsibility, by all users of money. That helps to make the free-market system more open: you might say more democratic.'[9]

But have Muslims established an interest-free economy anywhere or, at the very least, opened a successful zero-interest investment fund in an industrialized country that could be taken as a model? The answer to both questions is, unfortunately, no, although a Dr al-Naggar appears to have established a successful rural profit-and-loss-sharing savings bank in Egypt in the 1960s. This failed, however, when it was taken over by the state under President Nasser and radically remodelled so that it ran on overambitious top-down lines. 'The sad reality is that … there is not a single Muslim country which is running its financial institutions without resorting to interest. The fact is that no one knows how to do it and when political pressure mounts, they can only resort to some kind of subterfuge,' writes Shaikh Mahmud Ahmad in *Towards Interest-Free Banking.*[10]

Why is this? Fazlun Khalid blames western-educated Muslim economists like Chapra for advising Muslim countries to 'set up central banks and issue worthless paper money … They wield enormous influence on the rulers of Muslim states who are committed to the west-engineered development model.' Chapra is particularly suspect because he wrote in 1992 that Muslim governments were 'juristically permitted' to charge interest in particularly difficult circumstances, and also perhaps because he advises the Saudi royal family, which permits Western banks to operate extensively in its country.

Khalid thinks there is not a single truly Islamic bank operating anywhere at present and says that those banks that claim to be Islamic either charge interest or do things that are also condemned as usury by Islam, such as creating money by issuing loans greatly in excess of the amount of savings they hold on deposit, just as conventional banks do elsewhere in the world. The use of paper money, cheques and credit cards also amounts to usury because it leads to inflation.

Accordingly, the Murabitun movement has minted gold coins in Scotland, Spain and Germany and is using them to enable its members and others to trade throughout Europe without needing cheques, credit cards, or paper money. 'Special markets are being organized in which there are three zones: a white zone, in which paper currency can be used, a grey zone, for either gold or paper currency, and a green zone, restricted to gold and barter. We've got to start from where people are, but we obviously want them to move out of the black zone as time goes on,' Khalid told me in 1995. 'The prototype of these markets was held in Birmingham in 1992, and they have since been held in Granada, Amsterdam, and Zürich. Umar Vadillo, who lives in Scotland, is the driving force behind them.'[11]

Despite Islam's failure to provide a suitable model, interest-free community banks do exist and are functioning successfully in the Nordic world. In Denmark in fact they are offering the conventional banks such strong competition that improper means may have been used to get one of the most expansionary of them closed down, as the story in the next panel reveals.

But the best example of what a community bank can achieve and how the interest rate problem can be handled is provided by the Lankide Aurrezkia (Working People's Bank) which operates largely in the Basque country in Spain. It is impossible to describe how this bank came to be and how it operates without also telling the story of the Mondragon co-operatives, which now employ 21,000 people in the same area and in whose expansion the bank played a crucial part.

The bank and the co-operatives owe their existence to a local priest, José María Arizmendiarrieta, who was so unimpressive when in 1941, aged twenty-six, he was appointed to work among young people in Mondragon, a steel town of some 8500 inhabitants, that some of his parishioners wished the bishop would reassign him. 'He spoke in a monotone with intricate and repetitive phraseology diffi-cult to understand. He hardly even [read] with grace,' someone who became a close colleague wrote forty-five years later.[12]

One of Father Arizmendiarrieta's duties was to teach classes in reli-gious and human values at a school run by the town's steelworks for its apprentices. This was the only secondary school of any type in Mondragon, and demand for places far exceeded the supply. Father Arizmendiarrieta asked the steel company to expand the school, offering to help raise the extra cost. The company refused, so the priest decided to open a technical school of his own. He had boxes placed on street corners in which people could post offers of labour or cash; when they were opened it was found that a quarter of the town's households had offered concrete support.

The school opened in December 1943 with twenty pupils and added a higher class each year; by 1952 there were 170 students, and eleven members of the first intake had just completed an external engineering degree from the University of Zaragoza. These – the first

Mondragon workers' children ever to graduate – had been meeting Father Arizmendiarrieta each week, and it was through them that he developed his plans. However, he also held hundreds of meetings with other groups; in 1956 it was estimated that since he had come to the parish, in addition to his teaching he had conducted a study session on average every 2.7 days and over two thousand small group discussions.

Five of his eleven disciples went to work with the steel company. When the company decided to increase its capital by issuing more shares, they asked that the workers be allowed to subscribe for them. The company refused, convincing the five that it was impossible to democratize this particular capitalist enterprise from within. Accordingly they decided to start their own company and set about raising money from friends. Eventually they raised eleven million pesetas from a hundred people on nothing but the strength of their personal promises. This was equivalent at the time to $362,000 – a huge sum from a working-class community – and in 1955 it was used to buy a bankrupt factory making paraffin stoves in Gazteiz (Vitoria). The plant was moved to Mondragon and opened in 1956 with twenty-four employees under the name Ulgor (a composite of the initials of the five men) to make copies of a British-made Aladdin stove the group had purchased in France and stripped down; only some time later did Ulgor regularize its position by buying the Spanish rights.

Demand for stoves was strong, and Ulgor soon began designing its own, buying an existing foundry in the town so as to be able to make all the parts. A few months later the firm added a range of electrical equipment to its product line and then, after opening a second factory, bottled-gas cooking stoves under the brand name Fagor. By the end of 1958, Ulgor had 149 worker-co-operators and its success had inspired several other co-ops to set up in Mondragon and elsewhere in the region.

At this point Father Arizmendiarrieta suggested that his ex-students establish a bank so as to be able to tap local savings to finance the co-ops' expansion. 'Our initial reaction was one of annoyance, and we literally sent him packing,' one of Ulgor's founders said later. 'We told him, "Yesterday we were craftsmen, foremen, and engineers. Today we are learning how to be managers and executives. Tomorrow you want us to become bankers. That is impossible."' Undaunted, the priest drew up the bank's constitution and by-laws, concocted the minutes of a fictitious founding meeting, and forged two of his disciples' signatures, and – lo and behold – the Lankide Aurrezkia bank was formed as a co-op to be run by representatives of its own staff and that of its member-co-ops. It was recognized by the Spanish government in July 1959 and opened two branches, one in Mondragon, the other in Elorrio (then in a different province), just so that it could continue to operate should one province decide to revoke its licence and close it down. Persuaded of its potential importance, four of Ulgor's founders joined its board, one as president, another as chief executive. The fifth had already left Ulgor to found his own company.

In many ways Lankide Aurrezkia was, and is, the equivalent of an industrial holding company because each co-op signed a contract of association with it that set out in some detail how the co-op would operate. For example, wages paid by member-co-ops were tied to those in the bank by a clause that stipulated that their minimum rate of pay be no more than 10 per cent above or below the minimum paid by the bank to its staff and that their top rate not be more than three times their minimum. Each co-op also had to supply financial data to the bank every month and full accounts and details of future plans every year and was subject to a detailed assessment and audit by the bank every four years.

Naturally, all a member co-op's funds had to be banked with the Lankide Aurrezkia, and the contract of association also set the maximum and minimum amounts that anyone joining that co-op would have to provide as his or her share of its capital: not less than 80 per cent or more than 120 per cent of the bank's own joining fee, which at the time was equivalent to roughly a year's wages for anyone on its minimum rate. (New entrants could borrow the required sum free of interest and have deductions made from their wages until the amount was repaid; as the minimum Mondragon wage was usually above the equivalent in commercial companies, this entailed little hardship. However, a firm principle of the co-ops was always that worker-co-operators must risk their own capital.)

Finally, the contract of association set out how the profits of the co-ops were to be divided. Ten per cent had to go to charity, as required by Spanish law, a minimum of 20 per cent had to be retained by the co-op itself, and the balance was to be allocated to the co-op's workers and lodged in individual accounts, to be withdrawn in full only when the worker retired; anyone leaving prematurely or being sacked could lose up to 30 per cent. In the first year in which this system operated, 1960, workers were allowed to take 10 per cent of their co-op's profit in cash; between 1962 and 1965 this fraction rose to 30 per cent, equivalent to more than a month's wages. However, since then these cash payments have been abolished, and the only top-up to their wages the workers now receive is interest, up to a maximum of 6 per cent, on whatever funds they have invested with their co-op. As David Morris says in the best recent report on the way Mondragon operates, 'this disbursement formula means that the enterprise effectively controls 90 per cent of its net surplus. The individual capital account might be considered a long term, low interest loan to an enterprise that might not have the collateral to be able to borrow money outside.'[13]

What did the co-ops get in return for signing such a restrictive contract with the bank? Two massive advantages. One was and is low-cost funds. According to Morris, about half the capital of the member-co-ops is made up of loans from Lankide Aurrezkia, for which they pay interest at rates that are sometimes as much as 5 per cent lower than the prevailing market rate. This is possible because the top salaries in the bank were, at least until recently, significantly lower than those paid by banks outside and because the bank has automatic access to the surpluses of its member-co-ops. The bank is effectively the only source of capital open to the co-ops apart from the savings of their own members.

The other advantage the co-ops get from their association is first-rate advice and guidance on whatever they wish to do from the bank's consultancy division. This covers marketing, exporting, production techniques, industrial buildings, personnel, legal affairs, and audit and management control systems. In extreme circumstances, however, the bank does not limit itself to merely giving advice, and in the depressed period in the early 1980s when the Mondragon co-ops collectively made a loss for three years running, it intervened extensively, sacking managers, changing product lines, trimming wage levels, merging member-co-ops or transferring workers between them, and, when it was finally satisfied, making concessionary loans. In 1983 alone, thirty-four out of the 100 co-ops underwent this sort of treatment, which was highly successful – indeed in its entire history only three Mondragon co-ops have ever closed, two in special circumstances. Conventional firms in the Basque country have not survived so well; between 1975 and 1983 the region lost a fifth of its manufacturing jobs.

The new bank was successful in attracting private savings from the start, and by 1966 it was operating 21,653 accounts. 'Bankbook or suitcase' was Father Arizmendiarrieta's slogan – save or emigrate. By 1987 the bank had 600,000 depositors and $3 billion in assets. In its early days, however, most of its funds came from the co-ops, particu-

[main text continues p.168]

163

RURAL BANK OFFERS INTEREST-FREE LOANS

'We started our bank here in this room in January 1975 and took the first deposits across this table,' Inger Marie Ebbesen told me in the living-room of her dormer-bungalow in Grølsted, a small Danish village half-way between Århus and Viborg. Outside on three sides of the yard are the brick outbuildings where her husband, Jørgen, raises pigs. 'Ellen Clausen, my sister-in-law, and our two husbands were the first directors, and we started with just three or four accounts.'

Mrs Ebbesen had had no experience of running a bank when they began. 'But I had worked in the accounts department of a bacon factory, and that's about the best commercial training you can get in Denmark,' she says. Another thing that helped was a wave of anger some of her neighbours felt when the JAK Co-operative Bank, where some had kept accounts since the 1930s and which charged no interest on certain cate-gories of its loans, was taken over in 1972 by a commercial bank, Bikuben, after running into liquidity problems. 'The introduction of pay-as-you-earn income tax in 1969 had affected deposits from the JAK bank's salaried customers, and it lost some big municipal accounts as a result of a local government reorganization,' she explains.

The merged bank had been part of the wider JAK movement ('Jord, Arbejde, Kapital' – land, labour, capital), whose members were not pre-pared to see the no-interest principle it had stood for being forgotten. Many of them, like Ebbesen's team at Grølsted, helped set up at least twenty local co-operative savings banks – fælleskasser – to replace it, mostly in rural areas. All these micro-banks were legally barred from accepting deposits or making loans to people who did not live in the parish in which they were situated or the parishes immediately adjoining them. All were – and are – independent, controlled by their own boards of directors, who set the terms on which loans are made.

'The JAK movement was set up in 1931 by the great Danish thinker Kristian Engelbrecht Kristiansen, who had seen as a child the difficulties his parents had faced in paying interest after they had been forced to farm very poor, heather-covered heathland after moving out of Holstein during the German takeover. He believed that real capital was created when barren land was made fertile, just as his parents had done, and that money was merely a means of exchange and a standard of value that in itself produced no return. The charging of interest therefore led to the concentration of wealth, the increase of indebtedness, and the growth of unemployment. One of JAK's first projects was to issue its own currency, backed by the capital represented by its members' land, in order to reduce indebtedness. This circulated widely in this part of Denmark until the government prohibited it in 1932,' Ebbesen explains.

All the new fælleskasser had similar rules: loans could only be made to members, and members had to be shareholders. Each share at Grølsted cost 1000 kroner (approximately £100), paid no interest, and could not be cashed in, although it could be sold to other members. These shares represented the capital that was at risk if the bank ever failed, and their total amount determined how much the bank could lend, since the law

The official opening of Tallow Credit Union office in October 1976, Sheila Ryan is third on the left.

prohibited it from increasing its total loan book to more than twelve times its share capital. No matter how many shares they held, each member had only one vote, but members who risked their capital in this way could borrow one-and-a-half times the face value of their shares for up to twenty years, depending on the additional security they provided, and could top up these loans whenever half of them had been repaid, subject only to a setting-up fee and 4 per cent a year service charge to cover the cost of administration.

Alternatively, members operating current accounts at the Grølsted bank could get an interest-free 'turnover loan' on the basis of their average balance, subject to the setting-up fee and an administrative fee of 1 per cent a quarter. Therefore if one had maintained an account with an average balance of 10,000 kroner for a year one could borrow 10,000 kroner to be repaid by quarterly instalments over two years, or 20,000 kroner if one could pay off the loan in a year.[14] One-year time deposits entitled members to consideration for longer-term loans, such as mortgages, for up to thirty years, with a service charge of only 2 per cent a year, but the board naturally varied the number of these they approved according to the level of available funds. They also demanded suitable security.

Essentially, then, the Grølsted bank either lent you as much of someone else's money for as long as you had placed a similar sum in your current account for it to lend to other members or, with its time deposits, operated a queuing system rather like that once used by those Irish and British building societies that required members to build up a substantial sum over the years before they could even be considered for a house loan. It would also lend you back the money you had put at risk in buying your shares, provided you put up additional security.

As a result of a change in the law the bank was able to convert itself in the late 1980s into an andelskasse – a full-service bank offering a cheque-book account exactly like the commercial banks. It boomed and had to convert a detached house about a hundred metres from the Ebbesens' farm into offices so that it could cope. 'We were opening an average of five new accounts a day and seemed to be taking on a new member of staff every two months,' Ebbesen says. 'Both costs and earnings grew rapidly. High costs can kill a business such as ours; operating accounts is expensive.' To help spread these costs the bank began accepting interest-bearing deposits, particularly pension funds, and lending them out at standard bank interest rates. And, since it was now legally permitted to do so, it began advertising membership to people living outside its area. Most of these new shareholders either had family links with the Grølsted district or lived in places where there was no local JAK bank. The bank became one of the largest in the movement, and Ebbesen was elected president of the JAK National Association in its diamond jubilee year, 1991.

Naturally the growth of the bank and the prominence of its manager attracted the attention both of its conventional competitors and of the regulatory authorities. In 1990 its auditor recommended that someone with conventional banking experience be brought in to run the business, and as a result Jens Jensen joined in May 1991, succeeding Ebbesen at the end of that year. 'We had had big losses in 1986 and 1987, because a builder to whom we had lent money could not sell his houses. A loan to a camping-goods warehouse also went bad. However, our reserves were adequate to cover the situation,' she says. 'Handing over the management suited me, because I wanted more time to involve myself in promoting the movement generally.'

But in September 1992, only nine months after Jensen had taken over, the bank was closed by government order. 'We were expanding rapidly, and this meant that we were becoming a substantial threat to the established financial system. This, and the jealousy of some of the other JAK banks, is the reason we were closed,' Ebbesen says quietly. 'The government inspectors claimed that more people were entitled to no-interest loans than our share capital allowed us to provide as a result of the losses and said that we needed to sell more shares to make things up. This was impossible, because the shares at the time were trading at less than their nominal value. So, at a meeting that only the manager attended, the bank was given an ultimatum: start charging interest on all new loans in order to rebuild the capital base.'

An extraordinary general meeting of the nine hundred shareholders was called to discuss this demand, and Ebbesen is adamant that something could have been worked out, given the level of goodwill and support that most depositors felt for their organization. Capital injections from other banks in the JAK system were also a possibility. But the meeting was never held: the bank was closed down the day beforehand. Why? 'That's what I'd like to know! There were no discrepancies, and everyone will get 100 per cent of their money back,' she told me as we peered through the windows of the empty offices nine months afterwards. 'I've been made to feel like a criminal, and they've been going through the books for technical infringements of the rules. It's been very difficult, because most of my neighbours were depositors. Do you know, one inspector actually said that they could not permit a bank to operate in a ploughed field,' she says, pointing at the rich brown farmland that runs almost up to the office door.

She agrees that if the bank had refrained from paying interest to depositors and from making conventional interest-bearing loans and had thus stayed small, it would not have been closed down. However, she has no regrets about trying to expand when she did. 'The circumstances were right: salaries in Denmark had gone up and inflation had stayed low, so people could save a lot. You've got to take these chances when they come. After all, the bank had been trading for fifteen years and the movement for sixty. If I'd have continued as manager everything would have been all right. Our deposits would have increased to 100 million kroner and then grown more slowly.'

When I spoke to her last, in May 1996, Ebbesen was confident that she would be allowed to re-open the bank before the end of the year. 'It's quite clear we should never have been closed, because enough loans have been repaid by borrowers to allow the depositors to get all their money back,' she said. She was also determined to spread the JAK idea throughout the European Union: 'Since 1988, any bank setting up anywhere in the EU has been required to have 5 million ECUs capital behind it. This means that it is now impossible to start a bank the way we did. However, a bank that is registered in one EU country is permitted to trade in them all, so my idea is to run training courses here on the farm so that people can set up banks in their own countries which are part of the JAK system. I've already started working with groups in Belgium and Holland.'

Inger Marie Ebbesen, Thorsovej 92, Grølsted, 8882 Fårvang, Denmark; tel. +45 86871095.

167

larly Ulgor, and 75 per cent of its loans went back to other co-ops in the group to fund their expansion. Indeed the bank's rules initially prevented it lending money except to its member-co-ops.

The way in which the bank operates can best be shown by describing the role it plays in the establishment of a new co-op. If a group approaches the bank with an idea of its own or one selected from a list of possible projects the bank maintains, it will pay the salary of the member of the group most likely to become factory manager to work on a feasibility study in conjunction with members of the bank staff, including a 'godfather' whose responsibility it is to see the project through its early days. If the study shows that the project is promising, the bank will lend 60 per cent of the required capital. Half the rest is covered by a low-cost (3 per cent) long-term (ten-year) loan from the Spanish government, and the final 20 per cent has to be found by the members of the group themselves. Seventy per cent of any losses the project makes in its first two years are converted into an additional loan by the bank, to be repaid over the following seven years. The godfather gets a seat on the new co-op's board.

The big advantage of this approach for the bank is that each feasibility study builds up its expertise and provides information and ideas that may be useful for future studies. The advantage for the new co-operators is that they get help and guidance from a team that has handled previous start-ups and ought therefore to be able to save them making costly mistakes. Indeed one estimate suggests that the value of the services provided by the bank to a new co-op is roughly equivalent to the amount of capital it lends.

This way of doing things is certainly a far cry from that in Ireland and Britain, where most small business start-ups are attempted by people who have never opened or run their own business before. In fact some people with start-up experience are actively discriminated against because if their start-up failed they are likely to be refused a loan on the grounds of their 'bad record'. It is therefore scarcely surprising that, according to Barclays Bank figures, only 40 per cent of start-ups are still trading after their first three years.

As the Mondragon bank is actively involved in the management of its co-ops and shares risks with the people working in them, and since the interest rates it charges co-ops have, at least in the past, been largely independent of those on the Madrid money market and capable of adjustment, they are better seen as a combination of payment for services rendered and a share in the co-ops' profits than as pure interest as normally understood. Interest rates represent a financial

[main text continues p.170]

GOING DUTCH KEEPS INSURANCE PAYMENTS LOCAL

The payment of household and motor insurance premiums causes a serious and growing loss of national currency to almost every British and Irish community, but there is a way by which this can be reduced. Henk van Arkel, the director of the Dutch non-governmental organization Aktie Strohalm, lives in Soest, a village within commuting distance of Utrecht, in a thatched house he bought from a farmer who had built himself a spanking new residence across the road. Insuring a thatched building can be as difficult and expensive in the Netherlands as anywhere else, so van Arkel joined the local insurance co-operative, Statuten Soester Onderlinge Brandverzekering UA, which had insured the house for the farmer. 'There are five hundred of these co-ops throughout Holland', he explains. 'The way they work is that they collect premiums from their members based on the value of their properties and cover a proportion of the risk themselves. That keeps quite a lot of the money in the community. The rest of the risk they cover by sharing it with other local co-ops by re-insuring with a mutual insurance company a lot of them own, SOBH.'

Van Arkel thinks that the system works well because with only 425 members in the Soest co-op, one's fellow-members would soon know if anyone made a false or inflated claim, and be very unhappy about it. 'It would be reflected immediately in the rates of premium we all had to pay,' he says. 'The cost of insurance through these co-ops varies quite a lot because of their claims experience but it is normally cheaper than with the commercial companies.'

The co-op, which was founded by farmers in 1885, naturally has to maintain reserves to cover it if claims are greater than its share of the annual premium income. 'We've got 400,000 guilders [£175,000] set aside,' he says. 'I don't know how big reserves the co-op kept before 1944. It didn't take out re-insurance until then.'

SOBH, Meerndijk 11, 3454 HM de Meern, Netherlands.

Henk van Arkel estimates commercial insurers would charge him £500 a year for fire and storm damage cover on this old-style thatched farmhouse. Instead he pays £130 to a local co-operative insurance society.

performance target for a Mondragon co-op, not an absolute obligation to pay, as there is no question of the bank forcing it into liquidation if it is unable to cover them. Instead the ailing co-op is likely to be reorganized and, if necessary, refinanced, thus sharing the financial pain between the bank and the worker-co-operators.

The Mondragon system is therefore reasonably (if messily) close to the risk-sharing, profit-sharing, no-interest ideal, although, as the concept of interest is still omnipresent, a Muslim might not be happy with it. The individual co-ops are in effect interest-free too, as the rate of interest they pay to their worker-members for the use of the capital they provide on joining and contribute from their share of the profits is flexible and depends on the co-op's performance in a particular year: it is thus more akin to a dividend. The only guarantee the co-op gives to its members about their capital is that its value will be increased each year in line with the cost of living; and as this is a group of people giving a guarantee to themselves, they will have to find the resources themselves, perhaps by taking lower wages, if their co-op makes inadequate profits for the promise to be kept.

An equally valuable feature of the Mondragon system is that as its investors are also its workers and members of the local community, they are not solely interested in the financial return they get on their capital but in the whole range of social and economic benefits a project generates. This has enabled it to avoid the acute conflict between the interests of investors and those of the community. As a result, Lankide Aurrezkia represents the best working model for a community enterprise loan fund that we have – despite the fact that the Mondragon experiment is now unfortunately heading the wrong way, as we will see in the final chapter.

How, then, should a community set out to build its own local system? Its first step is obviously the establishment of a credit union if it has not got one already. The primary purpose of this would be to enable people to borrow to purchase consumer goods or to undertake house repairs without causing a leakage of interest payments and service charges to the outside world. The only decision the community needs to make before setting it up is whether it should charge interest. My personal view is that since most of the things members would buy with their loans would provide benefits year after year – freezers and greenhouses, for example – it is entirely right that they should pay for these benefits in addition to repaying the loan. As far as I am concerned, interest payments are acceptable so long as they stay in the community: it is only with business investments that problems arise.

[main text continues p.176]

BACK TO BASICS WITH BUILDING SOCIETIES

One method of recycling an area's savings that has almost disappeared in the past hundred years is the local building society. In 1900 there were 2286 building societies in Britain, almost all collecting savings and lending them out again within a limited area and thus reducing the amount of interest payments and capital that leaked out of the districts in which they operated. By the end of 1995, however, only 79 were left, and the biggest seven of these had not only become so national (and in some cases international) in their operations but also, with the major banks, so dominant in the mortgage market that only 14 per cent of all house loans were still being provided by the 69 remaining building societies with strong local or regional roots. Many of these were expected to disappear too. Replying to a 1994 survey by an analyst with the Union Bank of Switzerland, John Wrigglesworth, 70 per cent of building society chief executives said they thought most of the smaller local societies will have been absorbed by national ones by the end of the century.

Such a change is not inevitable, though. If enough well-motivated people opened accounts in their local building society they would be able to prevent its amalgamation, no matter how big a bribe a national society offered members to secure their vote to take it over. But this would merely prevent further losses: reversing the trend is likely to be much more difficult, since the EU now requires new societies to have a capitalization of 1 million ECU (which the British government gratuitously made more onerous by rounding up to £1 million), thus making it almost impossible for people in places that have lost their society to start a replacement. The days in which a building society could be dreamed up over drinks after an Ecology Party conference and launched by persuading ten people to invest £500 each – as the Ecology Building Society was in 1981 – have gone. 'That road seems closed,' Bob Lowman, the present general manager of the society, told me. 'The government seems to be moving the goalposts all the time. Societies can do many more things these days, but they are much more tightly regulated.'

Two approaches might enable communities to get around this EU restriction, however. The simplest would be for an existing building society to accept an invitation from a community to set up a branch in their area on the understanding that it would not move capital in or out of that area and would restrict itself to granting mortgages using the area's savings. Such a policy could become an attractive marketing strategy for an existing society once a reasonable number of people begin to accept the desirability of investing their savings in their own area.

The other approach goes back to the origins of building societies. The first society for which records exist was founded in the Golden Cross Inn in Birmingham in 1775 and was soon followed by others in the growing industrial towns of northern and central England. They were set up by working-class men who drank in the same pub (for the first fifty years of the movement every building society was linked with a public house).[15] These were all 'terminating' societies: they built the houses themselves and wound themselves up when everyone was housed; the last one was dissolved as recently as 1980. Each of the twenty-five or thirty members undertook to pay a fixed monthly subscription, and whenever the group had collected an agreed amount – enough to build a house – it would be allocated to a member, either by drawing lots or by competitive bidding, the successful bid going back into the kitty towards the next share.

Originally a member's share was interest-free, but as the pace at which shares became available was rather slow, some terminating societies began to borrow from non-members so that they could allocate shares more quickly. This enabled everyone in the society to be housed sooner but meant that members had to pay extra subscriptions to meet the interest payable to non-members. This was worth doing, because members would otherwise have continued paying rent for much longer.

The main problem with the terminating societies was that new members could not join after the society had started unless they could afford to put in a lump sum equal to the amount the others had already subscribed. In 1845 the first 'permanent' (i.e. non-terminating) building society was set up to overcome this drawback. It also allowed people not actually wanting to be housed to put their money on deposit and reclaim it whenever they wished, thus making their savings available to members needing housing rather more flexibly than with a terminating society. In other words, the permanent societies were, and are, deposit-takers, and deposit-taking is the activity that a society formed today would not be allowed to perform unless it had access to £1 million of capital. 'But if a new society was proposing to take its members' savings as shares rather than deposits, I would be able to register it under the Industrial and Provident Societies Act,' says Malcolm Lynch. This would mean that anyone saving with the new society would only be able to get their money out after another member had been found to purchase their shares and not, as with the existing societies, on demand.

This would be a drawback, but even so it means the way is open to launch a local building society that preserves the non-interest feature of the original terminating societies. Each year, groups with twenty members each could be enrolled by the society, each member committing himself or herself to saving by monthly instalments a twentieth of the cost of an average house in their area each year. If local house prices increased, the sum they would be obliged to save annually would be put up accordingly. At the end of its first year each group would have collected enough for its first member to buy a house, and a celebratory dinner could be held at which the amount was allocated by auction, the successful bidder being the person who offered to leave the highest proportion of the money in the pot to go towards the house-share for the next auction. The rules of the society would stipulate that successful bidders doubled their monthly payments once they were in their new house, thus giving the other members the benefit of the money saved by that member no longer paying rent.

Ten or eleven months later the price of a second house would become available and could be allocated in the same way. As time passed, the intervals between house-sums becoming available would become shorter, and – depending on how big a bid members were prepared to make in the house-sum auctions so they could buy their house sooner rather than later – the whole group could be housed within twelve to fifteen years. Subscriptions would then stop, and the group would have become owner-occupiers at a far lower cost than if they had had to take out mortgages. The disadvantage of the system – that some members would have to wait over ten years for a house – would be minimized if each group included a proportion of people young enough not to need to move into a home of their own for several years.

The building society would not terminate when the first group or groups had been housed but would continue to look after successive years' groups of savers. For example, if a member who had not yet bought a house fell on hard times and was unable to save for a period, the society could arrange for them to leave their original group and join a later one instead. If a member needed to withdraw from the system because their circumstances had changed, the society would advertise their shares and transfer them to whoever in the group they had belonged to offered the best price for taking their place. As the years passed, membership of a group would become increasingly valuable, as the time between each house-sum coming up for auction would get shorter and shorter. Indeed, if the society's rules allowed, members would be able to recover most of their money by buying a house-sum at one of their group's regular auctions and then paying off all the double subscriptions due until the group was scheduled to be wound up from the house-sum itself. Similarly, once a member had purchased a house, they would be able to recover their money by selling the house and paying their outstanding subscriptions in a lump sum from the proceeds of the sale. In short, techniques could be devised for ensuring that a reasonable degree of flexibility was possible, even though the society could not act as a deposit-taker.

Even ignoring the interest savings, it would be well worth the effort to launch such a society. Although the Ecology Building Society is national in its operations – and has other objectives, such as allowing its members to restore derelict properties and thus save the materials and energy embodied in them – in one case at least it has given an indication of the good a local society would be able to do. Some years ago it made a number of loans to enable families to buy miners' cottages in a village in Cumbria that other societies would not touch. As a result the school and the post office, which had been under threat, were able to stay open, and the whole community was reinvigorated.

Another approach to the provision of zero-interest housing loans has been developed by the Dutch non-governmental organization Aktie Strohalm ('Last Straw Action') for use in the South African townships, although it could well be applicable elsewhere. The townships suffer, among other things, from a shortage of houses and an almost non-existent local economy. This means that most residents with jobs have to travel to work outside the townships, and unemployment within them is high.

Several international agencies have offered funds for building houses, and Aktie Strohalm was asked to suggest a way in which their construction could be used to develop the townships' internal economies – because if the aid funds were spent on hiring a contractor in the conventional way, he would almost certainly be from outside the township and bring all the necessary materials and labour in. The township would get new houses, but nothing more. Part of Aktie Strohalm's suggestion involves using a township credit union to run the project; at the time of writing, however, it seemed unlikely that the idea would be taken up.

The first step would be that the credit union announced, with a great fanfare, that it would make interest-free mortgages available to families wishing to purchase houses, shops or workshops on a development it was about to start. The announcement would add that the only people eligible for the new mortgages would be those who, by the time the first building units were finished, (a) had saved, say, 10 per cent of the purchase price in special township tokens (TTs) that would be issued to pay the building contractors for their work, (b) were already resident in the township, and (c) had a regular savings account in credit with the credit union.

Contractors tendering for the first few units would be asked to price their bids in TTs on the basis that they could exchange the TTs at the credit union for 95 per cent of their face value in rand, if they so wished. However, if the publicity was successful, families wishing to qualify for an interest-free mortgage would be happy to buy the TTs from the builder at or above their face value in rand. The public demand for them should also ensure that shops and building material suppliers would be prepared to accept them at face value in payment for goods and building materials, and construction workers would consequently be able to accept them as wages. The credit union should be prepared to open special TT savings accounts, which would pay no interest but give depositors preference when the next batch of mortgages came to be issued. The credit union would never sell TTs for rand and would only accept repayment of the special mortgages in TTs, ensuring that there is a continuing demand for them.

If the exchange rate of TTs for rand rose above parity, this would be a signal that the credit union could get a contractor to begin another batch of houses and thus put more TTs into circulation. On the other hand, if significant amounts of TTs were being brought in for redemption in rand, this would be a sign that too many TTs had been issued, and further building contracts should be deferred. The aim of the programme would be to build as many houses as possible every year while at the same time keeping the TTs' value at par with the rand. The credit union could of course reserve the right to alter the amount of the deposit as a percentage of the purchase price of the properties it financed in order to control the system. It should also be prepared to finance old as well as new properties, at least when the system had become established, to avoid distortions in the local property market.

Analytically, by holding the new money, township residents would be making interest-free loans to the families that get the mortgages. Their motive for doing so would be that they – or members of their families – wanted to get interest-free loans themselves at some time in the future. Obviously, interest-free loans ought to be repaid more quickly than conventional mortgages.

The credit union would incur costs operating the system, but in the early stages at least, each TT would be backed by a rand provided by a donor agency, and the credit union could earn interest on the backing funds by lending them out to its members or by depositing them in a bank. Once the TT was well accepted, fractional backing would become possible and the donors' money would be able to finance houses worth several times its rand amount. There is no reason why the TT should not reach the stage where it circulated in the township as commonly as the Rand, the only differences being that it would not be acceptable outside and would not attract interest if placed in a savings account.

There would be no risk to the credit union in operating the scheme. The worst that could happen is if all the TTs were presented for conversion into rand immediately they were paid out to the builder. In this case the houses would be built and paid for just as if the experiment had never been tried.

Ecology Building Society, 18 Station Road, Cross Hills, Keighley, York-
    shire BD20 5BR; tel. +44 1535 635933.
Aktie Strohalm, Oudegracht 42, 3511 AR Utrecht; tel. +31 30 314314.

A self-build housing project at Gledhow Bank, Leeds, financed by the Ecology Building Society. The rear of the building will be covered with a turf roof.

Once a credit union is running well and the directors feel they can take a further step without jeopardizing it, they could start a Dutch-style insurance club or open a building society to provide a home for the deposits that at present they have to send out of the community for investment elsewhere. But although Irish credit unions and JAK banks (see panel page 164) can rent out work space to community businesses, as in Tallow, they should not attempt to provide business loans. This is because the banking model is totally inappropriate for financing local enterprises, since it basically involves telling the borrower, 'You know your business – or at least you ought to be pretending to if you want a loan. In any case, it is not our job to give advice. If you want that, hire a consultant. We daren't risk even suggesting what you should do because if things turn out badly we could be held legally responsible, or the loan agreement could be cancelled by a court. What we want from you is just that we get our interest and capital payments on time, however high the markets push up rates and whatever happens to the world or the national economy. And just remember, if you fall behind badly we'll seize the collateral you've signed over today and take up the personal guarantees.'

Of course you just can't talk to a neighbour like that. If he or she is going to use a community's savings in a business, the community has to be as sure as it can be that the enterprise is well thought out and has the necessary human resources behind it. Nor can it simply limit its involvement to a pre-investment investigation. Even TILT, operating on its tiny scale, finds that it has to help and advise its clients regularly if it is to protect its capital, despite having investigated their projects thoroughly before it became involved. And if things go really wrong a community investment fund needs the legal right to step in to help sort out the mess, Mondragon-style. Appointing a receiver is not the answer, since their primary role is to recover the debt owed to the institution that appoints them, rather than reorganizing the operation to keep it open. In any case they are usually sent in far too late.

Every community therefore needs an enterprise investment fund, with a team of people of sufficient calibre to investigate and then help manage the businesses it puts its money into. Assembling such a team should be given higher priority than finding the capital to invest. These funds should see themselves as holding companies that share the management, the profits and the losses with the groups and individuals they work with rather than lending organizations that stand back from a project's problems, insist on a fixed rate of interest, and threaten to call in their collateral and wind up the operation unless it is paid. Where they should differ from conventional holding companies, however, is in looking for social dividend as well as a financial return. Only when there are many such bodies in which people feel enough confidence to invest their pension funds will we be able to feel happy that self-reliant local economies are genuinely beginning to re-emerge.

CREDIT UNIONS

In Ireland the national organization is the Irish League of Credit Unions, Castleside Drive, Dublin 14; tel. +353 1 4908911. It sends out field officers to run training courses for new groups in any part of the country. The courses, which can last from six months to a year before the group is ready to be registered, are free, as are the training materials. The league also arranges for groups to be twinned with existing credit unions, which provide help and support. There is also the Ulster Federation of Credit Unions, 121A Sandy Row, Belfast 12; tel. +44 1232 236301, for those who would prefer not to be affiliated with an organization with head-quarters in the Republic.

The first step for any group considering setting up a credit union in Britain is to purchase the Open University's excellent guide, *An Introduction to Credit Unions*, which contains an audio cassette and a mass of other material explaining how to go about it. The guide tries hard to distinguish between the two national organizations, which are not on speaking terms, and lists seventy-six credit union development agencies, mainly financed by local authorities, from which help can be obtained. The guide can be purchased from the Association of British Credit Unions Ltd, Westminster Business Square, 339 Kennington Lane, London SE11 5QY; tel. +44 171 5822626. It costs £9.60 post paid, but I suggest that those sending for it add £1.75 for a copy of ABCUL's booklet *Starting a Credit Union* and a further 70p for a copy of the Credit Union Act, 1979. The other national organization is the National Federation of Credit Unions, 35 Avon Avenue, Meadow Well, North Shields, Northumberland NE29 7QT; tel. +44 191 2572219; fax +44 191 2582921.

OTHER ADDRESSES

Mark Beeson, TILT Ltd, 44 High Street, Totnes, Devon TQ9 5SQ; tel. +44 1803 867099.

Glen Saunders, Triodos Bank, 11 The Promenade, Clifton, Bristol BS8 3NN; tel. +44 117 9739339; fax +44 117 9739303.

Pat Conaty, Aston Reinvestment Trust, Swan House (suite 2), Hospital Street, Hockley, Birmingham B19 3TY; tel. & fax +44 121 2364808.

UK Social Investment Forum, c/o Danyal Sattar, Vine Court, 112-116 Whitechapel Road, London E1 1JE; tel. +44 171 4881059; fax +44 171 3775720; e-mail danyal@gn.apc.org; http://www/bath.ac.uk/Centres/Ethical/UKSIF.

Malcolm Lynch, 20 Central Road, Leeds LS1 6DE; tel. +44 113 2429600.

David Ralley, ICOF Community Capital Ltd, 12-14 Gold Street, Northampton NN1 1BR; tel. +44 1604 37563.

Fazlun Khalid, Islamic Foundation for Ecology and Environmental Sciences, 57 Brecon Road, Handsworth, Birmingham B20 3RW; tel. & fax +44 181 9043898.

Notes

1 27 January 1994.
2 Letter, 3 February 1994.
3 'Pandora's Marketplace', 13 February 1993.
4 A. Culloty, *Nora Herlihy: Irish Credit Union Pioneer* (Irish League of Credit Unions: Dublin 1990), p. 77.
5 Quoted in the *Guardian*, 26 June 1993.
6 Telephone conversation.
7 Included in *Islam and Ecology*, Fazlun Khalid and Joanne O'Brien (eds) (Cassell: London 1992).
8 Published in 1985 by the Islamic Foundation, 223 London Road, Leicester.
9 In a supplement 'Islam and the West', 6 August 1994. The *Economist* also published a long essay on usury in its Christmas issue in December 1993.
10 International Islamic Publishers, K-20 D, Saket, New Delhi 17.
11 Vadillo can be contacted at the headquarters of the Murabitun movement in Scotland: Achnagairn House, Inverness IV5 7PD; tel. +44 1463 831523.
12 Jesús Larranaga (one of his students), quoted by David Morris, *The Mondragon System: Co-operation at Work* (Institute for Local Self-Reliance: Washington 1992), p. 11.
13 Morris, *The Mondragon System*. Material on Mondragon has also been taken from Morris's *The Mondragon Co-operative Corporation* (Institute for Local Self-Reliance: Washington 1992) and *We Build the Road as We Travel* by Roy Morrison (New Society Publishers: Philadelphia 1991).
14 This is almost exactly the interest-free method of borrowing proposed by Shaikh Mahmud Ahmad in *Towards Interest-Free Banking*. His suggestion is that if someone wishes to borrow, say, £10,000 for a year, they would commit themselves to lending £1000 to the bank for ten years.
15 See Martin Boddy, *The Building Societies* (Macmillan: London 1986). Other historical material is taken from Donald McKillop and Charles Ferguson, *Building Societies: Structure, Performance and Change* (Graham & Trotman: London 1993).

5

Energy Makes the World Go Round

The provision of an adequate supply of energy from local resources is fundamental to greater self-reliance. Fortunately, most communities are able to develop such supplies.

I   GENERATING ENERGY

JUST AS THE HUMAN BODY adapts itself to the regular intake of 'hard' drugs, its systems coming to depend on them to such an extent that the user goes through a period of acute distress if they are suddenly withdrawn, so the use of 'hard' fossil energy alters the economic metabolism and is so highly addictive that in a crisis a user-community or country will be prepared to export almost any proportion of its annual output to buy its regular fix. Even in normal conditions a community in an industrialized country can devote a fifth of its external income to buying energy,[1] an expense that not only constitutes a serious drain on its resources but locks the community into the unpredictable gyrations of the world trading system. Consequently, any community that wishes to be more self-reliant must, at some stage, turn its attention to the slow process of reducing the extent to which it depends on whatever fuels, renewable or fossil, it brings in from elsewhere.

Stable, sustainable communities cannot be based on imported energy, for three reasons. One is that the use of fossil fuel on any substantial scale – and most energy imports are of the fossil variety – is not itself sustainable; it cannot continue for thousands of years without consuming its resource base as well as producing harmful environmental side-effects. The best estimates are that if the consumption of fossil energy continues at its present rate – an optimistic assump-

179

tion, since human numbers might well double over the next fifty years and the average amount of fuel used by each person is likely to increase – the world's known reserves of coal will be exhausted in 232 years, those of gas in sixty-five years, and those of oil in forty-three years.[2] Although it is reasonable to expect that large additional sources of fossil energy will be discovered and extraction rates may well go up, it is impossible to believe that adequate supplies of these three fuels will be available for millennia, which is what any reasonable definition of 'sustainability' requires. Moreover, even if supplies of fossil fuel were limitless, the capacity of plants and the oceans to absorb the carbon dioxide released when they are burned is not, and fuel consumption cannot continue at anything like its present level without causing highly damaging and potentially catastrophic changes in the world's climate.

The second reason for aiming for community energy self-reliance is that imported fuel supplies are unreliable. The output of British North Sea oil has been declining since 1987, and at present rates of extraction proven reserves will be exhausted by 2004 and imports will have to start again in 1996 or 1997. As a result, life in Britain will come to depend again on stability in the Middle East, which holds over 65 per cent of the world's known oil reserves. Since 1950 there have been five serious disruptions to oil supplies from the area: the Suez Crisis (1956), the Yom Kippur War (1973), the Iranian revolution (1979), the Iran/Iraq war (1980–8) and the Iraqi invasion of Kuwait and the subsequent Gulf War (1990–1). Gas supplies are even less secure than those of oil, although the enthusiasm that Irish and British electricity producers have recently shown for switching to it for generating electricity might lead one to think otherwise. British gas reserves are expected to be exhausted by 2002 if 1992 extraction rates are maintained. Consequently, if the British government's forecast that gas consumption will double over the next twenty-five years and 60 per cent of electricity will be generated from gas by 2020 proves correct, massive imports will be required. These imports will be piped in from Russia and the Middle East, as transporting liquefied gas by sea is very expensive. As a result, Britain will be exposed to the risk of its supplies being cut by civil unrest, local military conflicts and international disputes in any of the territories along the pipelines' routes.

Ireland's position is no better: Kinsale Head, its only known major gas field[3] (and indeed its only significant domestic fossil fuel source apart from peat) will be exhausted by about the year 2000, and the country is already importing gas from Britain through an undersea pipeline opened in 1995. 'We would envisage imported gas supplying almost all our requirements,' a Bord Gáis spokesperson told me.

The third reason for phasing out fuel imports is that energy prices are very erratic. The graph shows just how much oil prices have changed since this fuel started being put into widespread use in the last century. Swings since the early 1970s have been particularly wide and violent. Each substantial change affected the prices of all other fuels, even those that cannot easily be moved from place to place, because of the ease with which oil can often be substituted for them. In New England, for example, the price and supply of local firewood is entirely determined by the price of imported oil because people switch to burning oil to warm their houses in winter whenever it is cheaper.

Whenever energy prices change significantly, the whole structure of price relationships in the economy changes as well. This is because each product requires a different amount of energy for its production and distribution and so needs to be raised or lowered in price by a different amount. Energy price movements therefore make some goods and services relatively cheaper, and people begin to use more of them in place of the more costly ones, thus affecting the entire make-up of

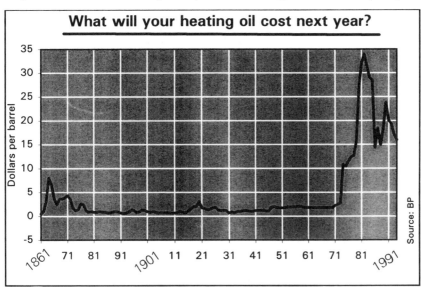

Graph 5.1 *Although fluctuations in oil prices since the early 1970s have been wild compared with their previous stability, they have been even more extreme for people outside the US who, because oil is priced in dollars, have had exchange-rate instabilities to cope with too. Communities depending on fuel from the outside are therefore running great but unquantifiable risks.*

an economy's output, encouraging expansion in some areas and contraction in others. This can be wasteful if machinery is scrapped and factories demolished before the end of their useful lives.

New energy price levels make new methods of manufacture commercially viable as well. For example, if the price of fuel falls, transport costs drop in comparison with other prices because the sector is relatively more energy-intensive. This makes it profitable to produce on a larger scale and to use additional energy in a transport fleet distributing the extra output over a wider area. Small, local manufacturers are driven out of business, and since it would take a long time before they re-emerged if energy prices rose again, we can see why higher levels of energy use are so addictive: a one-way ratchet effect goes into action, and it is very hard for an economy to revert to using less energy whatever prices do.

No stable, sustainable community can therefore exist without a secure, sustainable supply of energy at a steady price, and the only way that both security and price stability can be guaranteed is by having energy sources within community boundaries and under community control. But is energy self-sufficiency technically feasible for most communities? And, if so, does it carry a heavy cost penalty? After all, if it did this would seem to impede a community's efforts to produce a much wider range of goods and services for itself at prices that matched those from outside, the strategy we considered in chapter 2. In fact, however, moderately higher local energy prices are unlikely to create a competitiveness problem because the production techniques used in a community economy will generally require much less energy than those in the industrial system.

Moreover, electricity, the price of which will receive most attention within this chapter, is too high-quality a power to be used except in special circumstances for anything but a very limited range of applications, including lighting, microwave ovens, electronic equipment, motors, and methods of applying heat to limited areas such as welding. If local electricity is priced a few pence per unit more than that from outside, it will make little difference to a community's overall cost levels, provided its use is confined to these applications. Certainly no one supplying electricity to a distribution grid or taking it from one should ever use it for warming rooms or heating water, applications that an American energy expert, Amory Lovins, once referred to as equivalent to using a chainsaw to cut butter because of the waste of energy involved in generating electricity from fossil fuels.

In any case, what do we mean by the cost of an activity within a community? One aspect is obviously the amount of external currency that has to be earned to enable it to continue. When electricity is supplied through the national grid, apart from the wages of electricity workers living in the area, together with any rents, dividends and supply invoices the power companies pay locally, 100 per cent of whatever the consumers are charged leaves the area. With locally generated power from a renewable source, however, the only inescapable national-currency cost once the equipment has been installed is that of any spares too complex to be made within the area. Interest payments (a substantial part of the cost of power from most renewable sources), rents and wages could and should all go to local people. The external-currency cost of locally generated renewable power can therefore be very small.

This does not necessarily mean that the price of power to the consumer would be low, because local costs might be heavy, but there is no need for these costs to be paid in national currency. A wind farm, for example, could adopt Robert Swann's idea (see p.112) and issue its own currency notes, denominated in kilowatt-hours, to pay its staff and to cover the interest due to local people who had invested their national-currency savings to enable it to be built. If it then accepted these notes back in payment for its power, everyone in the community would be happy to use them as money, whether settling their electricity bills with them or spending them in shops.

The only real way in which locally produced energy can cost more than that from outside is in what economists refer to as its 'opportunity cost' – the cash value of the opportunities the community has to give up to bring its own power sources about. For example, it could be that the farmers growing willow to burn would have earned more cultivating another crop, or that the capital used to build a wind farm would have brought a higher financial return if it had been invested in something else. Communities will find these circumstances rarely arise, however, because energy projects should give as good a return on capital as any other scheme to serve the community's needs and because more profitable uses for a community's labour can only arise when it has achieved full employment.

Even if community members compare returns with those on investment opportunities in the outside economy, local energy projects should be an attractive place for their savings because of the low rate of interest mainstream banks, pension funds and building societies generally pay the small saver. Moreover, local savers will be aware that funds placed with institutions operating in the international economy are at risk if that economy breaks down, whereas an investment in a local power supply is about as safe as they can get. Nevertheless, if circumstances do arise in which there are substantial opportunity costs, people are going to have to decide what their priorities are: is a higher income stream from the external economy in the short term preferable to long-term community energy security?

Something that should make the decision to invest in local energy sources rather easier is the fact that world fossil energy prices are almost certain to rise sharply soon, despite the fact that in early 1994 the price of oil was down to only $14 a barrel, much the same level in real terms as it was between 1930 and 1970. In fact this low price was part of the problem: oil markets have been so weak for most of the period since 1982, because of the depressed state of the world economy, that very little capital has been invested in developing new fields, and there is now almost no capacity to accommodate even a modest increase in demand. When they come, these higher fossil energy prices will raise the amount of national currency that communities need to find to develop renewable power supplies. It therefore makes sense to develop those types of renewable energy now where the technologies are already so well established that their capital costs cannot be expected to fall much further. Wind power, small-scale hydro-electric power and some types of biomass energy (derived from plant matter) fall into this category. With other energy sources – photovoltaics, for example – huge capital cost reductions are likely within the next decade, and it is better to delay their exploitation.

The table in the next panel shows estimates of the national-currency and local-currency costs of the various methods of providing energy that communities might have open to them, calculated on the assumption that they are to be carried out on a community scale as opposed to a household or industrial one.

The table shows that even if all costs are treated as being in national currency, electricity from some forms of renewable energy is already entirely competitive with that from gas, oil and coal. This is despite the fact that fossil fuels are heavily subsidized since the full cost of the environmental damage they cause is not reflected in the prices power stations pay. Anyone who is surprised by these figures was in good company until recently because it was only in 1994 that the Department of Energy in Ireland learned how low renewable energy costs actually were. The department had asked companies to submit bids saying how big a government grant they would need to induce them to sign contracts to supply electricity from non-fossil sources if they were guaranteed an inflation-proofed average price of 4p per unit for fifteen years. Fifteen million pounds was set aside to cover the grants, but in the event not a penny was paid because more than enough proposals were submitted that were commercially viable without them. The department, which had obviously been under a seriously false impression about the true cost of renewable power, signed contracts for 50 per cent more capacity than it had intended.

No community anywhere is without some source of renewable energy that it can develop – indeed very few will find they have only one. Most will have several, like Hatherleigh, a small market town near Okehampton, Devon, whose energy prospects were assessed in 1993 by two firms of consultants, Terence O'Rourke PLC and Pell Frischman Water, under contract to the British government and the EU.[4] The consultants found that the town would have no problem meeting all its electricity and heating needs entirely from renewable sources, but only if several were exploited and consumers were pre-pared to pay somewhat higher prices for their power. The area's most abundant renewable energy resource was the solar radiation falling on its walls and roofs. Very little of this was exploitable, however, because the installation of solar-heating panels or arrays of photo-voltaic cells on buildings 'would conflict with the historic character of the town', most of which is a conservation area. The fact that many buildings were listed for preservation and could not be changed also meant that there was little scope for using passive solar energy, since this involves designing and constructing buildings so that the sun's rays are used in ways that reduce the need for artificial heating and lighting.

The next most abundant resource, wind energy, was also judged to be of limited potential because the area's average wind speed was below 6.5 metres per second, currently considered the minimum commercially viable speed if high rates of interest have to be paid to outside investors. If local savings had been available to finance the project, however, this cut-off point could have been reduced because the interest rates could have been lower while remaining attractive to local people, and the payments would have stayed in the area. 'The ability of renewable energy projects to facilitate the local retention of wealth is a potentially significant indirect benefit and worthy of fur-ther research in its own right,' the report says.

Local involvement would also perhaps overcome a second problem with wind energy in Hatherleigh: a wind farm's visual impact. The town's windiest site is the Moor, a prominent ridge to its east, and

[main text continues p.188]

BALANCING EXTERNAL COSTS AGAINST LOCAL ONES

A good approach when assessing a community's renewable energy options is to break down the estimates for the capital and running costs of the various possibilities into their national-currency and local-currency components. At first sight this might seem to make life more complicated because there are now four figures, not two, by which projects have to be compared: national-currency capital cost, local-currency capital cost, national-currency running cost, and local-currency running cost.

How can any one of these figures be related to the other three? Obviously a project with a low national-currency capital cost is better than one with a higher one, other costs being equal. But other things never are equal, and for each pair of projects with the same national-currency capital cost, the levels of local-currency capital cost, local-currency running cost and national-currency running cost will differ. How can comparisons be made?

The first step is to decide how much more national currency it is worth spending on capital equipment now in order to have lower national-currency running costs in the future. The conventional answer is to say that if a community's investors can earn more by putting the extra money in an outside project than would be saved from a power plant's national-currency running costs by spending it on better equipment, that is where the capital should be invested, provided the level of risk is the same. Consequently, someone who thinks the world economy is likely to break down seriously enough to cut off their income from external investments will favour putting extra capital in the local power plant, while a neighbour who holds a more optimistic view about the mainstream's future will not. You and I, of course, have reservations about this approach, since we think that, as a community, we should be looking for a much wider range of benefits than the purely financial return. Even so there is no hard and fast way of relating national-currency capital and recurrent costs in community projects in an uncertain world. Some sort of trade-off has to be made, and the outcome will vary according to the circumstances of the time and the community's attitude to the risk of external disruption.

The relationship between local-currency capital cost and local-currency recurrent cost is simpler. Both are mainly made up of wage bills, one to build the plant, the other to keep it running. If there are unemployed people in the community it makes sense to use as many hours of their labour as are necessary and available for local-currency wages now to reduce the plant's need for labour in the future. This is because labour cannot be stored, and if people who would like to have worked do nothing, a potential community resource has been lost. It should always be possible to find alternative work in the future to replace whatever is saved by the extra done now.

In other words, a project should take on as much labour and other inputs as it usefully can from people who are prepared to accept payment in local-currency notes. The cost of this labour should not be converted into national currency for project comparison purposes, except to the extent that the people involved would have been doing something to earn or save themselves national currency if the power plant project had not come along. No exchange rate should be used if no exchange would have been possible. The same applies to comparisons between local-currency running costs and national-currency ones: local running costs should only be expressed in national-currency terms to the extent that they represent resources that if used in some other way could have been sold on an equally secure basis for national currency.

What all this means in practice is that projects should be compared initially on the basis of the total national-currency investment required per unit of installed capacity and also the national-currency cost per unit of output generated. This enables those with the worst national-currency figures to be eliminated and a final choice made between projects for which enough local-currency-paid labour is available for their construction on the basis of their local recurrent costs.

Local and external costs of renewable energy sources

1. CAPITAL COSTS PER KILOWATT OF INSTALLED CAPACITY

	EXTERNAL	LOCAL	TOTAL
HYDRO	£550 for turbine & generator	£450–£950 depending on extent of site work	£1000–£1500
WIND	£825 for turbine tower	£175 for access road and provision of foundations	£1000
WOOD-CHIP CHP	£80 for diesel engine & generator, assuming 100kW capacity	£120 for gasifier & installation; £100 for planting coppice	£300

In addition to electricity, this system would also supply the equivalent of 1.5kW as hot water for every kW produced. For the hot water to be used, however, more capital might be needed for a distribution system. However, no allowance has been made for this as distribution costs such as the cost of connecting to the grid and grid usage charges are not included in the wind and hydro figures.

METHANE FROM BIOMASS CHP	£330 for pumps, gas engine, generator	£500 for tanks, sitework	£830

This system would also supply the equivalent of 1.8 kW as hot water for every kW of electricity produced. It has the additional advantage of dealing with problem wastes and produces valuable by-products. Both CHP systems have the advantage over wind and hydro that they can be operated at a variable output whenever there is a demand.

2. RUNNING COSTS PER KILOWATT-HOUR PRODUCED

	EXTERNAL	LOCAL	NOTES
HYDRO	0.4p (spares)	0.6p (maintenance)	operating 2600h/year
WIND	0.55p (spares & insurance)	0.8p (maintenance)	operating 2600h/year
WOOD-CHIP CHP	0.5p (diesel fuel) 0.5p (spares)	2.7p (wood-chips cost) 1.0p (maintenance)	operating 1500 h/year. More coppice would need to be planted for longer.
METHANE FROM BIOMASS CHP	0.5p (spares)	3–6p (depending on transport distances)	Based on a plant operating 350 days/year 60 tonnes biomass/day

Sources : Wind & hydro, Irish Energy Centre ; Wood-chip CHP, Rural Generation Ltd ; Biomass CHP, Mary O'Donnell.

objections would undoubtedly be raised if an outside company ever proposed to erect windmills there. The reaction might be different if a community company suggested the same thing, but with no sign of one emerging, the consultants decided that the only contribution the wind could make to Hatherleigh's needs was to drive small individual turbines on isolated farms to supply their electricity.

Hydropower was considered to offer poor prospects too. 'Without significant civil works, only schemes at existing mills and weirs dating from the nineteenth century and earlier would offer sufficient potential energy,' and even on those sites – there were six, with a total capacity of 230 kW – projects were 'unlikely to be cost-effective'.

So where was Hatherleigh to get its power? From agricultural sources: the coppicing of willow trees specially grown on farms, together with the production of gas from farm slurries, sewage sludge, and abattoir waste. The report states that the conversion of a tenth of the 7944 hectares of farmland to coppice would produce almost 8400 tonnes of dry wood-chip each year, more than enough to fire a power station producing 9600 MWh/year, the total electricity requirement of the town, as well as a considerable amount of hot water that could be used to warm workshops, greenhouses, homes, and offices. The consultants estimated that if the energy in the hot water was distributed free rather than being sold, the cost of the electricity would be about 10p per unit. Electricity from the biogas digester would be more expensive – upwards of 16p per unit – unless a use could be found for the hot water and an allowance made for the fact that the digester disposed of what would otherwise be problem wastes.

The consultants stress that Hatherleigh is not unusual in the abundance of its renewable energy resources. 'A not-dissimilar volume and variety of accessible resources would be found in the hinterland of many rural settlements. This conclusion applies not only to West Devon and other parts of the West Country but to other areas of the European Union such as Brittany and much of the Irish Republic.' Two other findings of the Hatherleigh study would apply elsewhere too. One is that the scope for the large-scale, centralized, commercial development of renewables is limited and that the available resources can best be developed on a community basis. 'Options for community engagement in the development, ownership and operation of a renewable energy project in Hatherleigh should be kept under review,' the report says. 'With the two most promising renewable energy resources both being farm-based, the farming community and its associated business and co-operative structures are likely to form a focus for specific projects in the locality.' The other finding was that renewable energy could provide an important means of rural renewal. 'A higher aspiration for renewable energy production would ... make a significant contribution to the European Union's efforts to promote sustainable development, diversify rural economies and improve the effectiveness of the Common Agricultural Policy.'

At a national level there is no doubt that the long-term potential of renewable energy is considerable. 'In principle, renewables could supply all the energy needs even of advanced industrial nations assuming that there is a serious commitment to energy conservation,' Dave Elliott of the Network for Alternative Technology and Technology Assessment (NATTA) at the Open University wrote in his report 'Towards a Renewable Energy Strategy for the UK'.[5] 'The government's Renewable Energy Advisory Group recently suggested that in theory, renewables could supply 1100 TWh/annum, two or three times the UK's electricity requirements, at a cost of less than 10p/kWh. To that must be added a heat contribution. A more ambitious scenario produced by Cambridge University's Department of Applied Economics suggests that we might expect up to 50 per cent total energy contribution by 2040 in the UK, while a scenario produced by the Stockholm [Environment] Institute for Greenpeace has renewables supplying 62 per cent of West Europe's energy by 2030, rising to 100 per cent by 2100.'

Let us look in more detail, then, at the forms of renewable energy most likely to be suitable for community-scale exploitation in Ireland and Britain.

1. WATER POWER

During the past twenty years, electricity from small hydropower plants – that is, under 5 MW – has become entirely price-competitive with that from power stations powered by fossil fuels, even by conventional accounting standards. And, while several community-scale projects have recently been carried out in Ireland and Britain, there is considerable scope for many more.

Over twenty thousand sites in the two countries had waterwheels at some time in the past, and very few of these are still used. Ireland, for example, once had 1800 watermills. In the early 1980s, when experts searched two thousand six-inch maps looking for their locations and for other places where water power might be developed, they found that only eighty-five sites of 3500 they considered worthy of visiting were still used for power. A report published by the

Department of Energy in 1985 gives the experts' assessments of the head, flow rate and power potential of the operational sites, together with details of the best 483 unexploited ones.[6]

According to this study, a total of 38 MW of capacity could be developed, a figure that Fiacc Ó Brolcháin, secretary of the Irish Hydro-Power Association,[7] thinks is about right. 'I've been going around the country for some time saying that [private generators] have about 10 MW of hydro-power installed and there's another 30 MW we could develop unless the price of electricity went much higher and made a lot more sites feasible,' he told me. (In addition, the state-owned ESB has 512 MW of hydro capacity, including its pumped storage station, Turlough Hill. At present, hydro supplies 5 per cent of Irish electricity.) 'However, there are a lot of sites which are in the report which ought to have been left out and a lot more which ought to be in,' Ó Brolcháin added. My own experience bears this out: there were once five watermills within a mile of my house, not one of which is mentioned in the report. Three of these stood together in a small valley to which water was channelled from a nearby river; after a preliminary survey, a friend who is a water-power engineer estimated that if the canal was reopened and a modern high-pressure turbine installed, it could generate 250 kW.

The key determinants of a good water-power site are the volume of water, the proportion of the year for which it flows, and the distance through which it falls. A single cubic metre of water falling one metre in one second generates 9.8 kW, provided the turbine or waterwheel though which it passes is 100 per cent efficient. In practice, of course, this is never the case. Also, although low-head turbines such as the Kaplan, in which the moving water pushes round propellers, can convert as much of the water's energy into useful power as those for higher heads such as the Pelton wheel, in which a high-pressure jet of water is directed into cups mounted on a spinning wheel, they are more expensive because they need to be bigger to cope with a much larger volume of water to give the same amount of power. They also need to be built to closer tolerances and shaped more carefully to suit the speed of the water passing through, because if turbulence develops it wastes a lot of the water's energy.

Obviously one cannot decide whether to fit a high-head or low-head turbine: that depends on the site. The traditional overshot mill-wheel is surprisingly efficient – it can extract 70 per cent of the water's power – but is unsuited to generating electricity because of the slow rate at which it turns. One could of course fit a gearbox to speed up the rotation, but this itself would waste energy, and if one tried to speed up the wheel the water would be thrown out of the buckets by centripetal force, also leading to inefficiency.

Electricity was not generated from water power until the 1880s, and there was almost no technological development of small-scale systems between 1930 and the oil crisis in 1973 because the market for turbine sets in industrialized countries collapsed when people who might have ordered them found it cheaper and easier to get their power from the national power grid. Many manufacturers went out of business or began making pumps. Even before 1930, small-scale hydropower was at a serious price disadvantage in relation to larger water-power schemes because of the cost of the control system required for reliable AC output. According to *Micro-Hydro Power*,[8] the best book I know for anyone considering a small-scale system, in the old days the controls for a 15 to 20 kW water turbine often cost more than all the rest of the installation and, on a 10 kW system, might have consumed 10 per cent of the output. DC control systems were cheaper and simpler but meant that the power was unsuitable for the most readily available electrical appliances.

It is only within the past twenty years that this control problem has been overcome, and electronic systems are now available at a reasonable price for even the smallest system. Progress has also been made on standardizing small, low-head turbines – and most sites offer only a limited head – and presenting them in such a way that the construction work needed to house the turbine and channel the water is greatly simplified. For example, a Dublin firm of engineers has developed the Polyturbine, which is suitable for sites with heads from 1.5 to 5 metres.[9] The beauty of this machine, which was conceived by a Swede, Evald Holmen, is that the contractor building the turbine house and the water channels running to and from it needs to erect very little shuttering before casting them in mass concrete. Instead the correct shapes are made up in glassfibre at the factory and placed in position on site, and concrete is poured around them to hold and strengthen them. This cuts site costs considerably. Moreover, because the channels and turbine chamber are lined with the smooth side of the glassfibre-reinforced resin rather than concrete, the water moves through with very little friction.

The Polyturbine – like similar systems from several other makers – is modular: only one size of turbine is made. This is capable of handling between one and three cubic metres of water a second; if the amount of water available is greater than that, another identical turbine is installed alongside the first. Adjustments to suit the differing heads from site to site are made by adding extra sections to the water intake channel. As a result the standard turbine and generator for a site with a 1.5-metre head costs £30,000 and produces 25 kW from a 2.5 cubic metre flow, while that for a 5-metre head site costs only £8000 more and delivers 114 kW, a much better bargain.

A small water-power site will probably cost about £1000 per kilowatt to develop, although that cost and the number of units a kilowatt of generating capacity converts to each year vary widely from site to site because of differences in the amounts of site work required and the length of time when there is enough water for power production. Traditional watermills had ponds if there were times of year when there was inadequate water for the mill to operate: a mill-pond enabled the energy of twenty-four hours' water flow to be used in seven or eight.

Séamus Langan, a pub owner who installed two Polyturbines near the site of an old mill at Ballinrobe, County Mayo, in 1995, will not say how much his installation cost, although he does say that the site work went more easily than he had expected: he had feared that the contractors would run into hard limestone. Even if he was prepared to quote the cost, however, it would be of little relevance to other people because the main investment that made his project possible was the digging of a mill-stream as a relief project 150 years ago at about the time of the Great Famine. Nevertheless his story is interesting.

Langan was a small farmer until he bought the Valkenburg bar in Ballinrobe in the early 1970s. He still had some fields, one of which ran between the Robe River and the mill-canal, but was not alive to the possibilities of water power until the late 1970s, when an English engineer working for a company that made an ill-fated attempt to develop an Irish-made range of wind-turbines pointed out the potential of the site.

Langan could do nothing to develop the site immediately because he did not own the water rights, which were still attached to the mill that stood derelict and rotting in the next field, one wall torn down years before by workmen taking machinery out. Eventually, however, the mill came on the market, and Langan bought it. He then had to seek permission from four governmental bodies to go ahead with plans prepared for him by Colm Walsh of University College, Galway, where the first experimental Polyturbine had been installed.

The first body he approached was the regional fisheries board, which helped him to adapt his plans so that fish in the Robe River would not be affected by the project. 'At some times of year the level of oxygen in the river is low, and so fish will be attracted to the disturbance created as the water re-enters the river after passing through the turbines,' Langan's son, Barry, told me when he showed me round. 'If they went in too far they would be killed, so we have had to fit screens to stop them. We only have to have them on when the water is low and take them away at other times because they interfere with the flow of water from the turbine, creating a back-pressure and reducing its efficiency.' The other stipulation the fisheries board made was that fish screens be fitted to the turbine intake as well and that some water from the canal be allowed to flow through to the old mill so that any fish in it could get away.

The next set of negotiations was with the Office of Public Works, which is responsible for river drainage, so that it could satisfy itself that the proposed works would not cause flooding. No problems there; but the final step before Langan could apply to Mayo County Council for planning approval was rather protracted: he had to persuade the ESB to take his power at a time when its huge coal-burning power station at Moneypoint had just come on stream and had considerable excess capacity. 'The ESB fellows were very nice but they just weren't interested,' Langan says. Eventually, however, agreement came through, and, with documentary evidence of the approval of the three bodies, he was granted planning permission without further trouble in 1987. 'It might be more difficult to get planning permission now,' he says. 'The anglers around here have become much more militant and are worried about the condition of the rivers.'

No site works were carried out until 1992 and only then to stop the five-year planning permission lapsing. Langan explains the delay by saying he was negotiating for an EU 'Thermie' grant towards the cost of the project but was unsuccessful. 'I think the money went on that wind farm in north Mayo instead,' he says. He then delayed actually fitting the turbines, which have a total capacity of 100 kW, for almost three years because he hoped to be able to get a grant under a scheme outlined by the Minister for Energy in October 1993, in which the ESB would buy 75 MW of electricity from renewable sources. In the event neither he nor anyone else got a grant, but he was awarded a fifteen-year supply contract, and the turbines were commissioned early in 1996.

In Britain anyone going through a similar process has to obtain the consent of the National Rivers Authority unless they are simply putting a turbine into the river itself beside an existing weir. 'If you

[main text continues p.196]

193

TOWN INSTALLS TURBINE TO CUT
OLD PEOPLE'S POWER BILL

If Bandon, County Cork, is any guide, communities are prepared to back the right sort of renewable energy project with cash and enthusiasm.

In May 1992 four friends bought a bankrupt earthmoving contractor's yard near the centre of the town at a liquidator's auction with a bid of £65,000. 'We had no money and had to get round to the bank quickly to arrange a loan so that we could put the 10 per cent deposit down,' says one of the four, Paddy O'Sullivan, an electrical contractor. His three colleagues were Paddy Connolly, a builder, John Perrott, a civil engineer, and P.J. McLoughlin, a pharmacist. 'The yard covered about 1.5 acres and was surrounded by ruined buildings, but we weren't interested in that,' O'Sullivan says. 'What we wanted was the seven-foot weir on the Bandon River beside the yard, which went with the property. Our idea was to put in a turbine to generate electricity to heat and light St Michael's, an old people's home run by a local voluntary group, and save them £14,000 a year.'

After paying the deposit they had to raise not just the balance of the purchase price but also the cost of building and installing the turbine, a 48-inch Francis producing 70 kW built by Paddy Belton of Richfort, County Longford, which eventually worked out at £120,000. 'We asked people for interest-free loans for five years, and the first big one we got was for £10,000 from the Bandon Co-op [which makes butter with milk from five hundred farms, besides supplying feed and fertilizer]. This gave us the leverage to go to the two main banks in the town and ask them to match it, which they did.' Getting an interest-free loan from a bank is some achievement. Then a community group that had collected £26,000 to build a hall lent that too, on condition the group could get it back whenever they needed it. Another community group put up £10,000 on the same basis.

The four also began hunting for grants. 'We chased every grant there is and had a 95 per cent failure rate,' O'Sullivan comments. Eventually they received £60,000, including £30,000 from 'Leader', an EU rural development programme, and £10,000 from the Ireland-America Fund. In addition to the grants they received £20,000 in donations from local people.

While the fund-raising was going on, the team felt they needed to learn more about water power. Their original idea was to restore an old turbine beside the weir, which had been out of use for many years. 'We did a tremendous amount of consultation. We questioned every turbine owner in the country to pick up what we needed to know,' O'Sullivan says. Eventually they decided that restoration would not enable them to get the maximum power from the site and that they would need to install a new one to do so. John Perrott designed the installation and Paddy Connolly built it. 'We had to cut seven feet down into the rock to deepen the tail-race, as otherwise the flow of water out of the turbine would have been impeded and we would have lost power,' Connolly says. 'The most helpful person we met was Paddy Belton. His quality and prices were the best too. He's a marvellous man.'

194

Belton Engineering Works is mainly a welding shop producing anything from structural steelwork to spiral staircases. Paddy Belton builds turbines because he is fascinated by their geometry. 'I've always been interested in alternative energy. I was looking through my diaries the other day and found I'd been thinking about turbines back in the 1940s.' The first turbine he built was completed in the middle 1970s. 'It went into an old mill and it wasn't that successful, but still it was good enough so I could carry on.' These days his target is to produce a turbine in the 2 to 10 kW range for under £1000. 'The problem with turbines is that they are too expensive, and electricity is too cheap. The idea is that we'll supply plans and the people will do 50 per cent of the work for themselves. I hope to be taking out a patent later this year,' he told me in 1995. 'You can save a lot of money if the electricity is just used for heating because the electronic load controller is expensive.'

By December 1992 the Bandon installation was complete, and representatives of the ESB arrived to test it before authorizing its connection to the national grid. Paddy Belton was there, uneasy among the men in suits. 'We had problems getting the sluice gate down fully, and there was a lot of turbulence. I had guaranteed that the turbine would deliver at least 60 kW, but the ESB man taking the readings kept saying the output was only 12. Was it the turbulence? Had I miscalculated? Was the shape of the housing terribly wrong? But then the ESB man realized he was only measuring one phase of the three-phase supply, and the actual output was 62 kW. You can bet I was relieved.'

Apart from the sticking sluice gate, the only teething problem the installation experienced was that the turbine intake kept getting blocked by water weeds or fertilizer bags being carried downstream. However, John Perrott designed an automatic scraper to clear the intake screen every fifteen minutes, and since that was fitted the installation has worked perfectly, producing about 400,000 kWh a year. By mid-1995 none of this had gone to the old people's home: instead it was being sold to the ESB, and the income was being set aside to repay the £70,000 of interest-free loans. However, Paddy O'Sullivan was optimistic that the contractor's yard would soon be sold – this time without the weir and water rights – for £100,000. As soon as that happened, he said, the home would get its power directly, and only if there was a surplus would it go to the grid.

'The whole thing was Paddy O'Sullivan's idea,' Paddy Connolly says. 'He'd been talking to the previous owners before they went into liquidation.' Did they widen the membership of their group when their bid for the site proved successful? I asked. 'We did not. We'd worked together a lot before and we'd learnt from being involved in other voluntary organisations that involving more people means more suggestions but not a lot more help in carrying them out.'

plan to take water from a river, pass it through your turbine and then put it back, you need an abstraction licence,' says Commander George Chapman, secretary of the National Association of Water Power Users.[10] 'If you want to put in a new weir you need an impounding licence.' Planning permission is also required. 'The NRA is a statutory consultee, so they are automatically told about your planning application by the planning authority. That means that it's a good idea to speak to the NRA first.'

Installations under 20 kW are not worth linking to the mains because of the high cost of the protection equipment, Chapman says. 'The best thing is to find a way of using that power directly and sav-ing yourself the 8p a unit or whatever it would have cost you to buy.' In any case the price paid by the local regional electricity company (REC) would probably be derisory – about 2.5p a unit. At present, projects have to be big enough to warrant the trouble and expense of submitting them for non-fossil-fuel obligation (NFFO) contracts to get a better price. In 1995, contracts under NFFO, the scheme used by the British government to support the development of nuclear and renewable energy, paid 4.85p per unit for water power, inflation-proofed for the next fifteen years.

According to Chapman, this might be about to change. The RECs are increasingly prepared to recognize that power supplied on a limb of a network is more valuable to them than if it is supplied by Power-gen or National Power through the national grid, because they can save the capital cost of strengthening their distribution lines to that area and have lower line losses. Also, RECs are under increasing pres-sure from OFFER, the regulatory body for the electricity industry, to pay independent producers no less than they pay their own electricity generation companies. And after April 1998 the RECs will lose their monopoly over power distribution, and producers will be able to sell their output to anyone they like. 'A water or wind-power producer will be able to find a customer somewhere in a REC's area and just pay the REC to use its wires to get it there. OFFER will control the amount that the RECs can charge for that service,' Chapman says. 'The power the producer supplies will just be metered into the net-work and then out again at the customer's premises. This arrange-ment already exists for people with loads of over 100 kW.'

So, a British wind-power or water-power co-op should soon be able to supply its members with electricity through the existing distribu-tion network and, apart from the REC's distribution fee, bill them in its own energy-based currency.

Things might be about to change in Ireland too. When this book went to press in 1996, no one planning a renewable energy project could be sure whether they would be able to sell the electricity it produced to, or through, the national distribution system. This silly situation came about because the rules for the 1994 competition to supply renewable energy laid down that 'no other alternative energy projects for the supply of electricity to the ESB will be accepted during the [1994–6] period.' The Irish hydropower and wind energy associations both criticized this rule when it was announced, on the grounds that it would lead to a once-off spurt of projects rather than a continuous flow, making it much more difficult to get investors involved and an Irish wind turbine manufacturing industry established. In submissions to the minister in early 1995, both associations asked that a fair price be set for power from renewable sources so that developers could negotiate to sell their output and connect to the grid at any time. They also expressed concern about the charges being made for connection to the grid and wanted special assistance for smaller projects. 'Not very much has changed since we made our submission,' Sheila Leyden, secretary of the Irish Wind Energy Association,[11] told me at the end of 1995. 'We want some sort of rolling programme so that projects can be developed on a continuous basis.'

Small-scale hydro is the supreme renewable energy source: correctly carried out, an installation should do no harm to the environment and run for fifty years before it needs a major overhaul. The only problem with it is that, like Hatherleigh, most communities have insufficient sites to meet more than a tiny fraction of their electricity requirements this way.

2. WIND POWER

The crucial decision to be taken when considering wind energy is the site. A good one must have a high average wind speed, since the power available to the turbine for converting to electricity depends on the cube of the wind velocity. This means that the difference between an average wind speed of five and six metres per second will affect output by almost 72 per cent.

However, a convenient connection to the electricity network is also needed, and when Ireland's first wind farm was being planned in 1991, a coastal site with higher wind speeds was dropped in favour of an inland one close to the turf-fired power station at Bellacorick, County Mayo, because this minimized the cost of linking up to the national grid. A single 300 MW turbine such as might be purchased by a group of neighbours needs access to a 10 kVA line – the type used to supply a large farm or a small factory – if they plan to use the grid to distribute the power among themselves and to sell any surplus that occurs.

Good sites should also have reasonable road access so that heavy equipment can be brought in to put the tower and turbine up. A smooth topography is also desirable, since a cliff or a two-storey building can cause unpredictable turbulence. Some of the turbines at Bellacorick are close to a young pine plantation and produce less effectively whenever the wind is from that direction. As the power losses will obviously get worse as the trees grow, I can see them being purchased and felled.

Sites should also be chosen where the erection of a turbine will not upset the planning authorities or the neighbours: insensitive siting and poor equipment have already given wind farms a bad name. The £30 million farm with 103 Japanese-made turbines at Llandinam in Wales is particularly unfortunate, causing a noise that has been likened to moans from a mass crucifixion. In fact there should be no appreciable noise from a wind turbine, provided its blades and gearbox are properly designed. All modern Danish turbines produce less than 45 dB(A) at 350 m, little more than the level of background noise at night in the country, as the chart below shows; and special versions are available whenever anyone wants to erect a turbine particularly close to a house. In moderate winds one can stand right under any of the twenty-one turbines at Bellacorick and talk in a normal voice, while in higher winds the noise of the wind itself drowns out that of the turbines.

The only serious environmental drawback to wind turbines is visual. The Danish countryside is dotted with single turbines, or

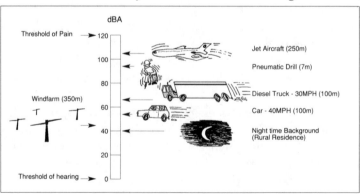

Common sound levels. (source: British Wind Energy Association)

groups of two or three, often erected by members of a 'wind guild' living close by. I regard these as acceptable additions to the rural scene; the only distracting feature is the movement of the blades, which in an otherwise stationary landscape tend to draw the eye. The wind farm at Bellacorick is acceptable too, adding interest to a bleak landscape in the way yachts add interest to a bay. A low-tension power line that has nothing to do with the farm but runs parallel to the road leading to Bellacorick as it crosses a long stretch of bog is much more unsightly.

But Llandinam, which supplies enough power for 21,000 houses, and the Altamont Pass in California are quite another matter. Here there is no question of the wind turbines becoming part of the landscape: they *are* the landscape, simply because there are so many of them. And because hundreds of blades are constantly rising into the sky, the angle of each forever changing its relationship with that of its neighbour, the overall effect is visually bewildering as the eye hunts vainly for repeating patterns. In his opening address to the conference of the British Wind Energy Association in 1993, Michael Jefferson, director of the British Energy Association, referred to Llandinam as 'involving unacceptable visual intrusion,' although he rated the acceptability of ten other wind farms as high. 'There are many potential sites for wind farms ... which are not of great landscape value,' he added.

In 1992, Bridget Gubbins, a leading opponent of proposals to site nuclear power stations on the Northumberland coast, went to Denmark and the Netherlands on a Churchill Scholarship to see what ordinary people living near wind turbines thought about them.[12] Naturally, opinions were mixed. Some thought the turbines beautiful, others hated them. One family living only three hundred metres from a wind farm at Vederso in western Denmark thought the twenty-seven turbines were too close to their house, although a group of three machines would have been acceptable. They also complained of a whistling noise from the turbines on quiet evenings when there was a low wind. 'We like to watch birds and have seen no harm done to them,' the husband said. 'We watch the migrating geese, and they avoid the turbines easily. I think people who say otherwise are misinformed.'

The nineteen-year-old daughter of another family also living three hundred metres from the nearest turbine of a 24-turbine wind farm in Låland thought the windmills nice to look at. 'Noise is not a problem,' she said. 'When the wind is from the north they can be quite loud, but then we are usually in the house with the windows closed. When there's a low wind we can hear them in the garden, but it's not loud.'

Gubbins found she liked the turbines more than she had expected, whether in large wind farms, singly, or in small clusters. 'The newest models were attractive to look at and have already become a normal part of the countryside in both countries,' she writes. 'The Danish sugar-bags available in all the supermarkets show a typical country scene where sugarbeet is grown, of a Danish single-storey farmhouse, trees, and adjoining wind turbine. Wind turbines are certainly more attractive than pylons, or wooden electricity poles and wires, which are found everywhere and which our eyes to some extent no longer perceive. The noise from the turbines I found negligible.'

My view is that if large wind farms are to be built they must be kept well away from favourite views. They could even be confined, if necessary, to offshore platforms and islands, where the higher wind speeds would compensate for the increased costs of erection, access, and grid connection. Convenient onshore sites, particularly those near houses, should be reserved for co-operatively owned turbines. This is done in Denmark, where the local planning departments divide their districts up into three zones. Zone 1 consists of particularly sensitive areas, where no turbines are permitted; in zone 2 – land close to houses – applications for single turbines or small clusters will be considered if they are owned by those living nearby; and commercial wind farms are confined to zone 3.

So, if a group of friends think that sites near where they live might have wind-power possibilities, how should they proceed? 'I spend a lot of my time talking people out of projects,' says Brian Hurley,[13] a wind energy consultant who lectures at Bolton Street College of Technology, Dublin. 'Sites generally aren't as windy as you think. If the group want to save money by doing some preliminary work themselves, they should look up their sites on wind maps of their area. In Ireland, Larry Staudt and I prepared a report for the Department of Energy in March 1988 called "Identification of Wind Energy-Rich Sites Best Suited for Wind Farm Development", which the department will usually give away to serious enquirers and which covers lowland locations near the coast but not those over 1000 feet elsewhere in the country. [In Britain, ETSU, the government's Energy Technology Support Unit based at Harwell, has done a wind survey of the whole country down to 1km squares, and supplies the results on maps or computer disks for specific areas.]

[main text continues p.202]

A BLUFFER'S GUIDE TO WIND TURBINES

Turbines start producing power at a wind speed called the cut-in speed, typically about 4 m/s. As wind speed increases, power output increases, until the maximum power output is reached, typically at a wind speed of about 12 to 13 m/s. The turbine design or its control system ensures that if the wind speed increases above this level, power output will not increase. This is to protect turbine components from forces larger than those for which they are designed; the additional energy available in higher wind speeds over a year would not justify the additional costs of using a larger gearbox, generator, bearings, etc.

At a higher wind speed, sometimes called the cut-out or furling wind speed and typically about 25 m/s, the control system stops the turbine. The maximum wind speed the turbine is designed to stand is called the survival wind speed. The levels of these wind speeds vary with turbine design and the sites for which the turbine is designed.

Turbines may be stopped on an instruction from the operator, when the wind speed exceeds the cut-out wind speed, or if the control system detects a fault. Most turbines have a mechanical brake mounted on one of the shafts in the nacelle [generator housing]. In addition, many turbines have aerodynamic brakes in which the blade tips, or the entire blades, twist to a position perpendicular to the plane of rotation, so slowing the turbines down.

Turbines may be upwind or downwind of the tower. Advantages of downwind design are that the blades can cone or flex in the wind without any danger of hitting the tower. This reduces the stresses in the blades and allows cheaper, lighter blades and a lighter structure to be used. Disadvantages are that a sudden drop in wind speed each time a blade passes behind the tower may cause vibration and fatigue of the blade and structure, and may also cause noise.

The capacity factor of a wind turbine is the ratio of average power output to rated power output for a given period. Turbines on windier sites tend to give higher capacity factors. Typical capacity factors are in the region of 20 to 30 per cent.

(From an article by Ciarán King in In the Wind, newsletter of the Irish Wind Energy Association.)

Most of Europe's wind-energy potential is in Britain and Ireland. The lighter shades on the map indicate wind speeds over 6m/s and the darker shades wind speeds over 7m/s.

'Otherwise, if anyone else has carried out wind studies nearby, the group should try to get access to their results. The Meteorological Office will also have some data. The EC has prepared a wind atlas of Europe, but this is very broad-brush.[14] I give free telephone consultations, and if people visit me with detailed maps I can usually give them broad guidance on whether it seems worthwhile taking the project further. If they want a consultant to undertake a site visit they obviously have to cover his expenses.'

Hurley suggests having three or four possible sites to show a visiting consultant. 'I normally rate them according to four factors,' he says. 'The most important is wind speed, of course. Next is access and the general suitability of the land. The third factor is the site's proximity to the electricity grid. And the fourth is the likelihood of getting planning permission.'

When the best potential site has been chosen, the next step is to erect an instrument tower exactly where the turbine will stand to record the wind's speed and direction for the next year at the height its blade hub will be. 'The test of a serious project is whether wind measurements have been carried out,' Hurley says. 'It's just like exploring for oil and gas: you choose the best site from maps and data other people have assembled, but you don't know if there's anything worthwhile there until you've drilled a test hole or, with wind energy, erected a test tower. You can get quite a surprise.'

Serious money has to be spent on these tests. Even if the group can erect the tower itself it will still cost between £1000 and £2000 and the instruments a further £1500. 'I never suggest that people get second-hand instruments,' Hurley says. 'That's for psychological reasons – it would be like saying their project wasn't worth researching properly – and because new equipment comes with a twelve-month guarantee. If you had to have a service engineer make a field trip to repair second-hand instruments, it might cost you as much as you'd saved. You'd also have lost readings while the equipment was down. In any case, a group should check the equipment regularly to make sure it's working and can expect to pay £30 a month to their consultant for the evaluation of the data it obtains.'

Even a full year's wind data is no guarantee that the site will be successful. 'Every farmer or fisherman knows how much a particular year's weather can vary from the long-term average,' Hurley says. 'But at least with a turbine you know that your readings are within 15 to 20 per cent of the mean. You can't say that about a year's water level readings in a river as a guide when planning water power.' So the next

 [main text continues p.208]

HOW THREE FAMILIES STARTED A MOVEMENT AND CREATED AN INDUSTRY

When OPEC tripled world oil prices in 1979, the Lauritsen family, who live in a rural area just outside Århus in Denmark, wondered what they should do. 'As we used oil to heat our house, we looked for ways in which we could save money and, maybe, help the nation too,' Per Lauritsen says. 'Ninety-six per cent of Denmark's electricity was being generated from oil at the time.'

There were not too many options to consider. There was no firewood they could cut on their property, and Lauritsen, who is an architect, had designed his family's house to be energy-efficient and to make good use of the sun. So the wind, which blows almost unchecked off the North Sea across the low-lying Jylland peninsula, seemed to be the best possibility, particularly as a long series of experiments in the area had shown wind power's feasibility. Eighty-eight years previously, in 1891, the 'Danish Edison', a secondary school teacher called Poul la Cour, had become the first person in the world to use wind electricity for lighting and heating, although so unreliable and costly were the carbon-filament light bulbs available at the time that he had had to electrolyze water and pipe the hydrogen this produced to gaslights in his school in Askov, a village in southern Denmark, and to the village itself.

The two world wars and the depression of the early 1930s stimulated further experiments, and by 1944 some reasonably reliable and productive wind-powered generating sets had become commercially available. After the war, however, as soon as normal coal and oil imports became possible again, the market for this equipment disappeared, just as it did for a small British turbine produced at the time, the Lucas Freelight. But the lessons of the war had not been lost on the Danish electricity distribution companies, which, after further research, built an experimental wind turbine in the middle 1950s with government support. This was sited at Gedser on the Falster peninsula, which stretches into the Baltic at the far south of Denmark. It worked well and produced 400,000 kWh a year from its 200 kW generator and 24-metre sails until it was closed in 1962 after accountants pointed out that its output was twice as expensive as that from a conventional station.

As a result of the Gedser turbine's 'failure', the Danish government ignored the potential of wind power when the cheap energy bubble burst during the first OPEC crisis in 1973. Instead it gave its atomic energy research establishment, Risø, extra funds. As a result, although Risø opened a test station for wind turbines in 1976, it was largely left to a few pioneers to try to commercialize them. One of these was a carpenter in west Jylland, Christian Risager, who built a 22 kW machine with twelve-metre blades made from glass-reinforced plastic. This met all the local electricity company's requirements, and although many obstacles were placed in his way, he was eventually able to couple it to the national grid.

Risager and his wife, Boe, set up a company in 1978 to manufacture the turbines, and by the time the Lauritsens became interested in wind energy, about twelve of the Risager machines had been erected around the country. Unfortunately, though, these turbines proved very unreliable, and claims for damages from the twelve owners, who had grouped themselves together in an association, Danske Vindkraftværker (DV) – Danish Wind-Power Stations – drove the couple out of business. Nevertheless the Risagers had shown what could be done, and other manufacturers entered the market.

The Lauritsens suggested to their neighbours, the Vangkildes, who are teachers, and the Sorensens, who are farmers, that the three families jointly buy a turbine to meet their energy needs and that any surplus electricity be sold to the grid. 'We had good relations with our neighbours and shared a snow-plough with them,' Inger-Lise Lauritsen says. A lot of money was involved: 350,000 kroner – about £35,000, or £12,000 per family – for a 55 kW machine; and although both the other families needed loans secured on their properties to raise this, they said they would go ahead.

The local electricity company (Denmark has 110 regional power distributors) was much less enthusiastic; in fact it said quite categorically that there was no question of its accepting their power. It took political lobbying, a debate in the Folketing (parliament) and the direct intervention of the Minister for Energy before the grid connection was made.

But at what price, and on what basis, was their power to be purchased? 'All previous wind turbines had been owned either by companies or by individuals. Ours was the first needing a connection which was owned by a group of people who wanted to use some of its power for themselves,' Per Lauritsen says. 'It took two years of negotiations, but the agreement we reached has formed the basis of all subsequent group connections. Essentially, we delivered all the power we produced to the public network, for which we were paid 85 per cent of the household price, and we bought back all the electricity we needed at the full price. We used the public network to bring the power to our homes.'

This agreement opened the floodgates. Per was almost overwhelmed by people telephoning to ask him to help them set up their own turbines. He joined DV and was elected to the committee. 'I lost him to the movement,' Inger-Lise says. A total of 377 turbines was installed in 1979 and 1980, and wind-power guilds were set up all over the country, drawing on a rural co-operative tradition that is very similar to that in Ireland.

'The only limitation was that all members of a guild had to live in the same electricity supply area and within three kilometres of its turbine,' says Flemming Tranæs, DV's chairman in 1993. 'The idea was that if anyone in the area around the turbine suffered any inconvenience from it, it should be those who enjoyed its advantages. Well-to-do people from the cities were not to be allowed to invest in turbines and gain the advantage of cheaper electricity without being affected by any noise or visual disturbance at the turbine sites. This approach fits in well with the co-operative idea: that you establish your enterprise in the area where you live and among the people with whom you share your life, for good or bad.'

Everyone connected with wind energy in Denmark – and DV had more than 9100 members at the end of 1995 – believes that had the Lauritsen group not been able to negotiate such favourable terms, wind power guilds would not have developed and the Danish wind energy industry would have been far less successful. In 1994, Denmark had 40 per cent of the world market for wind turbines and generated 4 per cent of its electricity from the wind, two-thirds of which came from collectively owned machines.

Certainly the emergence of the guilds – which are partnerships rather than co-ops because Danish law does not allow the members of a co-op to set the interest they pay on its loans against their personal income tax – was a crucial factor in generating political support for the development of wind power. The first fruit of this was the adoption by the Folketing of the 1981 Energy Plan, which gave the green light to wind power by making grants available for the first time covering one-third of an installation's cost.

In 1984 the grants were replaced by a subsidy of 15.5 øre (1.5p) plus VAT for every kilowatt-hour supplied to the grid. As a result, the buying price in 1994 was between 60 and 65 øre per kilowatt-hour, depending on the price of power to the consumer in the area where the turbine was located. This was equivalent to roughly 6.5p per unit, including a 27 øre (2.7p) state subsidy. According to Johannes Poulsen, the managing director of Vestas, Denmark's (and the world's) largest turbine manufacturer, this price was enough to give a 15 per cent return on the capital invested.

Not everything was plain sailing, however because some power companies charged unreasonable amounts for connecting turbines to their grids and cut the payments for the power they bought by deducting the fixed charge that would have been payable if a wind turbine had been an electric motor of the same capacity. When DV published a report on these abuses in 1984, the government announced that it would introduce a law governing the relationship between turbine operators and power companies. This was the last thing the power companies wanted, and they hastily offered DV a ten-year agreement under which grid connection costs were shared between utility and producer and the buying price was paid with no deductions.

'The resistance of the electricity companies to wind power arose because they were opposed to anything that could prevent them using nuclear energy,' says Flemming Trænæs. 'They wanted central management of electricity production. Turbine owners can tell incredible stories about the way power companies did whatever they could to prevent the erection of wind turbines. However, our association got as much press coverage for these cases as possible, and gradually the politicians and the public came to see that the companies were determined to carry through their own energy policy, not that of the government or Folketing. After the 1984 agreement, however, things went well. Nevertheless we deliberately selected the fourth of May – the anniversary of Denmark's liberation from Nazi occupation – as the date of DV's foundation because of the level of official mistrust and resistance the concept of wind energy met.'

The guilds also played an important role in ensuring turbine quality. 'There were a number of confrontations between the association and some of the first manufacturers in the market,' says Flemming Tranæs. 'Some wanted to make money quickly, others had products that were simply not good enough. In two cases, after long, unsuccessful negotiations, we had to expose firms in the monthly trade magazine Naturlig Energi, and in both cases the businesses ceased trading shortly afterwards.'

Having the association behind them certainly helped the Lauritsens. In 1981 they learned that blades had broken off at least two machines of the same model as theirs. 'We stopped ours for fear that someone would be hurt until the makers, Vestas, came and fitted new blades free,' Inger-Lise says. Then, in 1985, their turbine's brakes and gearbox gave trouble, so Vestas bought the machine back at the price they had paid in part exchange for a new model. 'It suited Vestas to get it back to preserve their reputation. They used it for research,' Per comments.

Today Naturlig Energi publishes a nineteen-page performance table each month for the majority of the turbines installed in Denmark. As this shows the amount of electricity each installation has produced and states whether there have been any technical problems, it naturally keeps manufacturers on their toes. 'It's certainly harmed the sales of firms that promise people wonders but cannot back their claims up with actual data for their product on a good, windy site. The table also decisively demonstrates the importance of siting turbines well,' Tranæs says.

How have the Lauritsens, the Vangkildes and the Sorensens fared financially as a result of owning their own turbine? 'It's difficult to say we've made money,' Per Lauritsen says, although he agrees they have definitely had lower heating bills. This is because they use almost three-quarters of their installation's 120,000 kWh annual output themselves: they took out their oil-fired central heating and replaced it with an electrically driven heat pump system, which they share with the Vangkildes, while the Sorensens have electric water-filled radiators. This level of consumption is much above average: normally 1000 kWh would be taken as enough electricity to meet one person's domestic needs for a year.

There is no doubt, however, that installing the turbine changed the Lauritsens' lives. In 1983, Per and a friend, Ole Johansen, submitted a successful proposal to the Danish Energy Commission for grants for the construction of a wind farm to demonstrate Danish turbines to foreign buyers. The farm, which won the partners the 1985 Energy Prize, now has forty-five turbines, worth about £3 million, producing enough power for about eight thousand people. In 1992 a third partner, Jørgen Dinesen, joined them in opening a wind park with grants from the EU near Sines in Portugal. Each turbine there is computer-controlled, and Per regularly monitors their performance on the computer in his office at home.

The wind-power movement has done well too. At the end of 1995, DV's members owned 2090 turbines, almost two-thirds of the Danish total, and there were 52,500 people in the turbine guilds associated with it, although many wind guilds had voted not to join. Flemming Tranæs is worried, however. 'The idealists as a percentage are getting fewer and fewer. In many new guilds that are being established, enthusiasm for working in a co-operative in your local community and the environmental benefits of wind power are no longer so important: what makes people get involved today is the prospect of a good investment and a reasonable rate of return.'

Looked at from another perspective, however, these changes merely indicate that wind energy in Denmark has ceased to be a fringe activity. It has entered the mainstream and is successful and mature.

Danske Vindkraftværker, Egensevej 24, Vålse, 4840 Alslev, Denmark; tel. +45 53831322; fax +45 53831202.

Naturlig Energi, Vrinners Hoved, 8420 Knebel, Denmark; tel. +45 86365465; . fax + 45 86365626.

The three couples who pioneered wind-energy co-ops in Denmark, with their turbine in early 1996. From the left, are Aage and Erna Sørensen, Inge-Lise and Per Lauritsen and Hans and Mary Vangkilde. 'If the picture had been taken in 1980, there would have been nine children as well,' Per Lauritsen says.

step, which would normally be carried out by the consultant, is to compare the wind data with that obtained for the same period at the nearest meteorological station to get some idea of how the particular year's readings compare with those of an average year. The site readings, together with the meteorological figures, could then be sent to the manufacturers of the turbine the group is considering so that they can quote for a suitable machine.

'A year's set of wind measurements is likely to cost anywhere between £3000 and £8000, depending on how much you can recover if you sell the tower and equipment afterwards,' Hurley says. 'As the smallest wind turbine I would recommend that anyone install these days would be a 200 kW model costing about £200,000, you've got to look on the cost of the measurements in the same way you would regard survey fees if you were buying a house for a similar sum.'

Once a suitable site has been located and tested, the group can decide what make and type of wind turbine to buy. 'Wind technology is now mature,' Tom Pedersen, a representative of Vestas, told a packed meeting of sober-suited businesspeople, civil servants and bankers in Dublin early in 1994. 'The typical Danish concept of a three-bladed, fixed-speed turbine is based on sound principles, and over the years we have refined the design to such an extent that the average availability when installed is over 99 per cent. The only development going on at Vestas now is to increase the size – we have a 1.5 MW machine on the drawing-board, as this will be more cost-effective – but we have become very conservative. In fact I think we are now even more conservative than the utility companies themselves.'

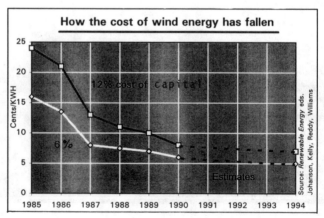

Graph 5.2 *As the size of wind turbines has increased, the cost per kilowatt of capacity has fallen. Given a good site, they are now entirely competitive with electricity from other sources. The data used here is based on experience with wind energy in California.*

As a result, Pedersen argued, groups shopping for a wind turbine did not need to worry about the technology embodied in it. What was far more important was the credibility of the manufacturer. 'The relationship between a wind-farm developer and a wind-turbine supplier is not just a straightforward sale but more like a twenty-year marriage,' he said. 'The main thing that developers need to satisfy themselves about is whether the supplier is financially strong enough to fulfil any warranty obligations and to be around to supply spare parts for many years into the future.' This was subtle sales talk, of course, emphasizing the points on which Vestas scores over smaller, younger, less well-capitalized rivals, whose equipment might not have the same lengthy record and therefore be less acceptable to banks and insurers; it was the wind-power industry's equivalent of 'No one ever got sacked for ordering IBM.'

Nevertheless he was broadly correct: generating electricity from the wind no longer involves the use of risky, experimental technologies. Moreover, it produces power at lower financial and environmental costs than any other form of renewable energy apart from small-scale hydro and, as the chart shows, already produces electricity at a comparable cost to that from a new coal-fired power station if the latter has to bear the European Commission's proposed combined carbon and energy tax. Within a few years wind will be the cheapest source of electricity apart from that from gas-fired power stations if promised drops in capital and maintenance costs occur.

But although Danish designs are effective and reliable, not everything is settled for all time in wind turbine design. Even in Denmark itself, as Pedersen explained, manufacturers are split over whether the blades should be 'stall-regulated' (fixed in position on the hub of the machine), which is cheaper and less complicated, or 'pitch-regulated' (able to alter their angle of incidence to the wind), which, although dearer, and potentially less reliable, enables more energy to be extracted from the wind by a given turbine on a particular site. It also allows the blades to be aligned with the wind in storms, reducing stresses on the whole turbine and tower structure.

Other Europeans and the Japanese have generally followed the Danish design policy, but American companies such as Carter, Enertech, US Windpower and ESI have drawn on aerospace technologies and materials to produce machines of between a third and a half of the weight of most Danish turbines. There were teething problems with some lightweight designs, particularly with the drive-train, which, apparently, have yet to be completely overcome.

The third step is financing, which will present much more of a problem in Ireland and Britain than in Denmark where wind guilds are so common that prospective members can readily borrow almost all the money they need for their share of the investment from their local bank. All they have to do is sign a standard agreement that their share of the income from electricity sales will be paid directly to the bank to discharge the loan; no additional security is usually required, although the bank will probably want details of the make of turbine and proof that it is insured.

Membership of a wind guild is restricted to residents of the parish in which the turbine will be erected and the parishes immediately adjoining it. All members do not necessarily invest the same amount, but each family's share of the investment and hence of the income from power sales is limited to 1.5 times their average annual electricity consumption, with an overall maximum of 9000 kWh. This limit is imposed because up to that level a member's earnings from electricity sales are completely free of income tax. Voting in the guilds, however, is based on the traditional co-operative principle of one member one vote, regardless of the size of investment.

Viola Jørgensen, a member of a wind guild in Vederso that owns three 75-kW Vestas turbines, told Bridget Gubbins: 'The association started in 1986. The cost of a share is 3400 kroner [about £300], and most people took out a loan [for the balance of the investment required, about £5000] from the local bank, to be paid back over ten years. We do it for fun and we make a little money. It's our money from our wind. Members include a headmaster, a janitor, a plumber – everyone you can think of. When our payments come in from the utility for our electricity, the local savings bank calculates how much money goes to each member and credits their accounts. This is the same bank we borrow from. Once the bank loan is paid off, members have almost free electricity.'

In Britain no financial institution has shown any readiness to help finance a wind co-op set up on similar lines, largely because they have not been asked. Mercury Provident, the ethical bank discussed in chapter 4, was commissioned by ETSU, the Energy Technology Support Unit of the Department of Trade and Industry, to look into the feasibility of a wind-energy investment fund but went off in the wrong direction. 'A financing gap exists between the maximum level a bank [branch] is prepared to lend (about £200,000) and the minimum level at which project finance departments of major banks are prepared to lend (about £2 million),' it reported in 1994[15] – a finding relevant to a far wider range of activities than wind energy. The result was that finance in the £200,000 to £2 million range was particularly difficult to obtain. 'With some banks charging minimum fees of £100,000 to arrange a loan, fees can be prohibitive for small projects,' it added.

Unfortunately, rather than investigating how wind projects could be structured on Danish lines so that no branch manager was asked to make a single loan of more than £200,000 but made lots of smaller ones to individuals, Mercury decided to set up the Wind Fund PLC in partnership with Triodos, the Dutch bank with which it later merged, to raise £5 million to provide share capital to wind farms. 'We found that share capital was even harder to obtain than bank loans,' Glen Saunders, a Mercury director, told me, explaining that Mercury would be providing part of the bank loans that the Wind Fund projects required and that he was confident that other banks would put up the rest. The initial rate of return required by the Wind Fund is over 12.5 per cent, and projections in its prospectus show this rising to 48 per cent within fifteen years. Community projects should therefore look for finance elsewhere.

As far as I can establish, the Inishowen Energy Co-operative in County Donegal is further along the road towards the establishment of a community wind-power project than any other group in Ireland or Britain. The co-op, which was set up by Stan McWilliams, a farmer and nurseryman, and Barney Walsh, a community worker in Derry, aims to help local people become involved in the development of sustainable renewable energy sources. Immediately after its launch in May 1994 it showed videos and organized discussions in the main towns on the peninsula to alert people to the prospects for renewable energy. 'We knew there was going to be a lot of commercial wind energy companies prospecting the area, so we thought there ought to be some public discussion,' Stan McWilliams says.

A young German, Reiner Eschwey, announced at one of the meetings that he was already measuring wind speeds at Drumlough. He joined the co-op, and the data from his instruments was given to an American firm, New World Power, which agreed to give the co-op a seat on its board and 1 per cent of the revenue from a £5 million wind farm it is to build there. The co-op has also had discussions with two companies that use £10,000 worth of electricity a year to keep potatoes in cold storage, and McWilliams is optimistic that the cost-benefit figures are good enough to ensure that at least one of them will install a wind turbine to cut its consumption from the grid.

Besides publishing a detailed assessment of the prospects for developing several types of renewable energy in Inishowen,[16] the co-op has investigated two small hydropower sites and, in association with the county council, the prospects for growing coppiced willow and chipping it to heat a proposed community education centre. 'As a result of our contacts with the county council, they are already thinking about how they can become more involved in energy self-reliance and are looking at plans for an energy-efficient housing project,' McWilliams says.

3. BIOMASS

Inishowen's wind energy potential is exceptional, and most places will probably find, like Hatherleigh in England, that biomass (plants and plant residues) is their most promising renewable energy resource. In all probability too they will decide it makes sense for them to explore how they can turn their existing agricultural and forestry waste into useful energy before examining whether they should grow plants specially for energy as well. In Ireland and Britain, forest and sawmill residue, animal dung and cereal straw are the most common plant wastes with good energy potential, while willows and poplars are the species most likely to be planted for fuel.

Straw

In a sustainable agricultural system involving mixed (*i.e.* arable and pasture) farming it is doubtful if significant quantities of straw would ever be available for use as fuel because it would be used for feeding and bedding animals before being composted in a biogas digester. Many organic farms outside the main cereal-growing areas already find it difficult or expensive to get supplies.

However, in the prairielands of the east of England under the present unsustainable system of agriculture, every four tonnes of grain harvested by the combine leaves two tonnes of straw, with the energy equivalent of a tonne of coal, in the field. About twelve million tonnes of straw is produced here each year; and since only half of this is fed to animals or used for their bedding, there is a surplus of some six million tonnes. Although this contains calories equivalent to about 1 per cent of Britain's total energy consumption, until the law was changed recently it was burned off in the fields, causing a smoke nuisance and doing considerable damage to trees and hedgerows. This was principally because it was unsuitable for large-scale, centralized power producers, as it is bulky even when baled and therefore expensive to transport. Consequently, if straw is to be burned for energy, it has to be exploited on a local basis.

In any case, burning straw requires a special furnace because, like other types of biomass, 70 per cent of it becomes a gas when heated, and a mixture of ash and char is left that will only burn if more oxygen is made available. This characteristic makes it suitable for combustion in the gasifiers we will be discussing later; despite this, most of the research in Britain has been into ways in which it can be used to replace coal in standard furnaces. Two approaches have been developed: one is to chop it into short lengths and blow it in on top of the burning coal; the second is to turn it into 'wafers' so that it can be handled by conventional automatic stoking systems and replace coal entirely. This latter process may 'expand the use of straw as a fuel into the rural industrial markets and perhaps even into the domestic market,' according to an official ETSU report.[17]

There have been several commercially successful demonstrations of the use of straw as fuel in Britain. Two hospitals in Birmingham, the Queen Elizabeth and the General, blew it into their boilers and cut their coal consumption by half; Woburn Abbey has a furnace that consumes four hundred tonnes of straw bales a year to heat the main buildings; and an Ipswich company, Needham Chalks, is using two thousand tonnes of straw a year to dry up to forty-five tonnes of chalk an hour.[18]

However, as in other renewable energy areas, it is the Danes who have shown what can really be done. Twelve thousand Danish farms have straw-burning boilers, and the first straw-fired district heating system was built in 1979. Fourteen years later there were sixty throughout the country; many of these were in places where no district heating system had existed before, so that pipes had to be run to take heat to the houses. 'Even plants as small as 2 MJ/s, corresponding to roughly two hundred single-family houses, are economic,' Dr Jørgen Boldt of the Danish Energy Agency told a conference in Helsinki in 1993.[19] 'The plants are reliable and have an efficiency of 80 to 90 per cent, which is comparable to coal-fired ones, and they generate less pollution. They are economically competitive too. The initial and operating costs are higher than for oil-fired plants but the fuel costs are lower, even ignoring the energy tax.' (The Danish government has imposed a tax on oil to cover some of the environmental damage its combustion causes. The amount of the tax rises whenever the world price of oil falls, and falls when it rises, so that the consumer pays a near-constant price.) The combined effect of the energy tax and gov-

ernment grants towards the capital cost of renewable energy projects*
was to make district heating with straw 20 per cent cheaper than with
oil, Boldt said. Nevertheless only a fifth of the surplus straw was being
burned in 1992; but when the resource is fully developed it will provide 7 per cent of Denmark's energy.

Forest waste
About a third of the total above-ground mass of a conifer never
reaches the sawmill but is left to rot on the forest floor. This residue
can be burned as fuel, as can the early thinnings too small for pulping
or chipboard manufacture that are produced by some modern
forestry systems. In Sweden both types of waste are normally left
where they fall to dry out naturally during the summer months before
being chipped in the forest and taken away to complete the drying
process under cover. From then on they can be treated exactly like
chips produced in the specially grown plantations we will be discussing shortly.

However, two points need to be considered by any community
considering this resource. One is that, like straw, wood-chips are
bulky and so need to be burned close to the forest. The second is that
while the trunk of a tree is very little more than a combination of
water and carbon dioxide, its leaves and small branches contain most
of the minerals it has extracted from the soil during its life – which is
why leaf mould is so good for the garden. Consequently, if leaves and
twigs are taken away, the forest will lose nutrients and, unless these
are replaced or returned, will become less fertile. In other words, the
burning of forest waste will not be sustainable unless the ash is
returned. All forms of biomass energy share this nutrient-loss problem to a greater or lesser extent.

Animal dung
Surprisingly, a cow extracts only 10 to 15 per cent of the energy in
the grass she eats. The rest is passed out in her dung, a fact that
explains why slurry (the mixture of dung and urine that collects in
tanks or 'lagoons' near the sheds with slatted floors in which most
cattle now spend their winters) can be so damaging if it gets into

---

* These grants have been available since 1976 and in some cases run as high as 50 per
cent. The policy is to phase them out as soon as a technology becomes mature. Wind
turbines at first received a 30 per cent grant; it was then cut to 10 per cent, and now
none are given at all.

streams accidentally. Its high energy content means that a lot of oxygen is absorbed when it breaks down, and if the oxygen is taken from the water in a river, too little can be left for the fish and they drown.

'A medium-sized cattle-house produces about thirty-three tonnes of beef a year – and three thousand tonnes of slurry,' says Les Gornall, who has been working on ways of extracting the energy from slurry in association with the University of Ulster at Coleraine, County Derry, since 1978. '[That amount of slurry] contains methane of at least the value of the beef, together with three hundred tonnes of fibrous matter, which is almost all carbon and as good as three hundred tonnes of best anthracite. But at the moment farmers concentrate on those two lorryloads of beef and throw away the thirty lorryloads of coal.'

Gornall set out to develop a system that would allow slurry to decay in the absence of air to produce a methane-rich gas that could be burned as a fuel. This was scarcely new: the Italian physicist Alessandro Volta had shown in 1776 that methane was given off by decaying vegetation, and by the time Gornall started work the Indian and Chinese governments already had large-scale schemes under way to build digesters – tanks in which animal, human and plant waste rotted to produce gas for cooking purposes – in tens of thousands of villages. But these were countries in which labour was cheap and where higher temperatures enabled decay to proceed more rapidly. What Gornall and a number of other workers in Europe were hoping to develop were digesters that were reliable and cheap enough to be attractive to individual farmers in temperate climates with high labour costs.

His first big success came in 1984 when he won a contract to install a digester to handle the slurry from three hundred cattle kept by the Cistercian monks of Bethlehem Abbey at Portglenone, County Antrim. The gas was piped to the abbey itself to fire the central heating system; the fibrous residue was composted and sold for horticulture; and the remaining liquid was sprayed on the abbey's land. This returned most of the nutrients to the soil, eliminating the need for chemical fertilizers and allowing the monks' system of organic farming to continue. A waste problem became an asset worth £60,000 a year, and the digester is still running well.

Work on farm-scale digesters was going on simultaneously in Denmark, but results from the forty-odd farms on which they were installed were disappointing. This was partly because the digesters themselves were inadequate but mainly because the farmers gave attending to them a very low priority: they always felt they had some-

thing more important to do. As a result, three-quarters of the proto-
types fell out of use fairly quickly, and the national effort shifted to
developing bigger digesters that could serve several farms and thus
warrant a full-time manager. These centralized digesters had the
added advantage of taking less capital to build per farm and being better able to meet steadily rising environmental standards. The first was
built at Vester Hjermitslev in the extreme north-west of Denmark in
1984, and ten years later fifteen centralized digesters were in operation and another five planned or under construction. Nevertheless
Denmark was exploiting only about 3 per cent of its biogas resource
and only one of the first nine plants had achieved a break-even
income. Despite this, a 1992 Danish Energy Agency report concluded
that if the lessons from the existing plants were incorporated in new
ones they would be profitable without state grants, provided Denmark's taxes on fossil energy were maintained.[20] This seems to have
been borne out by a digester at Hashøj, south-west of Copenhagen,
which opened in May 1994 and which has significantly lower capital
costs and extracts more gas from its slurry than its predecessors. However, had such 'poor' initial results been obtained in most other countries, detractors would have had a field day and the effort would have
been abandoned as a flop. Instead the Danes learned from their experiences and by now have gone through five cycles of designing, building, and testing.

So far, centralized co-operatively owned digesters have not reached
Ireland or Britain, but that statement will be out of date by 1998 if
Mary O'Donnell's efforts bear fruit. O'Donnell was one of the
founders of Earthwatch, the Irish arm of Friends of the Earth. In 1991
she had left the organization and was looking for an activity, prefer-
ably in the environmental area, that would create jobs in west Cork,
where she lives. She and her husband, Jim, who runs a furniture manufacturing business, had been working with Jerry O'Sullivan, manager
of the West Cork Institute for Rural Development, of which Jim was
chairman, investigating the possibility of setting up a factory to build
modular farm-scale methane digesters using technology developed by
Professor Martin Newell of University College, Galway.

However, during an environmental conference she had helped
organize in Skibbereen, her local town, she was advised to take
another direction. 'It was one of those discussions which take place
out on the street at three in the morning after the pubs have closed,'
she says. 'I was with Richard Byrne from the Danish company Krüger-
Bigadan, one of the leading designers of biogas plants, and Iain

Maclean, then Cork County Council's environmental officer and now the head of the Environmental Protection Agency. "Forget about farm scale, Mary," Richard said, telling me about the problems that had arisen in Denmark. "Go for centralized digesters."'

And so she did. She knew Kieran McGowan, the head of the Industrial Development Authority (IDA), from the time he had worked for the Crafts Council of Ireland, and rang him up to arrange a meeting, at which she told him about her plan to turn waste into a resource. Why aren't these digesters used already? McGowan asked, and after she had told him he promised a £15,000 grant towards a feasibility study. This sounded wonderful, but IDA grants present problems because they cover a maximum of half the cost of a study and are only disbursed against receipted invoices after the costs have been paid. Where was she to get the money she had to spend to be able to collect the grant?

The West Cork Institute formed a special company, West Cork Biogas Ltd, to carry out the feasibility study, and O'Donnell became its project director. Skibbereen's credit union and its two banks gave the new firm £2500, and the institute provided it with office space and gave the rent back as their contribution. Other people sent office equipment. Her husband's furniture business paid her salary in a way that enabled it to be considered as part of the £15,000 needed to match the IDA grant. Three years later, as this book was going to press, her feasibility study had convinced Cork County Council and a local farmers' co-operative, Drinagh, to put up a further £30,000 between them to employ consultants to take the project through to the construction stage.

'We've mapped the potential sources of waste within ten kilometres of the proposed site,' she told me. 'There are sixty dairy and pig farms, and we will be taking paunch contents from a slaughterhouse. Eighty per cent of the material going into the digester will be slurry; the rest will be sorted household waste, sewage sludge – that's great for gas-making – and residues from a cheese factory. The county manager has promised to bring forward the construction of sewage treatment plants in the small towns in the area so that we can get the sludge. We've already started mapping for a similar plant in the north of the county, and we'll move to the east later.'

In O'Donnell's proposal, the gas from the digester will be used to generate electricity, and the heat from the engine's exhaust will be piped to greenhouses. Some of the fibre will be composted and sold to gardeners, and the rest will be mixed with wood-chips and briquetted to be sold as domestic fuel. The liquid from the digester will go back to the farmers' land, as it does at Bethlehem Abbey.

'Spraying digester liquor on the land is much better for the farmer than spreading slurry because, as it doesn't contain fibres, it can be sprayed over the whole farm, including growing grass,' she says. Moreover because its nitrogen content is readily absorbed by the plants, farmers have been able to cut their nitrogenous fertilizer purchases by over half. 'There's much less risk of pollution. Farmers often have to spread slurry in wet weather because their tanks are overflowing, and the streams suffer the run-off. But if there is a digester in the area, the slurry can be collected and treated and the de-gassed liquor delivered back to them when and where they want it.

'The biggest advantage of the liquor, however, is that, unlike slurry, it contains no weed seeds and no pathogens and there's less recycling of intestinal bugs. Studies of farms using it show their vets' bills are significantly down.' Other studies have shown higher milk yields, less lameness, increased fertility, and a longer grazing season. Grain crops sprayed with liquor are less liable to lodging.

Mary O'Donnell cannot praise too highly the Danish Energy Agency and the Institute of Agricultural Economics[21] for the help she received. 'They publish regular updates on technology and spent an extraordinary amount of time answering questions on every aspect of the project,' she says, adding that the west Cork digester project could easily be replicated elsewhere and that she and Les Gornall are working together on proposals for one at Castlederg, County Tyrone. These involve the construction of a 1 MW biogas-fired power station that will take slurry from two large farms with three thousand cattle between them. However, O'Donnell and Gornall hope that smaller farmers will want to participate too. 'I knew at the outset that this was a five-year project,' O'Donnell says of the west Cork digester. 'It's still just bits of paper, but there's still two years to go.'

Growing special energy crops
While it certainly makes sense to use waste products such as farm slurry or surplus straw to produce electricity or heat a house, is it equally sensible to grow crops such as oilseed rape (canola) or coppice willow as a source of power and heat? Industrial agriculture is now so energy-intensive and the price signals given to the market system so distorted by subsidies that it could easily be commercially attractive to use more fossil energy to grow energy crops than can usefully be recovered when they burn.

Just how easily is illustrated by rape oil, which, although it has a very poor energy-in/energy-out ratio, has been the subject of many demonstration projects to show how it can be used to replace diesel fuel. For example, a treated version of it was used to run part of Reading's bus fleet recently and in Ireland it powers food-delivery vans in Waterford. But according to a study prepared for ETSU in 1992, growing rape purely for oil to turn into biodiesel produces only 35 per cent more energy than the farmer puts in, a return that makes the effort a nonsense.[22] If the rest of the plant is used for energy too the ratio naturally improves, but the plant's performance is still very poor, and a 1990 Irish study found that more external energy was needed to produce a litre of rape oil than the equivalent amount of any other crop-based liquid fuel it investigated. Ethyl alcohol from sugarbeet proved a much better proposition both in energy and commercial terms, as the by-products of the process were very valuable.[23] A German study found that using biodiesel in a vehicle would cut its greenhouse gas emissions by only 25 per cent and that this gain had to be set against the damage done to the soil and the environment generally by the chemicals used to grow the crop.[24]

Yet in spite of rape oil's poor showing, governments have been urged by farming groups to provide subsidies to make its production and sale commercially viable. 'Rape seed oil is competitive with diesel fuel provided the EC crushing subsidy is available,' another Irish report said in 1991, arguing that as the subsidy was equivalent to 70 per cent of the cost of producing the rape seed and farmers could sell the extraction residue as cattle food for another 45 per cent, they would be able to sell the oil for 10p per litre, the cost of extracting it, and match the pre-tax-and-duty price of diesel fuel at the time.[25]

The coppicing of fast-growing trees like poplar and willow produces a much more favourable fossil-energy-in/renewable-energy-out ratio. According to Caroline Foster of ETSU, this type of short rotation can give thirty times as much energy in the form of dry woodchips as was used to produce them.[26] However, a lot depends on how well the crop grows and is managed, and it is generally accepted that a more realistic ratio is one to twenty. Foster's analysis not only took in the energy used to fence and plough the land, plant the crop, protect it from weed and fungal infestation with chemicals, cut it, stack it for drying, chip it and then transport the chips to the power plant, but also that which went into building the drying-shed and a share of the amount used to build the tractor and other equipment.

Unfortunately, not all the energy in the wood-chips can be

extracted as useful power. The most efficient way to use them is to turn them to gas in a gasifier (which burns some of the chips to heat the rest and convert their volatiles into gas) and then burn the gas itself in an engine that powers a generator. This process allows about 60 per cent of the energy in the chips to be captured – one-third as electricity, two-thirds as heat. In other words, the overall outcome of growing willow, chipping it, drying it and burning it in a gasifier has been to promote one unit of a high-grade form of energy like diesel oil to about four units of a higher grade of energy, electricity, and eight units of relatively low-grade energy, heat suitable for warming rooms.

Coppiced wood-chip production is therefore only worthwhile if all the heat can be used, a fact well known to Malcolm Dawson, who has been involved in the effort to turn specially grown willows into useful energy for longer than perhaps anyone else in Ireland or Britain. Dawson works at the Horticultural Centre at Loughgall, County Armagh, where experiments have been carried out since 1974. Under the system he evolved, short lengths of fast-growing willow are pushed into a ploughed and weedkiller-treated field a metre by half a metre apart. They root and sprout, and after three years the long, thin shoots are cut and bundled by a special harvester and the stumps left in the field to provide another crop. The bundles of willow wands contain 50 per cent moisture when cut and are allowed to dry for three months in the open before being taken to a covered storage area, where they are chipped. Drying continues – using exhaust heat from the generator engine in the final stages – until the moisture content falls below 15 per cent and the chips can be satisfactorily gasified. On average, each hectare of willow coppice produces the energy equivalent of six tonnes of oil a year. The highest yields are obtained if several willow species are grown together, as this gives better protection against pests and disease, and each type has slightly different requirements from the soil.

Dawson says that Northern Ireland has 200,000 hectares of rush-ridden rough grazing, which would be ideal for willow coppice, and he would like to see farmers' co-operatives set up to provide both electricity and heat to colleges, hospitals and factories in the area. 'Two-thirds of the energy in the willow is released as heat, so you've got to have a use for that to make this operation attractive. You've also got to be able to displace electricity bought at retail prices rather than just selling it wholesale to the grid.' He therefore sees the farmers' co-ops installing gasifiers and generators on customers' premises and running them under contract. 'The farmers will only get the max-imum value-added if they do the whole thing in-house. Willow needs to be grown on a collective basis because the farms around here aren't big enough to supply a gasifier alone and it makes sense to use the harvesting equipment on more than one farm.'

Dawson has been running a 100 kW gasifier and a generator at Loughgall for several years to heat and light an agricultural college and a number of greenhouses. He feels that the technology is now advanced enough for a demonstration project in an institution to go ahead, especially as wood-chips have also proved themselves as a source of heat and light in many communities in Sweden, which pipe the heat from house to house. I agree. When he arranged for the gasi-fier to be demonstrated to me, I was surprised at how quickly it began to make gas when starting from cold and how simple a device it was. Any competent welding-shop ought to be able to make one.

Unfortunately, few farmers with suitable land seem to be interested in getting involved in producing wood-chips because of subsidies for suckler cows and sheep. 'They are getting direct EC grants worth £300 per hectare. If we had that level of subsidy for short-rotation forestry we'd be flying,' Dawson says. As a result, if he can get a demonstration project under way, as he hopes, the coppice is likely to be planted by non-farming landowners.

While Malcolm Dawson has been testing willows for wood-chip, Mike Bulfin has been experimenting with poplars at the agricultural experimental station at Kinsealy, County Dublin. Alders and ash are being evaluated elsewhere. Other people have been testing relatively small gasifiers too, including Ben Warren of Bristol University's Mechanical Engineering Department, who has a 30 kW gasifier at Long Ashton Research Station outside Bristol. This is smaller than Dawson's, and Warren thinks it would be suitable for installation on farms of over fifty hectares. But what would the farms do with the heat? Use it for glasshouses? 'Well, we've got a lot of greenhouses here at Long Ashton, and the unit produces more than enough to supply them,' Warren says. As part of his work for a PhD he has been carefully calculating the energy-in/electricity-out ratio and has pro-duced much the same figures as Caroline Foster: 'I think the ratio is about one to four,' he says.

Three points should be made about this work. The first is that Dawson's technology for producing wood-chips is very much an industrial one, and the energy-in/energy-out balance would improve if more local inputs, such as labour and horses, were substituted for external ones, such as weedkiller and tractors. The next is that unless it is done with the aim of achieving community energy self-reliance it is silly to use fossil fuel, land and labour to produce wood-chips for burning in one part of the country when straw or forest lop-and-top and thinnings are still going to waste in another. The third is that the low-grade heat must be used. This will almost certainly involve building district heating systems to serve existing housing, as is done extensively in the Netherlands, Denmark, and Germany. In Denmark, for example, seven of the first nine centralized biogas digesters had networks of hot-water piping built to nearby villages for them. However, biomass-fired district heating systems (BMDH) have probably proved more successful in Austria than anywhere else in Europe, and in 1993 alone, 36 plants were installed, 22 by farmers' co-ops, 10 by private firms, and 2 each by power utilities and municipalities. The first system was built by a sawmill operator in the village of Feldbach in 1979, and many of the 200-odd systems in place at the end of 1994 were in quite small communities.

'Villages with BMDH plants usually have between 500 and 3000 inhabitants and are of a predominantly rural character,' says an important EU-financed report, 'Pathways from Small-Scale Experiments to Sustainable Regional Development', which looks at factors that affected the adoption of renewable energy technologies in four countries. 'Accordingly, the size of BMDH plants varies between a few hundred kW and up to 8 MW, with corresponding grids between 100 metres and 21 km. Almost two-thirds of the plants have a power of less than 1500 kW.'[27]

While most of the early plants were erected by people in the timber industry with wood waste to burn, farmers with a few hectares of trees who had been selling wood as one of their sources of income forced their co-ops to move into district heating when timber and pulpwood prices collapsed in the 1980s. This was particularly true in those parts of Austria with the poorest prospects of developing alternative activities for the rural population in tourism or industry. In these areas the farmers lobbied their political representatives especially hard and persuaded them to make 35 per cent capital grants and an equal sum in low-interest loans available to the co-ops. A large part of the rest of the plants' cost was then raised from the connection fees paid by the owners of the homes to be heated.

Even with grants and the farmers behind them the co-ops found it impossible to get a district heating plant built in some villages, because many of their inhabitants either distrusted the new technology or objected to the traffic or to the chimney it would require. In general the villages where plants were built were those where a lot of community activities were already taking place. Where a co-op built a plant in the face of local opposition, the financial result was often poor because, with a high proportion of people refusing to be connected, it had to build longer pipelines to sell its heat. 'We noticed that all the villages [with plants] we visited were characterized by numerous local associations of villagers sharing such hobbies as music, sports, preparation of local events, or the planting of trees and flowers in the village streets. Common celebrations and good communications within the village were another characteristic,' the report says.

Community cohesion was not enough by itself, however. Idealism was needed too, both from a plant's promoters and from its customers. 'BMDH is neither a very good business for the operators nor a cheap way to heat for customers,' the report says. 'What are the motivations of local actors to realize a project?' Interviews in eighty villages showed that many promoters were concerned about the environment, wanted to improve forest management, and believed that their plants might make an important contribution to autonomous regional development. Their customers participated because they were also concerned about the environment, wished to support local farmers and the development of their region, and also appreciated the time and work that centrally supplied heat saved them.

Although the Germans have found that the capital cost of installing district heating on a new housing estate is actually lower than fitting each property with a gas-fired boiler,[28] the attitude in Britain is that people are too individualistic to agree to buy their heat that way. As a result, two 5.5 MW wood-chip power stations to be built in 1996 by a regional electricity company, SWEB – at Eye in Suffolk and near Cricklade in Wiltshire – will waste over half their energy. 'We'll be using some of the heat to dry the chips before they go into the gasifier and are looking for other uses. It's not economic to pipe the heat to people's houses in Britain because of the availability of natural gas,' a spokeswoman for SWEB told me. 'Until recently we were penalized under the government's non-fossil-fuel obligation arrangements if we used the low-grade heat for anything at all.'

The wood for the chips will be grown under contract by farmers, and forestry waste will be used when available. However, straw will not be burned, even though the Eye plant will be in the heart of cereal country. 'It requires special arrangements in the furnace, and the supply could be erratic because it would not be grown under contract and would depend on demand levels in another industry,' the spokeswoman explained, leading me to think that although SWEB prides itself on being a leader in the renewable-energy field,[29] its plans for both plants are not far removed from the 'let's-have-a-few-big-power-stations-near-the-coal-fields-and-not-bother-with-a-lot-of-little-ones-near-where-people-live-so-that-the-waste-heat-can-be-used' attitude of the old Central Electricity Generating Board.

Policy in Ireland is no more enlightened. At the end of 1995 the Department of Energy invited companies to submit proposals to build and operate a biomass or biogas-fired power station of up to 30 MW capacity, with the output to be sold to the grid at 3.6p per unit. A grant of up to £7.5 million could be made towards the capital costs to make the project attractive. But the specifications made no mention of the station using its low-grade heat. 'We had a competition for a CHP [combined heat and power] project recently,' an official told me. 'In this case we haven't excluded it, but we haven't included it either. We're waiting to see what the industry will come up with.'[30] However, it would not be possible to favour a proposal that did use the low-grade heat: a district heating add-on would have to be commercially viable by itself.

Growing coppice timber specifically for fuel may have a limited future. This is because willows and poplars only capture about 2 per cent of the solar energy that falls on them when they convert it to wood, and if the heat from the wood is wasted, only 0.4 per cent of the sun's energy is still available by the time it becomes electricity. Compare this with the 18 per cent conversion rate of solar energy to electricity already possible with commercial photovoltaic (PV) cells and the 28 per cent that has been reached in the laboratory, and it becomes apparent that specially grown plants are a very poor way of harnessing the energy of the sun.

Modern PV cells already produce the amount of energy used in their manufacture in their first two to three years of life, and their cost and energy content is falling dramatically as production methods improve. Professor Martin Green of the University of New South Wales has been able to reduce the materials cost per watt of capacity from two dollars to ten cents by finding a way of making satisfactory cells containing higher levels of impurities.[31] As the first cells of the new type converted 15.2 per cent of the sun's energy to electricity, the growing of wood-chips for electricity will probably be doomed as soon as they enter volume production. This is just as well, as it will eliminate the danger that the rich will take over land for growing their fuel at the expense of the poor, who need it for growing their food. Moreover, if a totally different approach to PV technology claimed by Advanced Research Developments of Athol, Massachusetts, really stands up, the future of all other sources of power will be radically altered. ARD say they are about to produce a plastic film that converts almost all the incident solar energy into electricity at a cost of only one cent a watt.[32]

In the medium term, the best type of plants to grow specifically for energy purposes might prove to be algae. A system developed at the University of the West Indies in Kingston, Jamaica, and at the University of the West of England in Bristol involves growing *Chlorella* in transparent cylindrical tanks and then drying and milling it before mixing it with diesel oil and burning it in a diesel engine to generate electricity. The waste heat from the engine is used to dry the algae, and the carbon dioxide given off by the combustion is dissolved back into the liquid in the tanks so that the next crop of algae can take it up. Other nutrients are also recycled. It has been claimed that the algae convert 15 per cent of the sunlight entering the tanks to usable energy.

The cost of electricity generated this way is claimed to be 2.5p per kilowatt-hour when calculated on a typical commercial basis using a 10 per cent interest rate and assuming a fifteen-year supply contract. It has also been said that a 2.5 MW power plant using this system would need 7.5 to 10 hectares of *Chlorella* tanks to supply it, compared with the 1500 hectares of coppice that would be needed to supply the same amount of power, and that the diesel content of the fuel could be as low as 5 per cent. I have been unable to verify any of these claims, however because the two companies involved in the commercial development of the technique, Biotechna-Graesser Ltd[33] and Photosynthesis UK Ltd, either did not respond to repeated enquiries or said that while they had the information I was seeking, it could not be found. Biotechna-Graesser did say, however, that the technique was not yet in commercial use.

Future prospects
The electricity production and supply system that will probably emerge in the future is one in which consumers will use the national or international grid not so much as a source of supply but as a battery. Many households will produce their own electricity, with a combination of solar panels on the roof and biogas-powered generating sets. Whenever they have more than they need they will 'bank' the surplus by feeding it into the grid; whenever they need more power

than they are producing they will take the required surplus from the mains. Their meter will run both ways, buying power from them at rates that vary according to the time of day and the season and charging it out on several rates as well.

The biogas could be piped in from a neighbourhood digester, with the waste heat from the engine used to warm the house – an approach that might be better in rural areas, where the houses are dispersed, than that used by the centralized biogas plants in Denmark with their big generators and miles of insulated pipes. Fiat is already manufacturing a single-house-sized CHP system, the Totem, but this needs modifying to run on biogas.

At University College, Cork, Professor Gerry Wrixon has developed a combined electrical generation system that may become commonplace in the future. It consists of a wind generator and a bank of PV cells coupled to an engine running on biogas. 'If you look at these graphs,' he says in his presentations, 'you will see that when the wind is blowing it's usually overcast and we don't get much power from the PV system. On the other hand, when it is sunny there is often little wind. The two systems, wind and PV, complement each other to a remarkable extent. However, for the periods when there is no wind and no sun we have the biogas engine. If you have your own digester this means that you can store the gas until you cannot get electricity from anything else.'

A second change will be that the grid will become a common carrier for electricity rather than the distribution arm of a monopoly supplier. As a result, local generating stations will be able to send electricity through the existing network to their customers rather than selling it to a state or private monopoly. As we saw, this is already happening in Britain to a limited extent and will be extended further in 1998.

These changes in the way electricity is generated and distributed are likely to come about whether communities aim for self-reliance or not. At a gathering of more than two hundred executives from many of the world's leading power companies in Arizona in early 1995 a common theme was the way deregulation and technological change were changing the shape of their industry. 'New power generation technologies are undermining the massive power stations that most people imagine is the only way to make electricity,' David Lascelles wrote in his account of the meeting in the *Financial Times*. 'In future, consumers will be served by the small, independent power stations that are already springing up, often owned by newcomers to the business. This could lead to miniature home generators which enable each household to make its own electricity, and even feed its surplus back to the grid.'[34] If he is right, the two key questions are: will local, renewable resources be used to power these small generating stations, and will local savings provide the capital to build them? Only if communities act decisively will the answer to both questions be 'yes'.

11   SAVING ENERGY

1. SAVINGS IN TRANSPORT

Most communities will find it easier and cheaper to use less energy than to meet all their present power requirements with supplies from renewable sources. In most cases they will find they can make the biggest demand reductions in areas in which they consume the most.

In industrialized countries this makes the transport sector the prime area for cuts. In Britain, for example, conventional breakdowns of energy use show that 33 per cent of energy goes to power road vehicles, aircraft, ships, and trains. This compares with the 27 per cent of energy used by households, another 27 per cent in industry, and 13 per cent in buildings such as shops, offices, hospitals, libraries, and schools. In the United States 31 per cent of all energy goes to power the transport fleet; the Irish figure is 20 per cent. However, these conventional breakdowns regard the energy that goes into building docks, airports, roads, multi-storey car parks and the rest of the physical infrastructure a modern transport system needs as being used by the industrial sector. The energy used to construct the cars and planes, the ships and trains, and to build the factories that build the vehicles is treated the same way. And as still more energy is used for such tasks as lighting the streets and providing packing materials that are not allocated to transport in the conventional total, it is easy to see why a Spanish study has found that more than half the fossil energy burnt in Spain is consumed directly or indirectly by the transport sector.[35] This means that curbing transport activity is one of the most promising ways of reducing the use of fossil energy.

The amount of energy used for transport in industrial countries has risen significantly over the past forty years – not because more goods are being consumed but because roughly the same weight of goods has been moved over longer and longer distances as a result of the increasing concentration and sophistication of production. In Britain the number of freight tonne-miles grew by 150 per cent between 1952 and 1992, although the production of coal, steel and other bulk commodities fell. This trend towards moving things further and further would obviously be slowed or reversed if communities began to do more for themselves.

A study by Stefanie Böge of the Wuppertal Institute in Germany shows the potential in this direction. She took a very simple product, strawberry yoghurt, which can be made at home with milk and fruit from the immediate area, and worked out how far the industrial system meant its components had to travel before a small jar could reach the supermarket. The result? The incredible figure of 3494 km.[36] This huge total was not reached because the main ingredients had to travel very far to reach the dairy in Stuttgart. The milk, which comprised 78.9 per cent of the jar's contents, came from the surrounding countryside, and so did the sugar. The strawberries added some distance, though, since – quite unnecessarily – they were grown in Poland, where labour is cheaper, and sent for processing in Aachen, near the Belgian border. However, as the map shows, the real culprits were the packing materials because, although the jar only had to travel 170 km

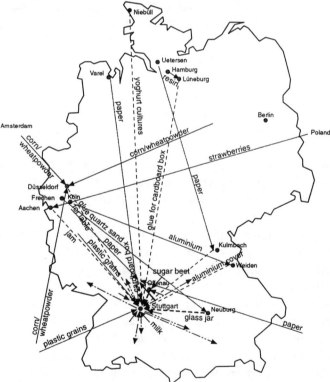

The journeys made by all the materials needed in the modern economy to get a jar of strawberry yoghurt onto a supermarket shelf.

from a glassworks in Neuberg, the quartz sand to make it had to be brought 400 km from Cologne, the paste for the label from Düsseldorf, the glue for the carton from Lüneburg, the plastic granules from Switzerland, the paper from Austria, the aluminium from Weiden, and so on, and so on. And most of these packaging components had to be made with materials such as starch, resin, pulp or alumina brought from somewhere else.

Böge calculated that the yoghurt maker could cut transport distances by over a third just by introducing standardized reusable jars that did not need to travel back to the original factory but could be refilled with other food products by other firms, and by adopting reusable crates for the jars, so that a new cardboard carton was not needed for every trip.

Under the present economic system, however, the least energy-efficient transport system, the movement of freight by road, enjoys substantial subsidies, which have enabled it to expand at the expense of rail freight – which only requires a quarter of the energy – canals, and coastal shipping. Böge quotes Dieter Teufel's 1989 study of the social costs of moving freight by road, which suggests that in Germany the tax on diesel fuel might need to be increased enough to raise its price to five times its present level to compensate citizens for the health, social and environmental damage that lorries do. I have been unable to trace similar estimates for Britain.[37] Teufel's calculation of the tax shortfall is as follows:[38]

Income from TAXES	6724 million
COSTS:	
Road expenditure	8730 million
Accident costs	5030 million
Accident-related distress	2600 million
Air pollution	6350 million
Noise costs (private dwellings)	9850 million
Other noise costs	2500 million
Congestion	2000 million
Water pollution from dangerous goods	3800 million
Water pollution from road salting	2800 million
Health damage to lorry drivers	1100 million
Other	1200 million
TOTAL COSTS	46,000 million
Subsidy given by public to road freight traffic (£17.5 billion Sterling at 1996 exchange rates)	39,300 million

Because he was just considering the social costs of moving goods by lorry and not the overall costs of the transport system, Teufel's figures leave out the considerable financial and environmental costs involved in the disposal of packaging materials as well as the environmental ones caused by their production. These costs should be ascribed to the transport sector, since without packaging, goods could not be moved safely over long distances.

In fact the closer one looks at transport the more subsidies appear, but as it is impossible to put reliable values on most of them, no one knows the overall total. All we can say with certainty is that transport subsidies are huge and that if they were removed, local manufacturers would be far better placed to compete in their local markets with bigger firms based elsewhere and goods would tend to be moved by lower-energy, less environmentally damaging forms of transport such as rail, canal, and sea.

There is very little that communities can do on a local level about road freight subsidies except campaign to have heavy lorries kept off certain roads. But in one area of transport – the use of the private car – energy consumption is under their direct control. Car travel, and consequently the amount of fossil energy it consumes, has increased sharply since the Second World War: in Britain the annual distance travelled increased tenfold between 1952 and 1992. Three-quarters of all journeys were under five miles. Car use itself increased car use by making it unsafe or unpleasant to walk or cycle and by reducing the frequency of public transport and lengthening its journey time.

So dangerous have many roads become in the past twenty years that driving children to schools well within walking distance has become a major parental chore. And while great-grandfather's pony ran on the renewable energy it grazed from under the trees in the orchard and pulled a trap made in the market town, the cars we use instead are entirely the products of the global economy, to which they tie us by their constant need for national currency to buy, insure, tax, repair and fuel them. Is it entirely accidental that car ownership is forbidden for the Amish, whose prosperous, socially cohesive communities are perhaps the best example of self-reliant communities in the industrialized world?

Any community moving towards greater self-reliance cannot avoid looking for ways to enable its members to live satisfactorily while running fewer cars. This means much more than maintaining or developing public transport. It means working closer to home. It means providing local delivery services, keeping the local shop open, and putting the travelling shop back on the road. It means car owners giving lifts to neighbours on a regular basis and, before they leave on a long journey, checking with agencies like those in Germany that enable people going in the same direction to travel along too. It means making the roads safe for pedestrians and cyclists, and establishing community car pools.

The German lift-arranging agencies advertise under M (for *mitfahrzentrale* – 'with travel centre') in the classified telephone directory, and three or four are normally listed in a sizable town. A driver planning a journey rings one of them three or four days beforehand and gives his or her name, address, telephone number, the registration number of the car, the destination, the time and date of departure, and the number of people they are happy to take. Drivers pay no fee to the agency. People looking for lifts then telephone in to see what is available, and if someone is going their way they have to call at the office to pay a fee, generally between 5 and 15 marks, depending on the distance, before they are given the driver's phone number.

'It's much safer than hitch-hiking,' says Sophie Wolf, who has used the system. 'The agency gives you the registration number of the car and advises you that if someone comes to the meeting-place in a different vehicle you should not go. If there is any doubt you can ask to see the driver's identity card.'

The agencies' rules stipulate that drivers must have adequate insurance, and be prepared to drop their passengers off at a bus stop or train station so that they can continue their journey. Passengers pay the driver something for their lift – the amount is left to be negotiated between them, up to a maximum set by the agency for the distance covered. This is generally about twice the fee paid to the agency. 'All the agencies' computers are linked,' Wolf says, 'so if I get a lift from Düsseldorf to Berlin, I may find myself travelling with a driver returning home there who registered with a Berlin agency before he left.'

The only long-distance lift-sharing agency in Britain is based in Newcastle-upon-Tyne. It was set up as Travelshare by a music graduate, Lindsay Gill, in March 1993 and later merged with a slightly older London agency, Freewheelers, and took its name.[42] 'We've got 16,000 members, roughly a quarter of whom are drivers,' Gill told me at the end of 1995. 'We've had a lot of press publicity, and membership is growing rapidly. There's a lot more interest in the idea than there was when I started.'

A year's subscription for both drivers and passengers costs £8, and passengers pay £2 for the telephone number of a driver going their way so that they can arrange a pick-up point and departure time. The agency suggests that passengers each pay 3.5p a mile towards the cost of the fuel. To increase security, members are issued with identity cards and the passenger is told the make, colour and registration number of the car that will pick them up. Same-sex lifts can be specified.

Lindsay Gill is in no doubt that it is better for Britain to have a single national agency, rather than a German-style network of local ones, because it keeps down overheads. 'Their computers are linked, so the Germans essentially have a single agency with a lot of outlets, which the users have to pay to support,' she says.

Lift agencies and car pools are only suited to longer journeys; and for the 75 per cent of journeys that are under five miles the bicycle is probably the best solution. The European city that has been most successful in getting people to use bicycles instead of cars is Groningen in the Netherlands, where, as a result of action by the local council, 50 per cent of journeys are now made on two wheels.[40] 'We are trying to find a balance between accessibility and livability by giving priority to the bicycle and public transport,' Marcel Bloemkolk of the Department of Town Planning, Traffic and Economic Affairs told me. 'We try to keep the use of cars to a minimum.' This is no easy task for an urban area with 170,000 inhabitants that serves as the regional centre for the whole northern Netherlands and to which more than 30,000 people travel by car to work each day.

The first steps were taken in 1979 when the council simply closed certain streets to traffic other than delivery vehicles, buses and bikes after what Bloemkolk admits was inadequate consultation. 'It wasn't the way we would do it nowadays,' he says. The closures meant that the inner city, which is about a kilometre in diameter, was divided into four sectors, and cars could not cross from one sector to another except by going out onto the inner ring road. The result was an outcry from car-owners and from retailers. 'The matter became heavily politicized, which was not at all helpful, and the retailers made things worse for themselves by putting advertisements in the newspapers suggesting that the city was surrounded by barbed wire. That must have cost them a lot of business,' Bloemkolk says.

'It was horrible at first,' Wilma Naaijer told me in her father's fabric shop, 't Binnehuis. 'People got lost in the new one-way system, and they could only park for two hours. We lost business, and shops in outlying towns advertised saying that they had no parking problems.'

On the other hand, there were improvements. Several streets were pedestrianized or narrowed, and the Great Market Place, which had in effect been little more than a traffic roundabout, became a public space once more. 'Under the 1979 plan public transport, including taxis, cyclists, and pedestrians, could move freely between the sectors,' Bloemkolk says. 'Retailers' income dropped until people got used to the new system. Some shops had to move, but that would have happened anyway in some cases.'

In Groningen today the council is eliminating the last parking spaces in the central area ('There are very few, but people drive around looking for them,' Bloemkolk says). Instead, car owners can pay a guilder (40p) per half-hour to park beyond the inner ring road and walk into the central area, or they park without charge on the outer ring and take the free and frequent bus service to the centre. The money collected from people parking close to the inner ring covers the operating costs of the buses for those who park further out.

Since almost everyone now walks, cycles or takes a bus into the central area, the planners have much more freedom about where retail developments within it should be. 'The shops were too concentrated before,' Bloemkolk says. 'They all wanted to be close to each other. Now we can offer them good sites in attractive streets that previously had a messy and worn-out appearance. You can do a lot more with a street if it has no cars.' Big shops like IKEA, which feel they need to be close to a car park so that customers can get bulky purchases away, are sited on the inner ring and allowed to have their own small underground car parks, for which their customers must pay.

While restricting the car has certainly cut the number of road accidents and made Groningen a more attractive place, it is hard to say how much energy it has saved. Council surveys show that car traffic is about 15 per cent lower and cycle usage 10 to 15 per cent higher than in cities of comparable size in the Netherlands, which, in comparison with anywhere in Ireland or Britain, look after their cyclists well. However, the strategy of both the council and the retailers, who now work closely together, is to use Groningen's new-found attractiveness to entice extra shoppers to travel there – mostly by car – from further and further away. 'The shopkeepers want more pedestrianized streets, and we think there is room for 20-40,000 square metres more retailing space on top of the 80-90,000 square metres we have at present,' Bloemkolk told me. 'We have to keep Groningen competitive. We're getting people from Germany now, especially when the shops there are closed on Saturday afternoons.'

Though its motives might be mixed, Groningen has a lot to teach other places about how to persuade people to cycle and to use public transport instead of their cars.[41] 'If you want to stimulate the use of bicycles, biking must be fast, comfortable, and safe,' says Bloemkolk, who is himself a member of the Dutch Cyclists' Union. 'We have therefore created a large number of special facilities for bicycles. The most important is a cohesive network of cycle routes beside main roads and along roads with little motor traffic. It is very important that the network is as fine-meshed as possible to cut distances and travelling time, so we've built bridges and cut-throughs for pedestrians and cyclists only. Cyclists can use almost all one-way streets in both directions; at traffic lights we give them waiting spaces in front of cars and allow them to turn right against a red light. Bicycle racks have been erected in the city centre and at bus and rail stations, and guarded bicycle shelters have been opened too, some with lockers, toilets, and phones. We've also started a campaign against bicycle theft.'

On public transport, Bloemkolk says that the council's planning policy has been to site buildings that a lot of people will be working in near existing bus routes and the railway station. It has also tried to integrate the different forms of public transport. 'They must form one network, from the train for long distances to local buses and taxis for transport in the city, and there must be as few delays as possible. We have special bus lanes and traffic lights, which can be changed by a transmitter in the bus.' Buses passing through the central area, however, are restricted to 15 km per hour to be safer for pedestrians. The plan is to replace the present diesel-powered vehicles on these routes with hybrid vehicles that will run on liquid petroleum gas most of the time but on batteries in the city centre to cut noise and emissions there.

Another city that has tried to promote the bicycle with great success is Davis in California, where roughly a quarter of all journeys are made on two wheels. (The best English city is York, which claims 10 per cent.) The policy dates back to the middle 1960s, when the University of California's Davis branch increased its student numbers sharply, with the result that many more bikes were being used on streets designed primarily for cars. In the city council elections in 1966, cycle lanes became the biggest issue, and a majority of candidates who supported their construction were elected. Now the city, which has a population of 50,000, a third of them students, has thirty-seven miles of cycle lanes running beside roads and twenty-nine

[main text continues p.236]

CAN HORSE TRANSPORT MAKE A COMEBACK?

Unlike lorries, horses make their own replacements, run on locally grown fuel, and only need simple accessories that are produced, often from local materials, in unsophisticated workshops. And if using them involves more work than their fossil-powered equivalent, that is a benefit rather than a disadvantage for people who wish to create incomes for each other rather than for financiers and factory workers long distances away.

For deliveries in towns or within a limited area, a two-horse dray is as cost-efficient as a four-tonne van, or so close as to make no difference, according to the most recent study, prepared in 1985 for the Shire Horse Society by an economist, Ian Webster, whose data was based on the experience of three of the dozen or so breweries that still keep horses for local distribution.[42] The figures he used are rather old now, but a study today would produce broadly the same result.

Webster assumed that both the van and the dray would travel twelve miles in a working day and distribute eight tonnes of goods on each of 240 days a year. The capital cost of the horses (£1100 each), their tack and the dray (£2600) was less than half that of the van (£9500) and so cost less in interest. They also cost less in depreciation: the horses were reckoned to have a working life of fourteen years and were written off over that period, while the dray, which could easily serve for 50 years, was depreciated over 25. This gave a total depreciation of £274, compared with £1902 for the van. Maintenance on the dray was much lower than on the van – £331, compared with £1727 – and its insurance was less too.

The only advantages that could be claimed for the van were that it was cheaper to garage and to fuel, and cost less for labour because, unlike the horses, it did not have to be fed, watered, and mucked-out at weekends. The £1400 difference in labour costs this entailed ·meant that the dray cost £22 a year more to run than the van.

Webster's actual figures were:

	TWO-HORSE DRAY	MOTOR VAN
A. Stabling or garage	1445	863
B. Insurance	160	220
C. Road tax	–	130
D. Wages	9369	7969
E. Depreciation	274	1902
F. Interest	264	809
G. Horsekeep	2244	–
H. Sundries	212	–
I. Fuel and oil	–	487
J. Tyres	–	170
K. Maintenance	331	1727
TOTALS:	14,299	14,277

If payments B, C, E, F, I, J and K go largely to recipients outside the community in exchange for the goods and services they supply, the dray is a much more self-reliant method of transport, since only 5.4 per cent of the costs associated with it leave the area, compared with 38 per cent for the van.

miles of separate bike paths. It also has an ambitious ten-year $21 million programme to build more.

But the pleasant, tree-shaded central area of Davis is unhealthily quiet, and the merchants have plenty of time to express their concern. The staff in the city planning office are worried too: their surveys show that while the number of bike journeys is not falling it is not growing either, although the city's population is expanding each year. As a result, cycling contributes a smaller and smaller percentage of all journeys made. The problem is that when Winger's department store in the city centre closed in 1986, a large shopping centre opened outside the city boundary. Sales-tax receipts in Davis, which are now a third or a half of those in comparable towns, slumped as people started shopping outside its borders. 'The reason the number of cycle journeys has not increased is that people need cars to get to the mall [shopping centre],' a planning officer told me.

Marcel Bloemkolk of Groningen sympathized with Davis when I told him the story. 'It's important to keep the central area compact. Groningen wouldn't want a megastore on the edge of town.'

2. SAVINGS IN THE HOME

Davis has, however, been much more successful in saving energy in the most important area under local control: the 27 per cent share of total energy consumption used in the home. Its technique is to ensure that all new houses are built to the most stringent energy-saving standards that California state law allows it to impose. This has not meant that houses built by developers are more expensive than they would otherwise have been: in any town the price of a new house is determined by what the market will bear, not the cost of construction, and if a developer has to spend an additional $5000 to reach a building code's standards, that is $5000 less he can afford to pay for the site. The landowner loses while the householder gains from lower heating, lighting and cooling bills and a higher resale value. The first houses in Davis to be built to the new standards now fetch 12 per cent more than conventional houses of the same age.[43]

So enthusiastic is Davis about the results it is getting from demanding high building standards that it publishes a monthly newsletter, the *Biketown Builder*, to keep contractors and others up to date with the regulations. Inspections of houses under construction are frequent and stringent, and the city has its planning officers devote a lot of their time to talking to architects and builders about possible improvements to their plans, not just for the houses themselves but the way they are laid out. Energy-efficiency should be designed in to a subdivision at the start rather than tacked on afterwards, a policy statement issued by Davis City Council stresses, before listing the features its staff will be looking for in planning applications. These include placing the buildings to take heat from the winter sun ('Building envelopes should be designed to provide solar access to the south-facing glazing of buildings ... on the winter design day of December 21, when the angle of the sun is 20.7 degrees') and to use the prevailing breezes in summer to keep cool. As a result, a minimum of 80 per cent of detached houses in a subdivision have to have their long axes running within 22.5 degrees of the east-west axis. Planting plans have to be prepared that provide shade for parking and play areas as well as the houses themselves, and paved areas generally have to be minimized to reduce heat gain. Another stipulation is that a convenient system of paths be provided for pedestrians and cyclists.[44]

If similar requirements had been adopted in Herefordshire it would have been much easier for David Olivier of Energy Advisory Associates to find a site for the highly energy-efficient demonstration house he started planning in 1990. Three potential sites had to be dropped, and on the fourth site, although the house had several of the features of the traditional cottages of the area – a long, thin shape, facing south, with a low slate roof and small windows at the rear – the council wanted a house facing the road, which happened to run to the north. A year's negotiations were required before the planners changed their minds. Construction should begin in 1996.

The principal feature of the house is that it will require only a tenth of the energy used to provide heating, lighting and hot water in a British house built to current standards. Moreover, since much of the energy the house does require will come from the sun – its south-facing roof will have ten square metres of solar collectors for hot water and fifteen square metres of photovoltaic cells for electricity, which will be banked in the grid – its fossil-energy consumption should be 3 per cent of that of a typical house. This is possible because it will have about four times the level of thermal insulation built in to a normal new house, together with much better windows, which will capture more heat from the sun each year than they lose. No European manufacturer was interested in making these, so the sealed glazing units will be imported from Canada and mounted in locally made frames of British timber.

Some of the house will be of local stone, and concrete blocks will be used for the load-bearing walls, as these take only a third of the energy used to make bricks. PVC, lead, insulation foamed with HCFCs and glues made with formaldehyde will be avoided, for environmental reasons. 'The amount of embodied energy in the materials for the house will be slightly less than for a normal dwelling,' Olivier says, a fact that leads him to hope that building costs for similar houses would be very little more than for conventional ones once their insulation levels and energy systems became mass-produced and therefore standard. 'There's negligible experience of building houses like this in Britain, but taking the Swiss and German experience as a guide, the extra cost should not be above 5 per cent in widespread use. Even in this country I know buildings which have gone half way towards the performance we are aiming for here with no extra cost.' One of these is a 1992 house in Charlbury, Oxfordshire, which has cut its total energy consumption, including that for lighting, cooking, and appliances, by 70 per cent. Another is a London house that has 200mm of insulation in the roof, 165mm in the cavities, and 250mm under the floor.

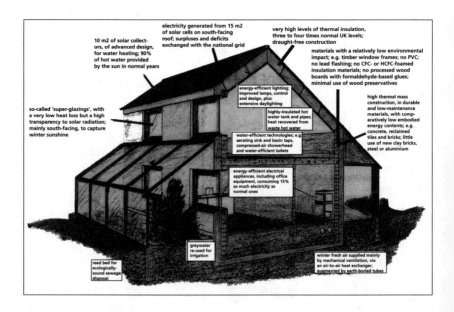

David Olivier's energy-saving house, which ran into planning consent problems.

Professor Owen Lewis, director of the Energy Research Group at the School of Architecture, University College, Dublin, agrees that the extra cost of a really energy-efficient house should be modest. 'It is greatly exaggerated by the building industry. I would say that 5 per cent is the upper limit, since, once you get the rate of heat loss down to a low level, you can make substantial savings because you do not have to install boilers, chimneys, and central heating systems.' (David Olivier's house has no central-heating system or wood-burning stove: cooking will be with either bottled gas or biogas.) 'At some point, however, you run into diminishing returns and it's not worth spending more.' In part this is because the occupants of the house and their lights and appliances will release enough heat to cover the remaining loss, much of which will be through the ventilation system as a result of the necessity to change the air continually.

In any case, it might be cheaper to capture replacement energy from the sun than to spend more on extra insulation. Susan Roaf's house in Oxford is said to be the first in Britain to generate more electricity – from the forty-eight solar panels on its roof – than its occupants will use in a year. Like Olivier's, it uses the grid as a battery, feeding the surplus into it when the sun is strong and drawing out at night. It is one of the developments that make Professor Lewis excited about the progress being made with photovoltaics. 'We're working with a Spanish firm that is building cells into its curtain-walling, which costs no more than any other good-quality cladding. It comes in six-metre-high units, which are fixed vertically. People tell us it is inefficient to place them this way because they need to be angled to capture the maximum amount of sun, but we tell them that since the electricity is essentially free the level of efficiency doesn't bother us.'

Given the minimal extra cost, could an Irish or British county council adopt Davis-style policies and demand much higher levels of energy-efficiency from the planning applications coming before it than those set out in the national building regulations? 'Yes, if the climate of opinion was right,' says a friend who is a senior planning officer. 'In fact a group of planners in Britain is already working in that direction.'[45]

But building new houses to much higher standards can only be part of the solution, as at current rates of demolition and new construction, over half Britain's housing stock will still date from before 1965 in thirty years' time and thus have been built before it was necessary to meet any legal insulation standards at all.[46] The average energy rating of British houses is between 40 and 50 on the government's misleading

[main text continues p.242]

CAR POOLS CUT MOTORING COSTS AND ENERGY USE
Cars are a problem for city-dwellers. It can be hard to find anywhere close to home to park them safely for long periods, and public transport is often more convenient for journeys to the office or shops because of parking problems at the other end. But for trips to the country and friends out of town, or for moving heavy items, it's nice to have one around.

Towards the end of the 1980s the three Petersen brothers in Berlin decided that it was silly for each of them to have his own car and began to share a common vehicle. Friends thought the same way too, and after a few months, seven people were sharing two cars. In 1989 the brothers decided they had better draw up some more definite rules about the way the costs were to be shared and set up a company, Stattauto, to handle what was becoming a booming business. ('Statt' is a word-play on stadt, 'town', and statt, 'instead of'.) By 1995 their firm had 2600 subscribers and had inspired or helped similar operations to get established in over three hundred German, Dutch, Belgian, Swiss and Austrian cities and towns.[47] There is at least one village system too, Dorf-Mobil Bad Boll, which draws its members from a rural area in Baden-Württemberg.

A new subscriber to Stattauto pays a deposit of 800 marks, refundable when they leave, and a 200-marks joining fee. They are given a key for a safe at all twenty-six stations around Berlin where the firm's cars are kept. When they need a vehicle, they ring to say what type they want, at what time, for how long, and the station at which they wish to collect it. The call is handled by a taxi company working under contract. A despatcher takes the call, checks the availability on computer and makes the booking.

'There are between three and five vehicles at each station,' says Bertolt Klessmann, chairman of the association representing Stattauto's subscribers. 'If all those at my nearest station are booked for the time I want, I ask the operator to check availability at the next-nearest station. If you have a planned life and know three or four days before when you are going to need a vehicle, the system works well. But if you ring up at 10:30 on a Saturday morning wanting a car at eleven o'clock, one might be hard to find. Weekdays would be much easier.'

When subscribers arrive at a station they insert a personal magnetic card into a reader, which records their name and the time and allows them to open a door giving access to the safe. They open the safe with their key, take the keys of the car they have booked, and drive away. 'The recorder is in case the car is stolen or there is an accident: the company can find out whose card opened the safe and when,' Klessmann explains.

The costs of using Stattauto vehicles are low. 'There's an hourly charge of between 2 and 6 marks, depending on the type of vehicle. The most common charge would be 3 or 4,' Klessmann says. 'There is also a charge for each kilometre of 27 or 28 pfennigs, which covers everything: insurance, taxes, repairs, engine oil, and fuel. The only other charge is a monthly fee of 10 marks, which covers the management costs. The rule is that subscribers should not return a vehicle with the fuel tank less than half full. They have to fill it up, and the receipt for whatever they pay is set against the rental charges. The only exception is when subscribers are going on a trip of over 500 kilometres: in this case they pay 17 or 18 pfennigs a kilometre and buy their own fuel. This makes sense because their fuel consumption can vary quite a lot according to how they drive.'

Subscribers return the cars to the station from which they borrowed them ('The company is trying to work out how it could handle one-way trips,' Klessmann says) and are responsible for seeing that they are left in a clean and tidy condition, although an 'auto-chef' – perhaps a student or a retired person – lives close to each station and gets a small allowance for making occasional checks on the cars. Subscribers pay monthly. They fill out a form at the station each time they return a vehicle, recording the hours they have used it for and the number of kilometres travelled. If the bill is not paid on time the company's computer declines to open the door to the key safe when they next present their magnetic card. Klessmann says that the only serious problem with the system is that some subscribers are late returning their vehicles and keep others waiting.

Experience has taught Stattauto how many cars it needs to have available at any time. 'Most of the cars are hired by subscribers to use during their free time – unlike car hire firms, which are busiest during working hours. We find that we need one car for every twenty-three subscribers in winter and one for eleven or twelve in the summer. There is a strong relationship between day length and car use.' The company is thus forced to buy new vehicles in the spring and sell the older ones in the autumn.

There is also a strong relationship between the length of time someone has belonged to Stattauto and the amount they drive. 'Their first year they drive quite a lot,' Klessmann says. 'The second year they will drive half the amount, and the third year half that again.' This means that one of the Petersens' aims in starting the company is being fulfilled: that cars are only being used when they are the best form of transport. 'When someone owns a vehicle, the main costs are fixed and they use it for the smallest things, like going two or three hundred metres to a shop. But if you are paying only according to how much you use it, you ask yourself each time you plan a journey if using some other form of transport might make more sense.' It also means problems for Stattauto: 'to stay our present size we have to increase the number of subscribers.'

Most of Europe's car-sharing groups belong to European Car Sharing, which allows their subscribers to use another club's fleet when they are away from home. 'Car sharing is one component of an environmentally compatible traffic strategy,' an ECS leaflet says. 'By combining bus, rail, taxi and car sharing, users can choose the most convenient, inexpensive and environmentally acceptable means of transport. Every car-sharing vehicle means four cars less on the road and an average saving of 28,000 car-kilometres per annum. The energy used for the mobility of a former car owner can be reduced by car sharing by almost 50 per cent.'

European Car Sharing, Feldstrasse 13B, 28203 Bremen, Germany; tel. +49 421 71045; fax +49 421 74465.
Dorf-Mobil Bad Boll eV c/o Jobst Kraus, Pappelweg 12, 7325 Bad Boll, Germany; tel. +49 716 43742.

Standard Assessment Procedure (SAP) scale, which ranges from 1 to a maximum of 100.* You might think that a house with a rating of 1 would lose all the heat put into it almost immediately while one with a rating of 100 would retain it indefinitely; but given the constant advances in technology, and since the laws of thermodynamics make it quite impossible to achieve a perfect level of insulation, any scale with an upper limit has to be misconceived. 'My house is off the scale: it comes out at about 250,' David Olivier says. 'Houses built under current building regulations are between 60 and 70, but that's based on how they are on paper, not necessarily how they actually perform when they are built. There are many low-energy houses in the UK whose energy performance is considerably poorer than the claims which were made for them at the design stage.'

How, then, can a community's existing houses be brought up to a reasonable level of energy-efficiency? Because it costs the municipally owned electricity companies of Denmark less to show someone how to save a unit of electricity than they would have to pay in interest to generate that unit if they had to build a new power station, they are generally reckoned to have had more experience than anyone else in Europe in getting their customers to cut power demand. According to AKF, the Danish Institute of Local Government Studies,[48] the main obstacle preventing households cutting electricity consumption is ignorance. In an experiment, three groups of households, none of which used electricity for room heating, were sent literature on ways they could save power and offered low-cost loans if they wanted to adopt any of the measures. They were also given a leaflet on how to read their electricity meters. As a result of these simple measures, group 1 cut its electricity demand by 7.4 per cent. Group 2 had the price of its electricity increased as well and its demand dropped by 8.3 per cent. Group 3 received the same treatment as group 2 except that its members were also visited by advisers; it cut its energy use by 10 per cent. These savings were achieved largely because people

---

* The Irish rating system simply states how much energy will be lost from the house per square metre of floor area per year, given the site on which it is built, and that certain temperatures are maintained inside. 'One problem with the SAP is that all the well-insulated houses get bunched together at the top end of the scale, so that people cannot distinguish between them,' says Bill Quigley, who set up the first company to offer domestic energy audits in Ireland and who devised the Irish system. 'With us, it is easy for people to calculate how much a well-insulated house will save them: all they have to do is multiply the rating by the floor area and the price they will be paying for their heating energy, and that gives them what it will cost to heat it for a year.'

Energy used by a typical British household	
HEATING (gas)	45 %
HOT WATER (gas)	16 %
LIGHTING (electric)	1 %
TV ETC (electric)	0.5%
COOKING (electric)	3 %
DISHWASHER (electric)	2 %
FRIDGE | FREEZER (electric)	2 %
WASHING-MACHINE | DRYER (electric)	0.5%
CAR	30 %

(source: New Scientist, 15 January 1994)

changed their habits: only a limited number of light-bulbs and appliances were replaced with more efficient types.[49]

Over a longer period, as more equipment became due for renewal, much deeper cuts would have been possible, as has been demonstrated by the Billsavers Project run by the Lothian and Edinburgh Environmental Partnership (LEEP). The project studied electricity use in a hundred low-income households for a year before supplying them with compact fluorescent light (CFL) bulbs and helping them get their appliances replaced or repaired. 'Significant savings are being achieved from installing CFLs, the most extreme example being overall savings/reductions of 70 per cent,' writes Robert Barnham, the project development officer. 'There are already cases where the replacement of an appliance is expected to result in first-year running cost savings matching the replacement costs. The most significant savings are through replacing fridges and fridge-freezers; though low rated in terms of actual wattage, they are on continuously and in certain cases older models are using up to ten times the energy of an efficient replacement model.'[50] LEEP is now looking at the potential electricity savings in a hundred middle-class and upper-class households and has a scheme under which families can buy CFL bulbs with loans from local credit unions. 'Development of an energy services company may be a longer-term opportunity incorporating advice, soft financing, retailing and contracting,' Barnham writes.

Bristol Energy Centre, set up as an offshoot of the Centre for Alternative Technology at Machynlleth in Wales to show what alternative technologies could do in an urban context, has already set up a company that aims to reduce not just electricity use but a household's total energy consumption. The centre believes that the main obstacles to a general improvement in domestic energy standards are the fact that many householders don't know what to do and that, even if they did, they would find it too much trouble to arrange for a contractor to do the work, particularly as they do not trust contractors anyway. On top of that, householders may not have the ready cash to pay for whatever needs to be done.

To tackle these problems, the centre formed the Energy Club in partnership with a regional electricity company, Northern Electric, and a firm of financial consultants, Lothbury Services Ltd, and launched a trial project in two communities outside Bristol, Yate and Nailsea, in October 1995. In the test, owner-occupiers were subjected to 'an intensive marketing approach' backed by a letter of support from the council, urging them to explore ways of cutting their energy bills by telephoning the Energy Club. 'With our computer software we can do quite a lot by asking people questions over the phone,' a club spokesman told me. 'We give them an estimate of the sort of savings they are likely to make, which are usually about £200 a year or 20 to 30 per cent of their energy bills, and some idea of how much it is likely to cost. If they are still interested we carry out a survey and organize contractors to do the work for them. If necessary we can arrange the finance through a personal loan over five years from a high-street bank. The current rate of interest is 14.6 per cent, and the savings they make should be enough to cover their repayments.'[51]

The club is nothing if not ambitious and expects 'to have delivered total energy packages to more than 2.5 million households' after five years' full operation, saving members 'some £500 million per year' and cutting carbon dioxide emissions by some 1.4 million tonnes of carbon equivalent annually.[52] 'We can bring houses up to 60 or 70 on the SAP scale,' the spokesman told me. 'Just how many houses we do will depend on how many other people see the commercial opportunity and come in. No government grants are involved.' When I pointed out that cheaper loans would be available from a credit union and that this would keep the interest payments in the community, he reflected the widespread attitude in Britain that credit unions are only for the poor and said that bank loans were 'more appropriate to the sector in which we are operating,' *i.e.* owner-occupiers. However, they were looking at credit unions as a possible source of loans for people living in social housing when they developed schemes for them.

Much higher standards of energy-efficiency can be achieved in existing houses than the Energy Club expects to make. In Schiedam in the Netherlands, for example, the local council has superinsulated an estate of 448 flats built in 1956 and in need of renovation. It insulated the external walls by covering them with 150mm of expanded polystyrene, followed by metal mesh and a concrete rendering. (This is the most efficient way to insulate any existing building – far better and easier than lining the walls with insulation inside. Visitors to the former East Germany can scarcely have failed to notice how extensively the technique is being used there to improve the housing stock.) An additional 70mm of insulation was put in the roofs, existing balconies were glazed, and the windows were replaced with double-glazed, argon-filled units with a heat-reflecting silver oxide coating, fitted in timber frames.

New space-heating systems were also installed. 'These measures brought the flats up to the standard of the best new Dutch buildings, and they use 90 per cent less energy than the average for the Dutch housing stock,' David Olivier told me.[53]

The latest British estimate is that if every household adopted all the energy-saving techniques open to it, including fitting full double-glazing, putting 150mm of glass-fibre in the loft, draught-proofing, insulating the walls, and changing over to the most efficient light-bulbs and domestic appliances, total domestic energy use would fall by almost 40 per cent, even if people did not take all their savings in the form of lower fuel bills but allowed themselves the luxury of warmer rooms as well.[54] Moreover, if householders did the installation work themselves they would get at least a 15 per cent return on most of their spending. If they had to employ contractors, the majority of their money would give an 8 per cent or better return.

The obstacles to energy-saving are not therefore technical or financial. They are essentially social – and that is where community attitudes and actions come in.

FURTHER INFORMATION

For a good recent all-round guide to energy issues try *The Future of Energy Use* by Robert Hill, Phil O'Keefe, and Colin Snape (Earthscan, London, 1995). Magazines are the best way of keeping up with what is happening in this area. The *Safe Energy Journal*, published by Friends of the Earth, Scotland, to promote the use of renewable and sustainable energy sources, gives an excellent overview, although for some readers it devotes rather too much space to the problems with nuclear power. (£16 a year, £8 unwaged, from 72 Newhaven Road, Edinburgh EH6

5QG.) *Renew*, published by the Network for Alternative Technology and Technology Assessment (NATTA) at the Open University, covers renewable energy
alone, in a lively manner and some depth; for anyone seriously interested in community energy I regard a subscription as essential. (£15 a year, £10 unwaged,
from NATTA, Energy and Environment Research Unit, Faculty of Technology,
Open University, Walton Hall, Milton Keynes, Buckinghamshire MK7 6AA.)
New Review, which calls itself 'the magazine of new and renewable energy', is an
attractively produced full-colour publication issued by the Energy Technology
Support Unit on behalf of the Department of Trade and Industry in Britain. As
one might expect, it is a good source of information about British renewable
energy policy and ETSU's activities. (Free from ETSU, Harwell, Oxfordshire
OX11 0RA.)

RENEWABLE ENERGY SOURCES

The book to buy or borrow is *Renewable Energy: Sources for Fuels and Electricity*, edited
by Johansson, Kelly, Reddy, and Williams (Island Press, Washington, 1993; distributed in Britain by Earthscan). The Renewable Energy Enquiries Bureau at
ETSU (tel. +44 1235 432450; fax +44 1235 432923) has a huge collection of
research reports available on loan and, perhaps by the time this book appears, via
the Internet. The Irish Energy Centre (Shinagh House, Bandon, Co. Cork; tel.
+353 23 42193; fax 41304; e-mail joanne@reio.ie) also sends out information to
enquirers free of charge.

A vast amount of information on renewable energy sources is available through the
Internet. On the World Wide Web, a good place to start is Solstice, the on-line
information server for the US Center for Renewable Energy and Sustainable
Technology (CREST). This is at http://solstice.crest.org. The UK Solar Energy
Society lists British Web sites at http://www.demon.co.uk/tfc/uk-ises_jumplist
.html, and the Student Solar Information network has a fourteen-page list of
renewable energy information sources at http://demon.co.uk/tfc/ssin.html. There
are many discussion groups. I subscribed briefly to Bioenergy (send the message
'SUBSCRIBE BIOENERGY *' with your e-mail address where the * is to MAJOR-
DOMO@CREST.ORG) but soon dropped out because the number of postings was so
high. Another discussion group, Alternative Energy, is equally busy. Join by sending the message 'SUBSCRIBE AE' to LISTSERV@SJSUVM1.SJSU.EDU.

CONTACT ADDRESSES

British Photovoltaic Association, c/o IT Power, The Warren, Bramshill Road, Eversley,
Hampshire RG27 0PR; tel. +44 1734 730073; fax +44 1734 730820; e-mail
itpower@gn.apc.org.

The British Wind Energy Association is at 89 Kingsway, London WC2B 6RH;
tel. +44 171 404 3433; fax 404 3432. Full membership costs £30 per annum and
includes copies of *Wind Directions*, the quarterly magazine published jointly by
the European and British Wind Energy associations. Alternatively, subscriptions
to the magazine alone cost £12 in the UK and £14 to the rest of Europe. Members of the Irish Wind Energy Association (see note 11) get it automatically.
Windpower Monthly has more advertising and pays more attention to the world
beyond Europe. Subscriptions cost £35 from Vrinners Hoved, 8420 Knebel, Denmark; tel. +45 86 365 900.

Methane Gen is a bi-monthly magazine on digesters, published by Methan O'Gen, a new company that makes digester parts. Subscriptions cost £17.50 a year from Tooracurragh, Ballymacarbry, Co. Waterford, Ireland; tel. +353 52 36304.

Mary O'Donnell can be reached at Business Development Unit, The Sutherland Centre, North Street, Skibbereen, Co. Cork; tel. +353 28 21011; fax 22084.

Les Gornall's business is Practically Green Environmental Services, 13 Thornhill Park, Magherafelt, BT45 5JQ; tel. +44 1648 32615. He supplies Ajax engines, which run on untreated bio-gas.

Malcolm Dawson's work on woodchip combined heat and power systems is being commercialized by Rural Generation Ltd, Henshaw Farm, Todmorden, Lancs., OL14 8QR, tel. +44 170 6814911.

ENERGY SAVING

David Olivier, Energy Advisory Associates, Moore Cottages, Bircher, Leominster, Herefordshire, HR6 OAX; tel. +44 1568 780868.

Bill Quigley is at the National Irish Centre for Energy Rating Ltd, 3 Bushfield Place, Dublin 4; tel. +353 1 4970133. The centre carries out energy audits on properties and uses the information to provide costed proposals for saving energy.

Notes

1 This figure is quoted by Paul Hawken in *The Ecology of Commerce* (Harper-Collins: New York 1993), citing the Rocky Mountain Institute as the source. A letter to the RMI produced a copy of its *Community Energy Workbook* and a compliments slip but nothing to indicate which of its studies produced this finding. However, Paul Harwood's report *A Domestic Energy Audit of Newport, Pembrokeshire* showed that in 1986 the average household in this small town was causing an 'energy cash leakage' of £747 out of the local economy for its cooking, heating and lighting and that this could readily be cut by two-thirds. This sum, of course, ignored the cost of the energy required to run the community's vehicles and the value of the energy used to make the products its members bought. As roughly 27 per cent of all energy is used in the home for cooking, lighting and space-heating and the rest is bought by households either directly at the petrol pump or indirectly through their purchases and taxes, this would mean that each household spent £2700 on energy a year in 1986. As the average after-tax household income that year was £192.32 a week or £10,000 a year, this makes the figure of a fifth look reasonable.

2 *BP Statistical Review of World Energy*, June 1993.

3 A small gas field, Ballycotton, was discovered in 1990, but no more recent finds have been reported.

4 *Hatherleigh Community Renewable Energy Study* (draft final report 1995), Terence O'Rourke PLC, Everdene House, Wessex Fields, Deansleigh Road, Bournemouth BH7 7DU; tel. +44 1202 421142; fax +44 1202 430055.

5 Available from NATTA, c/o Energy & Environment Research Unit, Faculty of Technology, Open University, Walton Hall, Milton Keynes, Buckinghamshire MK7 6AA; tel. +44 1908 654638; fax (Dave Elliott) +44 1908 654052.

6 *Small-Scale Hydro-Electric Potential of Ireland* (Department of Energy, Dublin).

7 IHPA, 13 Marlborough Road, Dublin 4; tel. & fax +353 1 6680043.

8 P. Fraenkel, O. Paish, V. Bokalders, A. Harvey, A. Brown, and R. Edwards, *Micro-Hydro Power: a Guide for Development Workers* (Intermediate Technology Publications: London 1991). Another guide that is particularly strong on the preliminary assessment of a site's potential is *The Development of Small-Scale Hydro-Schemes, Part 2* (Department of Energy: Dublin n.d.).

9 Polyturbine Ltd, Unit 16, IDA Enterprise Centre, 111 Pearse Street, Dublin 2; tel. +353 1 6711209; fax +353 1 6711746. The Polyturbine can be described as a single-regulated Kaplan because the propeller blades are not adjustable when the machine is in operation as they are in the double-regulated variety. This means that it produces slightly less power from a given flow of water than the latter but at a significantly lower capital cost.

10 The Rock, South Brent, Devon TQ10 9JL; tel. +44 1364 72185. The NAWPU can supply a list of consultants, manufacturers, lawyers and others who may be useful to anyone developing a water-power site in Britain. It lobbies on behalf of small hydro-electricity producers and publishes a bulletin twice a year. Membership is £20 annually.

11 Irish Wind Energy Association, Arigna, Co. Roscommon; tel. +353 78 46229; fax +353 78 46016.

12 Her report is called *Living with Wind Farms in Denmark and the Netherlands* and is available from North Energy Associates, 2 Old Bakehouse Yard, Morpeth, Northumberland NE1 1AS; tel. +44 1670 516949.

13 Hurley Staudt Associates, 63 Greenlawns, Skerries, Co. Dublin; tel. +353 1 8490396.

14 The 656-page handbook covers regional wind resource assessment and the local siting of turbines and explains how to correct calculations for the effects of rough terrain etc. It is accompanied by a diskette containing wind statistics. It costs 875 Danish kroner from the Department of Meteorology and Wind Energy, Risø National Laboratory, PO Box 49, 4000 Roskilde; tel. +45 42371212; fax +45 46755619. Risø also publishes an extensive list of free research reports in English on wind energy.

15 The report (ref. ETSU K/FR/00082/REP) is available from ETSU, Harwell, Oxfordshire OX11 0RA; tel. +44 1235 432450; fax +44 1235 432923.

16 *Inishowen Renewable Energy Study: Wind and Biomass in North-West Ireland* (1994), Inishowen Energy Co-op, Colpey, Muff, Co. Donegal.

17 L.P. Martindale, *The Potential for Straw as a Fuel in the UK* (ref. NI/84), ETSU, Harwell, Oxfordshire.

18 See 'Straw as a Fuel: Current Developments in the UK', *ETSU Technology Summary*, 073, June 1991.

19 The paper, *Bioenergy in Denmark*, is available from Dr Boldt at the Danish Energy Agency, 11 Landermærket, 1119 København K; tel. +45 33926700; fax +45 33114743.

20 *Update on Centralized Biogas Plants*, October 1992.

21 Institute of Agricultural Economics, Gl. Køge Landevej 1, 2500 Valby; tel. +45 36442080; fax +45 36441110.

22 F. Culshaw and C. Butler, *A Review of Biodiesel as a Transport Fuel* (ETSU-R-71) (HMSO: London 1992).

23 W. Dunne, *Liquid Fuels from Conventional Agricultural Crops* (Teagasc: Dublin 1990).

24 *Ökobilanz Rapsöl*, available from Umweltbundesamt, Bismarckplatz, 1000 Berlin 33.

25 T. Thomas, *Fuel Oil Seed Rape* (Teagasc: Dublin 1991).

26 'The carbon and energy budgets of energy crops', *Energy Conversion Management*, vol. 34 (1993), no. 9-11, pp. 897-904.

27 'Express Path' Summary Report (CEC contract no. EV5V-CT92-0086), March 1995. The technologies are biomass use in Austria, Denmark, and Greece, wind power in Denmark, and solar heating in Austria and Greece.

28 David Olivier, 'Continental efficiency', *Building Services*, March 1991.

29 In 1993 it published a report (ETSU resource study 287) on the future prospects of the renewable energy resources in its supply area, which runs from Avon through Somerset, Devon and Cornwall to the Isles of Scilly. This concluded that between 6 and 12 per cent of present electricity consumption could be met from renewable resources by the year 2000 and that nearly two-and-a-half times the present consumption could be supplied in the longer term.

30 Telephone interview, January 1996.

31 *Renew*, issues 92 and 93.

32 *New Scientist*, 20 August 1994.

33 20 New Bond Street, London W1Y 0RY; tel. +44 171 4954812.

34 David Lascelles, 'More than one way to go', *Financial Times*, 15 March 1995.

35 Antonio Estevan and Alfonso Sanz, 'Hacia La Reconversion Ecologica del Transporte en España', Centro de Investigacion para la Paz, Madrid.

36 *Road Transport of Goods and the Effects on the Spatial Environment*, July 1993.

37 The most recent British study (September 1995), *Reforming Road Taxation*, compares the total costs of the road transport system (not just freight transport) with the tax revenue raised from it. It was commissioned by the Automobile Association from Professor David Newbery, Director of the Department of Applied Economics at the University of Cambridge. It shows that after meeting the cost of repairing the road network and servicing the capital tied up in it, vehicle fuel taxes should be three times higher than at present to cover the costs vehicle users impose on each other, the environment, and the community. This figure is likely to be a serious underestimate because of the low figures used for the contribution of the transport system to the damage likely to be done by global warming, and also for its noise and health effects.

38 Quoted by Wolfgang Zuckermann, *End of the Road* (Chelsea Green, Vermont 1991).

39 Freewheelers, 25 Low Friar Street, Newcastle-upon-Tyne NE1 5UE; tel. +44 191 2220090; fax +44 191 2615746.

40 Groningen is called 'the record-holder among cyclists' cities' in a useful, fact-filled report, *Greening Urban Transport: European Examples of Pedestrian and Cycling Policy*, published in 1994 by the European Federation for Transport and Environment, Rue de la Victoire 26, 1060 Bruxelles; tel. +32 2 5376639; fax +32 2 5377394. The lessons learned in seventeen other cities in seven countries are presented as well.

41 Material in English available from the Public Relations Office of Groningen City Council (Postbox 7081, 9701 JB Groningen; tel. +31 50 672169; fax +31 50 672225) includes *Hand on Heart: a New City Centre for Groningen*, which describes the measures taken and includes maps and colour pictures, and an illus-

trated policy statement, *An Integrated Town Planning and Traffic Policy*, issued in 1992.

42 Details are given by Keith Chivers (ed.), *History with a Future: Harnessing the Heavy Horse for the Twenty-First Century* (1988), Shire Horse Society, East of England Showground, Peterborough PE2 0XE; tel. +44 1733 390696; fax +44 1733 390720.

43 David Roodman and Nicholas Lenssen, *A Building Revolution: How Ecology and Health Concerns are Transforming Construction* (Worldwatch paper no. 124) (Worldwatch Institute: Washington March 1995).

44 *Energy-Efficient Subdivision Design: General Plan Policy Interpretation*, July 1992.

45 This is the County Planning Officers' Society, c/o Lancashire County Planning Dept., P.O. Box 160, Eastcliff County offices, Preston, PR1 3EX.

46 Estimate by William Gillis in T. Markus (ed.), *Domestic Energy and Affordable Warmth* (Watt Committee report no. 30) (Spon: London 1994).

47 The first car-sharing club, Auto Teilet Genossenschaft (ATG), was set up in Luzern in Switzerland: Auto Teilet Genossenschaft, Postfach, Mühlenplatz 10, 6000 Luzern; tel. + 41 41 524655; fax +41 41 529349.

48 AKF, Nyropsgade 37, 1602 København; tel. +45 33110300; fax +45 33152875. Many of their publications are in English or have English summaries. The American power companies also have considerable experience in getting people to use less electricity, and the Results Center (IRT Environment Inc., PO box 10990, Aspen, Colorado, 81612–9689, USA) collates their results and publishes its findings.

49 Anders Larsen et al., *Virkemidler og Elbesparelser* [Measures for Savings in Electricity Consumption] (AKF: København n.d.).

50 'Energy saving pays off', *Safe Energy Journal*, September-November 1995, pp. 14-15. Robert Barnham can be contacted at LEEP, 72 Newhaven Road, Edinburgh EH6 5QG, Scotland; tel. +44 131 5554010; fax +44 131 5552768.

51 Telephone interview, December 1995.

52 Press release, March 1995.

53 Telephone conversation, 1996. See Olivier's article 'Continental efficiency', *Building Services*, March 1991.

54 L. Shorrock, *Potential Carbon Emission Savings from Energy Efficiency in Housing* (information paper 15/95), Building Research Establishment, December 1995.

6

Life from the Land

Modern industrial agriculture cannot be continued for very much longer because of the damage it is doing to the soil and the way it is undermining its genetic base. Community farms are part of the answer, locally owned shops another.

THERE ARE THREE POWERFUL REASONS WHY communities should produce almost all their own food. The first of these is that only by buying food produced locally from local resources can one be reasonably sure about the safety and content of what one eats. Its importance became all too clear early in 1996 when millions of Britons heard with horror that they might have been infected with CJD, the fatal human equivalent of mad cow disease, as a result of eating beef fed with meal made from diseased sheep carcasses. When newspapers revealed that cattle farmers had been prevented from learning exactly what was in the meal they bought for their animals and that beef by-products were used to make jams, jellies, biscuits and a wide range of other foods few people would ever have suspected, confidence in the conventional agro-industrial food system disappeared.

The second reason we discussed briefly in chapter 2. It is that any community which depends for its survival on buying its food from the outside world has to be able to sell, year after year, to the outside world enough of whatever it produces to earn the money to eat. This means the community is permanently exposed to the risks involved in selling its products on extremely unstable markets in the face of fierce competition from thousands of other producers all over the globe. Moreover, because it will starve without an income, it cannot refuse to sell its goods even if the prices offered for them are ridiculously low. It also has no control over the prices it pays for the goods it needs. In other words, the exchange rate between the goods it supplies and the food and other necessities it brings in is fixed externally, and the international trading system determines the level at which the community's members live. They are dependent on, and hence at the mercy of, outside forces in the most fundamental and intractable way.

The reason few people in the industrialized world worry about being in such a powerless state is that, unless they are small farmers, the world agricultural system has operated in their favour for over a century by steadily reducing the length of time they have had to work to earn the money to buy the necessities of life. For them – at least until newspapers began to run stories with headlines like 'Droughts bring global food crisis' in the autumn of 1995[1] – the idea that food might run short seemed ridiculous: after all, one of the EU's biggest problems had been controlling its agricultural surpluses. Why should anyone want to give up such an advantageous situation until events leave them no alternative?

The third argument for greater local food self-reliance provides the answer. It is that the system that has provided this apparent abundance is fundamentally unsustainable and liable to sudden, catastrophic collapse. One reason for this unsustainability is of course the huge amount of fossil energy the system takes to grow, pack and transport our food. According to the Swedish Food Institute, 15.8 MJ of energy is needed by the industrial system to produce, transport and sell a 1 kg loaf, which provides our bodies with 10 MJ of energy when eaten.[2] Similarly, 1 kg of frozen peas takes 22.6 MJ to produce and distribute – ten times the amount of energy the peas contain. The figures for beef grown on fertilized pasture are similar: each kilogram delivers 6 MJ of energy when eaten but absorbs 64.2 MJ of fossil energy in the course of reaching the shop.

Fertilizers in fact represent about half the fossil energy required by conventional chemical agriculture[3] and between 5 and 10 per cent of the energy used in an industrial country. In Britain as long ago as 1978, transporting food to shops accounted for a further 5 per cent of national energy use.[4] Since that statistic was calculated there has been a 50 per cent increase in the distance food travels to reach our plates, so the amount of fuel used must have grown substantially.[5] Allowing for the energy used in processing, as much as a quarter of all fossil energy could now be consumed by the food sector.[6]

Another reason for the system's unsustainability is the damage modern agriculture does to the soil. It used to be said that liming land enriched the father and impoverished the son; this was because making the soil less acid with lime caused plant humus to break down, and release nitrogen for a few years, which produced luxuriant growth. However, when the nitrogen was exhausted, crop yields dropped to well below their former levels because of the deterioration in the soil's structure and composition. Only the annual application of a lot of farmyard manure to replace the humus could prevent the soil being spoiled. Artificial fertilizers also give higher yields for a number of years before an eventual decline because they too destroy the soil's structure and make it more liable to erosion. Indeed in some intensively farmed areas in southern England, twenty tonnes of topsoil is being lost per hectare per year,[7] far more than if the land was farmed traditionally or by modern organic methods. This erosion is serious, since according to one estimate a loss of even twelve tonnes of soil per hectare reduces yields by 8 per cent.[8] In south-east Asia, chemical farming methods are already ceasing to work: despite higher levels of fertilizer application, yields of 'Green Revolution' rice varieties are declining by 1 per cent year upon year.[9]

These reasons for the world food system's unsustainability are widely known, and just as widely ignored. However, very few people also know that the system is genetically unsustainable and might suddenly collapse, causing the deaths of hundreds of millions of people from starvation and leading to political, social and military consequences comparable to those of a nuclear war. Since this danger can only be minimized by community action and is unfamiliar even to many of those already involved in sustainable, low-input types of agriculture, I devote the next few pages to explaining how it arises and what can be done.

After the construction of the railways, farmers in Cornwall were able to take advantage of their milder climate to grow winter and early spring produce for markets all over Britain. One of their crops was cauliflower, and the type they grew was Old Cornish, which had been selected into several varieties from seed brought in from Italy in the 1840s. Unknown to the farmers, Old Cornish was resistant to ringspot, a fungal disease most common in Wales and in southern and south-western England that causes brown spots on the larger leaves, which eventually turn yellow and die.

In the 1940s, after a breeding programme at Seale Hayne Agricultural College in Devon, Sutton's Seeds and the Ministry of Agriculture introduced the growers to French cauliflower varieties. Within ten years the Old Cornish cauliflowers were no longer produced because the shoppers of the day preferred the dense white curds of the French variety to the loose yellow ones of the Cornish strain. No one held on to seeds of the Cornish type: the line was gone. Shortly afterwards, ringspot outbreaks were noticed, and today it is very much more difficult to grow satisfactory crops of cauliflowers in Cornwall. Growers have tried to find resistant French seed, but production disasters have been experienced in some areas. Rotation with other crops helps reduce the problem, as does feeding the soil heavily with wood ash or another source of potassium, but there is no chemical means of control. 'The new varieties caused the extinction of the best (and perhaps the only) real source of resistance to the disease – the Old Cornish cauliflowers,' Cary Fowler and Pat Mooney write in their account of this tragedy in their disturbing book *Shattering: Food, Politics and the Loss of Genetic Diversity*.[10] 'We will never know what other valuable traits may have disappeared.'

This story has two morals. One is that we may not have the option of switching to a sustainable, low-input agriculture free of artificial pesticides unless we preserve the seed varieties – or, at the very least, the genes – that made this form of farming possible in the past. (The preservation of animal genes is equally important, as the story on page 272 explains.) The other lesson is that chemicals are inadequate substitutes for natural resistance and that without genetic diversity we may well become unable to feed ourselves at all.

For thousands of years, the seeds people planted were not pure strains with little genetic variability but what are called 'landraces' – natural assortments of seeds adapted to local conditions. Although diseases or pests were present every year, only the vulnerable plants in the assortment in the field would succumb: most of the crop would survive because of the defences the landrace had developed during hundreds of years of exposure to its enemies in agriculture and many thousands of years in the wild. Today, unfortunately, the variability that produced this security is thought undesirable: modern growers want all their crop to look the same and taste the same, to behave in the same way in the field, after harvest, and in the kitchen. This means that they demand, for example, wheat seeds that produce plants that grow to the same height and in the same time and are ready for harvesting simultaneously. As a result, from the beginning of the nineteenth century onwards, plant breeders have been selecting particular characteristics from among the multitude available in landraces and in the wild and crossing and recrossing their selections until they arrive at a 'pure' line, a strain that breeds true – that is, without any variability – from generation to generation.

In a field planted with a landrace, if a pest finds one plant unpalatable it moves on to the next one that is not. There is no pressure on the pest to change. However, when thousands of acres of a pure line are planted, pests and diseases have no alternative but to adapt to overcome the various resistances the line has had bred into it. They do so remarkably quickly. In an experiment at the International Rice Research Institute (IRRI) in the Philippines, brown planthoppers, the most serious rice pest in Asia, were confined in a cage with Mudgo, a hopper-resistant rice variety. Most starved to death, but some produced a second generation. By the time the tenth generation had emerged, about three months later, the planthoppers were devouring Mudgo as readily as any non-resistant rice type. Plant diseases adapt with great speed too. The first race of wheat stem rust was identified in 1917; fifty years later, three hundred more races had appeared in response to the development of rust-resistant wheat varieties.

In the industrial agricultural system, a desperate race is being run between plant breeders and pests, and millions will starve if the breeders lose. The life of a plant variety, Lawrence Hills, founder of the Henry Doubleday Research Association, once said with only a slight exaggeration, has been reduced to that of a pop record. For example, Triumph, a barley bred in East Germany, quickly became one of the main varieties grown in Ireland after its introduction in 1982. By 1989, however, its resistance to diseases had been eroded and it was superseded by an English-bred variety, Blenheim, which by 1994 was needing to be replaced in its turn. When the inbuilt resistance of a variety ceases to work, pesticides can be drafted in to help it out, but the pests rapidly become resistant to those too: it was only six years after DDT was introduced that resistance to it began to appear. Indeed scientists are worried that resistance is developing among pests faster than they can devise new pesticides and that a number of very serious pests are about to become uncontrollable.

Plant breeders go to the landraces and to the wild plants from which they were originally developed for new resistance genes to build into their strains. Unfortunately, the collapse of traditional agriculture throughout the world and the success of the international seed companies in promoting their new varieties has meant that very few landraces are still being planted, and only then in extremely remote areas. Wheat was probably first cultivated in the Balkans or Armenia, and at one time the fields from Greece to India and south to Ethiopia displayed an enormous range of genetic variation. Within the past fifty years almost all those fields have been switched to uniform commercial varieties, and the richness of the genetic heritage they once contained has gone.

The value of what has been lost is illustrated by a story told by one of the first people to draw attention to the loss of genetic resources, Professor Jack Harlan of the University of Illinois, who collected a wheat plant in a Turkish field in 1948. He wrote years later:

> It is a miserable-looking wheat, tall, thin-stemmed, lodges badly, is susceptible to leaf rust, lacks winter hardiness ... and has poor baking qualities. Understandably, nobody paid any attention to it for fifteen years. Suddenly, stripe rust became serious in the north-western states and [the wheat I had collected] turned out to be resistant to four races of stripe rust, thirty-five races of common bunt, [and] ten races of dwarf bunt and to have good tolerance to flag smut and snow mould.[11]

Today, genes from that miserable-looking wheat are used in every programme to breed wheat for the north-west of the United States and have saved farmers there from losses running to millions of dollars. No-one knows what potentially valuable genes have been lost with the landraces. True, not all the genetic material they contained has gone, as, in part because of Harlan's warnings, concerned scientists set up the International Board for Plant Genetic Resources (IBPGR) in 1972 to collect varieties and landraces of commercially important food plants and store them in gene banks. More than 110,000 wheat varieties and landraces and 12,500 wild wheats are preserved at the International Maize and Wheat Improvement Centre in Mexico, and similar collections exist for potatoes, barley, maize, sorghum, rice, groundnuts, okra, cowpeas, sweet potatoes, beans, and other crops. But just what proportion of the original diversity these collections contain is an unanswerable question. Moreover, while the collections of internationally important crops are incomplete, plants of regional and local importance are still largely uncollected and ignored. Among these are twenty different oilseed crops grown in east Africa that are almost unknown in the outside world; and only a last-minute rescue by the Peruvian government saved varieties of Andean crops such as *Chenopodium quinoa* and *Chenopodium pallidicaule*, and tubers and root crops including *Canna edulis*, from passing into oblivion.

Just because genetic material has been collected does not mean it is safe. The world rice collection is kept under refrigeration by IRRI in an impressive building not too far from two active volcanoes and right in the centre of an earthquake zone. Fowler and Mooney describe visiting the international centre responsible for the storage of sorghum and millet at Hyderabad in India to find the refrigeration system broken and shirt-sleeved workmen tinkering with pipes and mopping up water in vaults where seed librarians normally had to cope with a temperature of minus twenty degrees Celsius. There have been many such incidents. Within the past few years a major collection of Peruvian maize was ruined when the refrigeration failed; and five hundred varieties of American cassava were lost in transit from one collection to another. In November 1988 a band of Shining Path guerrillas raided the International Potato Centre at Huancayo in the Peruvian Andes, where more than 4500 varieties of potatoes are preserved by being planted out and harvested each year; the raiders intended to kill the scientists who maintained the collection, and shot the head of security, but fortunately the scientists were away in Lima, where, concerned for their lives, they stayed for several months.

The US National Seed Storage Laboratory at Fort Collins, Colorado, is located between a nuclear reactor and a munitions factory. It is possibly the most important gene bank in the world but in the early 1980s was a shambles, its cold stores liable to power failures and its seeds stacked in cardboard cartons and sacks on the floor. Worse, its staff were drying samples to prepare them for storage at 36 or 38 degrees Celsius rather than the 15 degrees recommended. There is no evidence of any great improvement since then. In November 1994, Henry Shands of the US Department of Agriculture Research Service wrote that a quarter of the collection was not available to researchers, possibly because the items could not be found.[12] Another quarter had less than 65 per cent viability, and there was a twenty-year backlog in the programme of growing varieties outside to regenerate them. 'Gene banks are as prone to failure as their financial counterparts,' Fowler and Mooney comment, 'but their losses cannot be overcome by a printing press.'

These horror stories should not be interpreted as an attack on the gene banks but as a plea for many more of them, so that if one is destroyed nothing of consequence is lost. Unfortunately there are more fundamental problems with gene banks than running them properly and keeping them secure. One is that in the outside world, the pests and diseases are continuing to adapt and change, while the seeds, deep in their cold-rooms, are no longer developing and throwing up new variations. They have been withdrawn from the race they have been running against their enemies since the dawn of time. Consequently, if we rely on the banks exclusively we are bound to find some time in the future that the pests and diseases have developed a feature that our crops cannot resist because we have not given them the chance to evolve to do so.

A second problem is that a seed can only be stored in a gene bank for so long before it dies, the time varying from crop to crop and the temperature at which it is stored. Accordingly, when an arbitrary proportion – usually 15 per cent – of a sample in a gene bank has ceased to germinate, the rest is taken out and regenerated by being planted, and the new seeds produced are placed in the store. There are two snags with this procedure, however. One is that the seeds that have died cannot be assumed to be genetically identical to those that successfully germinated in the regeneration plot: some genetic information has inevitably been lost. The other is that 'genetic drift' takes place whenever a sample is planted and grown because of the different responses the plants show to disease, insects, weather and soil while they are growing. To demonstrate this, Dr Eric Roos, a plant physiologist at Fort Collins, took equal numbers of eight bean varieties and ran them through fifteen cycles of aging and regeneration. By the end of the experiment, six of the varieties had become extinct.

Seed librarians therefore face an acute dilemma. If they keep seeds for such a long time that only a small proportion germinate when they are regenerated, they will have lost the genetic material of those that died. If, on the other hand, they regenerate frequently to prevent these losses, other genes will disappear in the regeneration process itself. In other words, whatever they do, the librarians will be left with strains of seeds adapted to survive in gene banks but lacking many of the characteristics originally collected in the outside world.

Fowler and Mooney draw the obvious conclusion from this: that genetic diversity cannot be saved by seed banks alone, and their efforts need to be supplemented by community action. Diversity, they say, can only be saved with a diversity of approaches. 'No one strategy could hope to preserve and protect what it took so many human cultures, farming systems and environments so long to produce ... Diversity, like music or a dialect, is part of the community that produced it. It cannot exist for long without that community and the circumstances that gave rise to it. Saving farmers is a prerequisite of saving diversity. Conversely, communities must save their agricultural diversity in order to retain their own options for development and self-reliance. Someone else's seeds imply someone else's needs.' They also believe that diversity will not be saved unless it is actually being used. 'Only in use can diversity be appreciated enough to be saved. And only in use can it continue to evolve, thus retaining its value ... The need for diversity is never-ending. Therefore, our efforts to preserve this diversity can never cease ... No technology can relieve us of the responsibility to preserve agricultural diversity for ourselves and all future generations.'

What does this mean? Quite simply, that communities need to grow their food using seed they have saved themselves because only in this way can their crops adapt to local conditions and have some chance of developing resistance to whatever tricks the diseases and pests develop. In short, landraces are in; pure lines and F1 hybrids (seeds resulting from the first cross between two very different strains which produce vigorous, identical plants whose seed cannot be satis-factorily saved) are out.

Some growers in Ireland and Britain still save their own seed but many more were doing so until quite recently. In 1982 R.F. Murphy of the Kinsealy Research Station near Dublin began collecting the self-saved seeds that Irish farmers were using to plant crops in the cabbage and turnip family, but by the time he came to write his report two years later, 40 per cent of growers who had been saving seed when he started had ceased to do so, and he reckoned that all but a small fraction of the diversity that had been present in the past had been lost. 'We were right on the edge,' he says.[13] He was, how-ever, in time to rescue some interesting and potentially valuable plants from extinction. These included a unique cabbage from the Glen of Aherlow called 'Cut and Come', which, as it has several stems, looks rather like a wallflower. It can be harvested over a long period for spring greens and, as its name indicates, will put out new stems after being cut the first time. In the west of Ireland he found several landraces of a fodder cabbage known as Flat Dutch, whose seeds had been saved by families for over a century. These landraces had the advantage over the usual Dutch cabbage of being able to be sown in late summer, overwintered, and planted out the following April without risk of bolting. Bundles of these cabbages can still be seen in towns in the west of Ireland at springtime displayed in the street for farmers to buy.

Murphy's seeds are now housed in the vegetable gene bank at Wellesbourne, Warwickshire, where the world's main collections of radish, carrot, onion and brassica seeds are held. Dr David Astley, the bank's manager, accepts that change and genetic drift are inevitable when seeds are stored and regenerated by institutions such as his. 'The gene bank stock will come to differ from that outside. This makes re-collection necessary after a period of between ten and twenty-five years,' he told me.[14] But re-collection is only possible if the material is still there – in other words, if the seeds are still being used by farmers – and in most cases they are not. Wellesbourne was set up in 1980 as a result of a special Oxfam appeal, and in 1983–4 it sent staff to collect cauliflower seeds used by growers in Italy, where some authorities think the crop was first developed – Syria is another possibility – and it certainly displayed a great deal of diversity.

In 1993, ten years later, Astley sent a PhD student back to see what had changed. 'A large proportion of the variability had gone,' he says. This was largely because agriculture had become more commercialized and the reduced number of people still involved in farming needed to produce crops acceptable to supermarkets and other customers longer distances away. 'I'm told, however, that there are still landraces to be found well off the beaten track,' he says. 'If we wish to preserve the use of landraces in the areas they developed, it has to be in a system which develops good local seed production with quality control and where the landrace products are acceptable within a market economy. Such a system would need to be linked to research into the complexities of landraces and the farming systems which produce them.'

So far, Astley's staff haven't even been able to get seeds from everywhere in Europe the first time around, let alone re-collect them to capture any new genes and gene combinations for conservation and to see how varieties have changed since they were last collected and what has been lost. 'There are still areas in which no one has ever collected, and I'm still trying to arrange national collection programmes,' he says wearily. 'International efforts are piecemeal and fragmented because of lack of funds. I get upset when I hear people saying that the gene banks have enough material in them. It does considerable damage if fundholders perceive that collection is no longer important and regard proposals for collecting trips to Spain or Portugal as pleasure jaunts.'

While the EU has provided some funds for seed-collecting, thousands of varieties have been lost as a result of its policies. On 1 July 1973, only months after its entry to the Common Market, the British government introduced regulations under the Plant Varieties and Seeds Act, 1964, making it an offence punishable by a fine of £400 to sell seeds after 30 June 1980 unless the variety was listed on the official national list or that of another EEC government. The regulations were introduced as a result of lobbying by an international organization representing big seed companies, the Union for the Protection of New Varieties in Plants (UPOV), ostensibly to protect breeders from having varieties that had cost them a lot to develop being dishonestly 'adopted' by other seed firms and sold under other names. They required that all new varieties be submitted to the Ministry of Agriculture for a DUS ('distinct, uniform, stable') test to ensure that they were distinct in form and shape from other varieties, uniform in genetic structure, and stable – in other words, that they bred true. Testing cost £90 in 1976, when fees were first introduced, and had risen to £825 in 1995.[15] If the variety passed the test it was entered on the National List free (£245 in 1995) and stayed there provided an annual fee of between £10 and £30 (£150 in 1995) was paid. The seed company responsible for the variety could also be asked to maintain an inspection plot so the variety's uniformity could be checked.

If the regulations had been confined to varieties just coming onto the market that would have been fair enough. However, the legislation – and similar laws were enacted in the United States, Canada, Australia and New Zealand as a result of UPOV's activities – covered old varieties as well. This caused a crisis for many smaller, family-run seed companies, which, since they lacked the financial resources to run breeding programmes, tended to specialize in traditional strains. Most of these firms were unable to list their varieties because landraces, or any strains of seeds with some genetic variability, were automatically excluded by the DUS test's stability requirements. Realizing that their business would be so restricted that they would become unviable after July 1980, many sold out to their bigger rivals. The milling and bakery combine Rank Hovis McDougall bought up eighty-three small seed firms in one week alone.[16]

In any case, no firm was going to pay for a DUS test for a variety it only sold in small quantities; and since sales to professional growers generated nine-tenths of the average seed firm's turnover, only those varieties popular with farmers and market gardeners were generally considered worth registering. This was more than unfortunate, since amateur gardeners and organic growers require very different seeds than the mainstream professional. High yield, uniformity and the ability to travel well are some of the characteristics the commercial producer seeks, whereas the amateur, above all else, wants a crop with flavour. With peas, for example, a farmer orders a variety that does not have to be supported with sticks, in which every pod ripens simultaneously so that it can be harvested at exactly the right moment for the frozen-food market, and that has little leaf or vine to block the harvesting equipment. An organic or amateur gardener, on the other hand, wants a tall pea, to avoid getting an aching back from picking, that has pods ready for eating over a long period, and that is

261

[main text continues p.266]

LAST-MINUTE HUNT TO SAVE LOST
IRISH APPLE VARIETIES

One of Ireland's foremost experts on apples, Dr J.G.D. Lamb, visited old orchards over much of the country in the late 1940s recording and photographing the varieties growing there for his doctoral thesis.[17] 'Half a century ago we were still largely self-sufficient in fruit and vegetables. If you did not grow your own apples you maybe did without. This led to the development of cultivars of purely local fame,' he wrote in 1995.[18]

'In those days there was a countrywide network of county advisers in horticulture, many of whom had extensive local knowledge. I also consulted the statistical surveys of the counties published in the opening years of the nineteenth century, as several of these listed the apple varieties being grown at that time. When the same name was applied to an apple by orchard owners in different locations, I took it as a strong indication that the name was correct, especially if it appeared in the relevant statistical survey. In all I found seventy types of apple of Irish origin as living trees. Today, with the advent of the chain saw, how many survive?'

Anita Hayes, founder of Irish Seed Savers, is attempting to find out. 'Twenty-eight of the varieties Dr Lamb recorded are in the apple collection at Brogdale in England. Another four are being grown by the Armagh Orchard Trust. And we've found ten more since the campaign to find them began two years ago,' she told me in late 1995. 'One of these, Honeyball, was found by my postman, who had eaten it as a child and knew the tree was still there today. Another, Red Brandy, a scab-resistant variety Lamb found in Piltown, County Kilkenny, was relocated by one of our members, Joy Daniels, who asked elderly members of her family the name of a tree her father had prized.'

A third variety, the Ballyvaghan Seedling, which was widely grown in County Clare because it is so easy to propagate – it puts down roots easily if someone takes a cutting at the right time of year and just sticks it in the ground – did not appear on Lamb's list, as his survey omitted the western counties. It was rediscovered by Genevieve Tenthorney, a geographer surveying the Galway Bay area for University College, Dublin. Tenthorney's father grows apples commercially in Switzerland, so she was interested in an article Hayes wrote in the alternative magazine Common Ground about the missing apples. 'All around us are old unidentified apple trees,' Hayes wrote. 'Talk to the elders in your communities and see if they know anything about them. Watch them come September and see if they still fruit. Take a picture of them and dissect them and photograph them again to identify their inner structure. As important as identification and taste, find the stories attached to the trees.'[19]

So Tenthorney began asking people about old apple trees as she worked on her survey. Eventually she was taken to see a tree in an abandoned orchard in Ballyvaughan, and she immediately felt it was something special. However, it was only several months later, when she could taste its light yellow fruit with an attractive red flush, that she could confirm her intuition. 'It has a sharp taste when you first bite it, but it is marvellously sweet, with a long, lingering aftertaste, just like a fine brandy,' she says.[20] She photographed it, as instructed, and posted the pictures to Hayes, who passed them to Dr Michael Henarty, a pomologist at University College, Dublin. Henarty could not put a name to the tree himself, so he sent the pictures to a retired head of the department of horticulture at UCD, Professor C.J. Clarke, a friend of Lamb's and a fellow apple expert, who immediately knew what it was.

Hayes regards the hunt for the missing apples as a race against time, because most of the people who know the trees' names and their stories are elderly, while every year some of the remaining trees die or are rooted up. And, though Lamb and Clarke are in excellent health, their expertise will not be available forever. 'These men were way ahead of their time,' she says. 'It is so important that the old varieties are rediscovered and preserved before they and people's knowledge of them are lost altogether, because all the old records mention how disease-resistant they were, and you've got to have scab and canker-resistant trees for organic fruit production. They are part of local history and bring biodiversity into our lives in a practical way.'

A cooking-apple growing in Piltown that Lamb was unable to name illustrates the potential value of what was being allowed to die. 'It's a wind-resistant apple,' Hayes says. 'It carries its fruit right into the winter, long after its leaves have gone, and you really have to twist and tug to get the apples off.' Peadar MacNiece of the Armagh Orchard Trust, who is a large commercial grower, hopes that a really fine eater will be found in the hunt that he will be able to grow for the market. 'We can grow good cookers like Bramleys in this part of the country,' he says, 'but we haven't enough sun for any of the present range of eaters.'[21]

When varieties are rediscovered, cuttings will be grafted to rootstocks and planted in a new orchard Henarty has established at University College, Dublin. Grafted specimens will also be grown in the Armagh Apple Trust's orchard between Moy and Portadown, which already contains forty-two old Ulster varieties, many not covered by Lamb, and in a heritage garden Hayes is setting up for Irish Seed Savers that will produce trees for sale to members. Plant quarantine laws have prevented cuttings from the Irish varieties at Brogdale being brought back from England, but Hayes obtained permission to use tissue from them to culture into trees. Getting the old varieties widely distributed is important for their survival, she says, recalling that when Lamb and Clarke established an apple collection in Dublin containing some of the lost varieties in the 1950s, it was destroyed without warning by Dublin City Council when the land was needed for something else. By the time they knew what was happening, their trees had been bulldozed into a heap to burn and it was quite impossible to identify them.

Finding lost apple varieties is by no means Irish Seed Savers' only work. Anita Hayes sees it performing two main tasks. One is the maintenance, through use, of strains of plants that have been grown in Ireland for long periods. An example is the Delaway cabbage, a very dependable plant of the cut-and-come-again type whose seed ISS obtained from an eighty-year-old man who had been growing it for fifty years. Another is the

'Cut and Come' cabbage R.F. Murphy collected in the Glen of Aherlow; as soon as Hayes learned its seeds were in the gene bank at Wellesbourne, she obtained a quantity to grow herself to get enough to send out to ISS members. She is also propagating traditional types of potato obtained from the museum collection kept by Teagasc, the agricultural development agency, so that she can send out tubers to members to try. Their taste can be very different, she says. 'This year I was able to send samples of Lumpers, the potato people ate at the time of the Famine, out to schools so the children who were studying that period could eat them. They are horrible. They lie really heavily on your stomach, just like the books say.'

Irish Seed Savers' second task is to import traditional varieties from around the world that seem suited to Irish conditions, so that members can grow them and, by saving their seed and passing it to neighbours, slowly develop strains that do well in their part of the country. 'I'm working on nineteenth-century English and French melon varieties, and also, being an American, I've found a pumpkin which has grown really well outside, even through two horrible summers,' Hayes says. She talks about the thrill she gets moving along a row, selecting the plants whose seeds will be saved. 'It's a big switch from producing your own food to becoming a caretaker for a plant variety and looking, perhaps, for a lettuce able to survive strong winds.'

She thinks that most people have lost the community bonds and the spiritual joy that come from being in touch with the bounty of things that grow in the place they live. 'Most of us now have no connection to the earth or the food we eat, some of which may never have been touched by a human hand. But native Americans used to sing to their corn to get it to grow. An American seed saver once came across a patch of corn which was growing much better than anything else nearby and he asked the Indian who had planted it why that was. "It's because I remember the song," the Indian said. But the seed saver took seeds from the corn and when he grew them he found that the strain had a tap root which went several feet into the ground so it was able to get to moisture that was unavailable to the other farmers' plants. That seed was taken to Africa so that the taproot could be bred into native varieties, and the result was so successful that the breeder won a UN prize. That Indian hadn't just remembered the song. He'd saved the seed as well.'

Once, after Hayes had been to visit Lamb at his home in County Offaly, she was taken to the door by his wife, Helen. 'We thought it was too late,' she told Hayes as they said goodbye. 'But now perhaps it's not.' And so it proved. In February 1996, as a result of Hayes' work, the Lambs attended a lunch at University College, Dublin, to inaugurate the Lamb-Clarke Traditional Irish Apple Collection – the name given to the orchard being established by Henarty. Clarke, unfortunately, had phoned the previous night to say he was unwell. Peadar MacNiece brought cuttings of the varieties in the Armagh collection, and a representative of the Brogdale Horticultural Trust brought tissue from the apple varieties the two men had sent over to England years before so that they could be grown in Ireland again. Afterwards, two minibuses took the guests to Áras an Uachtaráin to be received by the President, who spoke feelingly of the importance of pre-serving this part of the heritage, not just of Ireland but the world.

Irish Seed Savers, Capparoe, Scarriff, Co. Clare; tel. +353 61 927357.

Armagh Orchard Trust, c/o MacNeice Brothers Orchards, Ardress East, Portadown, Co. Armagh, BT62 1SQ; tel +44 1762 851 381.

Common Ground (41 Shelton Street, London WC2H 9HJ) launched its 'Save our Orchards' campaign in 1989 and organizes Apple Day on 21 October each year. It tries to emphasize the links between apple varieties and the places they are associated with. Its publication The Apple Source Book includes a county-by-county gazetteer of apple vari-eties, recipes using specific varieties, and details of selected nurs-eries and orchards.

Brogdale Horticultural Trust (Brogdale Road, Faversham, Kent, ME13 8XZ; tel. +44 1795 535 286) has 150 acres of fruit tree collections, including 2300 apple varieties, 500 of pear, 350 of plum and 220 of cherry. Open to the public daily. The Book of Apples by Joan Morgan and Alison Richards (Ebury: London 1993) describes all the apples in the collection. It is available from Brogdale for £26.50, post paid.

Collecting and mapping old pears and apples in Ulster for the Armagh Orchard Trust in September 1995. From right to left: John Carruthers, from Lisbellaw, Co. Fermanagh, Peadar MacNeice, and Jean-Paul Drominiou from Brittany Fruit Growers.

best fresh rather than frozen. And yet, despite these different needs, as the seven-year notice period ran on, dozens of tall peas and thousands of other older varieties were gradually deleted from seed company catalogues and – the lesson of the Old Cornish cauliflower forgotten – allowed to become extinct.

The listing legislation also caused genetic material to be lost because only one strain of a traditional variety was allowed on the National List: all seed firms' versions were regarded as identical, although in many cases it was clear they were not. In the 1970s, for example, the Bedfordshire Champion onion was one of the most popular varieties with amateur growers, and versions of it were listed in various seed catalogues under such names as Bedfordshire Champion Hurst Reselected (a name that indicates that the basic variety still had some genetic variation within it and that someone called Hurst had tried to eliminate it), Golden Globe, Nuttings Golden Ball, Cambridge no. 10, Sutton Globe, and Up-to-Date. After July 1980 all these strains had to be sold as just plain Bedfordshire Champion, completely disregarding the fact that reselection, both intentional and as a result of their having been produced on seed grounds in different parts of the country, had taken place over the years to such an extent that some of the strains now had resistance to downy mildew, which the parent variety lacked.

Even if a popular old variety was registered, it only stayed so as long as the seed firm responsible for it thought it worthwhile paying the annual fee. In the years since 1980, as a result of cost-cutting, hundreds of vegetable varieties have been dropped from the list and thus made illegal to sell. At the time this book was being written, if these varieties still existed, anyone wanting to sell their seeds would have had to pay the full DUS test fee to get them restored to the list.

In 1995 – two decades too late – the British and French governments unsuccessfully asked the EU to relax its directive and allow unlisted seed varieties over fifteen years old to be sold in small packets to amateur growers. 'Our request is still on the table in Brussels,' a Plant Variety Rights official told me in 1996. 'We ran into trouble with the Dutch, who don't think that you can distinguish varieties for amateur growers. We're still hopeful.' Simon Hickmott, a full-time seed grower working for the Henry Doubleday Research Association (HDRA) near Coventry, is not: 'It will never happen,' he says.

Because HDRA is the only amateur gardening organization concerned with organic methods, it was the only one to know what the loss of the old varieties might mean and to kick up a fuss in the media

– a campaign, incidentally, that played a large part in enabling and encouraging Oxfam to open the gene bank at Wellesbourne. HDRA also took action itself. For example, to get round the restrictions on selling unlisted seeds, its founder, Lawrence Hills, organized a seed library and a network of members to grow old varieties for exchange with each other. It also wrote to seed companies asking to be kept informed of any varieties they planned to drop, so that these could be taken into the library. In 1977 it published the first edition of its *Vegetable Seed Finder*, listing firms from which listed older varieties might be purchased without breaking the law.

Almost twenty years later, these activities are still going on. HDRA's Heritage Seed Programme now has about seven hundred varieties in its seed library, and the four thousand members of the programme, who are not necessarily members of HDRA itself, are sent the catalogue annually so that they may order five of them – free, of course, as it would be illegal for them to be sold – to grow in their own gardens. They also get a quarterly bulletin, *Leaflet*, containing practical advice on seed saving, and a 'lost and found' section, so that they can exchange rare varieties. The rare seeds the members order are produced in the project's gardens at Ryton, near Coventry, and by members who have volunteered to act as 'seed guardians' and grow at least one variety for seed year after year. 'We had 160 guardians in 1995 and will have more in 1996,' Simon Hickmott told me. 'At the moment the number of people in the programme is growing very quickly, and we badly need more guardians to produce seed for them because having varieties grown in several different places does a lot to reduce genetic drift.'[22]

Drift is in fact very likely to affect seeds in the Heritage Programme, as Hickmott realizes. 'We differ from other seed banks in that we have a very short period between generations, with very little seed being left in long-term storage: seeds are only kept back as insurance against failures. This leaves many varieties open to change and evolution from their original characteristics, but we feel that our approach at least allows our members to use the seeds. Our emphasis is always on making varieties available which are essentially suited to the amateur grower.'

Seed Savers' Exchange in the United States is a much bigger operation, although in its early years it received a donation from HDRA to help it get going. It was set up in 1975 by a gardener, Kent Whealy, who had inherited some seed from his grandfather-in-law and shared the old man's conviction about their importance, and now has about

[main text continues p.270]

PURE NO MORE? SEED MIXTURES CUT CHEMICAL USE

One of the tragedies about the way the West Germans annexed East Germany was that the communist state's good features were jettisoned along with the bad. Agriculture was no exception. The GDR put a lot of resources into plant breeding and its barley varieties were grown throughout Europe. However, in East Germany itself they were rarely grown by themselves: instead the state farms planted mixtures of the advanced barleys in their fields because this enabled them to avoid using fungicides, which would have to have been imported from the West for precious convertible currency.[23]

This use of barley mixtures was based on work carried out in the early 1970s at the Plant Breeding Institute in Cambridge by Martin Wolfe and John Barrett, who showed that if three spring barley varieties were planted together the plants were healthier than if each was grown apart. This, the researchers found, was because if one strain lacked resistance to a particular fungus, each stem was further from infected stems of the same variety and shielded from them by the resistant types. Moreover, although one of the components of the mixture might have a better yield than the oher two in a particular year, it was impossible to predict which it would be, and consequently the blend gave the highest and most stable yield from year to year.

Although some Danish farmers used this information and grew mixed crops successfully, barley mixtures never caught on in the West because the maltsters, to whom all the best barley is sold, refused to take them. Malting is harder to control if the seeds in a batch do not have the same properties, and those in a blend obviously do not: they vary in size, nitrogen content, and length of time to germination. Western malting companies had no interest in overcoming this challenge, whereas the East German maltsters did. As a result, 92 per cent of the 350,000 hectares of spring barley grown in the GDR at the time of reunification was a mixture (the remaining 8 per cent was used to grow pure seed for blending), saving an estimated 400 tonnes of fungicide from being used each year. East Germany's valuable exports of malt and beer to the west were unaffected.

'This national-scale German experiment was highly successful, despite the fact that, as we discovered later, the crop diversity that they were using was much less than had been thought,' Professor Wolfe told me in early 1995. 'At the time of reunification the main problem was that the East German farmers had then to sell their harvested seed direct to mainly West German maltsters and brewers, who paid higher prices but were not prepared to buy mixed seed. This forced the barley growers back to monoculture of the preferred quality varieties with application, once more, of expensive West German fungicides.'[24]

According to Wolfe, who now works in the plant pathology department of the Federal Polytechnic in Zürich, some barley mixtures are still being grown in Germany to be sold to more open-minded maltsters, and there is also some interest in wheat mixtures there. An estimated 100,000 hectares of wheat mixtures is already being grown in the United States as a result of work by Dr Chris Mundt; and in Switzerland, where farmers are

The Wolfes (photo: Patrick Whitefield, *Permaculture Magazine*.)

paid a subsidy not to use fungicides, insecticides and straw-shorteners on their crops, there has been a rapid and successful shift to the planting of mixtures of winter barley in those cantons where mixed seeds are available. However, Wolfe is most excited about his department's collaboration with Dr Edward Gacek in Poland, where farmers already plant over a million hectares of mixed species, as opposed to mixed varieties. 'Roughly 700,000 hectares of barley/oats and about 500,000 hectares of barley/oats/wheat are being grown,' Wolfe says. 'This development occurred over the last thirty years, initiated and stimulated by the farmers themselves without the support of scientists and against a background of criticism from the communist regime.'

Wolfe hopes that plant breeders will now develop seed varieties specifically for mixing, as he thinks this would lead to considerable gains in output. 'Even more exciting could be the selection of different species for positive interaction,' he says. 'This is because species mixtures have two principal advantages over variety mixtures. First, there would be no development of pathogen races able to attack the component species simultaneously because most, although not all, pathogen species are specialized to a single host species. Second because different species utilize different factors in the environment, there is greater potential for "complementation" among species than among varieties. We, and others, have had highly positive results with, for example, different forms of cereal/legume mixtures such as wheat and beans. Indeed, in the Third World, maize/beans is a very common crop and there is the well-established grass/clover mixture in Europe.'

The ultimate mixed species cropping system is, of course, agroforestry. 'My wife and I are now establishing four experimental agroforestry systems on a small farm in Suffolk as a long-term retirement project,' Wolfe says. 'One of our objectives is to indicate the possibilities for drawing people back to the countryside, either directly to run such complex enterprises or indirectly to make use of their manifold products.'

Prof. Martin Wolfe, Phytomedizin/Pathologie, ETH Zentrum/LFW, Universitätstrasse 2, 8092 Zürich; tel. +41 1 6323847; fax +41 1 6321108; e-mail WOLFE@IPW.AGRL.ETHZ.CH.

five thousand varieties in its library. Many of these were not in government seed banks in 1985 when a study commissioned by a committee of Congress revealed, for example, that of the 1799 varieties of beans that Seed Savers' network of 630 farmers and gardeners were storing or growing, only 147 could be found in official collections.[25] And while Seed Savers had 554 varieties of tomatoes and five of spinach, the government had only 133 tomatoes and no spinach.

In Ireland people know only too well what happens when a country relies on a crop with a narrow genetic base. All the twelve or so varieties of potato grown in Ireland before the Famine in 1845 had been bred from just two introductions, and consequently the plant had an extraordinarily narrow range of genetic variability, particularly as farmers never grew them from seed but planted setts cut from the tubers, a process that made every plant exactly the same as the next. When the potato was first grown in Ireland in the late sixteenth century, it had left all its enemies behind in the New World and was described as being 'peculiarly exempt from blights and mildews' and 'more tenacious of life than couch grass.'[26] As a result it was particularly useful as a standby against summers so wet that most of the cereal crop was lost and is credited with preventing several local famines. In the west of Ireland, however, potatoes came to be grown on a huge scale by people whose holdings of boggy, stony land were too small to allow them to plant the crop in different places each year on, say, a four-year rotation, even had there been other crops to rotate them with. In most cases only the potato would grow.

As the years passed and trans-Atlantic sailings became more frequent, the potato's enemies made the crossing too. In the 1750s a dry rot arrived that would destroy potatoes in store. In the 1770s leaf curl, a virus disease spread by aphids that can reduce yields by 70 per cent, arrived. Then in 1795 came botrytis, a blue-grey mould that rots the leaves and stems, and in 1833 blackleg, a bacterial disease that poisons the plant, blackening the stems and rotting the tubers in the ground or during storage. And finally came blight. It was first reported in the Isle of Wight in June 1845 and had spread to every country in Europe by August. Whole fields became blackened and stinking almost overnight. There was nothing anyone could do.

As these diseases arrived, potatoes became progressively riskier to grow. In each of the three quarter-centuries between 1724 and 1799 there were five years in which the potato crop was bad, but only three or four of the fifteen total bad years were serious enough to be officially rated as famines, with relief works being organized on a wide scale. Between 1800 and 1824 there were nine years of bad crops, of which five were judged to be famines. The worst was in 1821, when a quarter of a million people died. Between 1825 and 1849 there were fourteen years of bad or disastrous crops, at least eight involving famine. Perhaps a million people lost their lives, and another million emigrated. The effects of the loss of life and the enforced emigration that Henry Hobhouse documents so well in *Seeds of Change*[27] will be with us for ever.

Had a gene conferring blight-resistance not been found among the thousands of types of potato that peasants were cultivating in the Andes and in Mexico and bred into our modern varieties, it is unlikely that anyone in Europe would be able to grow it today. The crop almost had to be written off again sixty years later as a result of potato wart disease, a fungus that causes spore masses like black cauliflower curds to grow from rotting tubers. The fungus spreads in soil, and even muddy boots or windblown dust are enough to take it from place to place. In 1908 the problem had become so serious that it was made a notifiable disease; the following year, however, a government inspector noticed that two varieties, Snowdrop and Golden Wonder, were never affected, and it was from these that all other resistant varieties have been bred. As a result, for the moment, wart disease is no longer a serious problem.

When Lawrence Hills told this story in a HDRA newsletter in 1980 he pointed out that it was only because a range of potato varieties was being grown that people found out that genetic resistance to wart disease existed, and in which varieties. If only one type of potato had been cultivated and the rest all kept in gene banks, rectifying the situation would have taken much longer than it did.

The potato is now threatened by blight again: a second form of the disease has crossed the Atlantic, and scientists fear that it will interbreed with the first and produce a hybrid so vigorous it proves uncontrollable.[28] Most other major crops face similar threats, and, according to Fowler and Mooney, current trends make it almost inevitable that at least one of them will become impossible to grow. 'If enough diversity is lost, the ability of crops to adapt and evolve will have been destroyed. We will not have to wait for the last wheat plant to shrivel up and die before wheat can be considered extinct. It will become extinct when it loses the ability to evolve and when neither its genetic defences nor our chemicals are able to protect it. And that day might come quietly even as millions of acres of wheat blanket the earth.'

The consequences of genetic inadequacy overcoming a major crop

[main text continues p.274]

ANIMAL GENES AT RISK TOO

In a rational world, cattle with the ability to produce rich milk from rough hill grazing on which other breeds would starve would be prized as a valuable resource. In the world as it is, a breed with that ability, the Kerry, almost died out and was only saved at the last minute. Its low point came in 1982, when there were only 110 cows and 96 heifers in Ireland and Britain. The number of these tiny black animals – they are no more than thirty-eight inches high at the shoulder – has doubled since then, but some of their genetic diversity has been lost, according to Dr Brian Bradley of the Department of Genetics at Trinity College, Dublin, who has studied them. 'They are much more uniform than they would have been had their numbers not dropped so low,' he says. However, the Kerry's value is now appreciated, and to minimize inbreeding and prevent more characteristics being lost, the Irish Department of Agriculture uses a computer program to advise owners on the bulls they should use to inseminate each cow.

The Kerry almost disappeared despite having a breed society to promote it and record pedigrees, a show record going back to the 1840s, and the proven ability to convert its feed into milk more efficiently than almost any other type of cattle. In tests as long ago as 1841, a Galloway cow consumed 21.75 pounds of hay a day, from which it produced 6.25 quarts of milk, which was churned into 0.65 pounds of butter. The Kerry ate 16.875 pounds of hay and gave 7.5 quarts of much richer milk, which turned into almost a pound of butter.[29]

The ability to produce rich milk from heather-covered hillsides gave the Kerry the title of the poor man's cow. However, the present secretary of the breed society, Raymonde Hilliard, who milks twenty-four Kerry that graze on frequently flooded roughish land outside Killarney, says that yields will increase to justify the use of good land if it is available. The bull calves are good for beef too, which is unusual in a milk breed. 'They just take a bit longer to reach weight,' she says. A slaughter weight of about 560 pounds at three years – tiny by Charolais standards – is regarded as fair. She sells in-calf heifers for about £650, but 'people want them for peanuts'.

Many other traditional animal breeds with potentially valuable characteristics for a sustainable, low-input system of agriculture are either still in difficulties or owe their present satisfactory numbers to the Rare Breeds Survival Trust in Britain. For example, Ireland's only native breed of pig, the Irish greyhound (so called because it was long and lean and noted for its speed and ability to jump), is extinct, and several British breeds including the Lop, Large Black, Middle White, Tamworth (notable for its golden-brown coat), Berkshire, and Gloucester Old Spot (originally bred to be reared in woodlands and orchards), would probably have gone the same way without the RBST. No breed has been lost since the Trust was established in 1973.

In particular, sustainable systems of agriculture and food distribution are going to mean an increased role for the horse. About a million heavy horses were used in Britain in 1920 – 775,000 on farms and the remainder in transport and distribution.[30] In 1990, however, according to a Ministry of Agriculture census,[31] there were only 4500 on farms and smallholdings, slightly up on the 1979 figure of 4375. 'I would say only about 10 per cent of them are in use,' says John Ward of the Shire Horse Society. 'Most are kept for breeding purposes. There are about 3500 mares, and because the market for pure-bred foals has been very depressed of late, most of them are cross-bred to produce jumpers and riding horses that can carry a little weight. A good mare will sell for about £2000 and a working gelding for £1500. You get a lot of horse for very little money.'

Because of their numbers, Shire horses are safe as a breed, but the Suffolk Punch is down to 350, and Clydesdale numbers are also low. 'The Suffolk Punch is classed as an endangered species. There are very few bloodlines available, but if you talk to the breeders they'll say they are not seeing any problems but are aware of the dangers,' Ward says. According to the Food and Agriculture Organization of the United Nations, a breed is endangered if there are fewer than a thousand breeding females and twenty breeding males, and critical if there are fewer than a hundred breeding females and five breeding males.

Shire Horse Society, East of England Showground, Peterborough PE2 0XE; tel. +44 1733 390696.

Rare Breeds Survival Trust, National Agricultural Centre, Kenilworth, Warwickshire, CV8 2LE; tel. +44 1203 696551. Membership costs £15 in the UK, £25 in Irealand, and includes copies of a quarterly magazine, The Ark.

Irish Genetic Conservation Trust, c/o Jim Martin, Department of Botany, Trinity College, Dublin 2, is primarily for scientists. Subscriptions are £10. However, it has close links with the Irish Rare Breeds Society, Derk, Dromard, Co. Sligo, tel. +353 71 66002, which is much more for practical breeders. The Society's directory of Irish rare breeds covers cattle, sheep, pigs and horses and costs £2.50, post paid.

Only three examples of the Kerry Bog pony were known to exist when John Mulvihill, who keeps a pub outside Killarney, began to take an interest in them in 1987. By 1995, when they were recognized as a distinct breed by the Irish Horse Board, twenty-two ponies had been discovered.

would be much worse than those of the collapse of the world's financial system. It is therefore imperative that each community re-create landraces suited to its area by planting and saving mixtures of seeds. This would give its crops a fighting chance to maintain resistance to pests as rapidly as the pests developed new ways of overcoming it. Communities should also establish their own branches of organizations like HDRA and Seed Savers, so that, just as with money and credit, they can exchange seeds locally and have an alternative, independent source of genetic material available should the mainstream multinational one fail.

'Who would survive if wheat, rice or maize were to be destroyed? To suggest such a possibility would have seemed absurd a few years ago. It is not absurd now,' Jack Harlan wrote as long ago as 1972. 'How real are the dangers? What is the potential magnitude of the disaster? One might as well ask how serious is atomic warfare. The consequences of failure of one of our major food plants are beyond imagination.'

Reducing external inputs
It is not enough for a community to grow its own food from seed it has saved: it also has to end its reliance on other external inputs as well. The following table[32] sets out how extensive the changes in agriculture need to be if communities are to become more self-reliant.

Switching to the sort of low-external-input system outlined in the table is not the same thing at all as reverting to traditional farming, and the difficulties and increased costs attached to doing so are less than most people imagine. This is because many of the problems associated with high-energy, chemical agriculture are created by the system itself and become much less serious when the approach and scale are changed. For example, the use of nitrogenous fertilizers makes pesticide applications almost inevitable because they encourage plants to make lusher, sappier growth, which is much more liable to insect and fungal attack and contains more free amino acids, substances particularly attractive to bacteria that cause decay. Avoid using artificial sources of nitrogen and you can usually avoid using artificial pesticides too. Another cause of pest problems is the larger fields needed by farmers if they are to use bigger, more powerful equipment, because the hedgerows bulldozed to create them were the predators' habitat. A low-input agriculture would make less use of power machinery and either restore the hedgerows or plant special areas in which predators could thrive.

LIFE FROM THE LAND

	SELF-RELIANT SYSTEM	CONVENTIONAL SYSTEM
SUN	Main source of energy	Supplemented by fossil fuels
WATER	Mainly rain and small irrigation schemes	Large dams, centralized distribution, deep wells
NITROGEN	Fixed from the air and recycled in soil organic matter	Primarily from inorganic fertilizer
MINERALS	Taken from soil and recycled	Mined, processed, imported
WEED & PEST CONTROL	Biological, cultural, mechanical and locally available chemicals	With pesticides and herbicides
ENERGY	Some generated or collected on farm	Dependent on fossil fuel
SEEDS VARIETIES	Most produced locally; thrive in difficult conditions	Most from elsewhere; need high input levels
ANIMALS	Integral part of farming	Produced in special units
CROP SYSTEM	Rotation and diversity	Monoculture
LABOUR	Labour-intensive; most work done by farmer's family	Low labour requirement; most work done by hired labour and machines
CAPITAL	Provided by farm family or community; any surplus reinvested locally	External loans or shares; any surplus sent away
MARKET	Primarily local	Primarily far away

In any case, just as we saw with renewable energy, food produced in a community using a low level of inputs from outside is highly unlikely to cost more than its brought-in equivalent if the community has unused resources such as land and labour and can express the costs of using them in local terms, perhaps through pricing them in its own currency. Even when this is not possible, food produced using low-external-input techniques need cost no more by normal accounting standards than conventionally grown food. For example, a study in 1979 of the costs and returns from producing winter wheat in Britain showed that the gross margin per hectare was £393 on the organic farms and £399 on chemical ones if the higher price paid for organic grain was ignored.[33] A similar survey of two hundred conventional, organic and biodynamic farms in Baden-Württemberg in Germany showed that organic methods can produce crops almost as heavy as chemical ones.[34] A lot depended on the quality of the soil, there being much less difference in yields on the better soils, and, as organic farming improves soil quality, the longer a piece of land was farmed organically, the closer to the chemical yield its output became. Winter wheat, for example, yielded on average 3.3 tonnes per hectare on an organic farm three years after it had been converted from chemicals but 4.2 tonnes after seventeen years. The average chemical yield for the area was 4.7 tonnes; and as this figure can be expected to fall slowly as a result of soil loss unless counteracted by the introduction of improved varieties, after a decade or two organic output may well surpass chemical output.

One particularly impressive 1993 study of four mixed farms in Minnesota showed that they produced net incomes for the families who ran them between 50 and 100 per cent above the average for the conventional, chemical farms in their area, despite the fact that their acreages were significantly below the local average.[35] Their higher profit margins came about because, although they used more labour, they spent nothing on buying fertilizers and pesticides, inputs that could make up about 40 per cent of their neighbours' total costs.[36]

Jules Pretty looked at the results of many similar studies for his book *Regenerating Agriculture*[37] and concluded that low-external-input farms could be more profitable than conventional ones because while yields per hectare were lower, their input costs were lower still. 'Generally, the loss in yield per hectare is some 5-10 per cent for crops and 10-20 per cent for livestock,' he writes. 'Livestock perform less well mainly because of the substantially lower stocking rates necessary for clover-based pastures. Grassland in Britain has very large amounts of nitrogen fertilizer added and it is almost impossible to match returns when switching to clover pastures. But there is good evidence to suggest that the animals are better off. In Germany, cows in "alternative" herds are more fertile and live longer.' What he might have added is that male farmers who don't use chemicals have higher sperm counts, which makes them more fertile too.[38]

Even if the low-input yield is lower, the loss in weight will almost certainly be counterbalanced by a gain in nutritional quality. A study by Werner Schuphan showed that vegetables grown organically with only natural compost as fertilizer gave on average 24 per cent lower

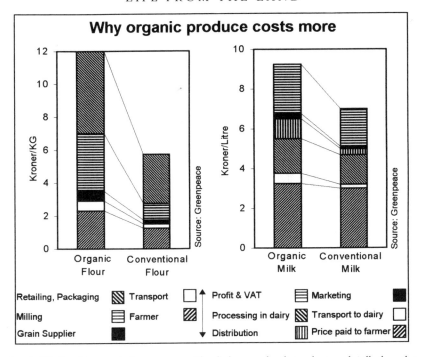

Graph 6.1 *Danish organic farmers are paid a little more for their wheat and milk than their conventional neighbours. The big difference between the price of organic and conventional produce in the shops is due to the higher mark-ups imposed by the distribution chain.*

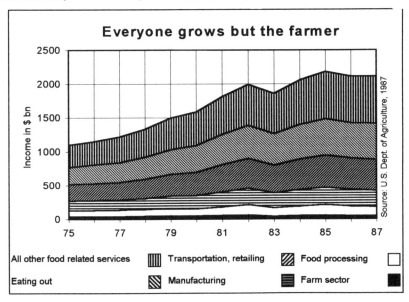

Graph 6.2 *Although the market value of food sold in the US doubled in 1975–85, the amount going to the farmer stayed almost constant, rising from $40 billion to $45 billion over the period.*

yields than their chemically fertilized equivalents but contained 23 per cent more dry matter.[39] In other words, the chemical fertilizer was causing the plant to water itself down. The organic vegetables were sweeter, as, weight for weight, they contained 19 per cent more natural sugars. They were also better food, containing 18 per cent more protein, 28 per cent more vitamin C, and 77 per cent more iron. Not unexpectedly, they also had a much lower proportion of undesirable chemicals, containing 93 per cent less nitrates, which can be turned into strongly carcinogenic nitrosamines by mouth bacteria, and 42 per cent less free amino acids, substances attractive to decay-causing bacteria.

So, although fertilizers, pesticides and herbicides are artificially cheap in the mainstream economy because their price does not cover the cost of the environmental damage they do (one American estimate is that a dollar's worth of pesticide does a dollar's worth of environmental damage, implying that a tax should be imposed on pesticides to double their price),[40] and the extra labour that low-input farming requires is artificially expensive because of the taxes placed on it, low-external-input food products should prove highly competitive with conventional chemical ones, especially if they are sold more directly to the customer.

However, it would be very difficult to use fewer external inputs if one intended to sell the produce through the conventional food distribution system in Britain. This is because of the grading standards imposed by the supermarket chains, which in 1994 were handling just over half of all fresh fruit and vegetables, a figure that had grown from 24 per cent in only a decade and was expected to reach 70 per cent by the end of the century.[41] To meet supermarket standards, growers were compelled to use fertilizers and sprays to achieve the highly uniform, cosmetically perfect fruit and vegetables the chains claim their customers demand. Despite the use of chemicals, however, large quantities of slightly blemished or misshapen produce had to be dumped: one estimate is that half of all organic fruit and vegetables and a fifth of all conventional produce is rejected on grounds of appearance alone.[42] Moreover, the range of varieties the supermarkets will accept is very limited, and those they specify have therefore to be grown on a large scale, creating pest and disease problems. Of the two thousand varieties of English apple, for example, only nine are widely sold.

Another problem posed for growers by the supermarkets is the huge quantities required for each chain's dozens of branches and their

[main text continues p.282]

RURAL REFINERIES REQUIRED TO REPLACE
OIL-BASED CHEMICALS

Although constructing a largely self-reliant local economy will not mean a return to the materials and technologies of the Middle Ages, it will involve picking up some strands of technological development where they were dropped earlier this century as a result of the increasing availability of oil and, to a lesser extent, coal. As David Morris, a co-founder of the Institute for Local Self-Reliance in the United States, puts it, sustainability and self-reliance necessitate moving from a hydrocarbon-based economy to a carbohydrate-based one – that is, from a system based on the consumption of the densely compacted remains of prehistoric plant matter to one based on fresh plant material; and he stresses the prospects this would open up for rural communities.

'One cannot know the future unless one knows the past,' Morris says. 'Little more than a hundred years ago, plant matter was a basic industrial raw material. The first commercially successful plastic was not made from oil but from cotton. What happened is that a billiard ball manufacturing company, Phelan and Collender, concluded that the rate of slaughter of African elephants was proceeding so quickly that it would soon exhaust the supply of ivory. They offered a $10,000 prize to whoever could create an ivory-like material that was also abundant and widely accessible.'[43]

Chemists had already learned that if cotton was treated with nitric acid an insoluble explosive, guncotton, was produced, but that if less nitric acid was used the product, though flammable, was not explosive and was soluble in a mixture of alcohol and ether. If the solvents were then allowed to evaporate, a hard, horny transparent substance was left that could be made workable by adding turpentine or camphor oil. In 1862 a prolific inventor, Alexander Parkes, showed a sample of the plastic, which he called Parkesine, at the International Exhibition in London; but although he realized its potential he was unable to commercialize it, and his company collapsed in 1868. However, two American printers, John and Isaiah Hyatt, were inspired by the ivory-substitute competition to carry out their own experiments and produced a plastic they named Celluloid, which was used to make buttons, dominoes, false teeth and eventually cinematic film, as well as billiard balls.

Other plastics and synthetic fibres based on natural materials soon followed. Count Hilaire de Chardonnet extruded dissolved cellulose through a fine nozzle to make rayon, and the first commercial rayon factory opened in France in 1889. This led to a cellulose acetate yarn, Celanese, which was introduced in the 1920s and had a third of the synthetic fibre market by 1940. In the 1930s cellulose acetate was moulded into steering-wheels, instrument panels and knobs for cars, uses that brought it into competition with Bakelite, the first hard, durable plastic, which was invented in 1909 and was made from phenols and formaldehyde, both of which were, or could have been, derived from wood. Cellulose is also the basis of Cellophane, which is made from wood pulp.

However, this development of a chemical industry based on natural feedstocks was halted by the growth in oil refining to produce petrol for motor vehicles. Refining left the oil companies with a lot of embarrassing waste gases, such as methane, ethylene, propylene, and butylene, and they undertook extensive research to find uses and hence a market for them. Gradually their laboratories developed products that, as they were cheaper and in many cases technically superior, replaced almost every- thing being made from plant material. Paint manufacturers found that petroleum-based resins gave them shorter, more predictable drying times than plant resins and that naphtha (white spirit) was a much cheaper thin- ner than turpentine, distilled from pine trees. American petrochemical output soared from only 10,500 tons in 1921 to 1.5 million tons in 1939. Being waste-based, these chemicals were remarkably cheap: their average price on the outbreak of the Second World War was only thirteen cents a pound.

By 1945 petroleum-based synthetic fibres such as nylon had only 0.5 per cent of the American clothing market, whereas plant-based synthetics, such as rayon and Celanese, had over 10 per cent. By 1980, however, as a result of the introduction of acrylic and polyester fibres, clothing made from oil had a 64 per cent market share. Plastics production also soared, from six million tonnes a year in the United States in 1965 to thirty mil- lion in 1990, while plastics derived from plant matter virtually disap- peared. Even Cellophane suffered: displaced by polymerized ethylene – polythene – its production dropped to less than a quarter of the postwar peak. Of all non-food products made from plant material, only paper and cardboard output continued to expand in the United States, although even this growth was less than it might have been because of competition from oil-based products, particularly polythene. Polythene envelopes have replaced paper ones for posting many periodicals, and polythene bottles have reduced the sales of cardboard milk cartons by 60 per cent.

Petrochemical consumption in the United States is now 109 million tonnes a year, seventy-five times its 1939 figure and almost sixteen times greater than the consumption of biochemicals. Morris, however, thinks the trend might be about to begin running in the other direction, for two rea- sons. One is that the cost of producing chemicals from plant matter is falling. The second is that environmental regulations have raised the cost of producing and disposing of oil-based products and also of disposing of plant wastes, encouraging farmers and processors to find uses for them, just as oil refineries had to do with their waste seventy years ago.

'Consider sawdust,' he says. 'About fifty million tonnes of sawdust are produced each year, creating a disposal problem. It can be burned inside the sawmill, but the dust particles are a fire and explosion hazard. It can be tipped in landfills, but sawdust is easily blown about and hard to han- dle. It can sit in piles in the sawmill yard but rain will eventually cause tannic acid to leach into the water table.' These problems, he says, stimu- lated a company in Missouri to open a plant for converting sawdust into fuel oil and activated carbon, which is used in waste-water treatment plants and as a toner in photocopiers. The same company claims that a second plant in New York state makes specialty chemicals from plant waste 30 per cent more cheaply than from oil.

'A 50 per cent recovery rate for agricultural wastes would generate 175 million tons of feedstock, theoretically sufficient to displace virtually all petrochemicals,' he comments, pointing out that the wastes have a much higher value as chemicals than as fuel. 'Lignin, which on average comprises about one-third of woody crops, has an energy value of $6 a ton and a chemical value of $120. Besides cellulose, a ton of wood can produce 350 pounds of lignin and eighty gallons of ethyl alcohol [ethanol].'

In contrast to the techniques used for manufacturing petrochemicals, the biological processes used for converting plant matter are inherently environmentally benign. 'Breaking down organic minerals like coal and oil requires high pressures and temperatures – breaking the carbon-hydrogen bond requires over 600°C. Most chemical processes also employ large quantities of strong inorganic acids or alkalis such as sulphuric acid and sodium hydroxide. These can result in effluents which harm the environment. The hydrogen-oxygen and oxygen-carbon bonds of cellulose are weaker and almost all bio-processes occur at 30-40°C, at near-atmospheric pressure and at near-neutral pH levels.'

A table in an important study, The Carbohydrate Economy: Making Chemicals and Industrial Materials from Plant Matter (1992), which Morris wrote with Irshad Ahmed, shows that vegetable-based chemicals are still much more expensive than petrochemicals in a lot of product categories: the difference varies from about 20 per cent for inks and 50 per cent for detergents up to 100 per cent for paints and 200 per cent for plastics.[44] Nevertheless products based on plant matter have gained market share because of a combination of 'green' consumerism and direct regulation. Detergents based on plant matter, for example, have benefited equally from the 75 per cent drop in enzyme costs over the past few years and the new bans on phosphates. Printers have two incentives for purchasing printing inks based on vegetable oils: first, regulations may soon be promulgated limiting the evaporative emissions of hydrocarbons from inks; second, inks based on vegetable oils reduce the need for clean-up chemicals, which may themselves create environmental problems. Paint manufacturers already face regulations on hydrocarbon compound emissions, which are an important ingredient in the formation of ground-level ozone.

'Biorefineries can become the backbone of a new rural economy,' Morris says. 'Because plant matter, unlike petroleum, is costly to transport, processing facilities will tend to be modestly sized and located near their raw material suppliers. Two hundred million tonnes of waste and virgin plant matter would be sufficient to supply seven hundred to two thousand new biorefineries. The higher estimate would allow one such facility in every rural county in the country.'

He sees the biorefineries being run by farmers' co-operatives and notes that several co-operative biorefineries are already operating in the US. 'Minnesota Corn Processors is the largest corn-to-ethanol producer in the state. The Dairyman's Co-operative in California converts whey into ethanol and whey protein concentrate. And a fledgling kenaf co-op is operating in Mississippi.'

unwillingness to assemble these quantities by buying from different suppliers; most chains will only deal with companies able to deliver to all their branches from a number of regional depots. Crop consolidators such as the East Kent Packers' Co-operative, which outgrew its name and now, having merged with a rival, Home Grown Fruit, grades and packs produce from growers all over England, were established by growers to meet the chains' requirements; nevertheless, orchards have been grubbed up and market gardens closed down throughout the country. It was usually smaller growers serving local shops who gave up the struggle. This was because three-quarters of the independent retailers with whom they dealt closed down between 1978 and 1993 as the supermarkets took their business.

Increasingly, the supermarkets have turned to imports to meet their needs. French apples – mainly the tasteless Golden Delicious – have 35 per cent of the British market, while British apples have only 25 per cent. In September 1994, although abundant home-grown supplies of apples, onions, carrots and green beans were available throughout Britain, Hugh Raven, co-ordinator of the Sustainable Agriculture, Food and Environment (SAFE) Alliance, a coalition of groups working to research and promote sustainable agriculture, found green beans transported 3600 miles from Kenya, apples brought 4700 miles from the United States, carrots brought 5100 miles from South Africa and onions brought 12,000 miles from New Zealand on sale in three central London supermarkets. As he told Charles Clover, environmental correspondent of the *Daily Telegraph*, 'it is madness to fly food half way round the world – like the American raspberries on sale here at the height of our raspberry season – when British growers are going out of business.'[45]

The overall effect of the replacement of locally owned bakers, greengrocers, butchers and provision merchants by retailing chains has been to push up the distance food has to travel. Raven, who estimates that food now travels half as far again as it did in the late 1970s, calculates that this increase was responsible for one-third of the rise in the total amount of freight carried on British roads. Crazy centralizations have contributed to this. Boots, for example, buys all the sandwiches sold in its branches from a company near Derby and delivers them overnight in its vans, while all dairy products sold by Safeway pass through a single distribution depot in Warwickshire, regardless of where they were imported or made.

But these distribution networks, along with the packing houses and the advertising and marketing activities that necessarily accompany them, are in fact the supermarkets' Achilles heel because they are costly to run. Indeed, as the chains have developed over the years, a larger and larger proportion of the price the consumer pays has to be used to cover the operating costs of the distribution system itself rather than paying farmers and growers for their output. Between 1982 and 1992, for example, food prices for consumers rose by 52 per cent but the prices paid to growers by the supermarkets increased by only 18 per cent.[46]

It is not just in Britain that increasingly powerful processing and distribution sectors have taken advantage of farmers and growers. In 1973, when there were 35,700 family farms producing pigs in Ireland, bacon factories were dotted all over the country, and of the price the shopper paid for a pork or bacon product, half on average went back to the farm.[47] By 1996, however, there were fewer than 700 pig farmers, although the total number of pigs reared had more than doubled. And, thanks to government policy, there were only six bacon factories of any size, three of these controlled by one company, Avonmore. As a result, only just over a fifth of the price of a packet of bacon was getting back to what had now become a factory farm rather than a family one. In the United States between 1980 and 1987, the amount the farmer received for his or her contribution to a box of corn flakes fell by a third, while the price to the consumer went up by the same proportion.[48] In West Germany in the 1950s, three-quarters of all spending on food went back to the farm; thirty years later, the proportion had dropped to a fifth.[49] In Denmark in 1991, as the graph on page 277 shows, 56 per cent of the pre-tax price of a bag of flour was absorbed by packaging, transport, and sale through the shop, 25 per cent went to the farmer, and 13 per cent went to the miller.[50]

The message is clear. Organic and other low-input producers need to short-circuit the supermarkets and sell to the public, either directly or, avoiding wholesalers, through a local shop. Either course would enable them to gain a larger part of the amount the customer pays for their goods while at the same time disposing of produce that, though safer and more flavourful than that grown with chemicals, the supermarkets would have required them to leave in the field.

Community agriculture

Community-supported agriculture (CSA) is an approach that low-external-input producers should consider adopting because it is not only a powerful method of direct selling but much more besides, as we will see shortly. It was born in Germany and Switzerland in the 1970s, became a popular movement in North America in the early 1990s, and has now spread back across the Atlantic to Ireland and Britain.

Robyn van En became one of those who introduced it to the United States almost by accident. In 1983 she had just moved to Great Barrington, Massachusetts, with her six-year-old son, planning to continue her training as a kindergarten teacher. 'I was looking for a house on about five acres to continue my flower farming,' she told me in the sitting-room at Indian Line Farm, her home about three miles outside the town, 'but this abandoned dairy farm and sixty acres was as cheap as a house on a lot.' When she got it the farm had been out of production for two years since the Willcoxes, who had farmed it since the late 1940s, had sold out to a speculative builder who wanted to build luxury houses on its thirty-acre upper pasture to take advantage of the view.

The Willcoxes had felt fortunate to get a buyer for the property at all. Dairying in Massachusetts, which in the 1930s supplied a large part of New York's requirements by rail, was in rapid decline because it had become so cheap to transport milk 1500 miles by road from Wisconsin that two-thirds of the milk consumed in the state was coming in from outside. Half of Massachusetts' milk producers went out of business between 1980 and 1993, 7 per cent quitting in 1988 alone. In many cases their land went unsold and is now reverting to forest, while their houses are either occupied as holiday homes for a few weeks a year or collapsing from neglect and decay.

Robyn van En bought the rump of the property from the builder and farmed a small part of it organically for two years, selling most of what she grew to a group of local families that had come together to buy their food staples collectively. This eliminated her marketing problems but left her finding all the working capital, carrying all the risk, and doing all the work. 'I knew there had to be a better way to farm,' she says, 'something co-operative, that allowed people to combine their abilities, expertise and resources for their mutual benefit while at the same time bringing the people who grew the food closer to those who ate it.'[51]

In the middle of her second growing season, in 1984, Jan Vandertuin, a Vermonter who had worked on several organic and conventional farms, returned to the United States from Switzerland and was taken out to Indian Line by a mutual friend. While he had been away he had helped set up Topinambur near Zürich, a collective producing vegetables for about 125 member-families and milk for even more. It had been modelled on two similar Swiss projects, Les Jardins de Cocagne near Geneva, which employed three full-time gardeners to supply organic vegetables every week to about 550 people, and Agrico near Basel, which had four people as well as a part-timer producing eggs, milk, vegetables and grain for more than 150 families. 'After talking for only a few minutes, Jan and I knew what we should do at Indian Line Farm,' van En says.

Because neither of them felt that they had sufficient horticultural experience to start on their own, they began to advertise for a qualified grower. In the meantime, they introduced the 'share the costs to share the harvest'

Robyn van En and Hugh Radcliffe bringing in the harvest at Indian Line Farm, Massachusetts. (photo: Clemens Kalisher)

concept to the area by getting thirty families to combine to harvest 360 bushels of apples from an old orchard where they would otherwise have been left to rot. They turned most of the fruit into apple juice, vinegar, and cider, each family paying $90 in advance to cover the costs. The following year, the missing component arrived when they were approached by Hugh Radcliffe, an experienced biodynamic gardener and a former research biologist at Cornell University who had come to believe that orthodox science was inadequate for understanding the living plant. In the autumn of 1985 he began preparing raised beds for spring planting on three acres leased from van En, and a prospectus was issued. This offered thirty year-round shares, each adequate for feeding two to three people, with a further thirty winter root-crop shares, designed for people who had their own vegetable garden for fresh produce in the summer but who did not grow enough potatoes, turnips, parsnips or other root vegetables to see them through the rest of the year.

'Distribution of the harvest will be twice a week in season and then once every two weeks for winter storage crops,' the prospectus read.

285

'The harvest will be divided into equal shares and made available at various pick-up points around the area. We plan to provide, per delivery, an average of 5 lb of vegetables/herbs twice weekly in season and about 20 lb every other week in winter.'

The costs of growing these were estimated at just under $21,000, which worked out at $557 per full share and $140 for a winter share, assuming all the shares were taken up. As at Topinambur, prospective members were also asked to provide two days' labour each during the year and to accept that the final price of their share could vary by as much as 12 per cent either way, depending on how things turned out. Members were also asked to demonstrate their commitment to the project by paying for their shares in advance if they were able to do so. Because of the success of the apple harvesting, most of the shares were sold without much difficulty, particularly as roughly $13 a week for forty-three weeks' supply of really fresh organically grown vegetables, which was what a full share was expected to provide, would be better value than any shop.

When production began, the gardeners and their assisting members planned to have everything picked by eleven in the morning on delivery days. 'If there were thirty-five shares each receiving two lettuces, one red leaf and one romaine, then that is what we would cut,' van En says. 'Most other things were picked according to what was ready or ripe.' These bulk items were weighed on an old railway goods scale and then divided into individual shares using nursery scales. Packed in dampened returnable muslin bags, each member's share of the harvest was available for collection from the farm at lunchtime or left by arrangement at one of several drop-off points in the town during the afternoon.

The following season's prospectus offered fifty-five full-season shares at $597 each and twenty winter shares at $160, giving the project an income of $36,000, 80 per cent of which was spent on labour. Even so, Radcliffe was paid only $13,500 for his thirty weeks of work during the growing season, a sum that a core group member later admitted was about half what he should have earned. In 1988 the cost of a full share was set at $300 by the simple expedient of halving the quantities members could expect to get, as some families found they had been receiving more vegetables than they could eat. As a result, 135 full-season shares were taken up.

It was at this point that things went wrong. So far the group had merely had a three-year lease on the land with the option to buy. As the third season drew to a close, everyone was keen that the option

 [main text continues p.292]

A FARM WHERE FOOD IS FREE

Indian Line Farm was one of two CSAs to be established in the United States in 1986. The other pioneer was the Temple-Wilton Community Farm near Wilton in New Hampshire, set up shortly after Trauger Groh arrived in the area from Buschberghof, a farm in the village of Fuhlenhagen about twenty miles east of Hamburg on which he had been working for the previous fifteen years. Temple-Wilton and Buschberghof were – and are – biodynamic farms run according to a system developed by Rudolph Steiner. According to Willy Schilthuis in his book Biodynamic Agriculture, this is based on

an awareness or sense that every living being has a link with the spiritual cosmic world and that it is the duty of every human being to guide the life of these beings in such a way that the links can take place undisturbed. Furthermore, [biodynamic farmers] work on the basis of the view that the Earth is a living organism and that a farm itself is a living organism.[52]

In practice, the main differences between biodynamic and ordinary organic agriculture are that biodynamic farmers plant according to the phases of the moon, make compost using two special preparations containing cow-horn, and spray their crops with six different extracts of such things as oak bark and yarrow leaves prepared with specific animal organs.

Buschberghof went biodynamic in the early 1950s, just as the movement was recovering from its suppression under Hitler. Its conversion did not shield it from the problems faced by other small farms, however, even though it had low input costs and was able to sell its produce for an above-average price under the biodynamic Demeter label. All food prices – biodynamic, organic, and conventional – fell steadily in relation to wages in Germany in the 1950s and 60s, making it increasingly difficult for the farmer, Carl-August Loss, to pay his workers and support his family. Like everyone else, he tried to cut his costs by mechanization and borrowed from the bank to purchase equipment. In 1968, however, he realized he was getting deeper in debt each year and that if he continued he would be made bankrupt and lose the farm, which had been in his family since the sixteenth century. Feeling that he would rather give his land away than have it taken from him by his creditors, he set up a land trust and transferred it to that.

At this point Trauger Groh appeared on the scene. He too was a farmer, but his land had been compulsorily purchased for a military airfield and he had cash to reinvest. The two men recognized that processing the milk and cereals the Buschberghof grew was likely to provide a better basis for supporting their families than buying another farm for Groh to work, so his capital was given to the trust and spent on building a cow-shed, a dairy with a flat above, a flour mill, and a bakery. It was also used to erect a large pink building in the distinctive anthroposophical style on a low hill outside the village. This contains two private flats, a big kitchen and dining-room, a library and meeting hall, and accommodation for twelve people with handicaps who, in accordance with Steiner's teachings and the farm families' feelings of social obligation, are looked after at the farm and work in the gardens, the dairy, or the house.

Since Groh and Loss had provided the trust with its land, stock, and equipment, it would have seemed wrong for them to have to rent it back to use it. However, they paid the trust an annual fee to cover the depreciation of the machinery and the repair of the buildings. 'The new farm started in a financially difficult position, with three families to support at a time when the market for biodynamic and organic produce was very limited,' Groh's daughter, Christina, says. 'The farm was slowly developed with the improvement of its soil, pasture and livestock ... At different times we sold our produce through a farm shop, wholesaler and weekly van-round. However, we found that a lot of time and energy was being spent on marketing.'[53]

In 1987 the families working the farm decided to adopt an idea Groh had just put into practice at Temple-Wilton. After discussions with their van-round customers and people who had been calling to the farm to buy their milk they set up an 'economic association for the care of plants, animals and man', with a target membership of about eighty families, the number they felt the farm could feed.[54] The farm has 210 acres, of which four are vegetable garden, 106 arable, and 69 permanent pasture. The rest is woodland. The farm team estimated that the 179 acres under grass and crops would feed 288 people on the basis of 0.25 hectares (0.62 acres) to feed each person. This figure turned out to be a little conservative.

The idea behind the association was that each year the farm would estimate its running costs for the year ahead and the subscribers to the association would pay these, not to obtain their food but to support the farm's work. Whatever was produced on the farm would belong to the subscribers, and they would get that free.

For the first year, 1988, 195 members subscribed. This was not enough to take up the farm's full output, and so the farm shop and other sales continued in parallel. Most of these subscribers came from the farm's milk distribution circles, groups of about ten families who picked up the milk on behalf of each other. The following year, however, 321 members signed up, and the farm shop and the remaining milk circles were discontinued. As at Temple-Wilton, each family decided how much it could afford to give each month to support the farm and paid that to the association's treasurer. It could then order as much food as it liked.

This system is still in use. 'There hasn't been any abuse. No one, for example, has ordered more than their household can eat to sell or give away,' Wolfgang Stränz, a chemist and language teacher, told me as we drove out to the farm on one of his monthly journeys to collect produce. 'That's because we are organized into groups of eight or nine families living in the same part of Hamburg and take it in turns to assemble the orders and make the collections. Everyone in the group would soon know if someone was taking advantage.'

In 1995 the budget for the farm was 500,000 marks, which means that, with ninety families participating, the average subscription was about 5500 marks or £2500. How much of its food did his family get for its contribution? I asked Stränz. 'Well, we buy tea and coffee, beer, salt and pepper, noodles, and rice. We eat tomatoes from the Canary Islands before the crop on the farm is ready. And every Sunday I go to the baker's for hot white rolls. But that's all. Everything else comes from the farm. The range of food we get is quite broad. There are nine different sorts of bread and seven types of cheese, for example.'

The old Loss farmyard is in the centre of the village. Wheat, dinkel (an ancient form of wheat popular on biodynamic farms), barley, oats and rye are stored in one of the brick-built barns facing the farmhouse, waiting to be processed in the mill in the same building. Not far away is the bakery, its big wood-fired oven still warm from a firing three days ago. In another of the barns a farmer is repairing equipment, of which there seems to be a lot, mostly fairly new. The pigs, who seem to be enjoying their carrots, are in a shed away from the road. Stränz unloads empty wooden crates he has brought with him from his car boot, each marked with a family's name, leaves the orders for the farmers to make up before the next collection in four days' time, and drives about half a mile up to the main building, beside which the hay-barn, cow-sheds and dairy have been built.

We take off our shoes and put on special boots before going into the dairy, where Christina Groh is separating curds for cheese-making from whey in a big stainless-steel vat. Her mother, Gisela, and her sister, Patricia, also live on the farm. She presses a switch and the whey is pumped outside into a wheeled tank so that it can be taken back down the hill to feed the pigs. While Stränz unloads holders containing the empty fruit-juice bottles that the farm uses for milk and loads up with filled ones, she proudly shows me the racks of cheeses maturing in the cellar below. She also makes butter and yoghurt. 'Before we joined the system, biodynamic butter was just too expensive for us to buy,' Stränz says. 'Now we even cook with it.'

Tobias Pedersen, the herdsman, walks past, and Christina calls him over. He is English and has only lived on the farm for about six months. He had very little German when he arrived but is now getting fluent. Later I meet his wife, Andrea, and one of their four young children. 'This is much more satisfying work than I could ever find in England,' he tells me. 'There I would have to look after a herd of at least two hundred animals and spend all my time at it. Here I look after just twenty, so I can do things properly and do a lot of other jobs on the farm.' The cows, which belong to the land trust, are Anglers, a rare red-coloured breed from the area. It is June, so they are grazing in a pasture not far away from the farm's wind turbine. In winter, however, they will be fed inside on hay. 'We don't use silage,' Christina says. 'Milk from animals fed on it has a certain taste and is not nearly as good for cheese-making.'

A lot of the straw from the cereal crops is used for the herd's bedding, and piles of manure are composting outside the cattle-shed. Seeing they are so well equipped and already using one form of renewable energy, I ask Christina if they have considered composting it in a biogas digester. She discusses with Stränz whether this would be in accordance with

Steiner's principles, and eventually they agree that it would but that the straw mixed with the dung might be a problem. I also ask if they have considered cutting their external inputs by replacing one or more of the farm's four tractors with horses. Yes, I am told, but suitable horses are hard to find and someone with the skills to work them even harder.

A garden surrounds the central building, an orchard adjoins it, and the vegetable garden is in the field below. Two polytunnels shelter behind a hedge, and there are swings and a sand-pit for young children: Patricia, Christina and the four farmers who run the farm all have young families. Patricia helps care for the handicapped residents – work for which the government gives a grant – and four or five biodynamic agriculture students are usually working on the farm at a time. In addition there is a paid employee, and the handicapped have two other carers.

Carl-August Loss had a stroke in the early 1990s and can no longer work. He lives with his wife in a pretty cottage in the village, bought and restored by the trust. His daughter and her husband are planning to build a house in the village to be near them, and they may take an active part in the farm.

As we drive back to Hamburg, dropping off some of the milk at a kindergarten on the way, Stränz says that association members feel very much a part of everything going on in Fuhlenhagen because they meet the farmers and see what is happening when they go out to pick up orders, and each group selects one of its number to attend the monthly management meetings there. They also attend the farm walks that are held each spring and summer, and some members work on the farm regularly during the week or for several weeks during the summer. Members can picnic on the property at any time.

However, the association is worried that although the farmers can live reasonably well on what they are paid, since they get their food free and their accommodation is provided, not enough financial provision is being made for when they retire. 'They will need to be able to buy houses and have decent pensions,' he says. 'Perhaps our subscriptions should be higher.' And today they are. Since my visit, not only has provision for pensions been added to the farm budget but a 5 per cent allowance has been added to it to build up a fund for new investments.

When we reach his house, Stränz puts the milk and the crates on some covered shelves outside his side door, and a few minutes later, drinking tea inside, we hear the bottles clinking as members of his group arrive to pick up their orders.

The Buschberghof is an inspiring example of what a CSA can be, but the real question is, can it be copied elsewhere? Part of the CSA's success is due to the trust, which has in effect subsidized food prices by not loading the farm's budget with rent for its land and buildings or interest on the money tied up in its livestock and capital equipment. How many Irish or British landowners would be prepared to turn over their land and capital to a similar trust and set up a CSA in the same way?

It is true that in America, Trauger Groh was able to find three families prepared to allow the Temple-Wilton farmers to use their land in exchange for whatever food they wanted for themselves, but the families did not give up the title to their properties and entered into the arrangement chiefly to stop their unused fields reverting to scrub. In places where such landowners cannot be found, groups keen to set up a CSA will have three alternatives. One is that their members will simply pay more for their food in order to cover rent and interest payments. The second is that the groups will set up a land trust along the lines set out in a later panel. The third is that they will find a way to use one or more of the techniques for creating local money and mobilizing local savings mentioned in chapters 3 and 4 to provide cheap or interest-free finance for their community farms.

But a much more important element in the Buschberghof's success than the subsidy is the set of beliefs that drive the farmers and their supporter-subscribers along. Without similar beliefs in the importance of the highest standards of care for nature, the land, crops, animals, and people, any attempts to replicate it are bound, at least in part, to fail.

Christina Groh examining her cheeses.

The main building at the Buschberghof.

should be taken up, and a valuer was called in to say what the price should be. 'He fixed a fair price for the land but put no value on the barn, saying that people didn't farm any more,' van En says. 'But the point was, the group had a use for it. They were packing everything on these tables here, and the root vegetable store was there at the back. As you've seen, it's a good, solid three-storey building, much better built than my house.'

The group would not improve on the valuer's figure, so van En refused to sell, and the group bought another site for their operations on the other side of Great Barrington. She continued subscription gardening with a new head gardener at Indian Line Farm in 1989 and 1990, until her work promoting the CSA concept throughout the United States became so demanding that she had to give one or the other up. So Indian Line is mostly hayfield and pasture again, although the garden plot is rented to an organic grower and the barn may be used for a community-supported brewery. This scarcely matters, however, because the system that Robyn van En, Jan Vandertuin and Hugh Radcliffe established there lives on, and at the end of 1995 there were six hundred community-supported horticultural or agricultural operations involving 100,000 people in the United States alone, taking several different organizational forms and producing a wide range of products. Even city-dwellers participate, contracting with a grower in the country to produce grain, meat, fruit, vegetables or milk for them.

The CSA idea entered Britain in 1990 when a Scottish soft-fruit grower, John Butterworth, read an article about it in the excellent Canadian rural-life magazine *Harrowsmith*. He had been selling some of his organic raspberries and blackcurrants to Dave Bellingham, a retired naval electrical engineer, and his wife, Eileen, who owned the two-acre walled garden at Sundrum Castle about five miles from Ayr where they were producing free-range eggs and growing vegetables that they sold from a van.

'The van round wasn't doing particularly well, and the Bellinghams felt they were getting insufficient output from the walled garden to enable it to do so,' Butterworth says. 'They asked me if I could help improve production, and I in turn approached a friend, Carol Freireich, a long-standing organic gardener, and the four of us formed Ayrshire Organic Growers as a workers' co-operative. We wanted to devise the best marketing system possible, and the *Harrowsmith* idea of local people buying shares in the operation of the farm seemed very attractive.'[55]

By sending out leaflets to friends, van-round customers, and local members of Friends of the Earth, they found twenty-five families prepared to subscribe £180 each for their vegetables, paying either in a lump sum or in three £62 instalments. The new system began in the spring of 1991, and a subscribers' meeting was held that autumn to review progress. The response was that, despite teething problems, the project had been well worth while. The main disappointment seems to have been the failure of the mange-tout pea crop because of faulty seed. Otherwise the burning issues subscribers discussed were how many outer leaves should be left on the lettuces and whether seven pounds of potatoes a week was too little or too much.

Forty subscribers signed up for the 1992 season, including all but one of the previous year's families, and fifty-three varieties of fruit and vegetables were grown. This huge range greatly reduced the risk of the co-op being unable to meet its delivery commitments because of crop failure, which was just as well because a gale blew the plastic cover of a polytunnel away, and a cold and wet early spring, a dry late spring and early summer and a wet autumn caused the potatoes and the onions to be affected by rot and some vegetables to crop badly.

It also points up a big difference in the approaches adopted at Indian Line Farm and at Sundrum. At Indian Line, all the produce belonged to the subscribers because they had hired the gardeners, rented the land, and provided the equipment. In the event of crop failure, the subscribers took all the risk. They had no guarantee that there would be any relationship between the shop price of vegetables and the total value of those produced on their behalf because there was no one involved who was able to give it. At Sundrum, on the other hand, the operation is owned by the co-op, not the subscribers, and getting families to pay in advance for their vegetables is little more than an efficient and effective financial and marketing tool.

Under the agreement signed annually between the co-op and its subscribers, the value of each week's delivery is calculated using the prices of non-organic fruit and vegetables that week in the Safeway supermarket in Ayr, where Eileen Bellingham works part-time as a cashier, and the co-op guarantees that if the total value of its deliveries for the year falls below £170 it will refund the difference. When it has to supply poorer-quality produce because of weather conditions or pest damage, it reduces prices below the Safeway figure.

'The customer does share the risk, in two ways,' Butterworth says. 'Firstly, we only guarantee £170 worth of produce, not £180. That's not a great difference but it does establish the principle that the farm is subject to risk and that the shareholders bear some of it. Secondly, we don't guarantee the exact quantities of each crop that people will get, and it's certainly possible that at some times of the year they'll be fed up with certain crops – runner beans, for example.'

Nevertheless, Robyn van En would not regard Sundrum as a true community garden. She thinks it important that growers be free from economic pressures if they are to do the best job they can. This means that the financing of the crops should be the responsibility of the consumers, who should also carry all, or almost all, of the risk. 'Paying a farmer or a gardener a guaranteed income establishes his or her professional status,' she says. 'During the first year at Indian Line Farm a freak thunderstorm dropped eight inches of rain in three hours. The mixed cropping and the raised beds meant that the winter squash was the only real loss. It was harvested prematurely, and members cooked or froze whatever they wanted. This translated into a $35 loss on each share purchase, but it would have been a $3500 loss on a family farm.'

In cash terms, about two-thirds of the Ayrshire co-op's produce is grown in the walled garden at Sundrum and in two polytunnels, with main-crop potatoes and carrots bought in from another registered organic grower in the area. This means that its produce is in effect coming from only five or six acres. 'We don't even have a tractor and borrow one when we need to,' Butterworth told me in early 1995, although they bought one later in the year. 'At present the operation isn't even generating a full-time job – we're all part-time – but that will come.' The shortage of growing-space was becoming a problem, and the co-op was planning to set up a land trust to acquire fifty acres near the walled garden to produce organic milk and meat and to ensure that only organic food had been fed to the animals responsible for the manure applied to the garden. This is highly desirable because of drugs such as Ivermectin, which is used to treat cattle for intestinal worms, lice and ticks and is excreted by them to go on killing organisms in the soil for a long time before it is broken down.

The co-op holds two meetings a year for subscribers, one in the winter so that they can help shape planting plans and give their reaction to the previous year's performance, the second in the summer so that they can see the garden and meet each other socially. Beyond this, most subscribers' contribution to the system is negligible, although one couple provides a day's labour each during July and August and has offered a low-interest loan, while another customer, who is in the pump business, has donated an irrigation system.

The co-op had eighty customers for its 1995 season and had lost only two of the original participants. Its subscription rate was still £180 for those able to collect from the garden, but for those who could not a £20 annual delivery charge had been introduced, which could be split among customers sharing the same drop.

After four seasons, Butterworth remained highly enthusiastic about subscription gardening. 'We have no waste. We don't have to conform to any pre-packed sizes for absurd cosmetic standards. We use minimum packaging, which is all reused – not recycled – and transport costs are kept to a minimum. From a financial standpoint we've a guaranteed market from one year to the next.'

At the end of 1995 there were three other subscription farms or gardens operating in Britain, according to Eric Booth of the Soil Association, but none was a true community effort on the American model. In addition, fifty or sixty organic growers were using the box system, under which a household agrees to take a box of vegetables, the contents varying according to whatever is in season, for a fixed price each week but does not pay in advance.

Among the pioneers of this system were Tim and Jan Deane of Northwood Farm, Cristow, near Exeter, who found out the hard way in 1991 that they were not going to be able to survive financially by growing ten acres of organic vegetables and selling them on the wholesale market. 'We had begun packing a few individual orders in addition to our wholesale commitments,' Jan says, 'but it didn't take us long to realize that this was not the road to prosperity either. Despite the higher price, the value of individual orders was generally

Ollan Herr and Mark Deary of the
Philipstown Trust farm, Dundalk.

too low to pay for the time it took to make them up; weighing out small quantities was extremely tedious; and people would telephone their orders at highly inconvenient times.'[56]

So they sent out a letter to friends, neighbours and existing retail customers offering to pack and deliver a weekly box of mixed vegetables at a fixed price, and twenty households signed up. By the end of the season more than forty boxes were going out, and when they circulated a questionnaire they were surprised to find that many people appreciated the convenience of not having to decide what vegetables to buy. From their own point of view the system overcame most of the disadvantages of packing to order, particularly as they could save time by estimating quantities by eye. Today they offer three sizes of box – £3.50, £4.50, and £5.50 – and allow their two hundred customers to say what types of vegetable they would prefer not to receive. 'We make it clear that we can't guarantee to make substitutions, but in practice it's usually quite easy to do,' Jan says. Some customers act as drop-off points so that several boxes can be delivered at the one stop. The boxes are reusable, and each carries the customer's name so that anyone who has failed to return two or three can be followed up.

In 1993 the couple had their worst growing season in the ten years they had been in business and had to buy in produce from other organic growers, severely eroding their income. However, if they had had to rely on the wholesale trade for distributing their produce they reckon they would have had to cease trading. 'Our customers often take the trouble to tell us that they appreciate the food we produce for them,' Jan says. 'When you are out in the leek field and you can no longer feel your fingers and toes and the rain is seeping through your waterproofs, that means a lot.'

The most ambitious community-supported agricultural project in Britain or Ireland is probably the thirteen-acre garden established by the Philipstown Trust outside Dundalk. The trust is the brainchild of Ollan Herr, who set up and runs a business making sluice gates and similar waterway equipment in the technology park attached to the regional technical college. He formed the trust to work towards local sustainability in 1992, immediately after the Earth Summit in Rio de Janeiro. 'Even before the world's leaders met we knew that nothing would be done and we would have to do any work ourselves,' he says.

Herr believes conventional farming is unsustainable, and the trust has among its wide-ranging objectives the encouragement of a gradual change-over to organic agriculture. However, he admits there were personal reasons for making subscription gardening its first project: 'I wanted my family to be able to eat organic vegetables, and I knew that I was never going to be able to grow them myself. I was buying them from a friend, Mark Deary, who was growing them and selling them from a van, and I was worried that if Mark got married, which didn't seem unlikely, his wife would suggest that he go back to teaching so that they could have a decent income. So to ensure that Mark could earn a decent living as a grower, I began to think about what could be done.'

As neither Herr nor Deary had heard of the CSA movement in North America or the subscription gardens in Britain, the details of the Philipstown project were developed from scratch. 'This had the advantage that we could evolve something that was exactly right for local conditions but the disadvantage that we were never able to say to the trust's board, "Look, it's working over there,"' Herr says. Deary learned his skills as an organic gardener by being a 'WWOOFer' – a willing worker on organic farms – which entailed moving from holding to holding and working for his board and lodging and perhaps a little pocket money besides. 'I really learned what a good day's work involved,' he says. John Butterworth says that WWOOFers give the Sundrum co-op substantial help.

Finding land for the garden took more than a year. 'People said it wasn't possible to make a living on a smallholding of, say, ten acres. We weren't being taken seriously,' Herr says. But in November 1993 they met a wealthy landowner who was prepared to rent them a derelict barn, farmyard and cottage together with three fields that had previously been used for grazing horses and had never been chemically farmed. 'That meant that we could go straight into organic production without any transitional period. We were lucky to get it,' Deary comments. 'The rent is £2000 a year, so we got no concessions.'

A leaflet was printed setting out the aims of the Philipstown Trust and outlining the garden project. Part of it read:

[This] is an invitation to membership of a community farm from which you will enjoy freshly grown vegetables in abundance for 8-9 months of the year ... We hope to attract 120 members in year one, each buying £208 worth of produce ... An August delivery might include tomatoes, peppers, peas and beans, potatoes and cabbages. A mid-winter delivery would have sprouts, leeks, cabbages and carrots. We will be growing more unusual varieties such as kohl-rabi and corn, too.

The £208 subscription was reckoned to provide sufficient vegetables for a family of five, and half-shares were available at £104 for smaller households. Prospective members were asked to pay half their subscription in advance and the rest by monthly banker's order, and also to make the project an interest-free loan of £100 (£50 for half-shares) for three years to cover its start-up costs. As if that was not enough, everyone was also asked to fork out £5 for a year's membership of the trust. 'To qualify for public funding [the trust] must be clearly seen as a community-based organization,' the brochure said. In any case, it added, the costs of newsletters, copying and postage had to be met.

Ambitious? Yes. Overambitious? Well, most of the trust's board feared it would prove to be so. Herr and Deary sold twenty memberships quite quickly and bought polytunnels, a tractor and other equipment with the money together with a £7000 overdraft Herr had personally guaranteed at the bank. It was only after they were fully committed – some would say overcommitted – that another forty subscriptions came in. 'It helped that we were both local and our families were well known in the town,' Herr comments. Help from official bodies was also important. An Bord Glas, the horticultural development agency, gave £1500, and the local employment creation agency, which originally said it could not help an agricultural project, eventually came up with a £3000 grant.

Production in the first season went remarkably well. This was in large part due to the long hours and great effort put in by Deary and his colleague Aidan Faughy. 'Aidan complements me because he's good with things like the tractor,' Deary told me towards the end of November 1994 when I bumped into him in Dublin. 'We've been working at least a sixty-hour week, and it's only now that I've got my old interests back and been able to think about other things.' Nine of the thirteen acres had been brought into cultivation, membership had risen to 105, and £9000 worth of vegetables had been sold.

As a result of donations and the grants, the financial results – a loss of just over £4500 after non-capital costs of £27,000 – were reasonable for a start-up, although the shortfall would have been greater had Deary and Faughy been properly paid. They got £140 a week each, which Herr realized was far too little. 'Mark runs the farm while I look after the financial side. He's worth a lot more than he's been getting. We've got to be able to pay him at least the average industrial wage,' he told me early in 1995, adding that with just over a hundred families signed up for the new season, he was optimistic that things would go really well.

They did not. An unprecedented drought saw to that. East winds and a dry April and May meant that the two men had to spend hours

 [main text continues p.306]

SOLVING THE LAND PROBLEM

A serious difficulty for many community projects is getting affordable access to suitable land. Robert Swann and Susan Witt of the E.F. Schumacher Society in the United States believe that this problem is part of a much larger one and that it will not be possible to build satisfactory self-reliant local economies unless land ownership ceases to be a legitimate arena for financial speculation. They argue that if land is treated as an ordinary commodity that can be sold to the highest bidder, any wealth generated by a community will tend to be absorbed by unproductive property investments rather than being used to increase local self-reliance. Witt writes in a Schumacher Society position paper:

When a region has excess capital, that capital can work to draw out the imaginative and entrepreneurial skills of its people and thus generate new businesses producing goods and services once imported from other regions ... When the capital is tied up in land, however, the local economy chokes up. Credit for the small business owner tightens. The region loses its diversity, which is the basis of a more sustainable economy and of a more environmentally responsible business sector.[57]

As mentioned in chapter 3, Robert Swann once worked with Ralph Borsodi, a leader of the back-to-the-land movement in the United States in the 1930s. In an essay, 'The Possessional Problem',[58] which, along with Henry George's book Progress and Poverty (1879), provides the intellectual foundation for most American community land trust thinking, Borsodi makes a distinction between things that are morally correct for someone to own and those that should be held in trust. For him it is moral to treat things one grows or makes as one's private property and to buy or sell them, but the land itself and the Earth's resources should be held in trust and their use regulated to benefit this and future generations.

None of the governments which now claim sovereignty over the Earth can vindicate in rational and moral terms ... the issuance of title [to land] 'in fee simple absolute'; therefore, we must face the problem of how land and other resources should be allocated ... Since capitalism takes private ownership for granted, it ignores both the question of its moral validity and its economic utility. As I see it, capitalism is from beginning to end a rationalization. To justify having everything privately owned, including what should be held in trust – the airwaves for instance, or mineral resources – its proponents have to accept all sorts of qualifications of the doctrine and all sorts of government intervention and regulation of business operations.

Many people have thought along similar lines and gone on to suggest that land and mineral resources be nationalized. This suggestion seemed as misguided to Borsodi as it does to Swann, who thinks that the centralized management of state-controlled land has been as big a disaster as the almost totally unregulated dealing in land on the open market. Instead Swann wants to see land and resources held in trust by democratic community organizations whose membership would be open to any resident of the district or bioregion. He suggests that one third of the directors of a trust would be elected from among the leaseholding members (those who are using the trust land), one third would be elected from non-leaseholders (the wider community), and the final third would be pro-

Community land-trust pioneer Bob Swann, May 1992.

fessionals such as land-use planners or lawyers appointed by the elected directors so that the trust could have the benefit of their expertise.

In 1967 Swann and Borsodi set up the International Independence Institute to promote, among other things, community ownership of land, and to support Vinoba Bhave and others in the Gramdan (Village Gift) movement, who walked from village to village in rural India appealing to landowners to give part of their holdings to community organizations to be leased to landless labourers. Many Indian landowners responded to the campaign, and the organizations set up to administer the land they gave were the forerunners of the community land trusts in the United States. Swann, who was active in the US civil rights movement, then worked with Slater King, a cousin of Martin Luther King, and New Communities, a group from Albany, Georgia, to set up a land trust for African-Americans in the rural south who were unable to get land to farm and so were forced to migrate to the northern cities to look for work. With donations and loans, New Communities bought 5000 acres and leased it out as individual homesteads and farms for co-operatives using the legal structure devised by the Jewish National Fund, which began to acquire land in Palestine at the turn of the century and now owns 95 per cent of Israel.

Not all went well, however. 'Through a series of tragic deaths, much of the original leadership was lost, and promised grants fell through,' Susan Witt says. 'As a result, New Communities took on more debt than was wise to purchase the land and were unable to repay the mortgage. They lost the property several years ago. But although the first land trust failed, it started a movement.'

Borsodi died in 1977 and that same year Swann established the Institute for Community Economics in Cambridge, Massachusetts, to promote community land trusts and the idea of social investment. In 1980, he and Witt, who was a colleague at the Institute, were asked to the Berkshires to start a community land trust there and were talked into staying. 'The prospect of living and working on a community land trust rather than just telling others to do it was very appealing to us,' Witt says. The new trust, the Community Land Trust in the Southern Berkshires, attracted some donations, took out a loan, and bought a ten-acre orchard outside the small town of Great Barrington the following year. It then leased out four house sites on part of the property, one of them to Witt and Swann for a house they built themselves. The trust has since used the lease fees to pay off the mortgage.

'The trust leases the rest of the orchard separately to a farmer who bought the existing trees and also owns the new raspberry canes, asparagus and fruit trees he has planted,' Witt says. 'No farmer could have paid as much for the orchard as was available for it on the housing market, and if it had not been bought by the trust but divided up into four one-house properties it would have gone out of horticulture. The lease fee the farmer pays is minimal, so the trust has secured an affordable source of food production in the region.'

If the farmer or the people who have leased house sites wish to move on, they can sell whatever they have done to improve the property. 'With a trust you don't own the land but you do own the house and any improvements such as planted trees,' Swann says. 'However, you cannot necessarily sell them at market value. To ensure that the land value is excluded from the sale price, an owner who wishes to sell improvements is obliged to offer them to the trustees, who are only obliged to pay replacement value.'

Since buying the orchard, the trust has acquired two other properties. One is an old house on the bank of the Housatonic River in Great Barrington that has been converted into office space for several community organizations. The other is Forest Row, twenty-one acres of woodland on the edge of the town. Most of this is to be preserved, but five acres has been used for eighteen moderately priced houses, each of which was designed and built specifically for the site leaseholder. 'Even with careful planning and the unit-holder's participation, the trust was unable to keep purchase costs as low as it would have liked,' Swann says. Accordingly, he helped set up a charity, the Fund for Affordable Housing, which used donations to subsidize the construction of two of the houses at Forest Row so that they were available to a lower income group.

Despite these successes and the establishment of more than a hundred similar land trusts throughout the United States, Swann and Witt are disappointed at the rate of progress. 'Unfortunately the accumulation of land in community land trusts has been very gradual,' they write in the position paper. 'It is true that each new piece of land in a CLT has its own story of hope and good work, yet there is no broad movement to decommoditize land. Environmentalism is the new religion of our age, but it is only a Sunday morning religion [because] we still reserve the right to sell the land we own and care for to the highest bidder. We have yet to fully imagine and embrace a culture in which land use is allocated by social and environmental contract rather than by checkbook.'

There are very few land trusts in Britain or Ireland. One of the oldest must be that set up on the island of Lewis by Lord Leverhulme, a founder of the Lever Brothers soap company which eventually merged with a Dutch margarine company to become Unilever. Leverhulme bought Lewis in 1917 and prepared ambitious plans for, among other things, developing the islands's fishing industry to supply his Mac Fisheries chain of fish shops. However, his ideas ran into fierce opposition from a powerful group of locals, and by 1923 he was ready to give up. In order to wind up his affairs, he offered to give his tenants and crofters, free of charge, full freehold titles to the lands they were renting from him. For various reasons, few of them took up his offer, but Stornoway Town Council accepted the deeds to the town itself, the parish of Stornoway and a small part of a neighbouring parish, and the Stornoway Trust was set up to administer Leverhulme's former property. Apart from land it has since sold outright to the council, the Trust has maintained the freehold of everything it took over. Only those who live on its property and whose names appear on the parliamentary Register of Electors have the right to vote in the elections for the ten positions on its board of trustees and, at present, the trustees, all of whom live locally, have a policy of giving the Trust's income from rents, interest and quarry royalties away to local charities and employment creation schemes. Recently, the trust has been granting long leases to quarter-acre house sites for only £50.

Three other land trusts have been set up in Scotland within the past few years; many more can be expected to be formed before the end of the decade as a result of an announcement early in 1996 by the Secretary of State for Scotland, Michael Forsyth, that the government was prepared to transfer its 260,000 acres of state-owned crofting estates free of cost to trusts if the 1368 crofter-tenants could show that the new bodies would not need a continuing financial contribution from the public purse. Indeed, the main reason for the offer was that the Exchequer was making losses on running the estates – largely, a Scottish Crofters' Union survey had shown, because of the Scottish Office's bureaucratic procedures. Another factor, however, was that crofters in Assynt, Melness and in Borve on the Isle of Skye had shown that trusts could take over holdings from private landlords and manage them more effectively.

'We had a first-class landlord. We regarded him as a gentleman and a friend,' John MacKenzie, who played a key role in establishing the Borve trust, told me. 'The family had charged the same rents – £5 a year for fifteen or sixteen acres plus the right to use common grazing – from the time the crofts were first settled in 1906.' As a result, there was little incentive for the crofters to take over the property. What changed the situation was the Crofter Forestry Act, which gave them the right to own any trees they might grow on their holdings. Previously, trees had belonged to the landlord. 'Our landlord, Major J.L. MacDonald, is a Skye man and speaks Gaelic, although he made his fortune in London as a financier. He was fiercely opposed to the Act, and as we wanted to be among the first crofters to take advantage of the grants available for afforestation because sometimes the early-birds get freebies from people anxious to make their schemes work, the idea emerged that we should buy him out.'

After some delay, MacDonald said that he wanted £40,000 for the 4000-acre property, much more than the £14,000 that twenty-one crofters could have expected to pay if they fought the purchase through the courts – in a previous case, crofters had been able to buy their holdings for fifteen times the annual rent. 'If the Major had been a bad landlord or an absentee one, we would have taken pleasure in fighting him, but we offered £20,000 and in June 1993 we heard he had accepted. The whole thing was very amicable. We gave him back the shooting rights out of goodwill, not that there's a lot to shoot here anyway. We got a short-term bridging loan from the Highland Fund to pay him and the local enterprise company paid our legal costs.'

Although by law they could never have been evicted from their holdings, actually owning them, albeit indirectly through a trust, seems to have made a big psychological difference to the people of Borve. 'It gives a feeling of freedom that no Act of Parliament could ever give,' MacKenzie says. In fact, holding the whole property jointly with their neighbours has given them something that the private ownership of individual parcels would not: the challenge of developing it as a whole. 'It would have been easy to have sat back and to have said, "Now we have what we wanted" and just carried on working at our daily occupations,' he continues. 'But the ownership of the land brings new responsibilities and new challenges. How could we as landowners protect the environment, improve the grazings and also generate some income from a source other than grazing animals?'

The crofters' first joint project was to plant a fifty-acre woodland of mixed native species along one of the property's boundaries. 'It will soon provide shelter for sheep and cattle and food and shelter for wildlife,' MacKenzie says. 'More forestry is at the planning stage on an area of the hill that is not of importance to the grazing stock. Now that the ownership of the crofting lands has passed to us it is our reponsibility to make sure that people stay on the crofts and that this crofting estate is a pleasant place to live in and provides a suitable environment in which to raise children.'

The psychological change that the new form of land ownership has brought about was mentioned in an editorial in the March 1996 issue of The Crofter, a monthly publication of the Scottish Crofters' Union. 'If you know crofters who are now part of a trust, one of the things that must have struck you is their confidence, and the respect with which they are now seen by others, and indeed by themselves. They have gone beyond the barrier of feeling that they as crofters are not capable of running their own affairs. They have proved that as crofters they can get on sufficiently well with each other to co-operate in the management of their estate. They have a pride in their achievement which sustains them through the unquestionable challenges that confront them in this exciting new era of land ownership.' One aspect of the new confidence is that crofters from Borve and Assynt have collaborated with Highlands and Islands Enterprise, the development agency for the area, and the government's Crofters Commission, to set up the Crofting Trusts Advisory Service, which helps crofters on other estates set up land trusts to take them over too.

But perhaps the most widely applicable form of land trust in Britain is the Stonesfield Community Trust in the village of Stonesfield, near Witney, Oxfordshire. This began when a freelance journalist, Tony Crofts, became concerned about the way outsiders were driving up rents and property prices in the village and wanted to ensure that there would always be affordable houses available for young couples from the area so that the local school would stay open. With two friends, a retired school teacher and the business manager of a successful local company, Solid State Logic Ltd, he set up the trust and gave it a quarter-acre site he owned in the village to develop. Solid State Logic put up £3000 to cover the legal expenses of setting up the trust and preparing the plans for the develop-ment of the site. 'We got permission for four houses,' says Crofts, who is now the trust's chairman. 'That greatly increased the site's value, and a bank lent us money secured on the property to pay for building the first two houses.'

A granny flat was added to one of the houses and a second was divided into two flats, so the trust now has six dwellings on the site. Then a second quarter-acre site became available and the district council gave the trust a one-year, interest-free loan of £80,000 to enable it to buy it. 'We had a track record. Stonesfield was the only village in West Oxfordshire that had built any affordable housing, even though the council had offered to give planning approval for the use of farmland for it. The council agreed to lend us the money within seven days. I cannot speak too highly of them.'

There are now five houses on that site, financed in part by Mercury Provident and the Ecology Building Society and in part by gifts and by pri-vate ethical investors who lend their money at a fixed rate for ten years. 'We advertised in The Friend [a Quaker magazine] for six weeks and that brought in about £85,000. Also, the Quaker Housing Trust converted £20,000 of its loan into a grant and attenders at the Witney monthly [Quaker] meeting made donations of between six and seven thousand pounds,' says Crofts, who is a Quaker himself.

'All the houses have been built and insulated to a very high standard, so that they are warm and comfortable to live in,' he adds. 'They were designed for maximum solar gain, and we'll put passive solar conservato-ries on four of them when we have the money. We are able to let them at below-market rates to people connected with the village because local people have covenanted to pay a sum each year to cover some of the interest charges, which are very high in the early stages of a loan. We've never had any government money; if we had, we wouldn't have been able to build to the standard we did and we'd never have owned the houses. Because we are a charitable trust, the tenants have no right to buy the houses, which will always belong to the village. When we get the loans paid off we'll be able to bring the rentals down to council-house levels and still have a good income, which we plan to use to re-boost social services here, which the government has steadily cut back. We're moving towards becoming the Independent Democratic Republic of Stonesfield. We intend to be a standing reproach to the government and the Treasury by showing that a high standard of social care is possible if you spend your money correctly. Devolution, local control and smallness are important to us.'

Other villages had asked the trust about how they could do something similar, Crofts said, but none of them had acted on it, because they felt unable to cope with the necessary fund-raising, which was 'pretty inten-sive at times'.

'They've all invited outside housing associations to come in and build the houses for them. This means that they will never own them. As far as I know, we're unique.'

Robert Swann and Susan Witt, E.F. Schumacher Society, 140 Jug End Road, Great Barrington, Massachusetts 01230; tel. +1 413 5281737; fax +1 413 5284472; e-mail efssociety@aol.com. A handbook of legal documents for establishing a trust is available.

The School of Living, which was set up by Borsodi in 1934 and has administered a land trust since the early 1970s, has published several pamphlets and booklets on them. A catalogue is available from RD1, Box 185A, Cochranville, Pennsylvania 19330; tel. +1 610 5936988.

The Institute for Community Economics (57 School Street, Springfield, Massachusetts 01105-1331; tel. +1 202 7468660) publishes the Community Land Trust Handbook at $12.

Tony Crofts, Stonesfield Community Trust, Home Close, High Street, Stonesfield, Witney, Oxfordshire OX8 8PU; tel. +44 1993 891686

Crofting Trusts Advisory Service, 6 Castle Wynd, Inverness IV2 3EQ, tel. +44 1463 718953

Scottish Crofters' Union, Old Mill, Broadford, Isle of Skye IV49 9AQ, tel. +44 1471 822529.

A group of houses built by the Stonesfield Community Trust.

each day taking the tractor to a nearby river for water to keep the seedlings alive. 'It was a particularly sensitive time,' Deary says. 'We were planting out the brassicas, and Aidan had to work on watering from 6 to 10 a.m., and then I would work from 6 to 10 at night. They survived but didn't grow. It was all we could do to keep them on a starvation water diet.'

'We kept thinking, "It must rain soon,"' Herr says. 'We felt that as soon as we spent money on an irrigation system the drought would break and we'd get a normal Irish summer.' But in mid-May they decided they could wait no longer, and Herr borrowed £8000 personally so that a well could be bored and a pump installed and they could order a sprinkler system from Italy. 'It was either that or see the farm collapse. As it was, we were unable to make six weeks' deliveries. We should have started supplying members in mid-May but in fact began at the beginning of July.'

Who was to cover the cost of the missed deliveries? Legally, the Philipstown Trust was liable, as its promotional literature had indicated to subscribers the amounts and value of the vegetables they could expect to get. But the trust had no money to make refunds, and in any case, what was it except an organization made up of the subscribers themselves? An extraordinary general meeting was held in September to sort the matter out and to consider how the project's other, more serious losses should be met. These arose because, with two full-time employees, the garden needed an income of £40,000 to break even, which essentially meant that it had to have two hundred subscribers paying £200 each. Even without the drought the project would have been lucky to have reached that number in 1995, although forty new families joined in the early part of the year. However, when the missed deliveries destroyed people's confidence the recruitment drive stopped in its tracks, and some faint-hearts even cancelled their monthly standing orders, cutting the number of participating families to 133.

Herr was extremely anxious before the meeting. How would the members react to what he had to tell them? How would they vote on a motion to wind the whole thing up? 'When we put the motion to liquidate, the people who had been criticizing us most fiercely earlier in the evening immediately swung round and wouldn't consider it at all,' he says. Instead the membership decided to convert their interest-free loans into grants and to write off the amounts owing for the missed deliveries. More importantly, thirty-three families said they would give £200 each to cover the shortfall in subscription income.

At the beginning of 1996, Herr and Deary were looking forward with confidence to the new season, particularly as, having seen the membership's rock-solid support, the International Fund for Ireland had promised to make the project a substantial grant to buy new equipment.

'We are eligible for support because our subscribers come from both sides of the border,' Deary told me. 'When we set the project up, I bought the equipment I thought I was going to need. Now I know what I need and it isn't quite the same thing.' Indeed, Deary had found that running a subscription garden was very different from growing for the commercial market. 'If you are growing to sell whole-sale you can plant and harvest all the crop at the same time. Here you need to have a little of each of a wide range of vegetables ready for picking every week. This means you have to have small plots of a wide range of things and makes planning quite complicated.'

Herr was reasonably sure that they could get membership up to two hundred during the year. 'The Dublin Food Co-op is going to subscribe for thirty memberships,' he told me. 'That will take us to up to about 165. Then a group of five families in Drogheda are joining, and a new group of ten families in Newry are coming in as well. With the people who said they were going to join last year but didn't because of the crisis, that should about do it. Two members of our board visited some CSAs in California recently and were surprised that they were smaller than we are. But Mark couldn't change a trac-tor tyre on his own, and if you're going to have two full-time workers and set the subscription at a reasonable level, the scale on which you have to operate is determined for you.'[59]

Purely from the perspective of developing a local economy it might seem that there is little to choose between a subscription garden that its members own, as at Indian Line Farm and Dundalk, or that the workers own, as at Sundrum, or a box system owned by the growers, as with the Deanes. All three solutions appear equally valid because they allow small-scale production to continue in circumstances in which it otherwise would have ceased, by eliminating at least two stages, the wholesaler and the retailer, from the conventional distribu-tion chain. They also save on transport and packaging. Moreover, all three systems give greater scope for job satisfaction than growing for unknown consumers long distances away. Circumstances rather than principle will normally determine which of the three variants, or what hybrid between them, is used in the beginning in a particular commu-nity. If an existing grower who already has land and equipment wishes to serve people living nearby instead of an unstable, highly competitive distant market, then a box system is ideal. And if this grower can persuade his or her customers to pay for their vegetables in advance, that's fine.

But in places such as Great Barrington or Dundalk in which there was no existing grower wishing to convert, consumers hoping to substitute organic vegetables for tired, well-travelled chemical produce and who also wish to stop purchasing power leaking from their community are going to have to act for themselves by renting the land, finding the capital, and recruiting and paying an experienced farmer. And in such circumstances they will inevitably have to carry most of the risk themselves, as the members of the Philipstown Trust found.

But building a local economy is not just about using local resources to meet local needs: it is also about building the local community, and in this respect a CSA owned by its members is likely to be much more effective than one run for the benefit of private owners with customer involvement being little more than a convenient marketing tool. The Sycamore Co-operative Garden in Julian, Pennsylvania, is typical of many in the United States when it states in its brochure that its prime objective is to 'foster the community of people who take seriously responsible stewardship of the land.' It relegates the production of 'fresh eggs and organically grown vegetables, herbs, fruit and flowers' to objective number two.

As Timothy Laird puts it in the introduction to his study of eighty-three CSAs in North America, community-supported agriculture 'tries to reconnect people with the land, and to reconnect farmers that are close to the land with the people who eat the food that they grow ... A [CSA] farm grows food not for sale, *per se*, but for the "community".'[60] The movement, then, is primarily about connecting people, and 63 per cent of the growers in Laird's sample said that this was the most successful aspect of their operations. Surprisingly, the benefit one would have expected growers to be most enthusiastic about – the financial stability being a CSA gave them – came a poor second and was mentioned by only 30 per cent, the same proportion that mentioned as a gain the fact that they were able to produce organic food. Over half the farmers said that community support was the most critical factor in their success, one grower telling Laird, who has himself managed two community farms, that a CSA needed 'an educated and committed group of folks who will see the larger picture [and are] not just out there for their own selves.' Others said that the best way to build a committed core group was to develop a sense of ownership among members, exactly what the Philipstown Trust has now done.

Many of the CSAs in Laird's study spoke of the difficulty of giving the grower a living wage, the former grower of a now-defunct CSA saying that 'the time and expertise required to grow the variety and quality needed by members is greater than the members can afford.' Another grower commented: 'People can't comprehend what it costs to grow food.' Despite this, most farms in the sample enabled the less-well-off members of their communities to participate in some way, sometimes by working a fixed number of hours for their share.

Philipstown enables people who could not otherwise afford to participate to pay for their subscriptions in the local LETS unit; it spends the units to employ extra labour at peak periods. 'It helped us and it helped the LETS,' Ollan Herr says. 'The LETS members had to find ways of earning the units they had spent with us, and that reinvigorated the local system.'

Early in 1996 the Philipstown Trust was negotiating to buy an old watermill site where a 10 kW generator has been installed and is selling power to the national grid. The buildings, part of which run underground, are to be renovated, and Herr's company will move in on one floor, its rent covering the trust's mortgage. The rest of the buildings will be used as a flour mill, grinding organic grains grown for the trust by small farmers under contract, and a bread and biscuit bakery, which will produce exclusively for the Dundalk area. The waste heat from the ovens will be used in the subscription garden's polytunnels, which will be on top. 'We'll be using our own electricity for power and only using the grid to balance out supply and our demand,' Herr says.

No decision has been taken yet on using the subscription system to help finance any of these, although Robyn van En thinks the approach could be applied outside the agricultural sector. 'A local small-scale baker worked out how many bread shares she would need to sell to afford the down payment on a 40-quart bread-mixer. Unfortunately she did not have all the interest necessary until after her deadline. Someone else has suggested a community-supported auto mechanic; if everyone paid in advance for a tune-up and an oil change, a mechanic would be able to buy the equipment he or she needs.'

In Britain, commercial organizations have already used the subscription approach very successfully outside farming. The first legal whisky distillery on the Isle of Arran in Scotland for 150 years was

 [main text continues p.314]

PUBS BREW THEIR OWN BEER
FOR ONLY NINE PENCE A PINT

In Britain, Australia and the United States the tide is already running strongly against large-scale, centralized production when it comes to beer. After a period in Britain in the 1960s and 70s when easier road transport and changes in brewing technology enabled at least one regional brewery and its tied houses to be gobbled up by a brewing chain every month, the reverse is now happening and a microbrewery serving free houses in its area, or a pub brewery just looking after its own needs, is opening on average every week. By the end of 1995 about 450 small breweries were trading, and well over a thousand different small-brewery beers were available. Some of these brewers were in the most unlikely places, including former cow-sheds owned by the National Trust in Devon, a disused sawmill in Hereford, an old foundry in Lancashire, and a converted carpet warehouse in Yorkshire.

Two factors explain the revival of interest in small breweries. One is that many drinkers are bored with the bright, fizzy, pasteurized and standardized keg beers the brewing giants substituted for the traditional cask-conditioned beers, which require much more knowledge and care from the publican, since the yeast they contain is still alive and they go on changing until they are served. The drinkers' dissatisfaction was channelled through the 37,000-member Campaign for Real Ale (CAMRA), which kept the taste for cask-conditioned beers alive and demonstrated to publicans that they could be an attractive commercial alternative to the mass-produced brews. 'Drinkers are now trading up to beers full of flavour and character,' says Jeff Evans, the editor of CAMRA's Good Beer Guide. 'Keg beer is fading fast and lager is past its peak.'

The second part of the explanation for the renaissance of small-scale traditional brewing is that if there is a demand for real ale it is best met from breweries close to where it will be consumed, as this enables significant savings in transport and marketing and allows the brewery to educate publicans and their staffs exactly how its product needs to be cared for and served. 'Many beers do not reach the customer in prime condition. It is absolutely essential that we are able to monitor our beer from fermenter to glass,' says David Roberts, who set up the Pilgrim microbrewery in Reigate, Surrey, in 1981. The best solution is for the brewery to be in the pub itself, as this eliminates transport and marketing costs altogether and ensures that the brewer is always on hand to see that the beer is served at its best. One of the conglomerates, Allied Breweries, has realized this and established its own 'Friar and Firkin' brew-pub chain.

'There were between six and seven thousand pubs that brewed their own beer in Britain before the First World War, but a shortage of raw materials put almost all of them out of business. Only three or four brew-pubs from that generation are still open today,' says David Smith, who runs a consultancy in York for people wishing to set up microbreweries and brew-pubs. 'Brewing on the premises is the best way to ensure that quality is maintained. It is also the least risky way of getting into the business: you have your market all ready and waiting for you in the bar. Most pubs will get through four or five barrels, each of 288 pints, a week, and with a four-barrel brew plant you can probably supply all your needs in-house. You also have to remember that a brew-pub not only attracts bitter enthusiasts but their spirits and lager-drinking friends as well.'

In 1988 Smith left Samuel Smith's brewery in Tadcaster to set himself up as a quality-control consultant to the growing number of independent breweries. He gradually became involved in advising would-be brewers how to start up, and by the end of 1994 he had been involved in the birth of twenty-four breweries, ranging in size from four to thirty barrels. His biggest brew-pub is in Jersey, with a capacity of twenty barrels. He argues that a brew-pub can deliver considerable savings over an independent microbrewery. 'Many pubs have outhouses where the brewing can be done, so there's no extra overhead for premises as there would be if you were starting a brewery. Another saving is that the landlord can often do the brewing himself and may not have to employ anyone specially. And there's a saving in capital: if you set up a microbrewery you're going to have to pay an extra four to five thousand pounds to buy a suitable second-hand van for deliveries. Many people overlook that.'

Breweries also have the problem of selling their beer. The Border Brewery in Berwick-upon-Tweed had to buy a pub to ensure that it could sell beer in its own town, and a largish 'small' brewery, Moles of Bristol, even bought up an entire chain.

Someone who knows the difficulties of not having secure outlets is Alan Gill, a former telephone engineer who set up what was at the time Britain's smallest brewery in a wash-house behind his home in Sutton-on-Trent, Nottinghamshire, in early 1992, using part of his redundancy money from British Telecom. 'I'm looking for a pub where I can brew as well,' he told me when I spoke to him in late 1994. 'Next week I'm moving from here to a ten-barrel brewery in an industrial unit until I can find a pub to buy and move the equipment there.'

Not that Gill had had too much difficulty selling the 2300 pints he was producing every week in the wash-house. 'There's a huge market I haven't attacked,' he said. 'I'm having to ration my customers now. I've got a 2.5 barrel plant here and brew four times a week. At present it's a struggle to make enough beer to get to break-even, and distribution is pretty inefficient as the van goes out from here only half or one-third full. Eight pubs take my beer on a permanent basis and another eighty or so as a guest beer. I sell beer through agencies, but the problem with them is the length of time it takes for my barrels, which cost £43 a time, to come back.'

The Cavendish Arms Hotel in Cartmell, Cumbria, took guest beers from real-ale breweries like Gill's until September 1994, when it began to brew its own. 'I had a normal week's supply of eight guest beers on the premises when we started,' says Nick Murray, the hotel owner's son, who runs the brewery, 'and I had to throw a lot of it away. We've only had four guest beers in the twelve weeks since then. It's been very good for business. There were three or four other pubs in south Cumbria which offered guest beers, but now we've got something that isn't available elsewhere.'

Besides exclusivity, there is another big advantage for pubs that brew their own: price. David Smith calculated that the price of beer from one of his installations is about £25 a barrel for materials and energy, which works out at less than 9p a pint. To this has to be added duty, which depends on the beer's alcoholic content but will typically add about £65 a barrel. 'You can reckon on a cash cost including duty of £85 to £90 a barrel,' he says. This is about half the price of a comparable bought-in beer – a difference of 30p a pint – although interest, depreciation and labour obviously have to be covered from this margin. The rest of the price of a pint is made up by the mark-up in the bar and VAT at 17.5 per cent. A brew-pub selling a pint at £1.50 will find itself paying 45p in VAT and duty to the government and 9p for materials, leaving 96p to cover its own costs. It is scarcely surprising that very few have failed.

It is surprisingly cheap for a pub to start beer production too. David Smith mentions a figure of about £15,000 for the installation of a four-barrel unit using second-hand equipment, the actual sum depending on the amount of work needed to prepare the premises. 'You can double that figure if you want to make the brewery a feature of the pub itself and install it behind glass, where the customers can see it, with wood cladding on the fermenters and copper tops on the mash tuns.' Alan Gill's ten-barrel brewery cost him £30,000 to open in his industrial unit, and Nick Murray spent 'around the cost of a small house'.

Lack of brewing experience does not seem to be an obstacle. Murray spent a week and £250 on a one-week brewing course at the University of Sunderland and then carried out four brews under David Smith's supervision. During the last brew with Smith, Murray trained his assistant, who now carries out brews on his own. 'It's not difficult if you've got a system,' he says. Gill was an enthusiastic home brewer when he worked as a telephone engineer and went on a three-day course at Malton Brewery, paid for by British Telecom as part of his redundancy package. 'I felt I needed a better back-up of technical knowledge,' he says. Since then he has taught courses of his own and says that at least six breweries have been started by people he has trained.

Gill and Murray have had few problems with officialdom. 'Although I'd been expecting difficulties, the environmental health officer was very helpful,' Murray says. 'He didn't require the brewery room to be tiled because he said that as we would be moving barrels around they could easily get cracked and that would create a health hazard. Four good coats of paint was all he required.' He finds Customs and Excise easy to deal with too. 'They come about four times a year to check that I'm paying enough beer duty. I have to keep invoices for all the materials I buy and issue invoices for all the beer I sell. That's all.'

Another approach to local brewing has proved successful in Birmingham, and the entrepreneur responsible, Robert McLauchlan, intends to sell franchises so that his model can be used elsewhere. Anyone able to use about eighty-five pints of beer, ale, stout or lager can go to McLauchlan's Ivy Bush Brewery in Edgbaston, select a recipe from the forty-odd available, and brew up the ingredients, which he provides, in a special small copper kettle under the supervision of an experienced brewmaster until they come to a rolling boil. 'No experience is necessary, and if ever anyone gets a brew that is not up to standard they can brew it again free of charge,' McLauchlan says. The process takes about an hour, after which the amateur brewer goes home. When his brew has cooled (and most of the Ivy Bush's customers are male) yeast is added and it is placed in a temperature-controlled fermenting-room for seven or eight days. The brewer then returns and bottles his creation to take it away.

'We sell only the ingredients and the use of the brewery. It is our customers who brew the beer, and consequently Customs and Excise have agreed that they do not need to pay duty,' McLauchlan says. This means that the price of a pint from the Ivy Bush can range from 35p for Pub Bitter to 90p for Extraordinary Barley Wine, although most brews work out at 59p, much more than the 9p a pint reckoned by David Smith to be the typical cost of the ingredients and energy used in one of his breweries. This margin has helped make the Ivy Bush a goldmine for McLauchlan. It opened in mid-1994, and by the end of that year more than a thousand permanent memberships had been sold at £40, enabling him to recoup its entire capital cost and build a second brewery. He had also sold an undisclosed number of temporary memberships at £2.50 for three months, despite charging this class of member 17.6 per cent more than the permanent ones for the ingredients for every batch of beer they brewed. Sales of reusable bottles at 29p each earned him even more; and since at least half of the £100,000 cost of each franchise he sells will be pure profit, he is being well rewarded for a good idea. The idea is not really new, however, as the Ivy Bush operates on exactly the same basis as time-share holiday accommodation, and it is certainly one that communities should consider adopting for a wide range of projects of their own.

Given their success in Britain, why have microbreweries and brew-pubs not come to Ireland too? (Ireland's first brew-pub opened in Dublin shortly before this book went to press.) 'I think the reason is that Guinness is a real beer and is not pasteurized. It takes 50 per cent of the market,' says Liam O'Dwyer, whose family owns a chain of pubs in Dublin and who was associated with an unsuccessful attempt to start a real-ale brewery, Dempsey's, between 1986 and 1988. The 25-barrel venture eventually closed, with the loss of £200,000. 'It sold into about fifty pubs, and the major problem it experienced was the lack of knowledge in the bar trade,' he says. 'There was an education problem. We'd train the staff in one pub and, being nomadic people, they'd move on.'

The Grist magazine is indispensable for anyone considering a small-scale brewery. Subscriptions are £26 a year from 2 Balfour Road, London N5 2HB; tel. +44 171 3598323; fax +1 171 3543962. It has a separate advisory service for people planning to set up and run small breweries.

David Smith can be contacted at 6 Church Street, Copmanthorpe, York YO2 3SE; tel. +44 1904 706778; fax +44 1904 705698.

Ivy Bush Brewery Ltd, 226 Monument Road, Edgbaston, Birmingham B16; tel. +44 121 4547447.

opened in 1995, partly funded by the sale of £450 'bonds', which meant that the purchaser would receive five twelve-bottle cases of a blended Arran whiskey in 1998 and five cases of a single-malt whiskey in 2001.[61] And, as the previous panel explains, capital contributions from prospective customers have financed a private, profit-making brewery in Birmingham.

The importance of locally owned shops

However many brew-pubs and CSAs are set up, it is not going to be possible for all local products to be sold direct to the customer. Local shops have therefore a crucial role to play if a district is to achieve greater economic self-reliance, and it is unlikely that they will be able to do so unless they are locally owned. This is because the big chain-stores do their buying centrally and will not be prepared to stock very different sets of supplies in each of their outlets. As a result the preservation – and in Britain, where so many villages have lost their shops, the re-creation – of locally owned retail businesses has to be given high priority. The city of Canterbury does not have a single sizable shop that is locally owned, while Dorchester, Thomas Hardy's archetypical market town, retains only two.

Ireland is much better off in this respect. Even tiny villages still have a food store, and in Westport, the town where I live, only a video shop and a shoe shop are not owned by local families. But local retailers are under pressure in Ireland too, particularly in the grocery trade, and this has forced many of them to add less value to the products they sell by doing less to them. The result is that even though they are still locally owned, a smaller proportion of the price the customer pays stays within the community. Twenty years ago, Hoban's, with its wooden counters and a system of wires and springs that catapulted money across the ceiling to the office for change, was the biggest grocery in Castlebar, Mayo's county town – that is, if it is correct to call it a grocery. It had a bakery at the back, which was renowned for its pork pies and also made a wide range of breads, fancy cakes, and pastries; and there was an abattoir at the side, which slaughtered cattle for sale in the butchery department of the shop. 'We didn't cure our own hams but we boiled and stuffed them and made excellent sausages and luncheon meat,' Art Mulloy, a former employee, told me. The shop also packed its own tea and roasted and ground its own coffee. In short, it was more than a big shop with over thirty employees: it was a food factory too, and since it closed in the middle 1980s – partly because of competition from supermarket chains but also because none of the owner's children was interested in taking it on – its work is being done elsewhere. Almost all the products the food shops and supermarkets in Castlebar pass over the bar-code scanners today are processed and packed outside the town, sometimes on the far side of the world.

It is going to be extremely difficult to re-create businesses like Hoban's but Derek Smith, a retired farmer, has established the non-profit Village Retail Services Association (ViRSA) to help communities in Britain retain or re-open their local shops. His efforts began when, in January 1991, the owner of the only shop in his village, Halstock in west Dorset, was defeated by high interest rates and announced that he was planning to close it. Smith and the other 350 villagers were stunned by what they regarded as another stage in their community's decline: their school had been closed five years earlier, and before that the church had been amalgamated with seventeen other parishes into a four-priest team ministry and the rectory and glebe land sold.

But the fate of the school and church had been decided by outside institutions: the future of the shop, Smith and his neighbours felt, was in their own hands, and they held a series of public meetings to decide what could be done. 'At the first meeting we came to the unanimous decision that we were determined to keep it open,' he says. 'At the second meeting, about two weeks later, we had our plans well worked out, which was just as well because the owner dropped the bombshell that he was closing down in three weeks' time. At that meeting sixty people undertook to lend a total of £15,000 interest-free to a special company, Halstock Village Shop Ltd, which was to run the new undertaking. Five days after that the company had leased premises which were converted, decorated, fitted out and stocked in what was left of the three weeks' notice we had been given. The old shop closed on the Friday evening, and the new shop was trading on the Monday morning.'

The shop was run by a volunteer for six months until a tenant, Brenda Erscott, took over. She put £12,000 of her own money into the operation and sub-rents the premises from the village company (which voted to convert itself to a co-operative at its first AGM) for £60 a week. As a result of a small difference between the rent she pays and the amount due to the owner of the premises, together with her payments for the company's stock, the original investors have been getting some of their loans repaid. 'They were given no guarantee that they would get their money back,' Smith says. 'The view from the outset was that people should not put up money they could not afford to lose. However, there was always a good chance of recouping half of the money if the business closed and the stock and fittings were sold off.'

Although the shop matches supermarket prices on basic lines, it made a net profit of £3665 on a turnover of £100,000 in 1993, besides paying Brenda Erscott a wage. But every penny she got was hard-earned. She opens between 7:30 a.m. and 6 p.m. each weekday and also on Sunday mornings. She takes Tuesday afternoon off and employs two regular part-time helpers and another occasional one for a wage bill averaging £100 a week. 'It's hard work and would not really be worth while without my post office salary of £4000,' she says.

Smith believed that Halstock's experience might be of value to other communities, and he set up ViRSA to pass along the lessons he had learned. 'Only a handful of villages have had any success with shop rescue operations, and fewer still have stood the test of time,' he says. 'It seemed to me that Halstock had the skeleton of a scheme which could be refined, widened and adapted to provide a repeatable model for other villages. Reinventing the wheel can be an expensive and time-consuming business, and the omission of a few spokes can easily lead to disaster.'

The Halstock model has two important features, Smith believes. The first is that people wishing to retain a village shop actually invest money in it, thus guaranteeing that they will give it their trade. 'Other methods of pledging working capital, such as reverse credit – in which customers advance cash to cover, say, their purchases for a month – are less durable because there is nothing to stop people with-drawing from the system by not replacing their capital after they have spent it some month. In any case, the amount of money reverse credit will raise is unlikely to be sufficiently large.' A community loan to help an existing shopkeeper out of his or her debts is also unlikely to be satisfactory unless the reasons the business got into debt in the first place are tackled. Too many rural shopkeepers have borrowed so much to buy their houses and shops that they cannot hope to pay their mortgages with what they earn from their businesses.

The second important feature is that the village shop committee actually owns or leases the premises and the refrigerators and fittings in it and finds a tenant to run the shop. 'This enables the villagers to decide who should be their shopkeeper, rather than vice versa,' Smith says. 'They have the chance of assessing the tenant's personality, retailing ability and financial standing before signing an agreement.'

Although running a shop with a volunteer staff might be necessary until a tenant can be found, he does not think it realistic for a community to plan to use volunteers to staff the shop indefinitely because people will lose interest. Nevertheless some villages – Letcombe Basset in Oxfordshire is one – have run shops with volunteers for ten or fifteen years.

Smith also advises against appointing a paid manager to run a shop on a village's behalf because the salary the business will be able to afford is unlikely to be sufficient to attract someone of the necessary calibre. In any event, he asks, who in the village is going to have the time and ability to supervise the manager? 'Renting gives the tenant the opportunity to make a profit by using his or her retailing skills without making a heavy capital investment in premises. If the tenant fails to make a go of the shop, the village still controls the premises and has the option of keeping them open, perhaps with volunteers,' he says.

After establishing ViRSA, Smith carried out a detailed survey of village shops in six counties to try to identify the factors that led to success. He came away convinced that the personality and ability of the proprietor was all-important. 'Every shop I visited had a supermarket within ten miles. One shop, with a turnover of £158,000, had two competing supermarkets within a mile. It was run with skill and efficiency by a husband and wife and showed the supra-importance of the shopkeepers themselves and what could be done in the face of intense competition.'

The second most important factor, Smith found, was that the shop include a sub-post office because this paid the shopkeeper a regular salary and brought customers to the premises. 'It may be that in villages with populations of well over six hundred people a shop can flourish without a post office, but this must be considered the exception rather than the rule,' he says.

Given a shopkeeper with retailing skills, a congenial personality and the stamina to work long hours, a village shop and sub-post office can be made viable with a customer catchment of only four hundred people, provided the community gives its support, Smith says. Such a shop needs a selling area of at least 500 square feet and a store of 150 square feet and should be available for a rent not exceeding £50 a week. Other overhead costs, such as rates, electricity, water, telephone, insurance, accountancy, and transport, can be expected to total £146 a week. Since a typical village shop makes a margin of 18 per cent on sales, an annual turnover of £55,555 is required before the shopkeeper gets any return for his or her time, apart from the payment for running a community post office, which, if it is open for twenty hours a week, amounts to £4257 a year. Smith therefore reckons that a minimum turnover of £70,000 is required before a village shop can be considered viable; but even at this level the shopkeeper would only earn £132 a week, including the post-office wage, before tax and social welfare deductions.

In ViRSA's first year, Smith advised twelve communities on saving their shops. One that followed the Halstock formula to the letter was at Talaton in east Devon, where the village shop had been caught in a vicious circle of falling custom leading to reduced stock leading to a further fall in trade, and had eventually closed after being run by the same family for three generations. 'Everyone thought it was too much of an institution to close,' one villager commented. On Smith's advice a questionnaire was circulated to test the strength of local support for retaining the shop, which determined that 80 per cent of the 140 households wanted it to survive. Then £6500 was raised from 120 villagers by selling £50 shop bonds and £10 membership subscriptions to the Talaton Village Shop Association, a registered co-operative. 'One motive to contribute which is often overlooked is that the value of people's houses in villages with shops is higher than in those without,' Smith says. The village group then rented the shop premises, which had been stripped to a shell, and volunteer carpenters, plumbers and painters fitted them out. The balance of the money was used to buy stock, fittings, a cash register, and cold cabinets. Thirty-five women now run the shop as volunteers, some doing as little as two hours a month.

Before it reopened, the Talaton association reckoned that its shop needed to take £1500 a week to survive. In fact Letcombe Basset survives on a fifth or a sixth of that level of business. 'We're only turning over between £250 and £300 a week because we only open for an hour each day,' says Anne Shone, who acts as co-ordinator. 'However, we do serve as a meeting place for the village, which I think is much more important than the amount of goods we sell.'

Smith agrees. 'Community shops are never going to take on the big supermarkets – some of them turn over less in a year than many supermarkets turn over in a day. However, they play an important role that out-of-town superstores can never fulfil. They are focal points and meeting places as well as being an important source of basic foods and household goods. Often they also stock something else that is lacking in most supermarkets: the best of local goods.'

In Ireland, where a much higher proportion of retail business remains in local hands, remarkably good results have been achieved by simply alerting people to what they stand to lose if they switch too much of their shopping to chain stores. Perhaps the most successful 'shop local' campaign is Communities Under Threat, which was launched in County Mayo in April 1993 by Brenda McNicholas,[62] a radiographer by profession and the mother of six children aged between eight and twenty-two who simply describes herself as a housewife in her campaign literature. 'I became involved through our local Integrated Resource Development (IRD) company in Kiltimagh, whose function is to use local resources and the initiative of local people to boost the local economy and help create jobs. At the first meeting I attended, there was a discussion on job losses, businesses closing and the leakage of money from the local economy because people were earning their money locally and spending it elsewhere. We felt that if the local economy wasn't supported, then talk of local development was pointless. We got an interested group together from around Mayo, and CUT began.'

McNicholas, who works unpaid although her printing and other expenses are paid by Mayo companies, including a big farmers's co-op, NCF, is normally invited to begin a campaign in a town by its chamber of commerce or a group of shop-owners. She holds a public meeting and then leaves behind a pack of specimen posters, speaking notes, circulars and leaflets which the local committee can use. One set of notes is for the local clergy – 'most of whom address the matter in church'. There is also a set of specimen news items for the next five issues of the parish newsletter. Other speaking notes are for talks to retailers, secondary schoolchildren and to the general public. All are very similar and make the point that £75 spent in the local economy generates £110-worth of business there because it passes from hand to hand, creating jobs and keeping the town alive. Money spent with a chain store on the other hand, is immediately lost and does nothing for the area. 'The quality of life we have in our small towns and communities around the west of Ireland is second-to-none – no hustle and bustle, no traffic jams, and a safe place in which to rear our children,' one leaflet says. 'Our towns and communities are the very essence of our country. We should support them, nurture and treasure them. But do we? ... It should be the aim of every town to be as self-sufficient as possible ... if all local services are supported, then you have a thriving economy, which not only creates jobs but also attracts new businesses and new people to live there.'

 [main text continues p.324]

STRICT RULES MAKE PRODUCE MARKETS WORK

Every Thursday morning Bríd McAuley unlocks the doors of Westport Town Hall, turns on the lights in the dark, echoing main room and, with a colleague, carries twelve folding tables from the stack in the kitchen and arranges them in a horseshoe along the two long walls and across the front of the stage. Then from her estate car outside she carries in boxes and sacks of herbs and vegetables she and her husband, Chris, have grown on their organic two-acre smallholding about four miles out of town. 'When we're at the height of the season I have to make two car journeys to bring in everything we have,' she says.

From nine o'clock onwards other people begin to arrive with things to sell. They stack bread, buns and cakes on the tables to the left of the hall, knitted goods and other crafts to the right, and vegetables at the top. Jams and lemonades go in the top left corner beside the free-range eggs – most of which are already ordered – and the plucked and dressed turkeys and hens. At the other end of the hall two women are setting out tea tables, where people will be able to sit for a snack. In the kitchen, sandwiches wait on trays, and the boiler is on for tea.

By ten o'clock everything is ready. More than a dozen customers rush in as soon as the doors are opened, to be sure of getting the items they want. An hour later the tea tables are full of customers talking and laughing, while the bakery and vegetable tables are almost empty, although the market still has another two hours to run.

Give or take a few details, this scene is repeated once a week in seventy-four other towns and villages in Ireland and 538 in Britain – the places in which Country Markets Ltd in Ireland and WI Markets in England, Wales and the Channel Islands have branches. The organizations are very similar, in that they grew out of the two national associations of countrywomen, the Irish Countrywomen's Association (ICA) and the Women's Institutes (WI), and the Irish body adopted many elements from the WI's operating manual when it opened its first market in Fethard, County Tipperary, in 1946. The first British market had opened in Lewes, Sussex, twenty-seven years earlier to enable WI members, unemployed people, pensioners and ex-servicemen to sell surplus garden produce. However, relatively few markets opened until the depression in the 1930s, when, after a request from the Ministry of Agriculture that the WI help feed the nation, a grant from the Carnegie Trust enabled the movement to expand.

That both original markets are still trading is in large part due to the rigid operating systems the two national organizations use. It is worth looking at these in some detail, particularly as, in Ireland at least, they are regarded as confidential. 'No business would tell anyone who asked exactly how it operated,' says Mary Coleman, chief executive (her job title is secretary) of Country Markets Ltd, the co-operative society of which every Irish market is a branch. 'Why should we?'

Let's start with the procedures for opening a new market. 'If any market member is approached by a person or a group in another area with a view to starting a branch market,' the Irish manual says, 'Country Market's Central Office should be notified immediately so that the Society's Secretary may attend any meetings to explain the Society's aims, rules and function.' In fact Mary Coleman will travel from Dublin to attend at least four meetings before any market opens. At the first she describes how the markets operate, and if after that enough people decide they want to go ahead, she will conduct a minimum of three workshops with them, covering the duties that those elected as officers of the local branch will have to take on, how goods offered for sale must be labelled and packed, and how the branch's records must be kept. Membership of the markets, while predominantly female, is open to both sexes in both countries.

After the workshops, those who attended are invited to become members of the Country Markets co-op by buying £3 worth of its shares, and if a minimum of twenty do so and undertake to make or grow goods regularly for the market, Mary Coleman is likely to recommend to the national committee of management that a new branch be formed and allowed to trade.

Nothing sold in a Country Market, not even the handcrafts, carries the maker's name: the label just carries a membership number and beside it, in red, the price. The person who sells it to you is unlikely to have made or grown it and will be most reluctant to tell you who did. Why the anonymity? Aren't market members proud of their work? 'Of course they are,' says Mary Coleman. 'But if the maker's name appeared on something, you could find that people who did not like that person would refuse to buy her produce. And if we allowed people to sell, for example, their bread and cakes as well as those made by other members, there would be a natural tendency for them to try to sell their own goods first. So it's best that everyone sells other people's produce. That way they can be completely even-handed and neutral about it.'

Members bring their goods into the market before it opens and present the market controller with a duplicate-book in which they have listed everything they have brought to sell. The controller not only checks the list against the quantities received but, in some markets at least, grades fresh fruit and vegetables according to their size and quality and checks the presentation of the goods. 'This grading is essential,' says the manual. 'As it is the quality of the produce, its freshness and presentation that attracts customers, the controller should not accept indifferent quality produce.' The controller might also discuss the prices members are proposing to charge so that everyone operates on the same basis and does not undercut local shops: 'the Society does not undersell,' the manual states. If a market goes by the book, the only prices not based on their shop equivalents are those for cooked products such as bread, cakes and jam, which are priced at whatever the jar or wrapping cost plus twice the price of the ingredients and heat. 'Regular 1 lb (454 g) jam pots must be used and make sure there is no brand name on them [as this would] leave Country Markets Ltd open to prosecution,' the manual says.

If a member takes away unsold goods at the end of the market, the controller amends both copies of the delivery note, taking one copy herself and returning the other in the duplicate-book to the member. Meanwhile the treasurer is totting up the takings to lodge in the bank. 'From the day a market starts, every penny must be accounted for whether it is received or paid out. To achieve this, all money received must be lodged in the bank and all amounts must be paid by cheque,' the manual emphasizes.

Members do not get paid on market day for what has been sold but receive a cheque for a month's markets some time later, from which a 10 per cent commission has been deducted. Most of this levy goes to cover local costs, such as the hire of the hall, but just less than a third goes to the head office, where it pays the secretary's salary, accountancy fees, and, most important of all, insurance, which covers accidents the public might suffer on market premises, the loss or theft of market money, and any claims that might arise if people become ill after eating food sold from a stall. For the additional sum of £1 each per year market members are also covered for any accidents that might happen to them from the moment they leave home on market business.

Most markets find the 10 per cent commission more than enough to cover the head-office levy and their own expenses, and the rules allow members to vote on whether the surplus should be distributed among themselves or used to promote co-operative principles, to pay for educational courses, or to support community activities. 'We usually use ours for community activities,' Lily Ryder, then chairman of the Westport market, told me. 'We're frequently approached for funds by groups like the street festival and the tourism committee.'

Not every market has been a success, of course, and some have closed down. Mary Coleman says the most frequent cause of problems is a lack of commitment to the co-operative principle. 'Many people have no idea what it means to be a co-operator. Dr Muriel Gahan, one of the founders of our first market, said that it took persistent good will. Of course people are going to have to work with others they might not like; but I can remember one lady telling me that she would regard it as her personal failure if she couldn't do so for two or three hours a week.'

Besides being secretive about their operating procedures, the Irish markets are also reluctant to speak about their total annual turnover. 'Quoting a figure might give people the wrong idea. They could think it was all profit, whereas when you've deducted members' costs and made allowance for their time, they are getting very little per hour,' Mary Coleman explains, ever fearful that the tax man might become interested. The British are not so shy, however, and as part of their seventy-fifth anniversary celebrations in 1994 proudly announced that their turnover had grown from £1 million in 1972 to £10 million in 1992, an average of £18,600 a year per market. This might not seem much, but it conceals huge differences in turnover between markets and between the earnings of people within them.

About twenty people sell goods through the Westport market each week, although the branch has more than forty members. 'You can get out of a Country Market as much as you put into it,' Bríd McAuley says. 'Some people just bring along a few jars of jam each week. For them it's primarily a social occasion. For others, however, the earnings are very important and it has become nearly equivalent to a part-time job. They might bake on Wednesdays, make jam at the weekend, and knit in the evenings. Mary Coleman told us when she came down to set this market up that it would only provide a small supplement to our families' incomes, but for some of us it's doing much better than that. But then you've got to remember that Westport is a particularly progressive market. If you go to some of them, it's just a few old ladies sitting around, which is fine if that's what they want. There's another market I can think of which people say reminds them of the war years and rationing. We've had some customers from there this morning, and they said that they never go to their local market because it's too depressing.'

No one may belong to more than one Country Market; and although I cannot spot it in the manual, the Irish markets also have a policy of refus-ing membership to people who live more than ten miles or so from where they are held. 'This is because we believe that they should set up their own markets and not get involved in driving long distances,' Bríd McAuley explains.

Mary Coleman, Country Markets Ltd, Swanbrook House, Bloomfield Avenue, Dublin 4; tel. +353 1 6684784.
Penny Annand, WI Country Markets Department, Reada House, Vachel Road, Reading RG1 1NY ; tel. +44 1734 394646.

The craft stall at Westport Country Market, May 1996. (photo: Frank Dolan)

'It's all very simple,' McNicholas says half-apologetically, 'but we've found that it's most effective that way.' It certainly is. According to figures compiled by the banks in Kiltimagh, the local traders' takings had risen by 40 per cent after the campaign had been running for two years. 'The locally owned SuperValu supermarket has increased the number of people it employs from five or six to eleven,' McNicholas says. 'What people are complaining about now is that there are not enough shops here.' As a result, she has been asked to launch campaigns elsewhere in Ireland, and a group fighting to preserve the high street at Totnes in Devon from the effects of a Safeway supermarket have also sought her help. She has no doubt that her efforts have been worthwhile. 'When you lose your high-street shops, you lose your community,' she says.

There are other ways of providing sales outlets for local products, of course. One of the best – a market under the auspices of the Irish Countrywomen's Association or in Britain of the Women's Institutes – is described in the previous panel. Another approach is to set up a co-operative that buys foodstuffs in bulk from wholesalers and producers and distributes it among the members. The Dublin Food Co-operative Society Ltd works on these lines. It was set up in 1983 after Eoin Dinan wrote to a number of people he had met in the anti-nuclear movement's successful campaign to stop the construction of an atomic power station in County Wexford, inviting them to a meeting in a friend's flat to discuss setting up an organization that would make it possible 'to shop in an ecologically sound way' and 'promote the rational use of the Earth's resources.'

Pauric Cannon, who is now the co-op's coordinator, was one of the sixteen people who attended. 'We had become increasingly aware of the critical link between a clean environment, nutritious food and healthy people,' he wrote in an article written to mark the co-op's tenth anniversary.[63] 'A wholefood consumer-owned co-op committed to organically grown food would, we firmly believed, provide a down-to-earth way of addressing the environmental threat.'

The meeting had been well planned, and everyone present was given a photocopied list of forty food products from which they could order. The idea was that if each person paid for whatever they wanted in advance and their individual orders were amalgamated, not only would the group be able to buy wholesale but by paying on the nail they would get the best possible discount from the supplier. A short time later the first batch of wholefoods was delivered, and the group

began to meet every month in a room on the second floor of a vege-
tarian restaurant to divide up what they had ordered. 'All the food
was weighed, packed and orders collated and assembled by members
organized on the basis of a voluntary help rota,' Cannon writes.

Eventually, however, when membership reached forty, it became
just too much work to carry sacks of rice and beans up four flights of
narrow stairs, and the co-op rented a small ground-floor room elsewhere until the regular queues of members along the pavement
meant they had to move again. In 1987 they moved for a third time,
to the large hall in Pearse Street it still rents on Saturday mornings. By
this time it had two hundred members and was holding fortnightly
rather than monthly advance-order collection days. Turnover was only
£7000 a year, however.

Sales reached £100,000 a year around the time of its tenth birth-
day in 1993, and members began to grow restive about still having to
order in advance. 'With over 500 members, the law of large numbers
must be starting to apply,' one wrote in the co-op's newsletter. 'I
would bet that the amount of rice and wheatgerm bought each week
varies very little. With five or fifty members, pre-ordering is essential,
but with the current number's purchasing power I suggest that it is
largely redundant.'

The chairperson's reply casts an interesting light on the co-op's
information systems and finances. 'The [advance order system] is the
only means of assessing the order requirements for the wholesaler. We
usually have at least £2000 worth of produce left over after each Collection Day ... We are unable to pay for goods until they are sold, so
we are unable to avail of the suppliers' discounts for prompt payment.' In other words, after ten years' trading the co-op had not
amassed enough capital even to finance the carry-over of £2000
worth of stock. This was because, in the interests of giving members
the cheapest possible prices, the mark-up to cover operating costs had
been set so low that the operation barely broke even, as the accounts
show. In 1991, for example, the year's surplus was a mere £40. On
the other hand, a survey showed that supermarket prices were 42 per
cent higher than the co-op's for an identical selection of goods.

The minimum-possible-price policy not only cost the co-op suppliers' discounts but meant that it lacked sufficient capital to run itself
properly. 'I don't think that the average member of the co-ordinating
committee has any idea of the problems we face and amount of
unnecessary work that has to be done just because we're not properly
set up,' Pauric Cannon told me in mid-1995. 'We're finding it increas-

ingly difficult to operate the co-op at its present size, because of the small storage space in our present premises and the difficulty of getting supplies in and out of the building. We'd like a building with enough space for storing and handling food which would meet food-storage standards.' As the co-op was planning to send out ready made-up orders to 'co-op clubs' – satellite groups of members who found it inconvenient or impossible to call in to pick them up – the need for suitable accommodation was particularly pressing. Cannon was also upset because the committee had decided to hold collection days every week rather than every fortnight, which meant twice the amount of work setting up in the hall and then putting things away again for, at that time, the same amount of business. 'Weekly collections have damaged the co-op from the social point of view too,' he said. 'People no longer come every collection day, so you can't be sure of meeting someone.'

When I contacted him six months later, he was much more optimistic. The co-op had had a financial crisis since we last spoke and had given itself such a fright that it had increased the mark-up on the goods it handled. 'We now charge 10 per cent on fair-trade products like Campaign tea and coffee,' he told me, '20 per cent on essentials like rice and pulses, and up to 30 per cent on luxuries. These rates are 3 to 4 per cent higher than they were a few months ago.' As a result, finances were much improved and the co-op even had £5000 in a special capital account to spend on equipment. However, they were no nearer getting a better building, and he did not think it was realistic for them to raise the money for one through higher margins. 'The mark-up will be put back down again as soon as the crisis is over. We're trying to set up an ethical investment organization; this will be independent of the co-op, but we're hoping that the co-op will be the recipient of one of its first loans, so we can get a building.' Other things were going well too. Advance ordering had been abandoned, membership was over six hundred, sales had increased by enough to make the weekly collection days worthwhile ('We're doing over £3000 worth of business a week'), and four co-op clubs were in operation, two of which were outside Dublin.

Over the years the co-op has established friendly links with the giant Seikatsu Consumer Co-op in Japan, which began in 1965 when a housewife persuaded two hundred women to buy their milk collectively and now supplies more than 220,000 households with a high proportion of their food. Apart from the disparity of scale, however, there are two significant differences between the organizations. One

Saturday morning at the Dublin Food Co-op, May 1996 (photo: Larry Boland)

is that Seikatsu members, 99.9 per cent of whom are women, pay the equivalent of £6 a month to belong to it until they have made a total investment of £1500. As a result, in 1995 their co-op was capitalized at over £100 million, the equivalent of £450 per member, a sum that has enabled it to employ eight hundred full-time workers, again mostly women, manufacturing, growing or delivering a wide range of products, which are always of high quality though not particularly cheap. Members of the Dublin co-op, on the other hand, pay only £4 a year for membership and expect low prices. As a result, their organization has very little capital per member and only one employee.

The other difference is social, and here Dublin scores much better. Seikatsu members are divided into groups, called *han*, of between six and thirteen people, which place a collective order once a month for delivery a week later. While there is a lot of social interaction among members of a *han*, they may have no contact with other Seikatsu members, although the co-op's regional offices do organize visits and social activities. In Dublin, by contrast, the range of people the average member unavoidably meets by buying through the co-op is much greater, if only because of the numbers present on collection day and the fact that members do not rush in, take their goods, and hurry out again, as they would at a supermarket. Collections are a time for meeting friends, and the refreshment area is often the most crowded part of the hall. In addition, if a member joins one of the seven teams of forty people that help weigh out orders in advance and operate the check-outs on a rota basis, they build up a camaraderie with people they would otherwise have never come across. They will also meet organic growers and craftworkers who sell from stands in the hall; and representatives of organizations like Greenpeace and Amnesty often put up a display.

'We may be ahead [of Seikatsu] as far as the social aspects are concerned,' Cannon says cautiously. 'They are more removed from their members. Nevertheless we've learned a lot from them, particularly about stock control and picking up point-of-sale data.' For many members, in fact, there is a close correlation between the Dublin co-op and their community. 'People have a basic need to feel that they belong to something,' Cannon says. 'Many people join a church for that, but when I go to church I never get to meet anybody. Here we're trying to become more aware that we're part of the whole community of nature by emphasizing the links between food and the natural world.'

Pauric Cannon was a property valuer, 'lubricating the wheels of the capitalist system', before the co-op entered his life twelve years ago. Does he regret the time he's given it? 'Not at all. I get a tremendous sense of satisfaction. It's really the people aspect, the range of people I've come into contact with, not just the Pearse Street community but people in Spain, Greece, the UK, the US, and Japan. We're all brothers and sisters, and it's wonderful to realize we're connected somehow, all working for the same thing.'

PRESERVATION OF GENETIC RESOURCES

Heritage Seed Library, Genetic Resources Department, Henry Doubleday Research Association, Ryton Organic Gardens, Ryton-on-Dunsmore, CV8 3LG; tel. +44 1203 303517; fax +44 1203 303517. A year's membership of the library costs £16 and includes a subscription to leafLET, an attractive and informative newsletter.

Genetic Resources Action International (GRAIN), Jonqueres 16, 08005 Barcelona, Spain; tel. +343 3105909; fax +343 3105952, e-mail grain@gn.apc.org GRAIN works for the sustainable conservation and use of agricultural biodiversity based on local knowledge and people's control over genetic resources. Subscriptions to Seedling, its quarterly newsletter which is especially strong on conservation work in non-industrialized countries, cost $35.

Seed Savers' Exchange, RFD 2, Princeton, Missouri 64673, is setting up a network of seed savers and plant collectors in eastern Europe before local varieties disappear as a result of the opening up of the markets in the former Communist countries to Western seeds firms.

LOW-EXTERNAL INPUT AGRICULTURE

The Soil Association, 88 Colston Street, Bristol, BS1 5BB, tel. +44 117 9290661, is the key organic agriculture organization in Britain. Supporters receive a quarterly magazine, *Living Earth*, for their £16 annual subscription. The organization also publishes *New Farmer and Grower* (£15 per annum in UK) for its farming members.

In Ireland there are two mainstream organic organizations, the Irish Organic Farmers' and Growers' Association, IOFGA (56 Blessington Street, Dublin 7; tel. +3531 307996) and the Organic Trust, Islands, Urlingford, Co. Kilkenny, tel. +343 5631411. There is also the Bio-Dynamic Agricultural Association, Kilderry, Peterswell, Co. Galway; tel. +353 9134138.

COMMUNITY-SUPPORTED AGRICULTURE

In Britain, contact the Soil Association, address as above. No organization has been set up in Ireland and the Philipstown Trust does not yet have the resources to handle enquiries. Robyn Van En can be contacted at Community Supported Agriculture of North America, Indian Line Farm, Box 57, Jug End Road, Great Barrington, Mass. 01230; tel. & fax +1 413 528 4374. An updated and expanded edition of her handbook, *Basic Formula to Create Community Supported Agriculture*, is due in Autumn 1996, priced at $15 including surface mail to Europe. A sample newsletter is $5.

RETAIL CO-OPERATIVES

Dublin Food Co-operative Society Ltd, Carmichael House, North Brunswick Street, Dublin 7; tel. +353 1 8721191; fax +353 1 8735737.

Seikatsu Club Consumers' Co-operative, 2-26-17 Miyasaka, Setagaya-ku, Tokyo; tel. +81 3 7060031. It has several publications in English, including a book, *I Among Others* (Seikatsu Club Seikyo Kanagawa: Yokohama 1991), that analyses the movement at a theoretical and practical level.

Notes

1 *Independent on Sunday*, 12 November 1995. A report by Geoffrey Lean inside carried the headline 'The food runs out: The world's cupboard is bare: Even Europe's grain mountain has vanished'.
2 P. Olsson. The statistics were quoted by the Industry Council for Packaging and the Environment (Incpen) in its report *Packaging Saves Energy* (1991).
3 *Green Fields, Grey Future: EC Agriculture Policy at the Crossroads* (Greenpeace: Amsterdam 1992) – much the best study of European agriculture, its problems and prospects that I have come across.
4 K. Blaxter, *Energy Use in Farming and its Cost*, Oxford Farming Conference, 1978.
5 See *The Food Miles Report* (SAFE Alliance, 38 Ebury Street, London SW1 0LU, September 1994).
6 Blaxter (*op. cit.*) estimated that 28 per cent of UK energy was used to grow, process and distribute food.

7 Richard Body, *Our Food, Our Land: Why Contemporary Farming Practices Must Change* (Rider: London 1991).

8 C. Arden-Clarke and R. Hodges, 'The environmental effect of conventional and organic/biological farming systems', *Biological Agriculture and Horticulture*, vol. 5 (1988), no. 3, pp. 223-287, cited in Greenpeace, *Green Fields, Grey Future*.

9 Interview with Dr K.G. Cassman, International Rice Research Institute, 1994.

10 University of Arizona Press, Tucson, 1990. A British edition was published the same year by Lutterworth under the title *The Threatened Gene: Food, Policies and the Loss of Genetic Diversity*.

11 J. Harlan, 'Seed Crops', in Frankel and Hawkes, *Resources for Today and Tomorrow*, cited in Fowler and Mooney, *Shattering*.

12 Quoted in the *Ecologist*, vol. 25, no. 5 (September-October 1995), p. 183.

13 Telephone conversation, 1995. Murphy's account of his cabbage collecting is on pp. 119-130 of the final report of the EC research programme, *The Collection of Land-Races of Cruciferous Crops in EC Countries* by Q. van der Meer et al., Wageningen, 1984.

14 Telephone conversation.

15 Letter from Plant Variety Rights Office, Ministry of Agriculture, Fisheries and Food (White House Lane, Huntingdon Road, Cambridge CB3 0LF), May 1995.

16 Kay Fennell, *The Seed Scandal* (Socialist Countryside Group: Sevenoaks 1987).

17 *The Apple in Ireland: Its History and Varieties* (RDS: Dublin 1951).

18 Introduction to a leaflet, *The Native Irish Apple Project* (Irish Seed Savers 1995).

19 *Common Ground*, July–August 1993.

20 Telephone interview.

21 Telephone interview.

22 Telephone conversation, 1996.

23 *Economist*, 10 August 1991

24 Letter, 23 January 1995.

25 Cary Fowler, *Report on Grassroots Genetic Conservation Efforts*, US Office of Technology Assessment, Washington, 1985, cited in Fowler and Mooney, *Shattering*.

26 Quoted by Henry Hobhouse, *Seeds of Change* (Macmillan: London 1992). I have also drawn material on the Great Famine from Austin Bourke, *The Visitation of God: the Potato and the Great Irish Famine* (Lilliput: Dublin 1993).

27 See above.

28 *Irish Times*, 3 May 1994 and 10 February 1995.

29 Cited by Leo Curran in *Kerry and Dexter Cattle* (RDS: Dublin 1989).

30 Keith Chivers, *History with a Future: Harnessing the Heavy Horse for the Twenty-First Century* (Shire Horse Society: Peterborough 1988).

31 Reported in *Heavy Horse World*, vol. 5, no. 2, summer 1991.

32 Adapted from Jules Pretty, *Regenerating Agriculture* (Earthscan: London 1995).

33 A. Vine and D. Bateman, *Organic Farming Systems in England and Wales* (Department of Agricultural Economics, University College of Wales, Aberystwyth 1981), cited in Greenpeace, *Green Fields, Grey Future*.

34 E. Böckenhoff et al., *Berichte über Landwirtschaft*, 64 (1986), 1, pp. 1-39, cited by Greenpeace, *Green Fields, Grey Future*.

35 *Profitability of Four Sustainable Farms in Minnesota*, 1994 (Land Stewardship Project, PO Box 130, 180 E. Main Street, Lewiston, Minnesota 55952; tel. +1 507 5233366).

36 *Alternative Agriculture* (National Research Council: Washington 1989), p. 39.
37 Earthscan, London, 1995.
38 'Organic farmers higher in sperm than other men', *Irish Times*, 10 June 1994.
39 *Nutritional Values in Crops and Plants* (Faber: London 1965).
40 David Pimentel, *et al.*, 'Environmental and Economic Costs of Pesticide Use', *Bioscience* 42 (10), 1992, pp. 750-60. All such estimates are flawed because they cannot be made without putting a price on the priceless.
41 Hugh Raven, Tim Lang, and Caroline Dumonteil, *Off Our Trollies: Food Retailing and the Hypermarket Economy* (Institute for Public Policy Research: London n.d.).
42 B. Norman, 'Making the grade', *New Farmer and Grower*, no. 26 (spring 1990).
43 'Getting the most from our resources', *Economic Development Review*, vol. 10, no. 3, summer 1992.
44 Published by the Institute for Local Self-Reliance, 2425 18th Street NW, Washington, DC 20009-2096. See also the pamphlet *Rural Development, Biorefineries and the Carbohydrate Economy* by the same authors, published by the ILSR in September 1993.
45 10 October 1994.
46 *Off Our Trollies*, p. 31.
47 *Business and Finance*, Dublin, 27 August 1992.
48 Peter Goering, Helena Norberg-Hodge, and John Page, *From the Ground Up: Rethinking Industrial Agriculture* (Zed Books: London 1993), p. 34.
49 Greenpeace, *Green Fields, Grey Future*.
50 M. Jörgenson et al., cited by Greenpeace, *Green Fields, Grey Future*.
51 Interview, November 1993.
52 Floris Books, Edinburgh, 1994.
53 Christina Groh, 'Community-supported agriculture: a new approach to marketing', *New Farmer and Grower*, spring 1991.
54 Trauger Groh tells the story of the Temple-Wilton farm in his book *Farms of the Future* (Biodynamic Farming and Gardening Association: Kimberton, Pennsylvania 1990), written with Steven McFadden.
55 Telephone interview.
56 Telephone interview.
57 *Land, the Challenge and the Opportunity*, March 1993.
58 Available from the E.F. Schumacher Society, Box 76, RD13, Great Barrington, Massachusetts 01230. The essay appears as a chapter in Borsodi's book, *Seventeen Problems of Man and Society*, (Anand: Charotar, India 1968).
59 Telephone interview.
60 Timothy Laird, *Community-Supported Agriculture: A Study of an Emerging Agricultural Alternative* (Graduate College, University of Vermont 1995).
61 Advertisement, *Guardian*, 18 March 1995
62 Brenda McNicholas, Communities Under Threat, Kiltimagh, Co. Mayo; tel. +353 94 81109.
63 *Dublin Food Co-op Newsletter*, no. 9 (spring 1993).

7

New Attitudes for New Times

The market economy relies on competition to control the way businesses behave. As this will not work in a community economy, new approaches and attitudes need to be found.

IN THE MAINSTREAM ECONOMY, great stress is placed on individual achievement, and unless we can reduce or shift this emphasis which has given the industrial system so much of its shape, we will fail to develop a satisfactory alternative. To put this more directly, if we simply begin to use a selection of the methods by which communities can become more self-reliant without changing our attitudes to the balance we strike between community goals and personal ones, we are bound to get disappointing results. Fortunately, as we will see, a new balance does not mean we will have to make significant personal sacrifices. Quite the contrary: we will gain personally by moving towards it.

In part, the industrial system's emphasis on the individual is a by-product of the Protestant reaction to the Catholic teaching that the church was the road through which the individual reached Heaven. Protestantism taught instead that salvation depended exclusively on the individual's unmediated relationship with God, and eventually almost everyone in the western world, Catholics included, came to feel that they were individually responsible for their spiritual destiny. From feeling that one should look after one's own future in the next world, it wasn't too big a step to believe that one ought to do the same in this, particularly after 'the father of economics', Adam Smith, wrote in *The Wealth of Nations* in 1776 that if each of us pursued our personal advantage in the economic sphere we would be led by an 'invisible hand' to promote the interests of society more effectively than if we had set out to do so. But those who wear Smith's mantle today have forgotten or deliberately overlook that part of what he meant by the invisible hand was the acceptance by everyone, businesspeople included, of a set of social values to which they conformed and which in certain cases were given force by the law.

The disregard today's economists display for the social component of the invisible hand is not accidental: the economics profession deliberately excludes morality and social and psychological factors from its scheme of thought. All mainstream economists assume that people make decisions rationally on the basis of narrow, individual self-interest and that a national economy can be understood by aggregating all these individual decisions. In other words they assume, in Margaret Thatcher's famous phrase, that 'there is no such thing as society' to moderate or modify individual behaviour, despite the fact that sociologists, a breed economists heartily despise, have produced a great deal of evidence that it is social and group norms that are the main determinants of human behaviour.

Economists are forced to ignore the possibility that irrationality, prejudice, love, community solidarity, idealism, upbringing and even enlightened self-interest might help explain the way people behave, because if they abandoned their twin simplifying assumptions of rationality and pure self-interest and let some or all of these other possible factors stay in the picture, the world would remain so complicated that they would not be able to say anything definite about it. In many cases, of course, their simplifications seem to work, in that they enable them to predict what will happen with reasonable accuracy. However, it is a grossly unwarranted step to go on to say, as most economists do, that the real world ought to be modelled on their simplified theoretical one in order to be efficient and that any actual system, action or outcome that does not accord with what they would have advised under their assumptions is sub-optimal.

Unfortunately, few people realize that most economic pronouncements are so flimsily based. The result is that whenever an economist categorizes a proposal as 'uneconomic', it is abandoned as rapidly and with as little discussion as it would have been five centuries ago had it been described from the altar as immoral. Indeed, morality gives force to the economists' condemnations, just as it did the priests', because anything truly uneconomic involves waste – a moral issue in a world in which people go without.

Like priests, too, economists have affected the way the laity thinks, except that their teachings have made people less rather than more likely to put collective interests on a par with their own. This was demonstrated in a series of fascinating experiments carried out by two psychologists and an economist at Cornell University. In one test, first-year postgraduate students from a number of disciplines were given some money and asked to divide it between two accounts, one 'private' and the other 'public'. They were told that they would be able to keep any money in their private account at the end of the experiment but that money in the public account would be pooled, its total increased by a certain percentage, and then divided out equally among all participants. For the group as a whole it was obviously best if everyone put all their money in the public account, as this would create the maximum sum to be increased by the percentage, so everyone could share in the biggest possible distribution. From the individual's point of view, though, the best course was to put all the money in one's own account and to take the share of the pool provided by the suckers as well.

What did the students do? When the results were analysed, it was found that economics students had contributed, on average, only a fifth of their money to the public account, whereas other students put in half. Questioned afterwards, nearly half the non-economists said they had been worried about the fairness of their allocation, whereas more than a third of the economics students refused to answer this question or gave complex, uncodable responses. 'It seems that the meaning of fairness in this context was somewhat alien for this group,' the research team commented wryly.[1]

In a second experiment, each student was given ten dollars and asked to divide it between himself or herself and another student on the basis that if the other student disputed the division, neither would keep any of the money at all. If the dividing student believed in fairness, he or she would obviously split the money fifty-fifty, while anyone motivated more by self-interest would calculate just how little they could offer the other – fifty cents, perhaps – to avoid the distribution being disputed out of jealousy or spite. Each pair played the game only once, so the receiver had no incentive for disputing the first division in order to get better deals subsequently. And what happened this time? The economists again distributed the money significantly less fairly than students from other disciplines.

After another survey that showed that economics professors gave less to charity than other academics, the researchers conducted a fourth study that showed that it was the economics training that made people less public-spirited rather than the innate disposition of people who took up economics. This they did by asking three groups of students a series of questions about their responses to hypothetical situations over a number of months. Two of the groups were made up of first-year economics students: a hard-line group being taught microeconomics by an instructor with an interest in industrial organization and game theory and a softer one taught by a specialist in the development of Communist China. Members of the third stream, the control, were astronomy students. A consistent pattern emerged, with the hard-line group becoming more selfish than the second one, who in turn grew worse than the astronomy students as their course went on.

Just as Catholic attitudes were influenced by the Protestant teaching on salvation, it is not only economics students and professors whose approaches to problems have been profoundly affected by the anti-communal aspects of economic thought: public attitudes have been damaged as well by the constant repetition of economic teachings in the media. And since economics is not the neutral system of analysis it pretends to be but an ideology that, because of its built-in assumptions, can prejudice our approach to the real world even if we have never studied it, we need to try to counteract its baneful influence on our thinking processes. Otherwise our attempts to establish community-based economic organizations are likely to go wrong.

Sixto Roxas, a Filipino economist who was once vice-chairman of American Express International Bank, argues that the main problem with conventional economics is that it focuses its analysis on the interests of the individual and the firm rather than those of the family and the community. 'Neo-classical economics is not just a mathematical framework or analytical guideline to facilitate the understanding of reality: it is a full-fledged ideology and design for remaking the world,' he says. 'The world that we are living in today is being cunningly and insidiously organized to fall into a particular pattern of imposed development, a massive restructuring in the image of the enterprise system' that only engages itself in projects that are profitable to the promoters and that ignores humanity's other needs. 'What is left behind is a gigantic mess of virtually unsolvable problems: health, education, environmental preservation, care for the poor and the handicapped.' People are reduced to flesh-and-blood machines that earn wages and salaries and generate profits but whose non-economic existence is not recognized.[2]

To remedy this, Roxas proposes that a profit-and-loss balance sheet be drawn up for the community as a whole rather than just for the income-earners in its area. 'The enterprise paradigm has established an accounting system that measures revenues, costs and incomes for enterprise owners. A new community paradigm must do the same for communities.' National income figures such as GDP, he says, should be compiled from community accounts rather than, as at present, from the incomes of firms and individuals.

But while the implementation of Roxas's idea would be a great step forward, it would immediately run into the problem we discussed in chapter 2, namely that market prices cannot be relied on to provide us with correct values for all the benefits a community enjoys, particularly as these would include things like health and happiness. And what constitutes a community cost to set against such benefits? Certainly not the current cash price of the goods and services that had to be sent out of the community in exchange for those that came in. Nor the amount of the work community members did: indeed, fulfilling work ought to be counted as one of the gains. Only any harmful side-effects of the way the local economy was being run – such as increases in unemployment, induced ill-health, inequality, crime, stress, noise, pollution, soil erosion, and natural-resource use – would count as costs to be set against the gains.

Community accounting would therefore be very different from enterprise accounting and would yield very different results. Only one set of figures – those for incomes – would probably be expressed in monetary terms; the dozens of other indices that ought to be monitored would be judged by comparison with their levels of the previous year. Has unemployment fallen? Well, that's a movement in the right direction. But income inequality has increased? That's a step back. Can we set it off against the unemployment gain? No, except on the basis of personal ethical judgment: there is no measuring-stick, no system of units, to help us out. Roxas realizes this: 'If there is to be a shift in viewpoint, a system will have to be set up that looks at matters that usually escape individual enterprise accounts. This assumes a moral and not a mechanical universe.'

Many communities, particularly in the United States, have already started keeping such accounts, taking their lead from the Sustainable Seattle project, which began in 1980 and monitors more than a hundred factors that affect the quality and sustainability of human life in King County, the administrative area within which Seattle stands. Its 1993 report showed more factors moving away from sustainability than towards it. The county became less sustainable because, among other things, its population grew, it used more non-renewable energy, had more traffic, generated more waste, had more children living in poverty, had fewer people who could afford adequate housing, had more juvenile crime, had more babies with low birth weight, and had smaller wild salmon runs in local streams. On the positive side, however, there was an improvement in air quality, the streets became more accessible for pedestrians, less water was used, the proportion of those employed who worked for the ten biggest employers fell, more young people were involved in some sort of voluntary service, the libraries and community centres were better used, and there was wider participation in the arts.

Jacksonville in Florida followed Seattle's example, for largely the wrong reason: it began monitoring its quality of life primarily to show big companies that the city was a good place to set up in, rather than to help its citizens make it better for themselves. Nevertheless the programme has worked out well. It monitors seventy-four indicators, covering nine aspects of the city's life: education, economy, public safety, natural environment, health, social environment, government and politics, culture and recreation, and mobility – that is, 'opportunities for and convenience of travel within Jacksonville and between Jacksonville and other locations'. The indicators were chosen by several committees involving more than a hundred volunteers in 1985; and in 1991 another, larger group of people agreed on targets for the indicators to reach by the year 2000. In 1993 serious movements in the wrong direction included a big rise in the proportion of black people unemployed in comparison with the total population, fewer people feeling safe walking alone in their areas at night, an increase in the number of newly diagnosed AIDS cases, a decline in the physical fitness of schoolchildren, a decline in the number of people rating local government leadership as 'good' or 'excellent', and a drop in the number of people travelling by bus.

Several British local authorities are experimenting with the Seattle model.[3] However, just because this will give them a better idea of what is going wrong does not mean they will be able to put things right. Companies and self-employed people need to make profits to survive, but the mainstream economic system does not provide any method of linking those profits to the extent to which the firms that made them have helped the community to reach its goals. Indeed it is frequently the firms that cut costs by ignoring the common good that are the most profitable. Moreover, even genuinely community-spirited enterprises are only able to tackle problems revealed by civic audits to the extent that they can do so without seriously damaging their financial performance. In other words, communities are very limited in the extent to which they can employ business, perhaps the most powerful human force for transforming the world, to achieve the collective as opposed to the private good.

This is one of the industrial system's most serious failings, and as competition increases as a result of international free trade, each firm's freedom to act for the common good will decline. Instead the world market will dictate more rigidly what a manufacturer should produce, at what price, and with what technology. If a firm should try to resist the market's decision because its directors have moral scruples about, say, the emissions produced by a new chemical process, it will make lower profits than its rivals unless it can make a marketing feature out of its refusal to adopt the technique – as the Body Shop has done with its rejection of animal testing – and thus persuade enough people to pay its higher prices. In most cases, however, taking a moral stance would cut its profits and hence its ability to exploit commercial opportunities, giving its less moral competitors the advantage and jeopardizing its survival. As Adam Smith knew, only if the law imposes morality or public obligations on every firm can all firms afford to observe them.

Competition forces firms to don a commercial straitjacket and to act in a very particular way. It is more effectively totalitarian than ever a Soviet central planner was able to be, which is exactly what its supporters like about it because they believe that only one way of operating a company or an economy is 'efficient'. They are happy to admit that their definition of efficiency is entirely commercial and excludes social objectives because they think that non-commercial objectives should be tackled separately once maximum profits have been made. However, as these profits are likely to be made at the expense of social objectives, the ultra-competitive, maximize-profits-first-and-then-use-some-of-them-for-social-ends-later approach is a highly inefficient way of achieving them. What our communities need is a form of economy that gives the producers within it sufficient protection from outside competition for them to meet social objectives as well as their own.

We are a long way from such an economy at present. As a result, one of the largest and, in some terms, most successful examples of community enterprise, the Mondragon co-ops, have been unable to protect themselves adequately against the forces of international competition, even though they had no outside investors and had their own source of low-interest funds. 'The particular genius of the Mondragon co-operators is not that they have found a mechanism to make money or create wealth – something done all the time – or that they have discovered a way to institutionalize the establishment of new business,' Roy Morrison writes in *We Build the Road As We Travel*.[4] 'Those are only part of the means to the end of creating and strengthening the bonds of chosen and discovered community.' Unfortunately, since the early 1980s the wealth-creating means Morrison mentions have increasingly become the end, and the goal of strengthening community has been diluted or lost.

When the first Mondragon co-ops were set up, demand for their products was high because Spain was just entering the consumer age and the Spanish market was protected by high tariffs. As a result, 'management was easy, without great burdens, and profitability flowed with abundance,' according to Jose Maria Ormachaechea, one of the founders of ULGOR, the original enterprise that became a cash-cow for the system.[5] Even as late as 1980, the manufacture of domestic appliances, the co-ops' most important activity, was sheltered from foreign competition by a 35 per cent duty. By 1991, however, the barrier had been lowered to 5 per cent, and it disappeared completely with the creation of the Single European Market in January 1993.

As the tariffs came down in the 1980s, foreign competition increased and the Spanish consumer became much more discriminating. This made marketing and management more important activities within the co-ops than actual production; and the wages of younger people performing these functions – who, as a generation, were less committed than their predecessors to the co-operative ideal – had to be increased to persuade them not to move elsewhere. To make this possible, the old rule that no one could earn more than three times the wage of the lowest-paid had to be relaxed, first in 1973, when the limit was raised to a factor of 4.5, and again in 1983, when it was increased to 6.* Then, in mid-1992, relativity restrictions on managerial wages were lifted altogether, a move that inevitably damaged the solidarity between the worker-members of the co-ops. The heightened competition also caused the co-ops to concentrate on increasing

---

* David Morris points out that since virtually no one was employed on the basic scale, the actual wage differential was about 4.3 to 1, much less than in Spanish industry overall, where the ratio was about 15 to 1. In Britain, chief executives earned on average 18 times more than manufacturing employees in 1995, compared with 16 times more in 1994. In the United States the multiple was 28, while Sweden and Switzerland had the lowest differential, 9 to 1, according to Towers Perrin, a firm of pay consultants, quoted in the *Financial Times*, 23 November 1995.

labour productivity, despite the fact that unemployment in the area had risen to over 16 per cent. So, while the amount of capital employed per worker has increased substantially since 1985 and output has also gone up, the number of people in the manufacturing co-ops has been static.

In 1992 the co-ops signed contracts of association with a new organization, the Mondragon Co-operative Corporation (MCC), instead of with the system's bank, which now only makes about 15 per cent of its loans to them. The word 'corporation' in the new organization's title is significant. Since it was set up, the MCC has merged some of its smaller co-operatives by moving their worker-members and equipment into a single building. It believes that co-ops with forty to sixty members cannot compete, and any that cannot meet strict market criteria must die. It is also reducing the number of products produced by the co-ops as a whole, and has made profit-sharing between them mandatory. Joint ventures with private firms are increasingly important, and most of its new investment and new employment creation has taken place outside the Mondragon area in places with no co-operative tradition. Moreover, whereas in the past it would have been unthinkable for a worker not to have been a shareholder, this has become quite common as profit-driven rather than people-driven managers think it desirable to be able to hire and fire staff easily to cope with fluctuations in demand.

Much of the consciousness of being a partner with a group of others in one's own enterprise has been lost as a result of the MCC's increased power in relation to member-co-ops, the compulsory profit-sharing, and the bigger co-operative units themselves. 'The Mondragon co-operative system increasingly looks similar to some decentralized US corporations (e.g. Johnson & Johnson),' David Morris notes.[6] In 1995 it abandoned enough of its community and co-operative principles to raise $96 million by selling shares to outside investors on the stock market.[7]

It had little alternative. Making car parts for Volkswagen, Ford and General Motors and holding 35 per cent of the Spanish refrigerator market against competitors like Electrolux and Bosch, which also manufacture in Spain, impose extremely tight commercial straitjackets. Consequently, once the directors had decided that executives' wages in Mondragon should be equivalent to those outside, the organization was well on the road to becoming conventionally commercial. What other path could it have taken, given that three of the ways of breaking out identified in chapter 2 – lower wages, shorter distribution chains, and the protection afforded by being able to price part of the output in a community currency – were not available to it, and the fourth – access to cheap funds through a community bank – was no longer as important as in the past? Mondragon may still be a network of community enterprises, but it is not serving a community market. If it was, it would now be operating in a more stable, less competitive commercial environment under a very different set of constraints and obligations.

The chief obligation likely to be placed on community enterprises in the type of local economies we are hoping to build will be that if a business makes profits as a result of the community's help and sacrifice, those who own it should accept that those profits are not theirs alone: they are in part the community's profits too and should be used with that in mind and not spent or invested outside the community's boundaries. This is one of the things I had in mind when I wrote of the need to strike a new balance between community and personal goals. While some writers define community enterprises as businesses owned and controlled by community groups, I regard any business as a community enterprise if it supplies the wants or needs of a community and its owners accept that they have a moral obligation to balance their community's interests against their own.

It could be argued that if a local firm makes its profits in the mainstream economy using labour, capital and environmental goods provided by the community on a full-cost basis, its owners ought to be free to use its profits as they wish. But what is full cost? Isn't every successful business in the world today making additional profits because it has access to many, many factors for which it never pays the full amount? Indeed the industrial system might never have developed – and would certainly not have developed in the way it has – had businesses not been subsidized on a massive scale by taxpayers, society, and the environment. All firms therefore have social obligations which I suspect extend far beyond whatever they pay in tax and which, if recognized, cannot be discharged in the mainstream system because of the constraints imposed by the forces of competition.

Competition can work against society in other ways too. Under the conventional, profit-driven approach, shop-owners are under permanent pressure to increase their turnover, even if this means forcing rival shops to close down. This is because the conventional business world works on the basis of 'dog eat dog' rather than 'live and let live', and any shop that does not behave accordingly is likely to be weakened and then swallowed up by one of its competitors. But a business system that leads to rival shops closing down is scarcely likely to advance the community's interests, as it will mean a loss of choice and convenience for some people and a step towards monopoly for them all.

What we need then is a system that allows, say, a grocer who believes his vocation is to serve the people of his area rather than to maximize his profits to stay in business. Such a trader would have a very different approach to his work and extract very different satisfactions from it. He would pride himself on his standard of service, the quality of his goods, and their range. He would accept that only a certain amount of groceries could be sold in his district and that if he sold more, fellow-grocers, whom he would regard as colleagues rather than competitors, would sell less, damaging their prospects and those of their families, and that should they go out of business it would make life difficult for people who found it more convenient to shop with them. Consequently, if he needed to improve his income he would try to find ways of doing it that would not harm his neighbours. Perhaps this would involve buying-in goods imported from outside the community, such as coffee or tea, in a less processed state and processing and packing them in his shop, capturing as much added value as possible for himself and therefore for the community. Alternatively, he might find another activity altogether that could be run alongside his main business and that no one was already carrying out.

A change in the way shopkeepers and other businesspeople are paid by the community for their work might give them the freedom to work this way, as Dorit Seemann has found with her wholefood business in Hamburg. As with most new businesses, Seemann, who was at different times a bookseller, a kindergarten teacher and a shipping manager before she began selling organic food, found she was losing money when she opened in 1986. This was because if she put a sufficiently large mark-up on the volume of goods she was selling to cover her overheads, her prices immediately became uncompetitive. For five years she persisted with the conventional solution, which is to grit one's teeth and try to cover whatever losses come along in the hope that sales will increase by enough to make the business profitable before one's capital and credit facilities are exhausted. Then she re-launched her business under the title *Der Andere Weg* ('The Other Way'), inviting her customers to help cover the shop's overheads by paying fifty marks as a monthly subscription; those who did were able to buy goods at their actual cost. Enough people took up the idea to make it work; this radically altered her relationship with those she supplied because instead of setting her prices at the highest level she felt her customers would tolerate, the challenge was now to buy as well as she could on her subscribers' behalf and to make the shop and its services as attractive and convenient for them as possible.[8] The tension inherent in the shopkeeper-customer relationship had gone: Seemann was now her subscribers' agent rather than their adversary. Her customers benefited because anyone who spent more than 150 marks at the shop in a month was able to make a substantial saving and had every incentive to do all their business there. Subscribers felt they were part of the business, and the level of pilferage dropped. 'My customers are my friends now,' she says.

The potentially malign influence of competition on one level and its absence on another presents community-scale economies with a problem. In the world economy, competition is the main method of ensuring that businesses do not make excessive profits at the expense of their customers. In a local economy, however, competition of sufficient intensity for this method of profit control to be effective is unlikely to be possible. Some other system has therefore to be found both to regulate the forms that competition can take in activities in which a reasonable number of similar businesses operate and also to prevent monopolies and oligopolies making excessive profits in activities where they do not. The need for such a system is not new: in the Middle Ages the crafts guilds regulated competition between members' businesses, while the problem of monopoly was tackled by governmental and ecclesiastical authorities through the concept of the 'just price' – an idea that may soon acquire a new lease of life in a community context.

Production in the early Middle Ages was not geared to accumulation and profit but to guaranteeing the existence of every member of society. For St Thomas Aquinas, the period's leading thinker on how a balance might be struck between personal and community interests, trade was not the sin it had been for earlier Christian theologians but was dangerous because it tempted its participants to sin. Aquinas, who died in 1274, taught that a man had the right to sell his stock or output for enough to maintain his status in society and to keep himself and his family in reasonable comfort, but anything beyond that was sinful profiteering. Trading for the sake of gain was wrong.

Aquinas's approach enabled just prices to be calculated. 'Prices were only marginally affected by the action of free and uncontrolled market forces ... Two factors – public need of the article and due return for its manufacture and transportation – were sufficient criteria for determination of the just price,' the Russian medievalist Aron Gurevich writes in *Categories of Medieval Culture*.[9] 'Determination of the just price was in the hands of responsible and respected people who were mindful that the norms of truth and general justice were here involved.'

A good example is the Statutes of Kilkenny of 1367, which set out in detail how a just price should be calculated. 'It is ordered that the mayor, sovereign or other chief officer of the town should call before him two of the most discreet men of the place, as well as the merchant to whom the said wares belonged, and the sailors of his ship.' The merchant and the sailors were to state, on oath, the first cost of the goods and the expenses of transport. Then the mayor or chief officer of the town, and the two discreet men, were to name a price at which the wares must be sold.[10]

Other measures were also used to prevent profiteering. London had a regulation to prevent anyone buying up cargoes of essential goods in order to corner the market. When a shipment of coal arrived, it had to be sold retail for the first eight days, families being limited to fifty basketfuls. Only then, in order to empty the ship, could any remaining coal be sold wholesale. And, naturally, the shipper's retail margin was determined on a just-price basis.

The other regulatory force of the period, the crafts guilds, first appeared around 1100 in Italy, the Rhineland, Holland and Belgium and spread quickly. Guilds were both social and commercial in character. On the commercial side 'the crafts guilds ... were concerned with maintaining a steady volume of business for their members. Their chief aims were a satisfactory standard of workmanship, and a fair price for its products, and the restriction of the number of apprentices a master might keep, the hours he might work and the tools he could use,' Antony Black writes in *Guilds and Civil Society*.[11] 'The general aim was to prevent the expansion of one man's business at the expense of others.' In some guilds, if a member was able to purchase raw materials at a bargain price he was expected to share his good fortune with his fellow-members; and many guilds required that workshops be open to the street so that it was possible to check that the rules were being observed.

Opinions differ on whether the guilds maintained a fair balance between their members' interests and those of the wider community. The current consensus seems to be that the guilds became more self-serving as attitudes slowly changed in the decades immediately before the Renaissance. However, there is no doubt that the guilds were of great non-economic benefit to their members because they conferred social status and provided, as a result of the oath members took to each other and the frequent communal feasting, a network of colleagues and friends who could be relied on for practical and monetary help at times of illness, poverty, and death. Black says that the guilds enabled work to take on the character of a vocation, and Gurevich can scarcely contain his enthusiasm for the system:

Belonging to a guild was connected with a complex of emotions which a man shared with other members: pride in his guild whose reputation and authority he would jealously defend, participation in meetings and general decisions, assertion of his dignity as a fully fledged burgher vis-à-vis the town patricians and the nobles, and a feeling of superiority vis-à-vis the unorganized craftsmen, the apprentices, pupils, servants – the common people of the town. A master craftsman sought and found in his work not simply a source of material prosperity: his work gave him satisfaction in itself. Hence his work and his product could be a means of achieving artistic pleasure. Perfection in a craft was handed down from generation to generation, forming a tradition of excellence and pushing the productive and the artistic possibilities of the craft to their utmost limits. A craft was a skill, and a skill was artistry. The free work of a master craftsman within a guild was a means of asserting his human personality and heightening his social awareness.

The union of productive, ethical and aesthetic principles in the work of the master craftsman gave this work very high social significance. It provided a basis for the development of the human personality to the maximum possible in the corporate society of the Middle Ages. The burgher was a citizen of his community, an owner, a working individual. The multilateral nature of his social relations raised him above the representatives of the other orders of feudal society.

A modern organization that has unconsciously adopted some of the features of a craft guild is the Briarpatch in San Francisco, an informal network of small businesspeople who, as their by-laws state, 'are in business primarily to serve people' rather than to become rich. Significantly, the word 'serve' is underlined in the original. Another guild-like feature is that members' financial records are 'open to all for examination: employees, customers, suppliers and anyone else who is interested,' an echo of both the concept of a just price and the open-to-view workshops guild members had to maintain.

The network takes its name from the Uncle Remus stories in which, while Brer Fox and the other animals lead serious lives and depend on their cunning, Brer Rabbit has a wonderful life of fun and play in the briarpatch. It was set up in 1974 by people who had campaigned against business and government in the social, political and environmental upheavals in the late 1960s and then, in the early seventies, found that they were in business themselves. 'We didn't want it to be just business as usual. We didn't want to be like Dow Chemical [which made napalm for use in Vietnam]. We wanted to do business in a different way,' says Roger Pritchard, an Englishman who joined the network early on and who is now a small-business consultant and part-time co-ordinator of the fifty-member East Bay Briarpatch, which operates in Berkeley and Oakland, across the Golden Gate Bridge from San Francisco. 'We had a common ethic of honesty and openness, sharing, dedication to excellence in whatever we did, the idea of having fun in our business and basing it on what we cared about and were good at, and a policy of taking care of people who did business with us. We found that this was not the way business normally worked so we needed to support each other in making those principles work for us in business.'

This meant that they had to set up their own organization, 'but one with no officers and no prestige because for us, prestige equalled politics.' Briars aim for 'right livelihood', which, Pritchard says,

makes work a central human activity with the responsibility for its meaning resting squarely in your hands. It requires that you be honest with yourself and work diligently to develop your faculties and skills. Right livelihood empowers you to do what you are really good at and love to do, involves you with the outside world in a compassionate way, aims for non-destructiveness, and integrates work and personal life.

People who seek right livelihood are involving themselves in reducing consumption, conserving natural resources, cutting down pollution, eating more simply and nutritiously, opposing nuclear war, bringing more spirituality into their lives and developing personal support networks to help each other do these things. They find that their lives are more in balance, more centered, more simple, clear and focused. They are no longer strung out in that cycle of material consumption which is so meaningless all by itself.

There have only been three coordinators since the Briarpatch was set up. Claude Whitmyer held the post when I visited San Francisco at the end of 1993. 'Because the support of the naturally large family and the clan or community has been lost to us, we must consciously re-create it as the first phase in finding our right livelihood,' he says. 'There are three effective steps to begin the process. First, focus on the people in your life; second, find the right people to support what you want to do; third, give back more than you get.'

Briars define themselves as people who:

(1) have an insatiable curiosity about the way the world works;

(2) seek to do the work they love and make a living at it;

(3) believe it is more important to provide the highest-quality product or service than to get rich;

(4) prefer co-operation to isolation;
(5) prefer honesty and openness to deceit and secretiveness;
(6) believe in self-reliance and social responsibility;
(7) believe in simple living and environmental preservation;
(8) believe in openness and the sharing of resources;
(9) have been in business long enough to have a track record;
(10) believe that joy is essential to a fulfilled life.

Would-be Briars are expected to be in sympathy with these ten points, although there is no formal screening process. The network holds a 'brown-bag' lunch in San Francisco on the first Wednesday of each month, to which anything between ten and twenty-five members come along. They sit around in a circle, eat whatever they've brought in their bags, and talk about what their business needs are and what help or ideas they can offer other members. Less regular activities include parties, classes, workshops, and seminars. A directory of members is available and, 'when there is the energy necessary,' a newsletter.

A lot of problems are solved at these lunches and by what Whitmyer calls his 'telephone ministry', which gets between twenty and fifty calls a month. Women, who make up 59 per cent of the Briar membership, apparently find these phone contacts particularly useful. For anything more intractable, a volunteer consulting team is available free of charge for calling out to businesses on Wednesdays. The team helps fifty operations in a typical year. 'You can learn a lot from these visits without being told anything, just by looking at things like how clean the premises are and the state of the books,' Pritchard comments. The success of these three types of advice and support has been remarkable: only 5 per cent of Briar businesses fail in their first three years, in comparison with the US average of 85 per cent.

Anyone wishing to join the Briarpatch sends off to their nearest co-ordinator a one-page letter outlining who they are, what their business does, and what their three or four main problems are, along with a six-month subscription, the amount of which is entirely up to them, the average being $50. Pritchard or Whitmyer then telephone to make an appointment.

At the moment there are 150 paid-up members in the Bay area, down from as many as 600 in the early 1980s. Pritchard is not worried by this decline. 'There is a tacit assumption that if something is successful it goes on. That's very wrong. The time may come for letting it go.' He points out that when the Briarpatch was launched, the ideas behind it were very radical, but now they no longer have the same intensity because the mainstream business community has taken up so many of them. Whitmyer agrees: 'Before "quality circles" and "total quality" there was Briarpatch. Before "excellence and ethics" there was Briarpatch. Before "green business" and "green marketing" there was Briarpatch. The sudden burst of businesses claiming to be socially and environmentally responsible has been enough to make the most trusting among us a bit suspicious.'[12]

Pritchard would probably not be in business himself without the Briarpatch. He was teaching at a university in San Francisco when he developed an idea for a business and, since he had no commercial background, joined the network for help and support in setting it up. What he learned caused him to abandon the idea – 'it would have been a disaster' – and instead to start a business helping people to open or run socially responsible businesses. He did this by 'apprenticing' himself to a consultant in the Briarpatch to learn the trade – a typical and common example of Briars sharing. 'Eighty per cent of my work is morale-related, helping people who are freaking out or have lost their business nerve,' he says. 'Often business disasters are caused by personality problems or blind spots. I was involved recently with a clothing business in which the two partners were not speaking to each other, and after three attempts at mediation failed I helped them structure the divorce. In another case I found a businessman had not kept any books, so I got in a bookkeeper to prepare them; but a month later he was totally uninterested in what they said. Naturally the business failed, but at least that man had learned what he did not want to do and moved on, so it wasn't necessarily a disaster.'

Most Briar businesses are small – 58 per cent are single-person and 85 per cent have fewer than seven employees – and most of their owners want to keep them that way. Pritchard himself decided not to employ anyone in his consultancy because his perfectionism made him bad at delegating. Michael Phillips, who discusses right livelihood in his important book *The Seven Laws of Money*[13] and who played a key role in setting up the network, tells the story of a graphic designer, George DeWoody, who began turning away work when he had five employees because he wanted to continue to design himself and not supervise other designers.[14] Other businesses in the network, including a toy distributor and the Down Depot, which cleans feather-filled clothing and duvets, have turned down opportunities to open franchised outlets and yet have helped other people to open similar entirely independent operations. 'The scale issue is crucial,'

Pritchard says. 'The trouble is that the role models put about outside the network are all about high-flying entrepreneurs.'

Although the Briarpatch, like many of its members, does not advertise since its structure and resources prevent it handling enquiries, a number of articles have been written about it over the years, and similar networks have been set up elsewhere in the United States and in New Zealand and Sweden. Another story Michael Phillips tells is of a Swedish Briar, Sven Olmstead, and his experience with open accounts-books:

Sven builds homes, offices and factories for a fixed contract price and lets his customers see his financial statements. Sven explains the results: 'When clients see that I have lost money on a project, the client is very appreciative of the hard work and excess effort my company made to do a good job for them; these clients always come back to me for the next job. When I make a large profit it is visible and the clients also come back, insisting that I offer them low bids – after all, I "made lots of money on the last job I did for them".'

An attempt to start a British Briarpatch was made at the end of the 1970s in that hotbed of economic experimentation, Totnes in Devon, but it failed to take off, apparently because the number of potential member-businesses was too small. The consensus seems to be that a minimum of twenty members is needed to start a network and seventy to keep it running. The Business Network, which was set up in London by Edward Posey and Frances Kinsman in 1982 and ran for eleven years, did not set out to be a Briarpatch. Its purpose was to link 'people interested in transforming business so that it embodies a vision of the wholeness of life and for the human spirit', its brochure explained. 'It aims to foster a new holistic approach to business which reflects the interdependence of the individual, business, the community and the environment.' It did not, however, offer a consultancy service nor endeavour to help members solve their business problems. Indeed it was not set up for small businesses at all, and members were not drawn geographically from any one place. 'Our aim was to get mainstream business people to think of the spiritual dimension, of different ways of dealing with business,' Kinsman says.[15] What killed it eventually was that New Agers who wished to get into business came to outnumber the 'suits'. He decided to let it die when two merchant bankers who had been dragged somewhat unwillingly to a meeting by their wives or girl-friends were forced to participate in a circle dance, which both they and Kinsman found extremely embarrassing.

At present, outside the Briarpatch at least, very few people who run a small business are happy and fulfilled. Indeed most would admit they are serving a monster that allows them no part of the day as their own and that so dominates their thoughts that they cannot maintain other interests. Any time they take off from their work is ruined by worries about tasks they should be tackling. Problems accompany them to bed at night and are there when they wake in the morning. They become boring to be with and bored with themselves. I know because I was such a person.

Above all, the proprietor of a small business is alone. This is because they are unlikely to have anyone prepared to listen to them talk about the problems, opportunities and humdrum day-to-day activities of the business in sufficient detail and at adequate length to be able to give the business person both the chance to develop his or her thoughts by talking things through and the informed yet dispassionate and objective outside view they require. Too often, for lack of anyone else, the owner's husband or wife is forced to fulfil this function. This is generally a mistake, particularly when the family's income is threatened by the business's problems, for the home immediately ceases to be a refuge from the stresses of the commercial world.

'A one-man show is an indicator for disaster,' an official of the Industrial Development Authority once told me. He was right. Few people have all the skills, knowledge and personal characteristics required to start and manage a successful enterprise. Someone who is a first-rate sales person gets excitement from winning orders, just as an angler does from catching fish. Sales people are quite happy to spend hours trying to tempt a big customer to take their bait, but once the order has been won they may lose interest completely. The routine grind of assembling the goods, packing, invoicing, despatching and finally chasing payment is not for them, although, rationally, they know that it is every bit as essential as getting the contract in the first place. They'll probably work up enough motivation to do it if they have to, but when it comes to keeping records for irksome things like VAT they can always think of something more important to do – like ringing so-and-so to see if he needs more supplies yet – and the job will never get done. Similarly, anyone with a clerical or accountancy background might get great pleasure from keeping tabs on the stock and cash side of things but is unlikely to be an enthusiastic wheeler-dealer as well. And people who derive enormous satisfaction from making or designing things will normally find it hard to buckle down to either selling or keeping the books. A mix of distinct personality traits that is rarely if ever found in a single person is needed to run a business successfully. A selling business needs at least two people: one to sell and one to look after the organizational side. A manufacturing business has to have a minimum of three: one each for production, sales, and administration.

True, a business can employ people with the traits the proprietor lacks, but employees create almost as many problems as they solve because the operation has to trade on a larger scale to develop the extra turnover the increased wage bill demands. There are other drawbacks to employing people too; Claude Whitmyer recently wrote a book, *Running a One-Person Business*,[16] together with Michael Phillips and Salli Rasberry, a Briarpatch volunteer consultant, which includes a two-page table entitled 'Ten reasons not to hire an employee'. 'The responsibility of regularly paying someone else to work for you can become a horrible burden ... Gone are the days when you could use slow business periods to relax, take vacations or learn new skills ... You have to give up your own pace for the employee's pace ... [and] schedule your work in a more normal way,' are some of the phrases they use. But even if the business could support an employee or two, the difference in status between worker and boss means that the latter would find it hard to go to the former for advice. So, without a Briarpatch, all a sole proprietor can do is employ a consultant, assuming they know of one with affordable fees and the right attitude, or find a partner with a complementary set of abilities, a minefield in itself.

What I am arguing here is that almost every business is, by its nature, a collective enterprise, but the present system makes it very difficult to organize one as such, and in small firms a single person usually has to take all the risk and accept all the responsibility for whatever happens, despite being inevitably ill-equipped to do so. Naturally the strain causes many proprietors to crumble under the load, and in general only the ill-informed, the desperate or the greedy want to run businesses on their own. Indeed, given the pressures they impose and the miserable life-style they provide, the only rational reason for anyone to want their own business these days is to become rich as soon as possible and take early retirement. We recognize this motive when we speak of a self-employed person being 'in business for himself': we do not see any public service element being present in commercial life, nor, as we have seen, does a hypercompetitive system permit one. But Roger Pritchard thinks that many people who go into business to become rich are unsuited to it. 'We have found that people who go into business to make money are impatient, act badly, and alienate people. They don't have the patience and persistence to make a business work.'

Forcing those who get involved in small business to accept all the pain and take all the gain is obviously bad for both them and society. In the community economy, business must be a means of service that allows those who take it up to gain respect for what they do rather than being despised for being engaged in an entirely self-seeking activity, as at present. In such circumstances a different type of person would enter commercial life, someone who would gladly give up the owner's claim to 100 per cent of a business's profits if they did not have to carry 100 per cent of its burdens and to risk losing, through personal guarantees, 100 per cent of their homes. Why is there such a huge difference between the way we treat, say, a gymkhana society that covers its deficit with a dinner-dance and whose organizers feel free to ring up anyone and ask them to help out, and a local baker and confectioner who is expected to make a profit and who finds there is no one to help when she fails to do so? The answer, of course, lies in the ownership rather than the relative importance or pleasure-potential of the two activities. The horse show is a community activity, whereas the baker is seen as simply trying to make a profit for herself.

If we are concerned about increasing the range of economic activities in our communities we will have to devise a new type of communally owned commercial organization that will have some of the features of a craft guild, some of the Briarpatch, and some of an investment trust. Its main objective will be to serve the people of its area rather than to make profits for owners or investors. As a result it will be free to seek donations to balance its books and to call for volunteers to help and advise its paid staff. Public-service radio stations in the United States are run on approximately these lines, broadcasting worthwhile programmes, taking a limited amount of advertising, and covering their losses in an appeals week once a year. Mondragon as it was in its early years is another good model because it had a mechanism for limiting the wages paid in enterprises in its system and redistributing the resulting profits, thus balancing the interests of the individual shareholder-workers against those of the community as a whole. It also had a mechanism by which a group wishing to set up a collective business could be part-financed and advised how to do so by people who had already helped many other businesses establish themselves. Although Mondragon has been forced to change recently, it still has a lot to teach.

Thermo Electron, a diversified technology company in Waltham, Massachusetts, that makes everything from alternative energy systems to artificial hearts, seems to have either reinvented or copied part of the Mondragon model with great success, although to make profits for itself rather than to benefit a community. The company has launched several small high-technology businesses by combining 'the advantages of a large company with those of a start-up,' according to its president, George Hatsopoulos.[17] Innovators working within the company are given a small stake in their project, loans from the parent company, and all the technical and administrative support they need to get them past the point at which most start-ups fail. Then, when a project has proved itself, it is converted into an independent firm able to raise capital by selling shares, although Thermo Electron always keeps a majority stake. Between 1985 and 1994 it launched ten companies, and it plans to spin off another fourteen by the year 2000. Although 85 per cent of American start-ups collapse, 'We won't let [ours] fail,' Hatsopoulos says.

But perhaps the best current example of an organization close to the Mondragon model is Radical Routes Ltd, a co-operative of co-operatives with offices in Manchester and Birmingham that accepts loans from ethical investors under the Industrial and Provident Societies Act to re-lend to its twenty members. As well as finance, Radical Routes provides business advice and technical and personal support to members of its member-co-ops, which include Organic Roundabout, which each week in 1995 was supplying over a thousand families in the West Midlands with a box of organic vegetables. As a result it has not so far had a bad debt. However, in other ways it is a less suitable model because it makes interest-bearing loans rather than providing equity, and it is national rather than regional in scope; its members are as far apart as Leeds, Wales, and Cornwall.

Perhaps what is needed is a community co-op in which every family in an area could hold shares. The co-op would enter into partnerships with individuals and groups wishing to start businesses in its territory, conduct feasibility studies, help develop business plans, provide equity capital, and carry out those aspects of administration in which the principals were weak. Most importantly, these co-ops would support and advise those running the businesses in which they were involved and link them with the other activities they were helping.

If local markets are going to meet a diversity of needs they will have to have a diversity of small producers, and community co-ops are consequently going to have to become involved in a lot of small-scale projects, many of which will be home-based. Building an alter-native to the industrial system does not mean duplicating it in scale, technology, or location. In *Divisions of Labour*,[18] his study of life and work on the Isle of Sheppey in Kent, R.E. Pahl points out that in pre-industrial times 'work was carried out by households and was a com-bination of self-provisioning subsistence, wage labour and by-employ-ment ... Regular, full-time employment at a single job was exceptional in the 18th Century.' A mixture of activities was the norm then and is likely to become so again in a post-industrial period. Most people will do many more things for themselves and their fami-lies (for which of course they will not be paid), supplemented by work for their neighbours – either directly or through a community co-op company – for which they will be paid mainly in a local cur-rency. Some will work for industrial-system employers, for which they will be paid in national or international currency, such as the Euro, perhaps at home or in workshops close by.

This will affect housing demand profoundly. Most urban accom-modation has been built or converted on the assumption that people want to do little more than eat, sleep, and watch television. As they rarely provide room for a pram, let alone a bicycle, many properties will prove entirely unsuited to the new working patterns. In the coun-try, of course, more space is available; and it is significant that Jim Connolly, whose work helping unemployed people move from cities to the countryside is described in the next panel, sees access to a gar-den and a work-shed as among the principal gains for those who move out of town.

There will also be profound repercussions for the community and the family. 'Work done by members of households is the central process around which society is structured,' Pahl says. This implies that if work is no longer available to a household's members, the structure of society will collapse or change, as has been happening. Wendell Berry, the poet, novelist, university lecturer and Kentucky tobacco farmer, makes exactly this point in a 1988 essay, 'The Work of Local Culture',[19] in which he states that 'if there is no household or community economy, then family members and neighbors are no longer useful to each other. When people are no longer useful to each other, then the centripetal force of family and community fails, and people fall into dependence on exterior economies and organizations.'

And if the labour of a young adult is no longer needed, he or she will go away, rarely to return, breaking the local succession of the gen-erations. In many communities, children are educated to enable them

 [main text continues p.360]

THROWING RURAL DEPOPULATION INTO REVERSE

In 1845, just before the Great Famine, 13,000 people lived on Loop Head, a bleak finger of rock and acid soil sticking out into the Atlantic in County Clare. Today it has only 1300 inhabitants, and for twenty years after he set up his studio and foundry there in the early 1970s, Jim Connolly, a sculptor, watched the depopulation process continue, with house after house being boarded up and abandoned as the elderly occupants died or families moved away.

As the parish's population fell, the quality of life available to the remaining inhabitants deteriorated. Shops and pubs closed, and schools were amalgamated or lost teachers. Signs of dereliction were everywhere. Like many places in rural Ireland, Loop Head seemed to be caught in a vicious circle in which because some families left, others had to leave too. According to an estimate prepared for the west of Ireland as a whole by Dr Tom Boylan of University College, Galway, whenever four families leave an area, another family nearby loses its income and might have to move away too because of the reduced amount of local spending.

What could be done to stop west Clare's decay? There were no jobs in the area to attract incomers, so Connolly's first thought was that craft workers like himself might be a solution, as they brought their work with them and were practical, resourceful and resilient people. But then he realized that the unemployed were another group that could draw their income anywhere and that even if they stayed on the dole, fifty resettled families would pump at least £500,000 into the local economy and gain personally as well, not least by bringing their children into a clean, safe, crime-free environment where they would be in much smaller classes in school.

Excited by this idea, Connolly went on the radio early in 1990 to talk about it. 'I'd no notion of setting up an organization myself,' he says. 'I just wanted somebody to take up the idea. My attitude was "let this cup pass from me" ...' But when over a hundred letters from families wanting to move out to the country from city housing estates arrived at his home after the broadcast, he felt he couldn't just ignore them, and a few weeks later he began meeting families off the Dublin bus in Kilrush on Friday evenings, taking them to a bed-and-breakfast for the night, and then driving them around the district the next day so they could get an idea of what it was like and what sort of rented houses were available.

A lot of the expenses he paid himself. 'I hadn't realized how close people living on the dole are to the financial edge. They just don't have the money for anything extra. One woman sold her washing-machine to be able to buy the bus tickets for the journey down.'

At the end of the year six families with twenty-one children between them had moved west out of Dublin, and by early 1995, 161 other families had been resettled too, predominantly in Clare but with at least one family going to rural areas in sixteen other counties. Thirty-five families moved in both 1993 and 1994, a small fraction of the number of applications received. 'We've three thousand people on the waiting-list, and whenever we get any publicity, dozens more letters flood in,' says Paul

Murphy, who administers Rural Resettlement Ireland, the organization Connolly's one-man effort became, from a prefabricated cabin a short distance down the road from Connolly's house. 'Many, many more people could have moved if we had been able to find suitable houses,' says Murphy, a former Dublin bus driver who himself moved out of Dublin with his family under RRI's auspices. Connolly agrees and complains about the number of houses being bought up in coastal areas by wealthy people wanting holiday homes. 'Some of those houses would otherwise have been rented to us.'

To get around this problem, RRI has started a campaign to get every rural parish with a declining population to find a house for a resettled family each year for the next five years, and more than thirty parishes have already joined up. It is also building five houses in partnership with a voluntary housing organization and purchasing another five houses with 90 per cent grants from the government.

But finding enough decent, dry houses that are available to rent on a long-term basis at a figure that families living on social welfare benefits can afford will always be a problem, and one of Connolly's ambitions is to establish a £1 million revolving fund to buy up properties in need of repair, renovate them, and sell them on to migrants using shared-ownership mortgages. These involve the householder paying a rent for half the house and a mortgage for the other half. Already about thirty of the incomers are buying their houses with share mortgages from Clare County Council and other councils, and RRI has been trying to persuade Dublin City Council to give similar assistance to any of its tenants who surrender a council house and move to a rural area. It argues that for every family that leaves the city, the city gains by not having to build a new property for someone on its housing list.

RRI is also trying to involve the banks and the government in providing shared mortgages for low-income families who move to rural areas, and seems to be having some success. 'Although almost all resettled families are unemployed,' Paul Murphy says, 'the Bank of Ireland has agreed to make mortgages available to them at 6 per cent interest to cover a third of the price of a property if another third can be covered by a government grant and the balance by RRI's revolving fund. We plan to use money we've been promised from the United States through the Ireland Fund. The problem at the moment is that some officials in the Department of the Environment seem to be dragging their feet.'

Given the huge imbalance between the number of city people who apply to move and the supply of houses that can be found for them, how does RRI select the families it will assist in moving? 'We don't. It's a self-selection process,' Murphy says. 'The ones that write two or three letters and generally keep in touch are asked to get references for us from their children's school and their local authority. When we get those they go onto our active list, and we visit them to make sure that they have a positive attitude and are not just wanting to move out of desperation. We also ask them to take a course which takes two evenings a week for six weeks and covers such things as coping with change and cultivating a garden.'

Happy to have left the city: the Boland family. Anti-clockwise from left are Noeleen, Bernadette (10), Maria (8) Noeleen Jnr (6), Emma (5), Anthony, Rebecca (9), Anthony Jnr (11).

Indeed the prospect of getting a house with a patch of land on which they can grow things and perhaps a shed where they can do some carpentry or take up a craft are two significant reasons why many families want to move to the country.

So far only twenty families who moved out of the city with the help of RRI have decided that they made a mistake and have moved elsewhere. 'The main reason they left was that they were not well enough acquainted with the area before they came and consequently did not really know what they were letting themselves in for,' Murphy says. Antony and Noeleen Boland decided to return to Dublin after one of their children choked on a piece of meat and, unable to breathe, turned grey. Without a telephone and with their nearest neighbours over a mile away, there was no one they could turn to for help. Noeleen eventually managed to clear the child's windpipe with her fingers, but the close shave convinced her that she should not risk her children's lives by living in such a remote place any longer. Their return to the capital did not last very long, however: they moved back to Clare after joyriders drove a car into their garden.

Now the main thing Noeleen misses is the shops. The family has no car, and groceries are delivered on the back of a tractor. Antony, who misses Chinese takeaways, is still unemployed but is on the board of management at the children's school.

'Almost all the families who come have experienced long-term unemployment and the difficulties that inevitably go with it. Problems such as a lack of confidence and marital, emotional and alcohol difficulties will not be cured by a move to the country,' Jim Connolly says. 'People are not immediately better off when they get here: they are pursuing a dream. However, by taking a brave step you can boost your spirit and your sense of enterprise. Some are very buoyant – fabulous people.' Families with children in primary school generally experience fewer problems than those with teenagers. 'Younger children make new friends more easily. Teenagers are the problem because they miss the group with whom they have been going around,' he says.

Certainly giving up a comfortable, relatively spacious council flat on a secure tenancy and saying goodbye to everyone they know imposes severe strains on those going through it. 'Every family that moves experiences financial hardship too,' Connolly says, explaining why he has been trying to persuade the government to make grants of £1000 available. 'Furniture removal is not the only expense. Other immediate costs include bus fares from Dublin, fuel, the purchase of food, local travel, some decoration, and so on. These have to be covered by social welfare payments, and often these payments are delayed by the move so that families have to borrow from whatever source they can. The financial difficulties caused by the move have contributed to some families' decisions not to stay.'

The local reaction to the incomers is generally favourable. 'In a few cases individual families have turned out to be troublesome tenants and have left unpaid bills, but other families resettled in the same area do not seem to have suffered as a result. On the whole, families are judged on their merits, and there are many examples of how schools, shops, sports clubs and so on have benefited,' Connolly says.

While it has not yet agreed to the £1000 resettlement grant, the government's attitude to RRI has been positive, and it currently pays roughly half the organization's £80,000 annual running costs. These cover a staff of three in Clare: Paul Murphy, his secretary Michelle Cahill, and Derrick McDonagh, the field officer, who visits community groups, including those in parishes that have undertaken to house a family each year, investigates properties, and helps families settle in. There is also an office in Dublin, run by Catherine Stapleton. So far, individual benefactors have covered the deficit. After a visit in 1994 President Mary Robinson passed on a £25,000 award she had been given, and the prefabricated cabin was purchased using funds sent by a woman in the United States.

Clare County Council has also been very supportive, and both the assistant county manager and the county solicitor sit on the RRI board. 'I've got a fantastic board of directors,' Connolly says. 'I needed people of experience and standing to give the organization credibility, and when I asked the county solicitor to join he said, "I don't need to think about it. It's a privilege." The Bishop of Killala in County Mayo is also a member.'

Nevertheless Connolly is frustrated because, despite its support for RRI, he believes the government response to rural depopulation has been entirely inadequate. Projections published in 1994 suggest that the population of the west of Ireland is likely to fall from 551,000 in 1991 to 441,000 by 2011 as a result of outward migration and the drop in the size of the average family. 'The government has no policy towards the rural areas, and without such a policy huge areas of our beautiful countryside will become wastelands without people,' he says. Later, Paul Murphy mentions that a government report he has just received states that the vicious circle of decline is terminal in certain parts of the country and that their communities cannot be saved.

Connolly argues that both the depopulation of the countryside and the social disintegration in the cities – the crime, the unemployment, the drugs – are due to the economic system's failure to provide an adequate way of valuing resources and sharing them out. 'Money is not an accurate measure of value. The real wealth of Ireland includes space, peace, access to culture, natural beauty, and a million other things which have always been available to those with money but have not been included in the equation defined by the dominant economic order. I see this beautiful country around here and not a soul in it, but we could share it, in a practical way, with not just hundreds but thousands and maybe tens of thousands of families, to everyone's benefit. The philosophy whereby our country functions at the moment is "I'm all right, Jack." This is deadly and inhumane. To my mind, sharing is the only philosophy that counts. My personal concern isn't for the grass, or the lonely roads, or even the lonely houses: it's for the people who might live here and the fact that they could have better lives.'

RRI's work demonstrates the willingness of thousands of families to leave the city permanently to live and work in the countryside; and anyone who doubts that rural Ireland now offers a better life than its capital to those able to find a way of living there has only to visit a mainline station on a Friday evening to see the exodus of thousands of people, mostly students or singles in their twenties with jobs and flats in the city, on the extra trains 'home'. Dozens of long-distance buses carry many more. Everyone pours back into Dublin on Sunday night. 'It wasn't like this in my day,' a friend in his fifties remarks. 'We couldn't wait to live in Dublin. It was where all the life was and all our friends. Going to see one's parents was a chore. Now the life is in the country towns and the kids can't wait to get home.'

Rural Resettlement Ireland Ltd, Kilbaha, Co. Clare; tel. +353 65 58034; fax. +353 65 58242.

to move away. 'It is felt that this is what they should do … and this applies as much to urban families as to rural ones,' Berry writes. 'In the present urban economy, the parent-child succession is possible only among the economically privileged. The children of industrial underlings are not likely to succeed their parents at work and there is no reason for them to wish to do so.'

As the children depart, generation after generation, the old stories are no longer told and their birthplace forgets its history and loses its culture:

The loss of local culture is, in part, a practical loss and an economic one. For one thing, such a culture contains, and conveys to succeeding generations, the history of the use of the place and the knowledge of how the place may be lived in and used. For another, the pattern of reminding implies affection for the place and respect for it, and so, finally, the local culture will carry the knowledge of how the place may be well and lovingly used and, moreover, the implicit command to use it only well and lovingly. The only true and effective 'operator's manual for spaceship earth' is not a book that any human will ever write; it is hundreds of thousands of local cultures.

The message of this book is that techniques already exist or can be devised that will lead to a better balance between the industrial world and the local community, that regional cultures can be reinvented and restored, and that children can remain in their native place. However, this will only be possible if a handful of people in each of perhaps a hundred communities are prepared to commit themselves to bringing the rebalancing about. Except in a few exceptional communities, all the approaches described in this book have been used in isolation from each other, so that there has been no opportunity for synergy to build up. What we must do now is develop ways of using several techniques together so that their true potential can be found. There are tantalizing hints in some of the previous chapters of what this might make possible.

Only when a community has demonstrated that it can build an independent, parallel economy that works well will politicians support the new approach and large numbers of other communities have the faith to begin to build one themselves. For those who believe that the industrial economy is unsustainable and will continue to threaten livelihoods and democracy if left uncontrolled, there could be no more important task than working in their communities to demonstrate that there is an alternative path for the world.

Yet, strangely, we are reluctant to commit ourselves to doing so. Most of us old enough to be in a position of influence believe, or at least hope, that the environmental and social problems generated by the industrial system can be solved, that the present levels of unemployment and instability in the world economy will prove temporary, and that life will resume behaving in the way it did in our childhood, a way we feel we understand. We don't want to have to work out new patterns of behaviour and face new uncertainties. Nor do we want to turn our backs on the prospect of reaping the lavish monetary rewards that the mainstream system promises a chosen few. However, for as long as we chase well-paid jobs in the world economy or believe that the relative safety and certainty that people in many industrial countries once enjoyed can be re-created by politicians who fail to realize why the changes they have made since 1970 have been so destructive, we will put off attempting to build the small-scale economies we must have if we are to secure the future. We will also fail to adopt the radically different attitudes required to make such economies a success.

We cling to our hope that radical changes can be avoided despite the fact that the evidence for the mainstream's failure is all too apparent and that even government posts and jobs in profitable companies with dominant market positions are no longer secure. In Ireland in the past, for example, Guinness workers were widely envied their job security, high pay, and superior medical and other benefits. Today they are still highly paid, earning about three times the average industrial wage, but their job security has gone, even though the company still has 90 per cent of the Irish beer market, invests £40 million a year in its Irish breweries, and is hugely profitable: in 1992 it made £106 million before tax in Ireland on sales of £704 million. Yet despite this strength, Guinness has reduced its work force at its main brewery in Dublin from almost four thousand in the 1960s to nine hundred today by a combination of voluntary and compulsory redundancy schemes. 'We need to be competitive on an international level,' a company spokesman explained in 1993 when he announced a further redundancy programme that will cut employment at the brewery to five hundred by the end of the century.

Exactly the same has happened in the United States, where the five hundred biggest firms dispensed with the services of 4.4 million employees between 1980 and 1993. In Britain, hugely profitable companies not directly exposed to international competition, including British Gas, British Telecom, the bank chains and the regional power companies, have recently made tens of thousands of well-paid, well-pensioned employees redundant. The result is that for larger and larger numbers of people, secure jobs are just not available. According to Paul Gregg and Jonathan Wadsworth of the Centre for Economic Performance at the London School of Economics and the National Institute for Economic and Social Research,[20] only 35.9 per cent of the work force had secure, full-time positions in 1993, compared with 55.5 per cent in 1975. A two-tier job market was developing, they said, the lower tier characterized by 'higher labour turnover among the least skilled, the young, and the old and those in atypical employment.' Overall, the length of time people held a particular job had fallen by 20 per cent.

These changes are both the challenge and the opportunity. They mean that for many people, including large numbers of the middle class, the type of parallel, local economy we have been discussing is no longer some sort of cranky optional extra but in fact the only realistic way they can build a satisfactory future for themselves and their families.

But I think it unlikely that a satisfactory community will emerge if we set out to build a local economy solely because there is no realistic alternative. Other motives need to be paramount. Perhaps the industrial system's most serious defect is that it fails to recognize that human beings, first and foremost, are social animals who can only be happy and healthy if they belong to a wide range of groups, including a family, a community, a circle of friends, a region, and a country. Because of this failure, it has put a strong economy before a strong society and bribed us to tolerate the breakdown of social structures and our conversion into single, separate economic agents by offering us consumer goods in compensation. Indeed it has created a vicious circle in which the greater the inner emptiness we feel from being cut off from other people by the demands of our work, the harder we need to apply ourselves to that work in order to earn enough to buy the system's products, in the hope that they will alleviate our basic dissatisfaction with ourselves and the lives we are living.

We must escape this circle. Consequently, whatever we do locally, we must never forget we are trying to build a society rather than an economy. This means that idealism must be at least as important a part of our mental attitude as realism, and the prospect of joy and fulfilment for ourselves and our friends a much stronger motive than anxiety about what will happen if things continue as they are.

To the extent that the industrial system's emphasis on individual achievement and competition (which has been described as a process of achieving one's goals by preventing others reaching theirs) either bribes or forces us to do things that damage others, it has to be condemned. The way it makes people feel they are failures about outcomes that were never under their control is extraordinarily harmful too. In short, the system has damaged us psychologically with both its rewards and its penalties and has kept us from relating properly with one another. Robert Lane's paper 'The Road Not Taken', on the relationship between the recent increase in the incidence of mental depression and the breakdown of social links, shows how high the cost has been.[21]

The fact is that there is no such thing as an individual achievement. Each of us is not only the product of millions of years of evolution but was shaped and affected by other people from the moment we were conceived. As a result, the ideas, attitudes and skills we possess are never truly our own: they are the product of chance, history, genetic inheritance, and other people's influences. This makes our contribution, whatever it is, that of the lens: we have merely brought a particular set of factors to a focus. Had Einstein recognized this when, towards the end of his life, he said, 'Perhaps I pursued the "it" too much and not enough the "we"'?

Humans are only fully human when we are involved with each other, and the majority of us find happiness most easily through collective achievement. If we join our neighbours in the adventure of building a local economy that supplies and supports us all, true happiness, deep joy, is waiting to be found.

Notes

1 Robert Frank, Thomas Gilovich, and Denis Regan, 'Does studying economics inhibit co-operation?', *Journal of Economic Perspectives*, spring 1993.

2 'The victims of vanity', *Down to Earth* (New Delhi), 15 March 1994.

3 This is being done under the framework of Local Agenda 21, the community-level part of Agenda 21, the massive international plan to promote sustainable development adopted at the UN Earth Summit in Rio de Janeiro in 1992. The Sustainable Seattle approach was introduced to Britain by the Sustainable Development Unit of the United Nations Association (3 Whitehall Court, London SW1A 2EL; tel. +44 171 8391784; fax +44 171 9305893). A 1995 report, *Sustainability Indicators Research Project: Consultants' Report of the Pilot Phase*, on how seven councils – Hertfordshire, Merton, Oldham, Fife, Bedfordshire, Leicester, and Strathclyde – fared in their first year, prepared in association with the New Economics Foundation and Touche Ross Management Consultants, is available from the Local Government Management Board (Arndale Centre, Luton, Bedfordshire LU1 5BR; tel. +44 1582 451166; fax +44 1582 412525; price £15). The UNA has also helped hundreds of villages and parishes in Britain to take stock of their local services, facilities and environmental health using household and individual questionnaires devised and delivered by local people. A pack con-

taining manuals, IBM-compatible computer software, sample questionnaire material and access to a user help line costs £50.
4 (New Society Publishers: Philadelphia 1991).
5 Quoted by David Morris in *The Mondragon Co-operative Corporation* (Institute for Local Self-Reliance: Washington July 1992).
6 *Ibid.*
7 'Foreign players eye Mondragon', *The European*, 19 May 1995.
8 Talk given at 26th Deutscher Evangelischer Kirchentag, Hamburg, 15 June 1995.
9 (Routledge: London 1985), p. 277.
10 G. Coulton, *Medieval Panorama* (Cambridge University Press: Cambridge 1945), p. 291.
11 Methuen, London, 1984, p. 16.
12 Draft article, 'A home in the Briarpatch', *c.* 1992.
13 (Random House: New York 1974). 'Do the right thing and the money will follow' conveys the spirit of the book.
14 In 'A new way to do business', *Resurgence*, no. 98 (May-June 1983), reprinted by Mike Money in *Health and Community* (Green Books: Totnes 1993).
15 Telephone interview.
16 (Ten Speed Press: Berkeley, California 1989).
17 Quoted in the *Economist*, 18 February 1995.
18 (Blackwell: Oxford 1984).
19 In *What Are People For?* (North Point Press: San Francisco 1990).
20 Reported in the *Guardian*, 3 April 1995.
21 'The Road Not Taken: Giving Friendship Priority over Commodities' (October 1994); available from Professor Lane, Department of Political Science, Yale University, PO Box 208301, New Haven, Connecticut 06520.

The Future, and it Works

MALENY, THE SMALL AUSTRALIAN TOWN that is using more of the techniques discussed in this book than perhaps anywhere else in the world, lies a thousand feet up in the Blackhall Mountains, about fifty miles as the crow flies north of Brisbane. To get there, you turn west off the Bruce Highway at Landsborough and drive for eleven miles along a twisting road that climbs up from the coastal plain along a steep spur and, as it gets higher, provides superb views of the Sunshine Coast and Moreton Bay behind. Near the top, the carriageway narrows sharply as it skirts a cliff and there is an abrupt change in vegetation, the gum trees and coarse brown grass of the plain being replaced by rolling green hills and remnants of tropical forest. A little further on, the road turns down just before Bald Knob Lookout and runs past four or five guesthouses and restaurants before entering the town.

'When I came here in 1974, the road was narrower and even more winding, as it followed the original wagon track built to take local butter to market,' says Jan Tilden, who has a doctorate in sociology and works for *The Range News*, the local newspaper. The butter she refers to was produced in a co-operative creamery opened in 1904 by farmers who had moved into the area after the forests of cedar, hoop and Bunya pines, and southern beech had been logged in the last quarter of the nineteenth century. By the early 1970s, however, most of the local farmers had ceased dairying and switched to beef in response to a steep decline in world butter and cheese prices during the 1960s. The switch meant that fewer farm-workers were needed and cottages fell vacant as they and their families moved away. In other cases, holdings were amalgamated leaving farmhouses empty. Empty, that is, until the area was discovered by young, well-educated people from the cities looking for a simpler, less materialistic life. 'I was one of the first of the new wave of settlers to move to the Maleny plateau,' Tilden says. 'The old share-farmer's cottage I rented for $6 a week had no running water and unreliable electricity. The farmer who owned it was embarrassed to charge me anything at all.'

Jill Jordan, a psychologist who moved to Maleny three or four years before Tilden, says that the local people did not know what to make of their new neighbours. 'We were looked on as hippies and treated with great suspicion,' she says. Tilden agrees: 'They were tolerant if not exactly welcoming. If nothing else, we citified newcomers were a source of good gossip.'

One source of complaint among the incomers was the poor range of foods available at the single local supermarket, and early in 1979, at the suggestion of Lorna Wilson, who had arrived from the United States where she had been a member of a food co-op, a meeting was held to discuss how this deficiency could be overcome. After considerable heart-searching – 'None of us had any business experience,' Jordan says – the idea of a co-op was accepted and a core group of three men and three women formed to establish it. 'We wanted to eat lentils, brown rice and fresh vegetables, not the range of tired tinned produce then offered by the supermarket,' Tilden explains. 'At our first meeting paper was passed around and people wrote down what they ate and that became the basis for our stocklist.'

The decision to meet the group's needs by establishing a co-operative rather than a conventional private business was important for what was to follow. So was the core group's brave decision that, rather than operating from someone's home, they should rent a vacant shop on Maleny's main street, Maple Street, so that the general public could trade there too, and the venture could serve as a community information centre and meeting place. A small amount of capital was raised by selling shares, equipment and shopfittings were donated, and the business opened in January 1980, with Jordan as manager. Slowly, locals began bringing in surplus produce to sell, and after a year it was trading sufficiently well for her to draw a salary.

'Some long-time residents came on the [co-op] board right away, happy to have a local outlet for their eggs and vegetables,' Tilden says.

'One of them, George Cassells, who was in his early sixties at the time, became financial manager. This helped bridge the gap between old and new Maleny residents.'

The co-op's success made the group associated with it feel that they could tackle other things. When Jordan returned from a permaculture conference in Tasmania in 1983 with the idea of starting a credit union to recycle local savings, the level of enthusiasm was such that within five months, the Maleny and District Community Credit Union Ltd had opened on the opposite side of Maple Street under her management, receiving $53,000 in deposits on its first day. Three years later deposits topped a million dollars, and by 1993 it had 2500 members and had provided finance for thirty-three new businesses, which generated a total of seventy-eight new jobs. The internationally known Crystal Waters Permaculture Village, which is near Maleny, was one beneficiary.

'The credit union is the lifeblood of the community,' Jordan says. 'Many of the people who borrowed from it would have been unable to get loans from any other source. A proportion of its annual surplus is paid into funds for environmental and co-operative education. It also has a community development fund which the members decide how to allocate each year, and a community assistance fund, which can be distributed in times of hardship, such as a fire or an accident, to anyone in the community whether they are members or not.'

In 1987 news of Michael Linton's experiments with LETS systems reached Maleny through the permaculture movement, and Jordan paid her own fare to Canada to see how they worked. As a result, the first LETS in Australia opened in Maleny in October 1987. 'It took off with a rush. People were ready for it,' she says. At the end of 1995 the system had eight hundred members of whom five hundred trade regularly and contribute to a monthly turnover of 25,000 Bunyas – the unit is named after the local pine trees from which the Aboriginals collected edible nuts. 'LETS is not just an extremely powerful economic tool but a magnificent social one,' Jordan says. 'Older people often find themselves living alone on fixed incomes without the strength to undertake some tasks necessary for their dignity and survival. They feel useless, too, because, although they have built up a lifetime of skills, they have no way of passing them on to younger people. LETS changes all that. It allows the elderly to earn credits by teaching their skills and then to employ energetic young people to get the physical work done.'

In 1988 and 1989, several more co-ops were established. Wastebusters operates a recycling depot in collaboration with the local council. Mountain Fare, which trains women with no work experience, began by growing and marketing herbs, and then moved into catering and frozen-food production. All this activity encouraged the Queensland government to provide the capital to turn the old co-operative butter factory, which had closed in 1978, into an incubator unit for small businesses. This opened in 1991 with Jordan on the board, and two years later one firm established there had already outgrown it and moved into the outside world. Other businesses in the centre included a publisher and two food manufacturers – Pure Pasta Products, which uses organic grain, and Maleny Clean Cuisine, which makes sauces and chutneys from organic ingredients. The centre's manager gives technical and moral support to the tenant businesses, which share secretarial services. More recently, a telecottage has been established there to give tenants access to marketing and technical information.

At the end of 1995 there were eighteen co-ops functioning in Maleny, the most recent being a community radio station. There is also a club that serves as a co-operative training centre during the day and a venue for local musicians at night. 'It's fabulous,' Jordan told me. 'At the moment we are trying to work out how people can pay for their drinks in Bunyas.'

It would be wrong to suggest that these co-ops transformed the declining town of the early 1970s into today's vital, vibrant community by themselves, although they undoubtedly helped. Derek Sheppard, a former economic development officer with the Queensland government who resigned and moved to Maleny to escape sixteen-hour working days, suggests that an influx of retired people from the mid-1970s onwards played a much greater role in halting the town's economic decline. However, the growing number of what Sheppard calls 'superannualists' has created problems for those seeking to build an alternative economy in the town. 'The farmers are right-wing but they could work with the alternatives,' Sheppard says. 'The retirees are right-wing too but they won't accept attempts to find an alternative way. It's damn annoying. When we set up the club, the National Party fought the project every step of the way. And the folk festival, which is the biggest in Australia and brought two million dollars into the town, has had to move to Woodford ten miles away. The retirees won't accept that there are other people in the community who have to make a living.'

So, although the co-operative movement in the town has become, according to Jordan, 'an incredible political force', the growing right-wing element was powerful enough to deny her re-election to the council in March 1994 after she had served a three-year term. 'I was unseated by the very forces that I originally went into Council to get rid of! Ugh!' she wrote to me shortly afterwards. 'This shows how much there is to do in the local sphere in terms of education...'

This is certainly true. Catering for tourists provides a growing number of Maleny people with their incomes, and the idea that the town should reduce rather than increase its dependence on the outside world is still unfamiliar to most residents. 'There's no widespread realization even that it's a good idea to shop locally,' Sheppard says. 'We're only a half-hour drive from the coast, where big shops offer a wide selection.' And within the alternative sector itself, there is still much to be done. 'The LETS system is only marginally useful,' Sheppard comments. 'It has had no real impact on the availability of necessities like groceries and foodstuffs. Builders and plumbers are also hard to get for Bunyas because they can get all the work they can handle for national currency.' Moreover, the effectiveness of the credit union as an agent of change is limited by its small size. 'As it has only seven or eight million dollars capital, it has had to put a cap on its housing loans of $50,000. And yet a site here can cost $70,000,' he says.

Jordan and other 'alternatives' are trying to overcome these difficulties by getting as many people as possible involved in their various ventures. 'Constant communication is the key to success,' she says. 'It is imperative to inform the broader community about every phase of a project, so as to maximize their opportunities for involvement. Any organization should have a broad base to ensure its stability. We ask people to become involved and stress that the proposals should enable everyone to make more income.'

Having a broadly based structure is one of Jordan's four golden rules for successful community economic development. The others are:
- Start small, with the skills and resources available within the community. Better a small success than a grand failure.
- Draw on other people's experience. Have someone from your group spend time learning 'on the job' from a similar venture even if it means travelling to do so.
- Build up a system of mutual support within your organization and, as you bring up more organizations, between organizations.

This last principle is, in fact, crucial to what the co-ops have achieved. Any one venture, such as the food co-op, can only deliver limited results to the community as a whole, no matter how big it becomes. However, once several organizations are operating, a synergy can develop between them with each contributing to the others' success so that the whole becomes greater than the sum of the parts, and the range of possibilities open to people involved in them is radically transformed. 'We really began to notice this from 1989 onwards, particularly in relation to people's skills. There are numerous stories of individuals who had never written a business letter or touched a calculator before coming into one of the Maleny co-ops, who are now comfortable running their own micro- or mini-businesses or managing a multi-million-dollar operation like the credit union. We have created a community-enterprise culture, a whole new sphere in which people can function,' she says.

Tilden agrees. 'The last twenty years have been a time of rapid population growth and economic change in Maleny,' she says. 'The co-ops have prevented people feeling that they are powerless, that they have lost the plot. The enterprise culture here empowers people. As a result, when the Red Rooster [a fast food chain] opened, we were able to exert considerable influence over the way they operated, and their employees' conditions.'

But even given the synergy between them, the co-ops would not have survived and prospered without an appreciable input of unpaid, volunteer labour. 'The need for voluntary input has characterized all Maleny co-ops to a greater or lesser extent, particularly in the early days,' Tilden says. 'For some years now, all workers have been paid at union-approved rates but co-op directors are still volunteers and members are encouraged to give service to keep prices at competitive levels. Some people question whether our co-ops can be considered viable businesses when they rely on volunteers, but how is viability [to be] defined in a business struggling to be ecologically sustainable and socially just in an unsustainable and unjust global economy?'

'Maleny is a town made up of communities,' says Derek Sheppard who, with his wife Jo-anne, chose to settle in the town because of its focus on arts and crafts. Now, besides being a director of the radio station co-op, Access FM, and the arts co-op, he is a driving force behind Maleny District Community Learning Centre Co-operative Society Ltd, which is setting up a school modelled on the Sudbury Valley School in the United States, for pupils aged four to nineteen – and adults outside school hours – at which everyone will decide each day what they wish to learn. 'The depth and extent of the community in Maleny is quite wonderful. The commitment of people to ideals and their practical implementation together with the level of support which surrounds it all is exciting. It helps drive me on, even when the road becomes a bit bumpy,' he wrote in the Autumn 1995 issue of the Maleny co-ops' regular magazine, *Review*.

'Maleny will tolerate variations in people's behaviour and is remarkable for its support mechanisms,' he told me. 'If you've got a plan and you take it to the community, you'll get support – mostly of the moral variety – to make it a reality.'

In short, Maleny is a town where people can learn, extend and fulfil themselves by involving themselves with each other. Who can ask more of their home-place than that? 'Maleny is nowhere special,' Jill Jordan says, 'it's just the product of a process that can be followed anywhere.'

Sunlight uplands: the rolling countryside near Maleny, Queensland, Australia. (photo: Jan Tilden)

Additional Sources of Information

IN MOST CASES, the sources of the information and ideas in this book have been given in sufficient detail for readers to be able to follow them up. Sometimes, however, addresses have been withheld because the people or organizations concerned cannot handle large numbers of enquiries. In such cases, the need to do a little detective work in order to make contact should eliminate the least important requests.

In other cases, publications and organizations relevant to the theme of this book have not been mentioned because there was no suitable opportunity to do so. Some of the most serious of these omissions are filled here but the selection is inevitably personal and, even if space was unlimited, no list could ever be complete.

MAGAZINES

Many of the topics discussed in this book have been touched on at one time or another in *Common Ground*, whose rare blend of ideas and practical details made it one of the best small magazines in these islands. In June 1996, however, the key people running it decided that they wanted to take at least a year off. They may then re-launch it in another form, perhaps on the Internet. Write to them at Smutternagh, Knockvicar, Boyle, Co. Roscommon, from mid-1997 onwards to find out what is happening.

Most other wide-ranging magazines looking for a new type of society and economy confine themselves to discussing ideas. Those closest to the spirit of this book are *The Aisling* (Inishmore, Aran, Co. Galway; four issues a year for £10 in Ireland, £13 elsewhere), *Resurgence* (Salem Cottage, Trelill, Bodmin, Cornwall, PL30 3HZ; six issues a year for £16 in the UK, £20 elsewhere), *Fourth World Review* (24 Abercorn Place, London NW8; a minimum of £10 for a year's six issues) and, more radical than any of them, *Plain*, from the Center for Plain Living, whose editors manage without telephones and are attempting to produce, typeset and print the magazine entirely by hand. Each issue concentrates on a single topic; back issues have covered 'Bringing food closer to home', 'Exiting the information superhighway', 'Leaving money behind' and raising children without computers. A six-issue annual subscription costs $30 to European addresses from P.O. Box 100, Chesterhill, OH 43728, USA.

Two indispensible sources of information about what those 'creating the new social paradigm' are doing and thinking are *Turning Point 2000* (The Old Bakehouse, Cholsey, Oxon OX10 9NU; two issues a year for £5 to European addresses) and *Tranet* (Box 567, Rangeley, ME 04970-0567, USA, $30 for a year's six issues). Both

ADDITIONAL SOURCES OF INFORMATION

give brief details of new publications and coming events. *Tranet* is also available on the Internet at http://www.nonviolence.org/~nvweb/tranet. Keeping up with the development of community-oriented economic thought also means subscribing to the New Economics Foundation's quarterly, *New Economics* (1st Floor, Vine Court, 112-116 Whitechapel Road, London E1 1JE; a minimum of £8 a year).

The best Internet discussion group I've found dealing with the issues discussed in this book is FUTUREWORK. Subscribe by sending the message 'SUB FUTURE-WORK TOM SMITH' (replacing Tom Smith with your own first and last names) to LISTSERV@csf.colorado.edu.

PRACTICAL PUBLICATIONS AND ORGANIZATIONS

The Smallholder, a monthly magazine for the small farmer, contains a wealth of practical information on a wide range of topics. Subscriptions – from Hook House, Hook Road, Wimblington, March, Cambridgeshire, PE15 0QL – cost £19.95 in the UK, £28.75 in the rest of Europe.

Those keen on replacing fossil-fuelled horsepower with the natural type should subscribe to *Heavy Horse World*. Only a few of its articles are on working with horses but the advertisements are the place to look for animals, tack, implements and training courses. Four issues a year for £10 in the UK, £14.50 elsewhere, from Park Cottage, West Dean, Chichester, West Sussex, PO18 0RX.

The Permaculture movement is involved in many of the areas mentioned in this book but has only been mentioned in passing. The key book on the topic is Bill Mollison's *Permaculture: A Practical Guide for a Sustainable Future* (Island Press: Washington 1990), but as this was written for Australian climatic conditions, British and Irish enthusiasts need to supplement it with other books. A good catalogue of these is issued by Permanent Publications, Hyden House Ltd, Little Hyden Lane, Clanfield, Hampshire PO8 0RU, who also publish the quarterly *Permaculture Magazine*, an annual subscription to which costs £10 in the UK, £16 elsewhere. Irish readers should write to The Ark Permaculture Project, Burdautien, Clones, Co. Monaghan for *The Whole Ark Catalogue*, which not only lists the key books but also the tools and plants required for permaculture design. The British Permaculture Association is at PO Box 1, Buckfastleigh, Devon, TQ11 0LH. Its *Bulletin* keeps people up to date with what is happening. However, much the most inspiring permaculture-related magazine that I see regularly is *Agroforestry News*, published quarterly by the Agroforestry Research Trust, 46 Hunters Moon, Dartington, Totnes, Devon, TQ9 6JT. Each issue concentrates on one or more of the tree and shrub crops that can be grown in temperate climates, giving cultivation details and listing the available cultivars and the nurseries that supply them. Subscriptions cost £18 per year in the EU.

THE NEW ECONOMICS FOUNDATION
working for a just and sustainable economy

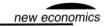

The New Economics Foundation is the leading UK think-tank focusing on the social and environmental dimensions of economic change. In recent years, NEF has introduced LETS to the UK, developed the social audit to assess the wider impact of business, and campaigned for new indicators of wealth and progress. NEF welcomes new supporters (£18 regular, £8 low/unwaged), who receive New Economics, a quarterly magazine charting the progress of this work and initiatives outlined in this book. A short guide to community action, 'Community Work', accompanies this book, setting out details of 'who, where and how' for a wide range of local initiatives in the UK. This is available free on request from NEF.

1st Floor, Vine Court, 112-116 Whitechapel Road, London E1 1JE, UK. Tel: +0171 377 5696; fax: +0171 377 5720; e-mail: neweconomics@ gn.apc.org.

INTERNATIONAL SOCIETY FOR ECOLOGY AND CULTURE: THE LADAKH PROJECT

The International Society for Ecology and Culture (ISEC) seeks to raise awareness of the social and environmental impact of economic globalization, while promoting ecological sustainability and community regeneration. ISEC's work is founded on twenty years' involvement in a range of societies at different levels of industrialization. It has been particularly active in Ladakh, or 'Little Tibet', providing information to counter the idealized image of Western consumer culture and exploring viable alternatives based on centuries of accumulated local wisdom. Publications include The Future of Progress: Reflections on Environment and Development and Ancient Futures: Learning from Ladakh. These titles are also available on video. ISEC's UK office is also the headquarters of the International Forum on Globalization (Europe) and Ecoropa (UK).

21 Victoria Square, Clifton, Bristol BS8 4ES, UK; Tel: +0117 973 1575; fax: +0117 974 4853. PO Box 9475, Berkeley, CA 94709, USA; Tel&fax: 510 527 3873.

AKTIE STROHALM
in search of a sustainable society

Aktie Strohalm provides the secretariat for LETSlink Europe, Holland and Flanders and is co-ordinator of Kiaros Europa's financial micro-alternatives programme. We belong to Kiaros Europa network and European Network for Economic Self-Help and Local Development. Our subsidiary the Institute for Sustainable Economy, is involved in research into sustainable alternatives in the macro and micro economy, innovation in financial micro-alternatives and the analysis of money flows.

Oudegracht 42, 3511 AR Utrecht, Holland. Tel: +31 30 2314314; fax: +31 30 2343986; e-mail: strohalm@intouch.nl.

Acknowledgments

THIS BOOK IS A COLLECTIVE EFFORT in that it could not have been produced without the help and involvement of dozens of people. Most of their names are listed here but a few have unfortunately been lost or forgotten. But whether named or not, I am extremely grateful to everyone for the time and trouble they took explaining things to me or supplying information, especially those who sent me suggestion after suggestion even though we had never met. Particular thanks must go to Antony Farrell of The Lilliput Press, who coordinated the project, Brendan Barrington, also of Lilliput, who carefully read the final proofs, Mari-aymone Djeribi (a.k.a. mermaid turbulence), who was responsible for the typography, Seamus Ó Brogain, who edited the text (a task he also performed for *The Growth Illusion*), Dana Marcell, who prepared the graphs, Amanda Bell, who assembled the index, and Mary Guinan, who designed the cover and the *Short Circuit* logo.

Extensive and wide-ranging contributions to the book were made by Gillies MacBain, Henk van Arkel, Paddy Corcoran and Hans Diefenbacher. Other valuable contributions came from Sven Giegold, Des Gunning, Karl Birkholtzer, Harry Bohun, Susan Minish, Joss Douthwaite, Leslie Douthwaite, George Douthwaite, Edward Goldsmith, Freda Rountree, Mary Sheehy, Greg Chamberlain, Eric Dammann, Tor Traasdahl, John Hille, William Lafferty, Aubrey Meyer, Shirley Jantz, Frances Milne, Tony Jaz, Toke Stevens, Paula Pace, David Gee, Ruth O'Brien, Tristan Donaghy and Kevin Donaghy.

The introduction could not have been written without help from Joanne Elliott, Margaret Day, Margaret Murray, Gustin Coyne, Regina King, Ann Day and Steven Royle.

Those involved in the section on local money systems were Ben Ryan, Lucillle O'Shea, Michael Corbett, Elke Corbett, Niall Herriott, Sacha Ryan, Paul Cassidy, John Mulloy, Iris Warhurst, Sabine Hiller, June Kerins, Hemmo Hemmes, Lucy Douthwaite, Tommy Simpson, Bill Walsh, Helen Gogarty, Michael Linton, Peter Furnell, Kiaya Seaton, Angus Soutar, Liz Shephard, John Bolger, Jyll Seyfang, Sandra Bruce, Paul Taylor, Steph Gahan, Edgar Kampers, Paul Glover, Edgar Cahn, Tom Greco, Walter Krause, Roy Davies, Hugo Godschalk, Henk Bor, Diana Schumacher, Pat Naismith, Irma van Baalen, Menno Houstra, Ursula Martin and Rob van Hulten.

Contributors to the chapter on local banking included Patrick Holohan, Brigitte Voss, Pat Conaty, Roger Cleary, Joseph Yewdall, Sheila Ryan, Mark Beeson, Connie Evans, Andy Langford, James Evans, Glen Saunders, Malcolm Lynch, Ronald Grzy-

ACKNOWLEDGMENTS

winski, Malcolm Bush, Joan Shapiro, Fazlun Khalid, Umar Vadillo, Luzita Ball, Inger Marie Ebbesen, Grace Perrott and Bob Lowman.

Help with the local energy section came from Dave Toke, Gavin Attridge, Dermot O'Kane, Seamus Langan, Barry Langan, Gerry Bracken, Paddy Connolly, Paddy Belton, Paddy O'Sullivan, Fiacc Ó Brolchain, George Chapman, Tadhg Dennehy, Peter Fraenkel, Sheila Leyden, Karl Cradick, Brian Hurley, Ciaran King, Per Lauritsen, Inger-Lise Lauritsen, Flemming Trænæs, Jorn Kristensen, Stan McWilliams, Les Gornall, Mary O'Donnell, Malcom Dawson, Ben Warren, Bernard Williams, Rosemary Kerrigan, Ramon Duran, Sean MacCarthy, Gerry Wrixon, Sophie Wolf, Lindsay Gill, Marcel Bloemkolk, Wilma Naaijer, Owen Lewis, Bill Quigley, Bruce Robins, Jobst Kraus, Bertolt Klessman, Robert Banham, Simon Roberts, Vicky Heslop, Brian John, Kitty O'Malley-Harlow, Daniel Prince, Hugh Babington Smith and Elizabeth Fordham.

The land and food section was researched with help from R.F. Murphy, David Astley, S. Jones, Anita Hayes, Genevieve Tenthorney, Peadar MacNiece, Renée Vellvé, Beth Burrows, Simon Hickmott, Maria Finckh, Marcus McCabe, Boru Douthwaite, Martin Wolfe, Raymonde Hilliard, Leo Curran, John Ward, Clare Hoare, John Mulvihill, Joan Stack, Molly D. Anderson, Hugh Raven, Antony McNicholas, Robyn Van En, Christina Groh, Tobias Pedersen, Wolfgang Stränz, John Butterworth, Dave Bellingham, Eileen Bellingham, Jan Deane, Eric Booth, Ollan Herr, Mark Deary, John MacKenzie, Tony Crofts, David Smith, Alan Gill, Nick Murray, Liam O'Dwyer, Robert McLauchlan, Elizabeth Baker, Art Mulloy, Derek Smith, Brenda McNicholas, Pauric Cannon, Brid McAuley, Chris Smith, Elizabeth Cullen, Lily Rider, Penny Annand, Mary Coleman and Jane Bickerstaffe.

Lesli O'Dowd, Perry Walker, Dorit Seeman, John Bradley, Roger Pritchard, Frances Kinsman, Jim Connolly, Paul Murphy and Antony Boland contributed to the final chapter, and the Epilogue on Maleny owes everything to Ted Trainer, Jill Jordan, Jan Tilden, Derek Sheppard, George Cassells and Wayne Ellwood.

Index

377

INDEX

Conservative Party (UK), 16
Consumer Credit Act, 137
Contranet, 105
Co-operative Bank, 149
co-operatives, xiii, 32, 44, 46, 136–7, 281, 353–4, 365; on Inishbofin, 7; Meitheal na Mart, 68, 77; WIR, 100–5; Mondragon, 160–3, 168, 170, 177, 338–41, 352–3; Soest, 169; biomass co-ops, 222–3; biorefinery co-ops, 281; Ayrshire Organic Growers Co-op, 292–4; Sycamore Co-operative Garden, 308; Talaton Village Shop Association, 318; Country Markets Co-op, 320–23; Dublin Food Co-operative Society Ltd, 307, 324–9; Seikatsu Consumer Co-op, 326–7, 329n; Maleny, 366–71
Copenhagen, 27, 216
Cork, city, 226
Cork, County, 194–5, 216–18
Country Markets Ltd, 320–3
Coyne, Gustin, 3
craft guilds, 343–5
credit unions, 125–32, 154, 174–8, 367, 369; joining, 126; risk, 127; benefits, 127; role, 128; interest rates, 128, 132
Credit Union Act, 130, 177n
CREST (US Center for Renewable Energy and Sustainable Technology), 245
Critchfield, Richard, 11–12
Crofter Forestry Act, 302
Crofter, The, 303
Crofters' Commission, 303
Crofting Trusts Advisory Service, 303, 305n
Crofts, Tony, 303–5
Crystal Waters Permaculture Village, 367
CSA (*see* community-supported agriculture)
currency (*see* local money systems)
CUT (*see* Communities Under Threat)

Daily Telegraph, 282
Daniels, Joy, 262
Danish Energy Agency, 216, 218
Danish Energy Commission, 206
Danske Vindkraftvaerker (Danish Wind Power Associations), 204–7
Dart, 136
Dasmann, Raymond, 53
Davis (California), 234–7
Davis, Milton, 150–2
Dawson, Malcolm, 220–1, 246
Day, Margaret, 2–3
Day's Hotel, 2
de Chardonnet, Count Hilaire, 279
Deane, Tim and Jan, 295
Deary, Mark, 297–8, 306–7
Death of Money, The, 15
Demeter, 287
Dempsey's, 313
Denmark, 15, 26, 46, 101, 160, 164–7, 198–200, 203–11, 213, 216–18, 222, 226, 240, 242, 268, 283
Derry, 215
DeWoody, George, 348
Diefenbacher, Hans, 24

Dinan, Eoin, 324
Dinesen, Jørgen, 206
Diss, Norfolk, 77
Divisions of Labour, 354
Doonmore Hotel, 2–4
Dorf-Mobil Bad Boll, 240–1
Dornbusch, Rudiger, 49
Dow Chemical, 346
Dublin, 20, 191, 200, 221, 238, 259, 262–4, 298, 307, 321, 324, 326–7, 355–9, 361
Dublin Food Co-operative Society Ltd, 307, 324–9
Duncan, Norman, 136–8
Dundalk, 296, 307–8
Dwellers in the Land, 53

Earthwatch, 216
Eastern Suburbs Business Enterprise Centre, 141–3
Ebbesen, Inger Marie, 164–7
Ebbesen, Jørgen, 164
Ecology Building Society, 171, 173, 175n, 304
Ecology Centre, The, 55n
Ecology Party, 171
Economic Reform Australia, 113n
economics; economic development of community, 153; economic disruption, 34; economic efficiency, 28; economic freedom, 15; economic globalization, vii–ix; economic growth, xi–xii, 58–9; economic localization, vii–x; economic management, 16; economic sustainability, 58; economic welfare, 19, 22, 24; economics   profession, 19–21, 26, 28, 33, 35–6, 48, 91, 122, 155–7, 183, 333–5; balance between local economies and world system, 31–47, 50–2, 56–9, 87, 341, 343, 360; effects of conventional economics, 122–3, 156, 333–5, 337; money economy *vs* real economy, 15; world economic system, vii, 15–17, 19–20, 25, 29, 31, 33, 47–9, 56, 332, 337
Economist, The, 25, 49, 159
Edinburgh, 242
EEC See European Economic Community
EFTA See European Free Trade Association
Egypt, 64, 159
Einstein, Albert, 363
Electricity Supply Board, 193, 195, 197
Elliott, Dave, 189
emigration, 40, 122
Emmett, Isabel, 62
energy, 50, 58, 179–245 *passim*; energy saving, 227–45 (*see also* wind power, hydropower, biomass energy)
Energy Advisory Associates, 237
Energy Club, 243–4
Energy Plan (1981), Denmark, 205
Energy Prize (1985), Denmark, 206
Energy Technology Support Unit, 200, 210, 213, 219, 245n
Enertech, 209
environmental damage, 23, 58, 251–3
Environmental Protection Agency, 217
Enz, Paul, 101
Erscott, Brenda, 315–16
ESB (*see* Electricity Supply Board)

379

INDEX